Science
AND
Development
OF
Muscle
Hypertrophy

Brad Schoenfeld, PhD, CSCS, CSPS, FNSCA

Lehman College, Bronx, New York

HUMAN KINETICS

Library of Congress Cataloging-in-Publication Data

Schoenfeld, Brad, 1962- , author.
 Science and development of muscle hypertrophy / Brad Schoenfeld.
     p. ; cm.
 Includes bibliographical references and index.
 I. Title.
 [DNLM: 1. Muscle Development--physiology. 2. Exercise. 3. Physical Fitness. WE 500]
 QP303
 612.7'6--dc23

2015035559

ISBN: 978-1-4925-1960-7

Copyright © 2016 by Brad Schoenfeld

Acquisitions Editor: Roger W. Earle
Senior Developmental Editor: Christine M. Drews
Managing Editor: Karla Walsh
Copyeditor: Patsy Fortney
Indexer: Patsy Fortney
Permissions Manager: Dalene Reeder
Senior Graphic Designer: Keri Evans
Cover Designer: Keith Blomberg
Photograph (cover): © Human Kinetics
Photographs (interior): © Human Kinetics, unless otherwise noted
Photo Asset Manager: Laura Fitch
Photo Production Manager: Jason Allen
Senior Art Manager: Kelly Hendren
Associate Art Manager: Alan L. Wilborn
Illustrations: © Human Kinetics, unless otherwise noted
Printer: Walsworth

Printed in the United States of America   10 9 8 7 6 5 4

The paper in this book was manufactured using responsible forestry methods.

Human Kinetics
P.O. Box 5076
Champaign, IL 61825-5076
Website: www.HumanKinetics.com

In the United States, email info@hkusa.com or call 800-747-4457.
In Canada, email info@hkcanada.com.
In the United Kingdom/Europe, email hk@hkeurope.com.

For information about Human Kinetics' coverage in other areas of the world,
please visit our website: **www.HumanKinetics.com**

To my father, may he rest in peace, for instilling the scientific method in me for as long as I can remember. You pushed me to learn, to pursue higher education, and to become a scholar. Wish you were around to see the fruits of your efforts. This is for you; I know it would have made you proud.

CONTENTS

PREFACE

The quest to develop a muscular body is an age-old one. Natives of 11th-century India first began using primitive dumbbell-like weights carved from stone to increase muscle size. Gyms were widespread in the country during this era, and by the 16th century, weightlifting had become India's national pastime. However, it wasn't until the late 1800s that Prussian strongman Eugene Sandow, often referred to as the Father of Modern Bodybuilding, brought muscle building into the public realm. Sandow toured the world displaying his well-muscled physique in stage show exhibitions to large audiences. Sandow also is credited with inventing the first resistance training equipment for the masses (implements such as dumbbells, pulleys, and tension bands), which furthered the ability to gain muscle.

Today, millions of people around the globe train with the goal of maximizing muscle mass. Some do so for purely aesthetic reasons; others, to enhance athletic performance. A recent focus has been on the health-related benefits of increased hypertrophy. Sarcopenia, the age-related loss of muscle tissue that affects as much as half the population over 80 years old, is implicated in debilitating functional impairment as well as the onset of a multitude of chronic diseases.

For many years, training and nutritional approaches to maximize muscle growth were primarily relegated to gym lore and personal anecdotes. Those seeking to increase muscle size were left to follow the routines of their favorite bodybuilders. Scientific evidence on the topic was scarce, and research-based guidelines were a product of gross extrapolations from limited data.

Over the past several decades, this has changed dramatically. An explosion in the number of studies investigating the hypertrophic response to training has occurred. A recent PubMed search of the phrase *skeletal muscle hypertrophy* revealed almost 500 published peer-reviewed studies in 2014 alone! Moreover, the techniques used to assess hypertrophic outcomes, both acutely and chronically, have become more advanced and widely available. As such, we now have solid evidence from which to develop a true understanding of the hows and whys of exercise-induced muscle growth.

This is the first book to synthesize the body of literature on muscle-building practices into one complete resource. All aspects of the topic are covered in extensive detail, from the mechanisms at the molecular level to the manipulation of training variables for maximal hypertrophic effect. Although the book is technically oriented, its primary focus is on applying principles to practice. Thus, you will be able to draw evidence-based conclusions for customizing hypertrophy program design to individuals.

Following is an overview of the content of the chapters:

- Chapter 1 covers hypertrophy-related responses and adaptations to exercise stress. It provides an overview of the structure and function of the neuromuscular system and the responses and adaptations of the neuromuscular, endocrine, paracrine, and autocrine systems. You'll learn about the role of fiber types in muscle growth; the ways hypertrophy manifests; and how intrinsic and extrinsic factors drive the accretion of muscle proteins.

- Chapter 2 delves into the mechanisms responsible for exercise-induced hypertrophy. Understanding the processes involved in building muscle is essential to developing strategies for maximizing growth. You'll learn how the mechanical forces are converted into chemical signals to mediate muscle protein accretion, how the exercise-induced accumulation of metabolites stimulates the hypertrophic response, and how structural perturbations in muscle affect tissue remodeling.

- Chapter 3 details the role of resistance training variables in hypertrophy. It is generally believed that the precise manipulation of these variables holds the key to the growth response. You'll learn how volume, frequency, load, exercise selection, type of muscle action, rest interval length, repetition duration, exercise order, range of motion, and effort interact to promote muscular adaptations, and how they can be altered to maximize muscle growth.

- Chapter 4 explores the impact of aerobic training in hypertrophy. This is a highly nuanced topic, and misconceptions abound. You'll learn how aerobic intensity, duration, frequency, and mode affect the hypertrophic response both when aerobic exercise is performed in isolation and when it is combined with resistance exercise (i.e., concurrent training).

- Chapter 5 looks at population-specific considerations that influence muscle building. The large differences in inter-individual hypertrophic response are the result of multiple factors. You'll learn how genetics, age, sex, and training experience affect the ability to increase muscle size.

- Chapter 6 provides practical information on exercise program design for maximizing hypertrophy. This is where the science of training becomes an art. You'll learn how to synergistically vary exercise selection to bring about complete muscular development, how periodization models compare with respect to promoting hypertrophic gains, and how to implement a periodized program to sustain results.

- Chapter 7 examines the role of nutrition for hypertrophy. Without question, dietary intake has a profound impact on muscle-building capacity. You'll learn the effects of energy balance and macronutrients on muscle growth, the impact of meal frequency on muscle protein synthesis, and the efficacy of nutrient timing for enhancing muscular gains.

Science and Development of Muscle Hypertrophy is the definitive resource for information  regarding muscle hypertrophy. An image bank of most of the figures, content photos, and tables from the text is available to instructors who adopt the book and can also be ordered by individuals from www.HumanKinetics.com/ScienceAnd DevelopmentOfMuscleHypertrophy.

ACKNOWLEDGMENTS

- First and foremost, to Roger Earle, for envisioning this project and providing all the necessary resources to ensure its quality. I am thankful for your trust in me writing the book, and for your continual guidance throughout the publication process. Without your efforts, this book would not have come to fruition. I am eternally grateful.

- To Chris Drews and Karla Walsh, for effectively and efficiently managing the development of this project so that everything ran smoothly. Your efforts were greatly appreciated.

- To my close friends and long-time colleagues Bret Contreras and Alan Aragon, for providing a stimulating scientific environment that continually expands my knowledge base. Our frequent discussions and debates have enhanced my ability to carry out research and furthered a better understanding of the practical implications of evidence.

- To my students, past and present, who perpetually inspire me to learn and grow, and to be the best I can be in my field. Your personal development and success are ultimately what makes my life so fulfilling.

Hypertrophy-Related Responses and Adaptations to Exercise Stress

To comprehend the many factors related to maximizing skeletal muscle hypertrophy, it is essential to have a foundational knowledge of how the body reacts and adapts to exercise stress. This chapter reviews the structure and function of the neuromuscular system and the responses and adaptations of the neuromuscular, endocrine, paracrine, and autocrine systems. Although these systems are discussed separately, they are integrally connected; their interactions ultimately mediate lean tissue growth.

Neuromuscular System

A detailed discussion of the complexities of muscle hypertrophy requires a fundamental understanding of the neuromuscular system—in particular, the interaction between nerves and muscles that produces force and results in human movement. Although a thorough exploration of the topic is beyond the scope of this book, this section provides a general overview of concepts that are referenced in later chapters. Those interested in delving further into the subject are advised to seek out a good textbook specific to exercise physiology.

Structure and Function

From a functional standpoint, individual skeletal muscles are generally considered single entities. However, the structure of muscle is highly complex. Muscle is surrounded by layers of connective tissue. The outer layer covering the entire muscle is called the *epimysium*; within the whole muscle are small bundles of fibers called *fasciculi* that are encased in the *perimysium*; and within the fasculus are individual muscle cells (i.e., fibers) covered by sheaths of *endomysium*. The number of fibers ranges from several hundred in the small muscles of the eardrum to over a million in large muscles such as the gastrocnemius. In contrast to other cell types, skeletal muscle is *multinucleated* (i.e., contains many nuclei), which allows it to produce proteins so that it can grow larger when necessary.

Skeletal muscle appears striped, or *striated*, when viewed under an electron microscope. The striated appearance is due to the stacking of sarcomeres, which are the basic functional units of myofibrils. Each muscle fiber contains hundreds to thousands of *myofibrils*, which are composed of many *sarcomeres* joined end to end. Myofibrils contain two primary protein filaments that are responsible for muscle contraction: *actin* (a thin filament) and *myosin* (a thick filament). Each myosin filament is surrounded by six actin filaments, and three myosin filaments surround each actin filament, thereby maximizing their ability to interact. Additional proteins are also present in muscle to maintain the structural integrity of the sarcomere, including titin, nebulin, and myotilin. Figure 1.1 shows the sequential macro- and microstructures of muscle tissue.

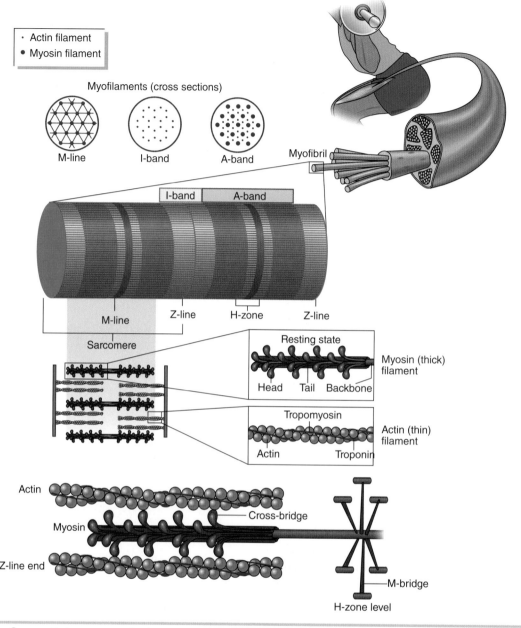

FIGURE 1.1 Sequential macro- and microstructures of muscle.

Motor Unit

Muscles are innervated by the nervous system. Individual nerve cells associated with muscular actions are called *motor neurons*. Motor neurons consist of three regions: a cell body, an axon, and dendrites. When a decision is made to carry out a movement, the axon conducts nerve impulses away from the cell body to the muscle fibers, ultimately leading to muscular contraction. Collectively, a single motor neuron and all the fibers it innervates is called a *motor unit* (figure 1.2). When a motor unit is innervated, all of its fibers contract.

Sliding Filament Theory

It is generally accepted that movement takes place according to the *sliding filament theory* proposed by Huxley in the early 1950s (329). When a need to exert force arises, an action potential travels down the nerve axon to the

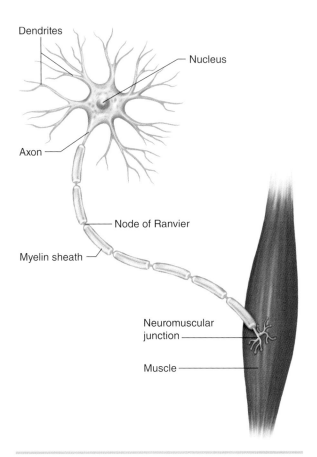

FIGURE 1.2 A motor unit.

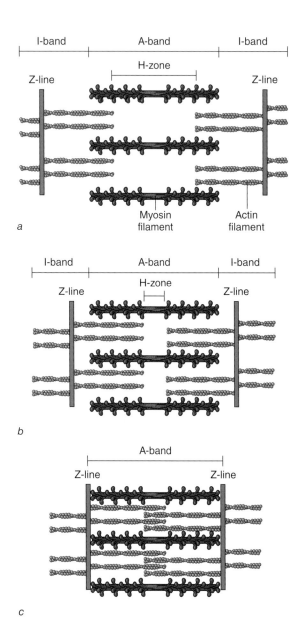

FIGURE 1.3 Contraction of a myofibril. *(a)* In stretched muscle, the I-bands and H-zone are elongated, and there is low force potential as a result of reduced crossbridge–actin alignment. *(b)* When muscle contracts (here, partially), the I-bands and H-zone are shortened. Force potential is high because of optimal crossbridge–actin alignment. *(c)* With contracted muscle, force potential is low because the overlap of actin reduces the potential for crossbridge–actin alignment.

neuromuscular junction, where the neurotransmitter acetylcholine is released across the synaptic cleft and ultimately binds to the muscle fiber's plasmolemma. This depolarizes the muscle cell, causing calcium to be released from the sarcoplasmic reticulum. Calcium binds to troponin, which in turn moves tropomyosin from actin binding sites so they are exposed to myosin. Assuming sufficient ATP to drive muscular contraction, the globular myosin heads bind to exposed actin sites, pull the thin filament inward, release, and then reattach at a site farther along the actin filament to begin a new cycle. The continuous pulling and releasing between actin and myosin is known as crossbridge cycling, and the repeated power strokes ultimately cause the sarcomere to shorten (figure 1.3).

Fiber Types

Muscle fibers are broadly categorized into two primary fiber types: *Type I* and *Type II*. Type I

fibers, often referred to as slow-twitch fibers, are fatigue resistant and thus well suited for activities requiring local muscular endurance. However, peak tension takes time—approximately 110 ms—to achieve in these fibers, thereby limiting their ability to produce maximal force. Type II fibers, also known as fast-twitch fibers, serve as a counterpart to Type I fibers. They can reach peak tension in less than half the time—just 50 ms—thereby making them ideal for strength- or power-related endeavors. However, they fatigue quickly and thus have limited capacity to carry out activities requiring high levels of muscular endurance. Accordingly, fast-twitch fibers appear white under an electron microscope, whereas slow-twitch fibers appear red as a result of their high myoglobin and capillary content. The greater myoglobin and capillary content in slow-twitch fibers contributes to their higher oxidative capacity compared to fast-twitch fibers. Table 1.1 summarizes the characteristics of the primary muscle fiber types.

Muscle fiber types are further distinguished according to the predominantly expressed isoform of myosin heavy chain; they are referred to as Type I, Type IIa, and Type IIx (784). Several other similar forms (commonly called *isoforms*) have been identified with intermediate staining characteristics, including Ic, IIc, IIac, and IIax (figure 1.4). From a practical standpoint, the c isoform typically comprises less than 5% of human muscle and thus has minimal impact on total cross-sectional area.

On average, human muscle contains approximately equal amounts of Type I and

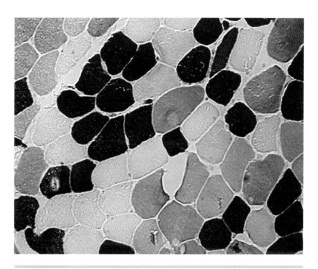

FIGURE 1.4 A photomicrograph showing Type I (black), Type IIa (white), and Type IIx (gray) muscle fibers.
Reprinted, by permission, from David Costill.

Type II fibers. However, a large interindividual variability exists with respect to fiber type percentage. The quadriceps of elite sprinters have been shown to have a predominance of Type II fibers, whereas quadriceps of elite aerobic endurance athletes are primarily composed of Type I fibers. Moreover, certain muscles are predisposed to higher percentages of a given fiber type. For example, the endurance-oriented soleus contains an average of more than 80% Type I fibers; the more strength-oriented triceps brachii contains ~60% Type II fibers (167).

TABLE 1.1 Characteristics of Muscle Fiber Types

Characteristic	Type I	Type IIa	Type IIx
Size of motor neuron	Small	Medium	Large
Contraction time	Slow	Moderately fast	Fast
Force production	Low	Moderate	High
Resistance to fatigue	High	Moderate	Low
Mitochondrial density	High	Moderate	Low
Oxidative capacity	High	High	Low
Glycolytic capacity	Low	High	High
Capillary density	High	Moderate	Low
Myoglobin content	High	Moderate	Low
Glycogen stores	Low	High	High
Triglyceride stores	High	Moderate	Low

Many experts claim that all Type II fibers are inherently larger than Type I fibers. However, there is evidence that women often display a larger cross-sectional area of Type I fibers than of Type IIa fibers (784). Research does indicate that the oxidative properties of a fiber, rather than fiber type, influence muscle size. Specifically, the cross-sectional area of glycolytic Type IIx fibers is significantly greater than that of the more oxidative Type I and Type IIa fibers. It has been speculated that the smaller size of high-oxidative myofibers is an evolutionary design constraint based on the premise that fibers have a limited capacity to hypertrophy and increase oxidative capacity at the same time (784). This is consistent with the hypothesis that competition exists between the turnover rates of structural (myofibrillar) proteins and those involved in metabolism (i.e., mitochondrial proteins), which is seemingly mediated by interactions between signaling pathways involved in either the synthesis or degradation of the respective muscle proteins (784).

Another often-proposed assumption is that Type II fibers are primarily responsible for exercise-induced increases in muscle size. This is largely based on studies showing that Type II fibers experience superior growth compared to Type I fibers after regimented resistance training (1, 119, 131, 382, 670, 723). When considered as a whole, the literature indicates that the growth capacity of Type II fibers is approximately 50% greater than that of Type I fibers (12), although substantial interindividual variability is seen in the extent of fiber type–specific hypertrophic adaptation (382). There also is evidence that the rate of muscle protein synthesis is elevated to a greater extent in the primarily fast-twitch human vastus lateralis muscle (~50% to 60% Type II fibers) compared to the primarily slow-twitch soleus muscle (~80% Type I fibers) following heavy resistance exercise (775). A caveat when attempting to extrapolate such findings is that high loads were used in a majority of studies on the topic, which potentially biases results in favor of fast-twitch fibers. Thus, it is conceivable that the superior capacity for hypertrophy of this particular fiber type may be a function of the models in which it has been studied rather than an inherent property of the fiber itself (548). The practical implications of this topic are discussed in later chapters.

Responses and Adaptations

Resistance exercise elicits a combination of neural and muscular responses and adaptations. Although an increased protein synthetic response is seen after a single bout of resistance training, changes in muscle size are not observed for several weeks of consistent exercise (683). Moreover, appreciable muscle protein accumulation or growth (commonly referred to as *accretion*) generally takes a couple of months to become apparent (509). Early-phase increases in strength therefore are primarily attributed to neural improvements (509, 585, 640). Such observations follow the principles of motor learning. During the initial stages of training, the body is getting used to the movement patterns required for exercise performance. A general motor program must be created and then fine-tuned to carry out the exercise in a coordinated fashion. Ultimately, this results in a smoother, more efficient motor pattern and thus allows greater force to be exerted during the movement.

KEY POINT

Early-phase adaptations to resistance training are primarily related to neural improvements, including greater recruitment, rate coding, synchronization, and doublet firing.

Neural Drive

Several neural adaptations have been proposed to account for strength gains during acclimation to resistance training. Central to these adaptations is an increase in *neural drive*. Research indicates that humans are incapable of voluntarily producing maximal muscle force (187), but repeated exposure to resistance training enhances this ability. Numerous studies have reported increases in surface electromyography (EMG) amplitude after a period of regular resistance training, consistent with a heightened central drive to the trained muscles (2, 3, 276, 519). Research using the twitch interpolation technique, in which supramaximal stimuli are delivered to a muscle while subjects perform voluntary contractions, shows that as much as 5% of the quadriceps femoris muscle is not activated during maximal knee extension testing before exercise. After 6 weeks of training, however, subjects increased activation by an additional 2% (371). Similarly, Pucci and colleagues (594) reported an increase in voluntary activation from 96% to 98% after 3 weeks of training of the quadriceps muscles. These results are consistent with research showing that trained athletes display greater muscle activation during high-intensity resistance exercise compared to nonathletes.

Muscle Activation

The findings of increased activation resultant to training are most often ascribed to a combination of greater *recruitment* (the number of fibers involved in a muscle action) and *rate coding* (the frequency at which the motor units are stimulated). It has been well established that muscle fiber recruitment follows the *size principle* (1, 12, 14, 16-19, 23, 33, 34). First explained by Henneman (301), the size principle dictates that the capacity of a motor unit to produce force is directly related to its size (figure 1.5). Accordingly, smaller, low-threshold, slow motor units are recruited initially during movement, followed by progressively larger, higher-threshold motor units as the force demands increase for a given task. This orderly activation pattern allows for a smooth gradation of force, irrespective of the activity performed.

Two primary factors are responsible for the extent of muscle recruitment: level of muscle force and rate of force development. Training with heavy loads requires substantial force production and therefore calls on both low- and high-threshold motor units to maximize force. Although there is an intent to lift heavy loads quickly, the actual velocity of the lift is relatively slow. As the intensity of load decreases, the required force production from

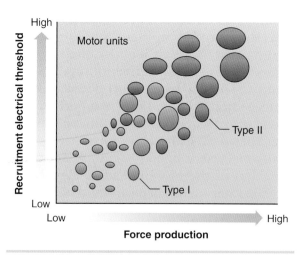

FIGURE 1.5 The Henneman size principle.

the muscle decreases, and fewer motor units are necessary to complete the lift given the same speed of shortening. By lifting a lighter weight quickly, however, most motor units are likely to be recruited even at loads equivalent to 33% of maximum (191). The extent of reductions in recruitment threshold from rapid contractions is greater for motor units in slow-contracting muscles, such as the soleus, compared with fast-contracting muscles, such as the masseter, one of the primary muscles involved in chewing food (191). The role of fatigue also must be considered with respect to recruitment. As fatigue increases during low-load contractions, the recruitment threshold of higher-threshold motor units progressively decreases even at somewhat slower speeds (321, 638, 801). It has been hypothesized that fatigue-induced reductions in motor unit threshold recruitment is an attempt by the neuromuscular system to sustain necessary levels of force generation to continue work output during repeated contractions (107).

The upper limit of motor unit recruitment is approximately 85% of maximal applied isometric force; recruitment thresholds during dynamic actions are even lower (191). This suggests that enhancements in motor unit recruitment likely play a limited role in strength-related training adaptations. The ability to maximally recruit all available fibers in a given motor unit pool is essential for maximizing the hypertrophic response to resistance training. After all, the stimulus for a muscle fiber to adapt is based on its recruitment. However, it is important to note that simply recruiting a fiber does not necessarily promote a hypertrophic response. For example, a substantial recruitment of the full spectrum of muscle fibers, including those associated with high-threshold motor units, is achieved by cycling to fatigue at 75% $\dot{V}O_2$max (638). Although this observation suggests that submaximal cycle exercise would promote substantial size increases across fiber types, research shows that muscle growth associated with aerobic exercise is limited primarily to Type I fibers (287).

Increases in force production above 85% of maximal voluntary contraction are thought to occur through greater discharge rates. Thus, an increase in rate coding would seem to be the most likely target for neural adaptation. Research is limited on the topic, but a study by Kamen and Knight (349) provides supporting evidence for training-induced enhancements in rate coding. Fifteen untrained young and older adults were tested for maximal voluntary contraction in knee extensions before and after 6 weeks of resistance exercise. By the end of the study, young subjects increased maximal discharge rate by 15%, and older subjects showed a 49% increase. Similarly, Van Cutsem and colleagues (782) showed that 12 weeks of resisted dorsiflexion training increased average firing frequency in the tibialis anterior from 69 to 96 pulses per second. In contrast, Pucci and colleagues (594) reported an increase of approximately 3% of maximal voluntary activation following 3 weeks of isometric quadriceps exercise, but no changes in discharge rate were noted. Differences in findings may be related to the methods employed for analysis.

Motor Unit Synchronization

Several other factors have been speculated to account for neural improvements following resistance exercise. One of the most commonly hypothesized adaptations is an enhanced synchronization of motor units, whereby the discharge of action potentials by two or more motor units occurs simulta-

neously. A greater synchrony between motor units would necessarily result in a more forceful muscle contraction. Semmler and Nordstrom (679) demonstrated that motor unit synchronization varied when they compared skilled musicians (greatest degree of synchronization), Olympic weightlifters, and a group of controls (lowest degree of synchronization). However, other studies have failed to show increased synchronization following resistance training or computer simulation (363, 846). The findings cast doubt on whether synchronization plays a role in exercise-induced early-phase neuromuscular adaptations; if it does, its overall impact seems to be minimal.

Antagonist Coactivation

Another possible explanation for exercise-induced neural enhancement is a decrease in antagonist coactivation. The attenuation of antagonist activity reduces opposition to the agonist, thereby allowing the agonist to produce greater force. Carolan and colleagues (125) reported that hamstring coactivation decreased by 20% after just 1 week of maximal voluntary isometric knee extension exercises, whereas no differences were seen in a group of controls. These findings are consistent with observations that skilled athletes display reduced coactivation of the semitendinosus muscle during open-chain knee extensions compared to sedentary people (30). The extent to which these adaptations confer positive effects on strength remains unclear.

Doublets

An often-overlooked neural adaptation associated with resistance training is the effect on *doublets*, defined as the presence of two close spikes less than 5 ms apart. Doublets often occur at the onset of contraction, conceivably to produce rapid force early on and thus generate sufficient momentum to complete the intended movement. Van Cutsem and colleagues (782) reported that the percentage of motor units firing doublets increased from 5.2% to 32.7% after 12 weeks of dynamic resisted dorsiflexion training against a load of 30% to 40% of 1RM. Interestingly, the presence of these doublets was noted not only in the initial phase of force development, but also later in the EMG burst. The findings suggest that doublet discharges contribute to enhancing the speed of voluntary muscle contraction following regimented resistance training.

Protein Balance

The maintenance of skeletal muscle tissue is predicated on the dynamic balance of muscle protein synthesis and protein breakdown. The human body is in a constant state of protein turnover; proteins are constantly degraded and resynthesized throughout the course of each day. Skeletal muscle protein turnover in healthy recreationally active people averages approximately 1.2% a day and exists in dynamic equilibrium; muscle protein breakdown exceeds muscle protein synthesis in the fasted state and muscle protein synthesis exceeds muscle protein breakdown postprandially (49).

Protein synthesis has two basic components: transcription and translation (figure 1.6). Transcription occurs in the cell nucleus through a complex process that is segregated into three distinct phases: initiation, elongation, and termination. The process involves the creation of a *messenger ribonucleic acid* (mRNA) template that encodes the sequence of a specific protein from the genome. Each phase of transcription is regulated by various proteins (i.e., transcription factors, coactivators) that ensure that the correct gene is transcribed in response to appropriate signals. Messenger ribonucleic acid concentration for a given protein is ultimately regulated by the myonuclear or the mitochondrial density and the transcription factors required for promoter activity (784).

Translation occurs in organelles called *ribosomes* located in the cell's sarcoplasm. Ribosomes can be thought of as large peptide factories that regulate the translation of genetic material encoded in mRNA templates

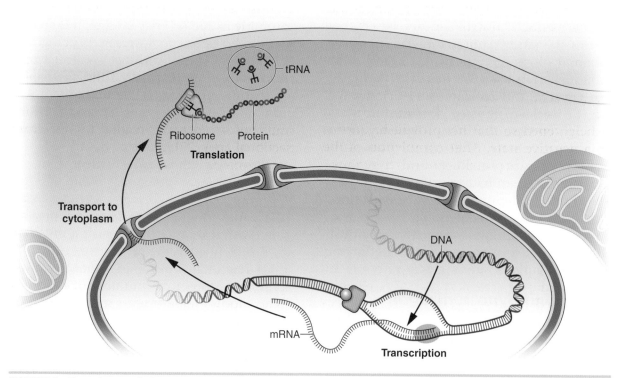

FIGURE 1.6 Protein translation and transcription—the basic processes of reading DNA sequence information and using it to build a protein molecule. The DNA sequence is read in the cell's nucleus, where a complementary RNA strand is built. That mRNA strand then moves to the cell cytoplasm, where it is used to manufacture the amino acid sequence of the protein.

into muscle proteins. Each ribosome is composed of two subunits: a smaller subunit that binds the mRNA and a larger subunit that integrates specific transfer RNAs along with their bound amino acids (137). After binding with mRNA, the ribosomes synthesize a corresponding peptide strand by joining amino acids to tRNA at the carboxyl end of the chain (137). The result is that translational capacity depends highly on the number of ribosomes in myocytes (11).

As with transcription, reactions are segregated into three phases: initiation, elongation, and termination. Each phase involves a distinct cluster of translation factors that are aptly termed *initiation factors* (eIF), *elongation factors* (eEF), and *release factors* (eRF) (the *e* stands for *eukaryotic*, referring to a cell that contains a nucleus and other cell structures). The availability and the state of activation of these factors determine the rate of translation of mRNA into muscle proteins (784). Translation initiation is believed to be the rate-limiting step in the protein synthetic response (463, 604). Not surprisingly, therefore, hormones and other growth factors that regulate muscle protein synthesis exert their effects by either increasing or decreasing the rate of translation initiation (137).

During a bout of resistance training, muscle protein synthesis is suppressed and *proteolysis* (the breakdown of proteins into amino acids) is heightened so that net protein balance is in a negative state. After completion of the workout, muscle protein synthesis is increased 2- to 5-fold along with nutrient delivery, and the effects last approximately 48 hours postexercise (575). The exercise-induced increase in muscle protein synthesis is primarily attributed to an enhanced translational efficiency (314, 551). Thus, when repeated bouts are performed over time and sufficient recovery is afforded between sessions, the net synthetic response outpaces that of proteolysis, resulting in an increased accretion of muscle proteins.

Hypertrophy

By definition, muscle *hypertrophy* is an increase in the size of muscle tissue. During the hyper-

KEY POINT

Muscular adaptations are predicated on net protein balance over time. The process is mediated by intracellular anabolic and catabolic signaling cascades.

trophic process, contractile elements enlarge and the extracellular matrix expands to support growth (656). Growth occurs by adding sarcomeres, increasing noncontractile elements and sarcoplasmic fluid, and bolstering satellite cell activity.

Parallel and In-Series (Serial) Hypertrophy Contractile hypertrophy can occur by adding sarcomeres either in parallel or in series (figure 1.7). In the context of traditional exercise protocols, the majority of gains in muscle mass result from an increase of sarcomeres added in parallel (563, 757). Mechanical overload causes a disruption in the structure of the myofibers and the corresponding extracellular matrix that sets off an intracellular signaling cascade (see chapter 2 for a full explanation). With a favorable anabolic environment, this process ultimately leads to an increase in the size and amounts of the contractile and structural elements in the muscle as well as the number of sarcomeres in parallel. The upshot is an increase in the diameter of individual fibers and thus an increase in total muscle cross-sectional area (771).

Conversely, an in-series increase in sarcomeres results in a given muscle length corresponding to a shorter sarcomere length (771). An increase in serial hypertrophy has been observed in cases in which a muscle is forced to adapt to a new functional length. This occurs when limbs are placed in a cast and the corresponding immobilization of a joint at long muscle lengths leads to the addition of sarcomeres in series; immobilization at shorter lengths results in a reduction in sarcomeres (771).

Research indicates that certain types of exercise actions can affect fascicle length. There are three distinct types of actions: concentric, eccentric, and isometric. *Concentric actions*

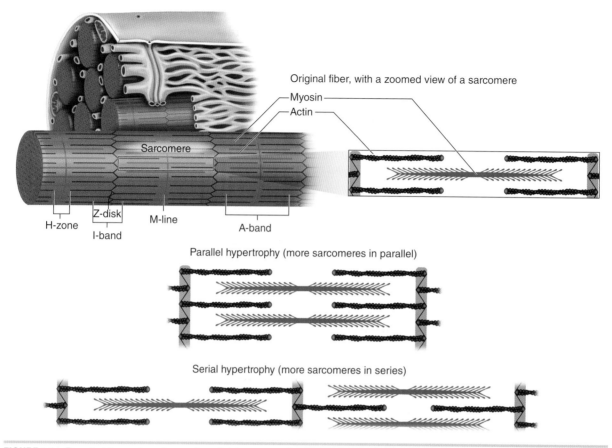

Original fiber, with a zoomed view of a sarcomere

Myosin

Actin

Sarcomere

H-zone

Z-disk

I-band

M-line

A-band

Parallel hypertrophy (more sarcomeres in parallel)

Serial hypertrophy (more sarcomeres in series)

FIGURE 1.7 Parallel hypertrophy and serial hypertrophy.

occur when a muscle is shortening; *eccentric actions* occur when a muscle is lengthening; and *isometric actions* occur when a muscle is producing force at an immobile joint. Lynn and Morgan (437) demonstrated lower sarcomere counts when rats climbed on a treadmill (i.e., incline) compared to when they descended (i.e., decline). This indicates that repeated eccentric-only actions result in a greater number of sarcomeres in series, whereas exercise consisting solely of concentric contractions leads to a serial decrease in sarcomere length.

With respect to traditional resistance exercise, there is evidence that serial hypertrophy occurs to an extent during the early stages of participation. Seynnes and colleagues (683) reported a 9.9% increase in fascicle length in a group of recreationally active men and women after a 35-day high-intensity resistance training program. However, a longer-term study by Blazevich and colleagues (80) found

that fascicle length changes were specific to the initial 5 weeks of resistance training, and that adaptations did not persist beyond this period. Evidence suggests that altering the style of training may affect changes in serial hypertrophy. Increases in fascicle length have been reported in athletes who replace heavy resistance training with high-speed training (22, 79). These findings suggest that performing concentric actions with maximal velocity may promote the addition of sarcomeres in series even in those with considerable training experience.

KEY POINT

Hypertrophy can occur in series or in parallel. The primary means by which muscles increase in size following resistance training is through parallel hypertrophy.

Sarcoplasmic Hypertrophy It is hypothesized that a training-induced increase in various noncontractile elements (i.e., collagen, organelles) and fluid may augment muscle size (441, 687). This phenomenon, often referred to as *sarcoplasmic hypertrophy*, conceivably enhances muscle bulk without concomitantly increasing strength (687). The sarcoplasmic component of muscle is illustrated in figure 1.8. Increases in sarcoplasmic hypertrophy are purported to be training specific—that is, lighter-load, higher repetitions promote greater accumulation of sarcoplasmic fractions compared to heavy-load, low repetitions. Support for this belief is based on research showing that muscle hypertrophy differs between bodybuilders and powerlifters (757). In particular, bodybuilders tend to display higher amounts of fibrous endomysial connective tissue as well as a greater glycogen content compared to powerlifters (440, 759), presumably as a result of differences in training methodology.

The chronic changes in intramuscular fluid are an intriguing area of discussion. Without question, exercise training can promote an increase in glycogen stores. MacDougall and colleagues (439) reported that resting concentrations of glycogen increased by 66% after 5 months of regimented resistance training. Moreover, bodybuilders display double the

glycogen content of those who do not participate in regular exercise (9). Such alterations would seem to be mediated both by enzymatic alterations and the greater storage capacity of larger muscles. The relevance to sarcoplasmic changes is that 1 g of glycogen attracts 3 g of water (130).

Training-induced increases in intracellular hydration have been demonstrated after 16 weeks of progressive resistance training (613). Subjects performed a bodybuilding-type routine consisting of 3 sets of 8 to 12 repetitions with 60 to 90 seconds of rest between sets. A total of 11 exercises were performed per session using a combination of free weights, cables, and machines. All sets were taken to the point of momentary muscular failure. Analysis by bioelectrical impedance spectroscopy found significant increases in intracellular water content, both at the midpoint of the study and at the study's end; results showed a moderate effect size. Conceivably, these alterations were mediated by increases in glycogen content, because osmosis-promoting properties would be required to maintain the ratio of fluid to proteins and thus preserve the integrity of cellular signaling. Although the study provides evidence that training does in fact promote an increase intracellular hydration (and, thereby, likely an increase in glycogen stores), what remains unclear is whether training-induced increases in intracellular hydration are specific to bodybuilding-type training or inherent to all types of resistance training. Bodybuilding-type training relies primarily on fast glycolysis to fuel performance, and carbohydrate is the primary energy source. As such, the body necessarily adapts by increasing its capacity to store glycogen and thus fuel the demands of future performance. On the other hand, the short duration of powerlifting-type training requires that fuel be derived from immediately available ATP and PC sources. The lack of need to substantially use carbohydrate during these bouts would seemingly diminish the need to ramp up glycogen storage capacity, and thus reduce localized fluid accumulation.

Although this line of reasoning provides a logical basis for training-specific alterations in sarcoplasmic volume, evidence that this

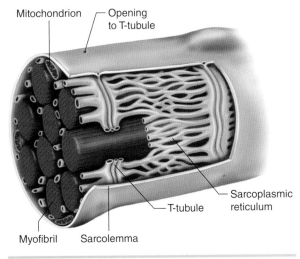

Mitochondrion — Opening to T-tubule

Sarcoplasmic reticulum

T-tubule

Myofibril   Sarcolemma

FIGURE 1.8 Sectional view of a muscle fiber showing the sarcoplasmic component of muscle.

occurs in practice is lacking. Burd and colleagues (105) found that training at 90% of 1RM induced greater early-phase postexercise (~4 hours) increases in sarcoplasmic protein synthesis compared to training at 30% of 1RM, but the low-load condition showed a greater increase at 24 hours postexercise. These findings are specific to myocellular protein fractions and do not reflect the long-term changes in hydration status associated with resistance training. Moreover, it is unknown whether such results would have persisted over time.

Importantly, there is no evidence that sarcoplasmic hypertrophy takes place in the absence of increased myofibrillar protein accretion. Resistance training–induced increases in myofibrillar hypertrophy occur in parallel with those of noncontractile elements. Thus, the often-cited opinion that bodybuilding-style training leads to nonfunctional hypertrophic adaptations is misguided.

Satellite Cells Skeletal muscle is a postmitotic tissue, meaning that it does not undergo significant cell replacement throughout

its life. An efficient means for regeneration of fibers is therefore required to maintain healthy tissue and avoid cell death. It is widely accepted that satellite cells are essential to this process. These myogenic stem cells, which reside between the basal lamina and sarcolemma, remain inactive until a sufficient mechanical stimulus is imposed on skeletal muscle (791). Once aroused, they produce precursor cells (myoblasts) that multiply and ultimately fuse to existing fibers, providing agents necessary for the repair and remodeling of the muscle (771, 855). This may include the co-expression of myogenic regulatory factors such as Myf5, MyoD, myogenin, and MRF4 (158) that bind to sequence-specific DNA elements present in the promoter of muscle genes; each plays a distinct role in growth-related processes (636, 696). Figure 1.9 shows the cycle of satellite cell activation, differentiation, fusion, and repair/remodeling following a sufficient mechanical stimulus.

It has been theorized that the most important hypertrophic role of satellite cells is their

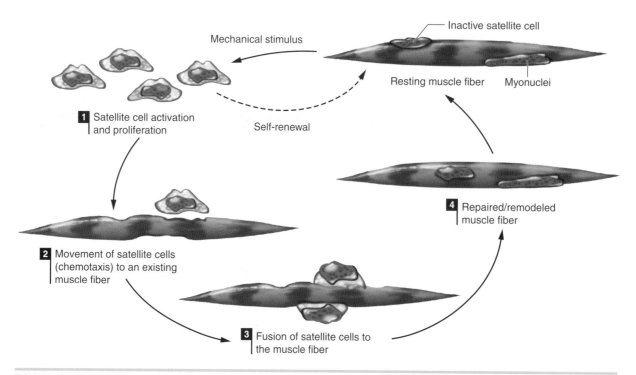

FIGURE 1.9 Cycle of satellite cell activation, differentiation, fusion, and repair/remodeling following a sufficient mechanical stimulus.

Adapted, by permission, from W.L. Kenney, J.H. Wilmore, and D.L. Costill, 2015, *Physiology of sport and exercise*, 6th ed. (Champaign, IL: Human Kinetics), 249.

ability to retain a muscle's mitotic capacity by donating nuclei to existing myofibers (see figure 1.10), thereby increasing the muscle's capacity to synthesize new contractile proteins (61, 512).

Given that a muscle's nuclear-content-to-fiber-mass ratio remains relatively constant during growth, the satellite cell–derived addition of myonuclei appears to be essential for sustaining muscular adaptations over the long term (765). This is consistent with the concept of *myonuclear domain*, which proposes that the myonucleus regulates mRNA production for a finite sarcoplasmic volume and any increases in fiber size must therefore be accompanied by a proportional increase in myonuclei (574). Considering that skeletal muscle contains multiple myonuclear domains, growth could occur by either an increase in the number of domains (via an increase in myonuclear number) or an increase in the size of existing

domains. Both events are believed to occur during the adaptive response to exercise, and satellite cells are believed to contribute significantly to the process (771).

KEY POINT

Satellite cells appear to be crucial to maximizing the hypertrophic response to resistance training. The primary role of satellite cells appears to be their ability to retain a muscle's mitotic capacity by donating nuclei to existing myofibers.

Although controversy exists regarding the precise hypertrophic role of satellite cells (470), the prevailing body of research indicates that they are crucial for the regulation of compensatory muscular growth (12, 542). Compelling support for this contention was demonstrated in a cluster analysis by Petrella and colleagues (574) that showed that people who were extreme hypertrophic responders (>50% increases in mean myofiber cross-sectional area of the vastus lateralis over the course of 16 weeks of resistance training) displayed a much greater capacity to expand the satellite cell pool compared to those who experienced moderate or negligible increases in growth. More recently, Bellamy and colleagues (67) showed a strong positive relationship between the acute temporal satellite cell response to 16 weeks of resistance training and subsequent muscle protein accretion. Correlations were noted in all fiber types, and expansion of the satellite cell pool showed the greatest associated hypertrophic increases in Type II fibers. These findings are consistent with research showing that hypertrophy is significantly impaired when satellite cells are obliterated by gamma irradiation (789).

It seems likely that satellite cells become relevant only when muscle growth reaches a certain threshold. Kadi and colleagues (348) found that increases in myofiber hypertrophy of up to 15% could be achieved without significantly adding new myonuclei; however, myonuclear addition was required when

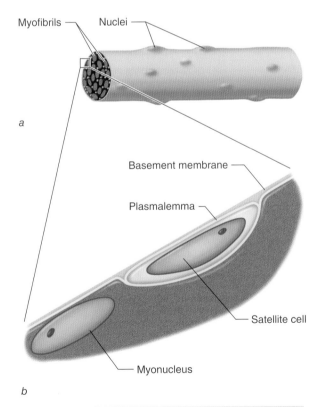

Myofibrils — Nuclei —

a

Basement membrane —

Plasmalemma —

— Satellite cell

— Myonucleus

b

FIGURE 1.10   *(a)* Single muscle fiber with myonuclei at the periphery. *(b)* Myonucleus and satellite cell. The satellite cell is separated from the fiber by its own plasmolemma and that of the fiber, but it lies within the basement membrane of the skeletal muscle fiber.

hypertrophy reached 26%, conceivably because of an inability to further expand the myonuclear domain. This observation suggests that satellite cell function might be particularly important in well-trained people because the size of myofibers would necessarily reach the upper limits of their myonuclear domain.

Interestingly, myonuclei are maintained over time even after long periods of detraining and the corresponding muscle atrophy. In animal models, a technique called *synergist ablation* is often used to study muscle tissue; the process involves a muscle being surgically removed so that other synergist muscles are forced to carry out a movement (see chapter 3). In an elegant design, Bruusgaard and colleagues (101) used synergist ablation to cause significant hypertrophy in the extensor digitorum muscle of rodents and a 37% increase in myonuclei count. Subsequent denervation of a parallel group of animals produced marked muscular atrophy, but the number of myonuclei remained constant (101). Work from the same lab showed that mice treated with testosterone propionate for 14 days elicited a 77% increase in muscle hypertrophy and a 66% increase in myonuclei count (199). Muscle fiber size returned to baseline levels 3 weeks after discontinuation of steroid administration. However, the myonuclei count remained elevated for at least 3 months, which amounts to over 10% of the animal's life span. These findings indicate that the retention of satellite cells associated with hypertrophic adaptations serves as a cellular memory mechanism that helps to preserve the future anabolic potential of skeletal muscle (199). Thus, the number of myonuclei might be limited to a person's ability to add muscle during the initial stages of overload, but the subsequent addition of satellite cell–derived nuclei associated with muscle protein accretion might facilitate increased synthesis upon retraining (266).

Hyperplasia

It has been theorized that exercise-induced muscle growth may be due in part to *hyperplasia*—an increase in fiber number (figure 1.11).

Evidence supporting the ability for muscles to undergo hyperplasia is primarily derived from animal research. Alway and colleagues (27) attached a weight to the right wings of adult Japanese quails that corresponded to 10% of their body mass. The contralateral limb served as a control. After 5 to 7 days of chronic stretch, fiber number was approximately 27% greater than that in nonloaded controls. These findings indicate a substantial contribution of hyperplasia to gains in lean mass. Follow-up work by the same lab evaluated a comparable

Single fiber

Split fiber

Split fiber

FIGURE 1.11 Muscle fiber splitting (hyperplasia).

stretch protocol except that loading was carried out for 24-hour intervals interspersed with 48- to 72-hour rest periods (36). Although significant increases in mean cross-sectional fiber area were noted in the stretched limb, fiber number did not change over the course of the study. Subsequent work by the same lab expanded on this study to employ progressive overload (37). Loading was increased from 10% to 35% of the bird's body mass over a period of 28 days. Histological analysis determined an 82% increase in fiber number at the study's end. These findings seem to indicate that extreme loading conditions can induce hyperplasia, at least in an avian model.

Whether hyperplasia occurs in humans using traditional training protocols remains controversial. A meta-analysis on the topic of 17 studies meeting inclusion criteria concluded that a stretch overload consistently produced greater fiber counts, and exercise-based protocols produced highly inconsistent results (358). Moreover, increases in myofiber number were substantially greater in studies that used avian (~21%) versus mammalian (~8%) models. MacDougall and colleagues (441) evaluated myofiber count of the biceps brachii in 5 elite male bodybuilders, 7 intermediate-caliber bodybuilders, and 13 age-matched controls. Despite markedly greater hypertrophy in the bodybuilders, the fiber counts of the groups were similar, indicating that heavy loading had no effect on hyperplasia. Paul and Rosenthal (563) proposed that the authors of studies showing evidence of hyperplasia may have misinterpreted the intricate arrangements of elongating fibers as increases in fiber number. These researchers noted the difficulty in attempting to analyze fiber count, particularly in pennated muscles in which fibers do not all lie in the plane of sectioning, and in muscles with multiple endplate bands and many intrafascicularly terminating fibers in series. The body of evidence suggests that the notion that new myofiber formation contributes to loading-induced muscle hypertrophy in humans is questionable. If any contribution does exist, its impact on increases in muscle cross-sectional area appears to be minimal (12).

Endocrine, Paracrine, and Autocrine Systems

Muscle protein balance is influenced, in part, by the neuroendocrine system. Various hormones have been shown to alter the dynamic balance between anabolic and catabolic stimuli in muscle, helping to mediate an increase or decrease in muscle protein accretion (708). Moreover, certain substances (hormones and myokines) are secreted locally, either in a *paracrine* (between adjacent cells) or *autocrine* (within the cell itself) fashion, in response to exercise to cause specific adaptations.

Responses and Adaptations of Hormones

Endocrine hormones are produced within glands, released into the blood, and then transported to target tissues where they bind to receptors either on the sarcolemma or in the sarcoplasm. Table 1.2 provides a summary of the primary anabolic hormones and their actions. There is clear and compelling evidence that basal concentrations of anabolic hormones influence growth and regenerative capacity of skeletal muscle (154); when anabolic hormonal concentrations are chronically suppressed, muscular adaptations are blunted. The following sections address the hypertrophic role of the primary anabolic hormones (insulin-like growth factor 1, growth hormone, testosterone, and insulin) and the resistance training–mediated alterations caused by those hormones.

Insulin-Like Growth Factor 1

Insulin-like growth factor 1 (IGF-1) is a homologous peptide that, as the name implies, has structural similarities to insulin. IGF-1 carries out intracellular signaling via multiple pathways (see chapter 2) (272, 623, 680). These signaling cascades have both anabolic and anticatabolic effects on muscle and thus promote increased tissue growth (643). *In vitro* research (studies done in a laboratory setting on extracted cells, not inside the body) consistently shows that IGF-1 incites protein synthesis, inhibits protein breakdown, and

TABLE 1.2 Primary Anabolic Hormones and Their Actions

Hormone	Actions
Testosterone	Directly increases myofibrillar protein synthesis and decreases proteolysis (the breakdown of proteins into amino acids), potentiates the release of GH and IGF-1 while inhibiting the activity of IGFBP-4 (an IGF-1 antagonist), and increases the number of satellite cells.
Insulin-like growth factor 1 (IGF-1)	Stimulates differentiation and fusion after myotrauma and helps the donation of myonuclei to muscle fibers. Although IGF-1 does directly influence anabolic intracellular signaling, it is not clear whether these effects are synergistic for exercise-induced muscle growth.
Growth hormone (GH)	Serves as an anabolic factor through its potentiating effect on IGF-1. Although some evidence exists that GH promotes anabolism independent of IGF-1, whether those effects have an appreciable impact on muscle development remains questionable.
Insulin	Causes a reduction in protein breakdown (as opposed to increases in muscle protein synthesis).

increases both myotube diameter and the number of nuclei per myotube (289). Despite its known anabolic properties, however, evidence suggests that a functional IGF-1 receptor is not essential for exercise-induced muscle hypertrophy (716).

Three distinct IGF-1 isoforms have been identified in humans: IGF-1Ea, IGF-1Eb, and IGF-1Ec. Both IGF-1Ea and IGF-1Eb are produced mainly in the liver and then released into systemic circulation. Other tissues express these isoforms as well, however, and the extent of nonhepatic synthesis increases in response to physical activity. In fact, contracting muscles produce the majority of systemic IGF-1 during intense exercise, and much of the circulating IGF-1 is inevitably taken up by active myofibers (92, 254). On the other hand, IGF-1Ec is a splice variant of the IGF-1 gene specific to muscle tissue. It is expressed in response to mechanical loading and then carries out its actions in an autocrine/paracrine fashion (254). Because IGF-1Ec is stimulated mechanically, and given that its carboxy peptide sequence is different from the systemic isoform, it has been termed *mechano growth factor* (MGF). (Because MGF carries out its actions locally as opposed to systemically, it is specifically discussed in the section on myokines and only briefly covered in this section.)

The age-related decrease in serum IGF-1 levels is associated with muscle atrophy (282); this suggests that a threshold exists for circulating concentrations of this hormone below which muscle mass is compromised. IGF-1 is a potent effector of the PI3K/Akt pathway (see chapter 2) and is widely thought to be necessary for activating the signal transduction required for the initiation of protein translation following mechanical loading (717). However, the extent to which systemic IGF-1 is involved in compensatory hypertrophy remains controversial, and some researchers dispute whether it has a primary role in the anabolic response to exercise (470, 542). Serum concentrations of IGF-1 are not necessarily correlated with postworkout increases in muscle protein synthesis (861). Furthermore, IGF-1-deficient mice exhibiting an 80% reduction in circulating IGF-1 levels do not exhibit an impaired hypertrophic response to resistive exercise (462). The inconsistencies in studies on this topic have yet to be reconciled.

The upregulation of systemic IGF-1 is delayed following exercise, and this temporal pattern of release coincides with later-stage satellite cell regulation (573). Hence, the primary hypertrophic effects of systemic IGF-1 may manifest in its ability to stimulate differentiation and fusion following myotrauma and thereby facilitate the donation of myonuclei to muscle fibers to maintain optimal DNA-to-protein ratios (771, 789). Whether the systemic IGF-1 isoforms have additional hypertrophic actions as a result of resistance training remains to be established.

Growth Hormone

Growth hormone (GH) is a superfamily of polypeptide hormones released by the anterior pituitary gland. GH is secreted in a pulsatile manner, and the highest non-exercise emission takes place during sleep. GH possesses both anabolic and catabolic properties (789). On one hand, it stimulates *lipolysis* (the breakdown of lipids); on the other hand, it promotes cellular uptake and the incorporation of amino acids into various proteins (791). Although there is evidence that endogenous GH plays a role in the regulation of skeletal muscle mass (789), at physiological levels its primary anabolic action appears to be specific to collagen synthesis as opposed to an increase of myofibrillar proteins (184).

The anabolic influence of GH on muscle tissue is thought to be carried out primarily via its potentiative effect on IGF-1 (789). Animal research shows that an increase in skeletal muscle mass associated with GH requires an intact IGF-1 receptor (365). These findings are consistent with studies showing significant increases in circulating IGF-1 levels following GH administration (38, 280, 619). In addition to mediating the release of systemic IGF-1 isoforms, GH also appears to increase the action of MGF. Klover and Hennighausen (370) found that removing the genes for signal transducers and activators of transcription (STAT), which are considered compulsory regulators of GH-induced transcription of the IGF-1 gene, led to a selective loss of skeletal muscle STAT5 protein, whereas hepatic expression remained unaltered (370). These findings are consistent with in vitro research showing that treating myoblast C2C12 cells with recombinant GH directly potentiates MGF expression prior to that of IGF-1Ea (331). In addition, the administration of GH in mice significantly elevated MGF, indicating that MGF mRNA expression occurs in parallel with GH release (330). Alternatively, GH-independent expression of IGF-1Ea and MGF has been observed in hypophysectomized (pituitary gland removed) rats following

synergist ablation (842), which implies that GH serves to potentiate rather than regulate IGF-1 function. Interestingly, there is evidence that mRNA levels of MGF are greatly increased when elderly men combine resistance training with recombinant GH treatment (280), but similar results are not seen in young adult men (38). Discrepancies in findings are not clear.

The claim that GH mediates hypertrophy solely via potentiating IGF-1 release remains controversial. Some researchers have suggested that the two hormones may confer additive effects (713, 789). The possibility of IGF-1–independent anabolic effects of GH is indicated by research showing reduced growth retardation in IGF-1 knockout mice compared to those lacking both an IGF-1 and GH receptor (434). Moreover, a reduction in myofiber size is seen in skeletal muscle deficient of functional GH receptors (713). These effects are thought to be carried out, at least in part, by later-stage GH-regulated cell fusion that results in an increase in the number of nuclei per myotube (713). The actions of GH also seem to cause a permissive, or perhaps even a synergistic, effect on testosterone-mediated muscle protein synthesis (795). Whether these effects are seen as a result of endogenous GH production within normal physiological levels remains speculative.

Testosterone

Testosterone is a steroidal hormone derived from cholesterol in the Leydig cells of the testes via the hypothalamic-pituitary-gonadal axis, and small quantities are synthesized in the adrenals and ovaries (108). Men have an amount of circulating testosterone approximately 10-fold greater than women, and this hormonal discrepancy between the sexes is believed to be in large part responsible for the greater muscularity seen in postpubescent males (289). The overwhelming majority of circulating testosterone is bound to either sex hormone–binding globulin (60%) or albumin (38%); the residual ~2% circulates in an unbound state. Unbound testosterone is biologically active and available to be taken up by bodily tissues; weakly bound testosterone can rapidly dissociate from albumin and become active (424). In its unbound form, testosterone binds to androgen receptors in the cytoplasm of target tissues. This causes a conformational change that shuttles the testosterone–androgen receptor complex to the nucleus of the cell, where it regulates gene transcription (795).

The anabolic actions of testosterone are irrefutable. The administration of exogenous testosterone produces large increases in muscle mass in both men and women regardless of age (73, 75, 696), and these effects are amplified when combined with resistance training (74). Elderly women display significantly greater exercise-induced growth when testosterone concentrations are chronically high versus low (277, 278). Kvorning and colleagues (400) showed that blunting testosterone production in young men by administering goserelin, a gonadotropin-releasing hormone analogue, significantly impaired muscular adaptations after 8 weeks of resistance training.

The anabolic actions of testosterone have been partly attributed by its direct ability to increase protein synthesis and diminish proteolysis (780, 860). It is also suggested that testosterone increases the release of other anabolic agents including GH (788) and IGF-1/MGF (675), while inhibiting the activity of IGFBP-4, which is an IGF-1 antagonist (780). Evidence also shows that the combined elevation of testosterone and GH is synergistic to increases in IGF-1 (795). Moreover, myoblasts have been shown to contain androgen receptors. Accordingly, evidence suggests a dose-dependent effect of testosterone on satellite cell proliferation and differentiation, and that higher testosterone concentrations increase the number of myogenically committed cells (289, 696).

There is some evidence that androgen receptors may play a role in the anabolic response to exercise (19). Androgen receptor concentration is diminished immediately after resistance training, but levels rise significantly over the ensuing several hours (795). This postexercise androgen receptor upregulation appears to depend on corresponding elevations in testosterone levels (719). These findings suggest that acute testosterone spikes may influence exercise-induced hypertrophic adaptations both directly and through its effects on androgen receptors,

although the practical relevance of such events remains questionable (see the discussion on acute versus chronic hormonal responses in the next section).

Insulin

Insulin is a peptide hormone secreted by the beta cells of the pancreas. In healthy people insulin regulates glucose metabolism by facilitating its storage as glycogen in muscle and liver tissue. Among other secondary roles, insulin is involved in muscle anabolism, stimulating both the initiation and elongation phases of protein translation by regulating various eIFs and eEFs. Insulin also exerts anabolic effects through activation of the *mammalian target of rapamycin*, universally abbreviated as *mTOR*. A serine/threonine protein kinase, mTOR plays a critical role in regulating cell growth and monitoring cellular nutrient, oxygen, and energy levels (see the PI3K/Akt pathway discussion in chapter 2 for more information).

Despite its anabolic properties (78, 221), the primary impact of insulin on exercise-induced hypertrophic adaptations is believed to be a reduction in protein breakdown (174, 243, 305, 362). The mechanisms by which insulin reduces proteolysis are not well understood at this time. Given that muscle hypertrophy represents the difference between myofibrillar protein synthesis and proteolysis, a decrease in protein breakdown would conceivably enhance the accretion of contractile proteins and thus facilitate greater hypertrophy.

It should be noted that in nondiabetic people, exercise has little effect on insulin levels and can actually blunt its release depending on intensity, duration, and preexercise nutritional consumption (391). Rather, the primary mechanism to manipulate insulin is through nutrient provision. Thus, its hypertrophic role is further explored in chapter 7 in the discussion of nutrient timing strategies.

Acute Versus Chronic Hormonal Responses

Exercise has been shown to significantly increase the release of anabolic hormones in the immediate postworkout period. Strong correlations have been shown between hypertrophy-type training and acute hypophyseal GH secretion (261-263, 273, 579, 736, 737), and the magnitude of these increases is sizable. Fujita and colleagues (237) reported a 10-fold increase in GH levels following blood flow restriction exercise (see chapter 2), whereas Takarada and colleagues (737) found that elevations reached 290-fold over baseline. It is believed that elevations are at least in part mediated by metabolite production (261, 273). An increase in acidosis from H+ buildup also may potentiate GH production via chemoreflex stimulation regulated by intramuscular metaboreceptors and group III and IV afferents (425, 796).

Performance of hypertrophy-type training also has been shown to significantly increase circulating IGF-1 levels (385, 386, 633), although these results have not been consistent across all trials (388). It is not clear whether such elevations are mediated primarily by corresponding increases in GH release or whether the exercise itself enhances acute production. Research on the acute testosterone response to resistance training has been somewhat inconsistent. Several studies have shown greater elevations in testosterone following hypertrophy-type resistance training versus strength-type protocols (108, 263, 273, 471, 701), whereas others failed to detect significant differences (385, 605, 731). It should be noted that sex, age, and training status profoundly influence testosterone synthesis (391), and these factors may account for conflicting results.

Given the positive relationship between anabolic hormones and hypertrophy-type training, researchers formulated the *hormone hypothesis*, which proposes that postworkout hormonal elevations are central to long-term increases in muscle size (262, 285). It has been proposed that these momentary hormonal spikes may be more important to muscle growth–related responses than chronic alterations in resting hormonal concentrations (391). Theoretically, hormonal spikes increase the likelihood that the secreted hormones interact with the target tissue receptors (161), which may be especially beneficial after exercise when muscles are primed for tissue anabolism. In addition, large hormonal elevations may positively influence intracellular signaling to rapidly reduce postexercise proteoloysis and heighten anabolic processes to achieve a greater supercompensatory response.

Despite a seemingly logical basis, a number of researchers have questioned the legitimacy of the hormone hypothesis (426, 576); they have proposed an alternative hypothesis that such biological events are intended to mobilize fuel stores rather than promote tissue anabolism (819). In particular, the anabolic role of acute GH production has been dismissed largely based on studies showing that injections of genetically engineered recombinant GH do not promote greater increases in muscle growth (407, 847, 848). Although this contention may have merit, it fails to take into account the fact that exogenous GH administration does not mimic the *in vivo* (within a whole, living organism) response to exercise-induced hormonal elevations either temporally or in magnitude. The intracellular environment is primed for anabolism following intense training, and it is conceivable that large transient spikes in GH enhance the remodeling process. Moreover, recombinant GH is composed solely of the 22-kDa isoform (200), whereas more than 100 molecular isoforms of GH are produced endogenously (531). These isoforms peak in the early postexercise period, and a majority of those isoforms are of the non-22-kDa variety (200). Recombinant GH administered in supraphysiological doses (i.e., a dose that is larger or more potent than would occur naturally in the body) actually inhibits the postworkout stimulation of these alternative isoforms (200), potentially blunting hypertrophic effects. Whether these factors significantly affect hypertrophic adaptations has yet to be established.

The binding of testosterone to cell receptors can rapidly (within seconds) trigger second messengers involved in downstream protein kinase signaling (162), suggesting a link between momentary postworkout elevations and muscle protein synthesis. Kvorning and colleagues (401) demonstrated that suppressing testosterone levels with goserelin blunted exercise-induced muscle growth despite no alterations in acute mRNA expression of MyoD, myogenin, myostatin, IGF-1Ea, IGF-1Eb, IGF-1Ec, and androgen receptor, suggesting that that testosterone may mediate intracellular signaling downstream from these factors. Both total and free testosterone levels in the placebo group increased by approximately 15% immediately postexercise, whereas those treated with goserelin displayed a reduction in total and free testosterone 15 min after the training bout, suggesting an anabolic effect from the transient elevations. In contrast to these findings, West and colleagues (817) reported that acute elevations in postexercise anabolic hormones had no effect on postexercise muscle protein synthesis in young men compared to those performing a protocol that did not significantly elevate hormones. Although these studies provide insight into general hypertrophic responses, it is important to recognize that the acute protein synthetic response to exercise training does not always correlate with chronic anabolic signaling (148), and these events are not necessarily predictive of long-term increases in muscle growth (765). This is particularly true with respect to the untrained subjects used in these studies, because their acute responses may be more related to their unfamiliarity with the exercise per se and the associated muscle damage that inevitably occurs from such training (49).

Several longitudinal studies show significant associations between the postexercise hormonal response and muscle growth. McCall and colleagues (469) investigated the topic in 11 resistance-trained young men over the course of a 12-week high-volume resistance training program. Strong correlations were found between acute GH increases and the extent of both Type I ($r = .74$) and Type II ($r = .71$) fiber cross-sectional area. Similarly, Ahtiainen and colleagues (18) demonstrated strong associations between acute testosterone elevations and increases in quadriceps femoris muscle cross-sectional area ($r = .76$) in 16 young men (8 strength athletes and 8 physically active people) who performed heavy resistance exercise for 21 weeks. Both

of these studies were limited by small sample sizes, compromising statistical power. Subsequently, two larger studies from McMaster University cast doubt on the veracity of these findings. West and Phillips (820) studied the postexercise systemic response to 12 weeks of resistance training in 56 untrained young men. A weak correlation was found between transient GH elevations and increases in Type II fiber area ($r = .28$), which was estimated to explain approximately 8% of the variance in muscle protein accretion. No association was demonstrated between the postexercise testosterone response and muscle growth. Interestingly, a subanalysis of hormonal variations between hypertrophic responders and nonresponders (i.e., those in the top and bottom ~16%) showed a strong trend for correlations between increased IGF-1 levels and muscular adaptations ($p = .053$). Follow-up work by the same lab found no relationship between acute elevations in testosterone, GH, or IGF-1 and mean increases in muscle fiber cross-sectional area following 16 weeks of resistance training in a group of 23 untrained young men (497). Although the aforementioned studies provide insight into possible interactions, caution must be used in attempting to draw causal conclusions from correlative data.

In a number of studies, researchers have attempted to directly evaluate the effect of the transient postexercise hormonal release on muscle protein accretion. The results of these trials have been conflicting. Madarame and colleagues (447) found a significant increase in elbow flexor cross-sectional area following unilateral upper arm exercise combined with lower-body occlusion training compared to identical arm training combined with nonoccluded lower-body exercise. Differences in GH levels between conditions did not rise to statistical significance, but the authors stated that this was likely a Type II error due to lack of statistical power. Given that comparable protocols have resulted in marked increases in postexercise hormones (261, 262, 273, 579, 736, 737), findings suggest a possible role of systemic factors in the adaptive response. It also should be noted that muscle cross-sectional area remained unchanged in the nontrained arm, indicating that the acute systemic response had no hypertrophic effect in the absence of mechanical stimuli.

Employing a within-subject design, West and colleagues (818) recruited 12 untrained men to perform elbow flexion exercise on separate days under two hormonal conditions: a low-hormone condition in which one arm performed elbow flexion exercise only and a high-hormone condition in which the contralateral arm performed the same arm curl exercise followed immediately by multiple sets of lower-body resistance training designed to promote a robust systemic response. After 15 weeks, increases in muscle cross-sectional area were similar between conditions despite significantly higher postexercise concentrations of circulating IGF-1, GH, and testosterone in those in the high-hormone condition.

Ronnestad and colleagues (625) carried out a similar within-subject design as that of West and colleagues (818), except that the high-hormone group performed lower-body exercise before elbow flexion exercise. In contrast to the findings of West and colleagues (818), significantly greater increases in elbow flexor cross-sectional area were noted in the high-hormone condition, implying a direct causal link between acute hormonal elevations and hypertrophic adaptations. Differences were region specific, and increases in cross-sectional area were seen only at the two middle sections of the elbow flexors where muscle girth was largest.

Evidence from the body of literature as to whether postexercise anabolic hormonal elevations are associated with increases in muscle growth remains murky. Although it is premature to dismiss a potential role, it seems clear that if such a role does exist, the overall magnitude of the effect is at best modest (658). More likely, these events confer a permissive effect, whereby hypertrophic responses are facilitated by the favorable anabolic environment. It is possible that the acute systemic response has a greater effect on satellite cell function as opposed to regulating postexercise anabolism, thereby influencing hypertrophy by enhancing long-term growth potential. If so, the hypertrophic effects of transient spikes

in hormones might be limited by genetic differences in the ability to expand the available satellite cell pool. This hypothesis remains untested. Importantly, no studies to date have evaluated the topic in well-trained people, so it cannot be determined whether those with considerable training experience respond differently to acute exercise–induced hormonal elevations than those who are untrained.

KEY POINT

The endocrine system is intricately involved in the regulation of muscle mass, although the exact role of acute hormonal elevations in hypertrophy is unclear. The chronic production of testosterone, growth hormone, IGF-1, and other anabolic hormones influences protein balance to bring about changes in resistance training–mediated muscular adaptations.

Responses and Adaptations of Myokines

The term *myokine* is commonly used to describe cytokines that are expressed and locally secreted by skeletal muscle to interact in an autocrine/paracrine fashion as well as reaching the circulation to exert influence on other tissues (580, 583). Exercise training results in the synthesis of these substances within skeletal muscle, and an emerging body of evidence indicates that they can have unique effects on skeletal muscle to promote anabolic or catabolic processes (see table 1.3) (530, 596, 682). Myokine production provides a conceptual basis for clarifying how muscles communicate intracellularly and with other organs. There are dozens of known myokines, and new variants continue to be identified. This section addresses some of the better studied of these agents and their effects on muscle hypertrophy.

Mechano Growth Factor

Mechano growth factor (MGF) is widely considered necessary for compensatory muscle

TABLE 1.3 **Primary Myokines and Their Respective Actions**

Myokine	Actions
Mechano growth factor (MGF)	Believed to kick-start the growth process following resistance training. Upregulates anabolic processes and downregulates catabolic processes. Involved in early-stage satellite cell responses to mechanical stimuli.
Interleukins (ILs)	Numerous ILs are released to control and coordinate the postexercise immune response. IL-6, the most studied of the ILs, appears to carry out hypertrophic actions by inducing satellite cell proliferation and influencing satellite cell–mediated myonuclear accretion.
Myostatin (MSTN)	Serves as a negative regulator of muscle growth. Acts to reduce myofibrillar protein synthesis, and may also suppress satellite cell activation.
Hepatocyte growth factor (HGF)	Activated by nitric oxide synthase and possibly calcium–calmodulin as well. HGF is believed to be critical to the activation of inactive satellite cells.
Leukemia inhibitory factor (LIF)	Upregulated by the calcium flux associated with resistance exercise. Believed to act in a paracrine fashion on adjacent satellite cells to induce their proliferation.

growth, even more so than the systemic IGF-1 isoforms (289). As previously mentioned, resistance training acutely upregulates MGF mRNA expression (366). Current theory suggests that this event helps to kick-start postexercise muscle recovery by facilitating the local repair and regeneration following myotrauma (254). In support of this view, Bamman and colleagues (56) recruited 66 men and women of varying ages to undertake 16 weeks of lower-body resistance training. Based on their hypertrophic response to the program, subjects were then categorized as either extreme responders (mean myofiber hypertrophy of 58%), moderate responders (mean myofiber hypertrophy of 28%), or nonresponders (no significant increase in myofiber hypertrophy). Muscle biopsy analysis showed a differential MGF expression across clusters: whereas MGF levels increased by 126% in those classified as extreme responders, concentrations remained virtually unchanged in nonresponders. These results imply that transient exercise-induced increases in MGF gene expression serve as critical cues for muscle remodeling and may be essential to producing maximal hypertrophic gains.

MGF is purported to regulate muscle growth by several means. For one, it appears to directly stimulate muscle protein synthesis by the phosphorylation of *p70S6* kinase (a serine/threonine kinase that targets the S6 ribosomal protein; phosphorylation of S6 causes protein synthesis at the ribosome; it is also written as p70S6K or p70^{S6K}) via the PI3K/Akt pathway (see chapter 2) (13, 14, 541). MGF also may elevate muscle protein synthesis by downregulating the catabolic processes involved in proteolysis. Evidence indicates that the activation of MGF suppresses FOXO nuclear localization and transcriptional activities, thereby helping to inhibit protein breakdown (259). These combined anabolic and anticatabolic actions are thought to heighten the postexercise hypertrophic response.

MGF also is believed to influence hypertrophic adaptations by mediating the satellite cell response to exercise training. Although systemic IGF-1 promotes later-stage effects on satellite cell function, local expression of the peptide has been shown to be involved primarily in the initial phases. This is consistent with research demonstrating that MGF regulates extracellular signal–regulated kinases (ERK1 and ERK2; also abbreviated as ERK1/2), whereas the systemic isoforms do not. It is also consistent with research demonstrating that MGF is expressed earlier than hepatic (liver)-

type IGF-1 following exercise (59, 255). Accordingly, MGF appears to be involved in inducing satellite cell activation and proliferation (309, 844), but not differentiation (844). This observation suggests that MGF increases the number of myoblasts available for postexercise repair as well as facilitating the replenishment of the satellite cell pool. However, other research challenges MGF's role in satellite cell function. Fornaro and colleagues (225) demonstrated that high concentrations of MGF failed to enhance proliferation or differentiation in both mouse C2C12 murine myoblasts and human skeletal muscle myoblasts, as well as primary mouse muscle stem cells. Interestingly, mature IGF-1 promoted a strong proliferative response in all cell types. The discrepancies between this study and previous work are not readily apparent.

Interleukins

The *interleukins* (ILs) are a class of cytokines released by numerous bodily tissues to control and coordinate immune responses. The most studied of these isoforms is IL-6, an early-stage myokine believed to play an important and perhaps even critical role in exercise-induced muscular growth. This contention is supported by research showing that IL-6 mice display an impaired hypertrophic response (682). IL-6 is also considered an important growth factor for human connective tissue, stimulating collagen synthesis in healthy tendons (31). Such actions enhance the ability of muscle tissue to endure high levels of mechanical stress.

Resistance training acutely upregulates IL-6 by up to 100-fold, and exercise-induced metabolic stress may further stimulate its production (213). Moreover, the magnitude of postexercise IL-6 expression is significantly correlated with hypertrophic adaptations (497). Contracting skeletal muscles account for a majority of circulating IL-6; additional sources are synthesized by connective tissue, adipocytes, and the brain (566). The appearance of IL-6 in the systemic circulation precedes that of other cytokines, and the magnitude of its release is by far more prominent.

It was initially thought that muscle damage was a primary mediator of the IL-6 response. This seems logical, given that damage to muscle tissue initiates an inflammatory cascade. However, emerging evidence indicates that myodamage is not necessary for its exercise-induced release. Instead, damaging exercise may result in a delayed peak and a slower decrease of plasma IL-6 during recovery (566).

The primary hypertrophic actions of IL-6 appear to be related to its effects on satellite cells, both by inducing proliferation (350, 772) and by influencing satellite cell–mediated myonuclear accretion (682). There also is evidence that IL-6 may directly mediate protein synthesis via activation of the Janus kinase/signal transducer and activator of transcription (JAK/STAT), ERK1/2, and PI3K/Akt signal transduction pathways (see chapter 2) (608).

IL-15 is another myokine that has received considerable interest as having a potential role in skeletal muscle growth. Muscle is the primary source of IL-15 expression, and exercise regulates its production. Resistance training, in particular, has been shown to acutely elevate IL-15 protein levels, apparently through its release via microtears in muscle fibers as a result of inflammation, oxidative stress, or both (596, 616). Type II fibers show a greater increase in IL-15 mRNA levels than Type I fibers do (529).

Early animal research suggested that IL-15 exerted anabolic effects by acting directly on differentiated myotubes to increase muscle protein synthesis and reduce protein degradation (596). A polymorphism in the gene for IL-15 receptor was found to explain a relatively large proportion of the variation in muscle hypertrophy (616). Moreover, recombinant IL-15 administration in healthy growing rats produced more than a 3-fold decrease in the rate of protein breakdown, leading to an increase in muscle weight and contractile protein accretion (596). However, recent research suggests that IL-15 may not cause the hypertrophic adaptations originally thought. For one, IL-15 mRNA correlates poorly with protein expression. In addition, hypertrophic effects of IL-15 have been observed solely in diseased rodents. Quinn and colleagues (595) demonstrated that transgenic mice constructed to oversecrete IL-15 substantially reduced body fat but only minimally increased lean tissue mass. Muscular gains were limited to the slow/oxidative soleus muscle, whereas the fast/glycolytic extensor digitorum longus muscle had slight decreases in hypertrophy. Given this emerging evidence, it is hypothesized that IL-15 serves to regulate the oxidative and fatigue properties of skeletal muscle as opposed to promoting the accretion of contractile proteins (583).

Research on other ILs is limited at this time. IL-10 has been implicated as an important mediator of processes that drive myoblast proliferation and myofiber growth (580). Other evidence suggests that IL-4 is involved in myogenic differentiation (637). IL-6 and IL-7 are also believed to play a role in muscle hypertrophy and myogenesis (567). Substantially more research is needed for developing a complete understanding of the roles of each of these IL isoforms (and perhaps others) with respect to exercise-induced muscular adaptations.

The acute effects of resistance exercise on ILs must be differentiated from chronically elevated levels of these cytokines. Evidence indicates that chronic low-grade inflammation, as determined by increased circulating concentrations of pro-inflammatory cytokines, is correlated with the age-related loss of muscle mass (489). Reducing chronically elevated inflammatory levels with nonsteroidal anti-inflammatory drugs has been shown to restore muscle protein anabolism and significantly reduce muscle loss in aging rats (618). Moreover, physical activity displays an inverse correlation with low-grade systemic inflammation (566): The acute elevation of ILs enhances anabolism, whereas the suppression of chronic IL production mitigates catabolic processes.

Myostatin

Myostatin (MSTN), a member of the transforming growth factor-β superfamily, is recognized as a powerful negative regulator of developing muscle mass (367). The MSTN gene is expressed almost exclusively in muscle fibers throughout embryonic development as well as in adult animals (669). A mutation of the MSTN gene has been shown to produce marked hypertrophy in animals. A breed of cattle known to be null for the MSTN gene, called the Belgian Blue, displays a hypermuscular appearance (figure 1.12), so much so that they are popularly referred to as Schwarzenegger cattle after the champion bodybuilder. Moreover, targeted disruption of the MSTN gene in mice results in a doubling of skeletal muscle mass (484).

The regulatory effects of MSTN are present in humans, as exemplified in a case report of an infant who appeared extraordinarily muscular at birth, with protruding thigh muscles (669). The child's development was followed over time, and at 4.5 years of age he continued to display superior levels of muscle bulk and strength. Subsequent genetic analysis revealed that the child was null for the MSTN gene, which conceivably explains his hypermuscularity.

There is conflicting evidence as to the quality of muscle tissue in MSTN deficiencies. Racing dogs found to be null for the MSTN gene were significantly faster than those carrying the wild-type genotype, suggesting a clear performance advantage (511). Alternatively, other research shows that a mutation of the MSTN gene in mice is associated with impaired calcium release from the sarcoplasmic reticulum (83). So although these mice are hypermuscular in appearance, the increased muscle mass does not translate into an increased ability to produce force. At this point the functional implications of alterations in MSTN remain undetermined.

MSTN carries out its actions via downstream signaling of the transcription factors SMAD2 and SMAD3, which in turn negatively regulate hypertrophy independent of the catabolic enzyme muscle ring finger protein-1 (MuRF-1). Early research indicated that atrophic actions of MSTN were attributed to an inhibition of satellite cell activation, thus impairing protein synthetic capacity (473). Moreover, in vitro research showed that MSTN blunted satellite cell proliferation and differentiation (857). However, subsequent research has refuted these findings, showing instead that MSTN inhibition increases muscle mass primarily by acting on muscle fibers as opposed to satellite cells, thereby increasing the cytoplasmic volume to DNA (804). The body of evidence appears to suggest that the primary mechanism of MSTN action in the postnatal period is the modulation of myofibrillar muscle protein synthesis (12), although it may still play a minor role in regulating satellite cell function (286). The negative regulation of muscle protein synthesis is thought to occur via a combined inhibition of the Akt/mTOR pathway (see chapter 2) as well as downregulation of both calcineurin signaling and the transcription factors MyoD and myogenin (784). Myostatin-induced inhibition of mTOR is self-perpetuating, because this downregulation in turn further amplifies MSTN signaling (250).

In addition to acutely upregulating numerous growth-related factors, resistance train-ing also downregulates inhibitory factors including MSTN (366). Untrained people show modest decreases in MSTN following a resistance exercise bout, and these reductions are more than 3-fold greater with consistent resistance training experience (516). However, MSTN does not seem to play a significant role as an inhibitor of exercise-induced hypertrophy in normal healthy adults expressing a fair amount of muscle MSTN protein and mRNA (366). Therefore, what, if any, effects these changes have on long-term increases in muscle growth remains uncertain (215).

Other Myokines

A number of additional myokines have been identified, and emerging evidence indicates that many may play a role in hypertrophic adaptations. Perhaps the most intriguing of these is *hepatocyte growth factor* (HGF), which exerts mitogenic actions on numerous bodily tissues including muscle. Evidence shows that HGF is critical for the activation of dormant

FIGURE 1.12 Belgian Blue, a breed of cattle known to be null for the myostatin gene.

satellite cells (11). To date, HGF is the only myokine shown to stimulate dormant satellite cells to enter the cell cycle early both in vitro and in vivo (748).

The active form of HGF is present in the extracellular compartment of uninjured skeletal muscle (746), and it is activated by mechanical signaling via the dystrophin-associated protein complex (11). Muscular contractions alter this complex, leading to nitric oxide synthase activation, which stimulates the release of HGF from the extracellular matrix and facilitates its interaction with receptors on satellite cells (11). There is also evidence that calcium–calmodulin signaling mediates HGF release from the matrix independent of nitric oxide production (747). Evidence shows that HGF is critical for the activation of inactive satellite cells (11). Interestingly, chronically high levels of HGF are associated with the upregulation of MSTN mRNA, which in turn may have a negative effect on the proliferative response and return satellite cells to quiescence (12). These data highlight the fine regulatory role that HGF seems to have in the growth process.

Leukemia inhibitory factor (LIF) is another myokine that has been shown to play a role in muscle hypertrophy (717). During exercise, skeletal muscle markedly upregulates the expression of LIF mRNA, likely as a result of fluctuations in intracellular calcium concentrations (96). Mice null for the LIF gene were incapable of increasing muscle size following muscular overload, but the growth response was restored following recombinant LIF administration (717). It is hypothesized that LIF exerts hypertrophic effects primarily by acting in a paracrine fashion on adjacent satellite cells, inducing their proliferation while preventing premature differentiation (96).

KEY POINT

Myokines are autocrine or paracrine agents that exert their effects directly on muscle tissue as a result of mechanical stimulation. Numerous myokines have been identified, although the specific roles of the substances and their interactions with one another have yet to be elucidated.

Many other myokines with potential hypertrophic effects have been identified in the literature, including fibroblast growth factor, brain-derived neutrophic factor, tumor necrosis factor, and chitinase-3-like protein 1. Myokines are a relatively new area of research, and the study of these substances is continually evolving. Over the coming years, we should have a much greater understanding of their scope and effects on muscle growth.

TAKE-HOME POINTS

- Early-phase adaptations to resistance training are primarily related to neural improvements including greater recruitment, rate coding, synchronization, and doublet firing. The extent and temporal course of neural adaptations depend on the degrees of freedom and complexity of the movement patterns.

- Muscular adaptations are predicated on net protein balance over time. The process is mediated by intracellular anabolic and catabolic signaling cascades.

- Hypertrophy can occur in series or in parallel, or both. The primary means by which muscles increase in size following resistance training is through parallel hypertrophy. Resistance training does promote changes in sarcoplasmic fractions, but it is not clear whether these adaptations are practically meaningful from a hypertrophic standpoint, nor is it known whether different training protocols elicit differential effects on the extent of these changes. There is contradictory evidence that hyperplasia occurs as a result of traditional resistance training; if any fiber splitting does occur, the overall impact on muscle size appears to be relatively minimal.

- Satellite cells appear to be crucial to maximizing the hypertrophic response to resistance training. The primary role of satellite cells appears to be their ability to retain a muscle's mitotic capacity by donating nuclei to existing myofibers. Satellite cells also are involved in the repair and remodeling of muscle tissue, including the co-expression of myogenic regulatory factors that mediate growth-related processes.

- The endocrine system is intricately involved in the regulation of muscle mass. The chronic production of testosterone, growth hormone, IGF-1, and other anabolic hormones influences protein balance to bring about changes in resistance training–mediated muscular adaptations. Although the manipulation of resistance training variables can acutely elevate systemic levels in the immediate postworkout period, it is not clear whether these transient hormonal spikes play a role in the hypertrophic response; if there are any such effects, they appear to be of minor consequence.

- Myokines are important players in exercise-induced muscular adaptations. These autocrine/paracrine agents exert their effects directly on muscle tissue as a result of mechanical stimulation. Numerous myokines have been identified, although the specific roles of the substances and their interactions with one another have yet to be elucidated.

Mechanisms of Hypertrophy

2

Increased muscle protein accretion following resistance exercise has been attributed to three primary mechanisms: mechanical tension, metabolic stress, and muscle damage (656). This chapter addresses each of these mechanisms and the theoretical rationale for its promotion of a hypertrophic response.

Mechanical Tension

Skeletal muscle is highly responsive to alterations in mechanical loading. Accordingly, a number of researchers have surmised that *mechanical tension* is the primary driving force in the hypertrophic response to regimented resistance training (232, 253). Mechanical tension alone has been shown to directly stimulate mTOR (316), possibly through activation of the extracellular signal–regulated kinase/tuberous sclerosis complex 2 (ERK/TSC2) pathway (501). It is theorized that these actions are mediated via the synthesis of the lipid second messenger phosphatidic acid by phospholipase D (316, 551). There also is evidence that phosphatidic acid can phosphorylate p70^{S6K} independent of mTOR (414), presenting another potential avenue whereby mechanical stimuli may directly influence muscle protein synthesis.

Research indicates that mechanosensors are sensitive to both the magnitude and temporal aspects of loading. Using an *in situ* model (i.e., examining an intact muscle within the animal), Martineau and Gardiner (454) subjected rat plantaris muscles to peak concentric, eccentric, isometric, and passive tensions. Results showed tension-dependent phosphorylation of c-Jun N-terminal kinase (JNK) and ERK1/2; eccentric actions generated the greatest effect; and passive stretch, the least. Peak tension was determined to be a better predictor of mitogen-activated protein kinase (MAPK) phosphorylation than either time under tension or rate of tension development. In a follow-up study by the same lab (455), an in situ evaluation of the rat gastrocnemius muscle showed a linear relationship between time under tension and the signaling of JNK, whereas the rate of change of tension showed no effect. This suggests that time under tension is an important parameter for muscle hypertrophic adaptations. In support of these findings, Nader and Esser (515) reported increased activation of p70^{S6K} following both high-intensity and low-intensity electrical stimuli of the rat hind limb; however, the response was not as prolonged following the low-intensity protocol. Similarly, in vitro research shows a magnitude-dependent effect on p70^{S6K} signaling when mouse C2C12 myoblasts are subjected to biaxial strain (229).

Mechanosensors also appear to be sensitive to the type of load imposed on muscle tissue. Stretch-induced mechanical loading elicits the deposition of sarcomeres longitudinally (i.e., in series), whereas dynamic muscular actions increase cross-sectional area in parallel with the axes (229). Moreover, the hypertrophic response can vary based on the type of muscle action. Isometric and eccentric actions stimulate the expression of distinct genes in a manner that cannot be explained by differences in the magnitude of applied mechanical force (229). These examples highlight the intricate complexity of mechanosensors and their capacity to distinguish between types of mechanical information to produce an adaptive response. What follows is a discussion of how mechanical forces regulate muscle hypertrophy via mechanotransduction and intracellular signaling pathways.

KEY POINT

Mechanical tension may be the most important factor in training-induced muscle hypertrophy. Mechanosensors are sensitive to both the magnitude and the duration of loading, and these stimuli can directly mediate intracellular signaling to bring about hypertrophic adaptations.

Mechanotransduction

Exercise has a profound effect on muscle protein balance. When muscles are mechanically overloaded and then provided with appropriate nutrients and recovery, the body initiates an adaptive response that results in the accretion of muscle proteins. Transmission of mechanical forces occurs both longitudinally along the length of the fiber and laterally through the matrix of fascia tissue (730). The associated response is accomplished through a phenomenon called *mechanotransduction*, whereby mechanical forces in muscle are converted into molecular events that mediate intracellular anabolic and catabolic pathways (see figure 2.1) (861).

A diverse array of tissue and substances help to carry out mechanotransduction including stretch-activated ion channels, caveolae, integrins, cadherins, growth factor receptors, myosin motors, cytoskeletal proteins, nuclei, and the extracellular matrix (229). Central

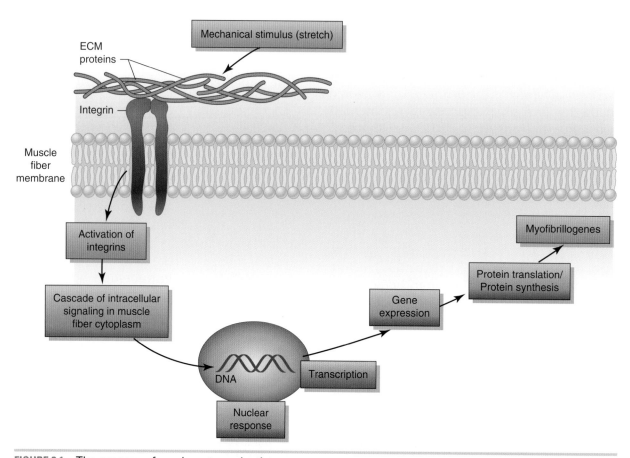

FIGURE 2.1   The process of mechanotransduction.

Based on P.G. De Deyne, 2001, "Application of passive stretch and its implications for muscle fibers," *Physical Therapy* 81(2): 819-827.

to the process are mechanosensors that sense mechanical tension and transduce the stimuli into chemical signals within the myofiber. Integrins have been identified as a primary mechanosensor. These receptors reside at the cell surface and interact with the extracellular matrix to facilitate the transmission of mechanical and chemical information from the outside to the inside of the cell (856, 861). Integrins mediate intracellular signal transduction as part of focal adhesion complexes that bridge the connection between the extracellular matrix and the cytoskeleton. Emerging evidence shows that an enzyme called focal adhesion kinase serves as a key player in signal initiation (165).

Once forces are transduced, intracellular enzymatic cascades carry out signaling to downstream targets that ultimately shift muscle protein balance to favor synthesis over degradation. Certain pathways act in a permissive role, whereas others directly mediate cellular processes that influence mRNA translation and myofiber growth (463). A number of primary anabolic signaling pathways have been identified, including the PI3K/Akt pathway, MAPK

pathways, calcium-dependent pathways, and the phosphatidic acid pathway (see figure 2.2). Although these pathways may overlap at key regulatory steps, there is evidence that they may be interactive rather than redundant (763).

Alternatively, muscle catabolism is regulated by four proteolytic systems: autophagy-lysosomal, calcium-dependent calpains, the cysteine protease caspase enzymes, and the ubiquitin–proteasome system (562). The 5'-AMP-activated protein kinase (AMPK) pathway is believed to act as a metabolic master switch in these systems. It is activated in response to environmental stressors (e.g., exercise) to restore cellular energy balance via an increase of catabolic processes and a suppression of anabolic processes (see figure 2.3).

Signaling Pathways

This section provides a general overview of the primary anabolic intracellular signaling pathways and their significance to skeletal muscle hypertrophy. Although huge strides have been made to elucidate these pathways, our understanding of their relative importance is limited at this time.

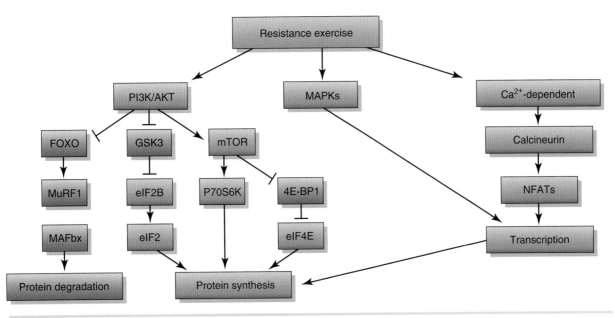

FIGURE 2.2 Primary anabolic intracellular signaling pathways.

With kind permission from Springer Science+Business Media: *Sports Medicine*, "Potential mechanisms for a role of metabolic stress in hypertrophic adaptations to resistance training," 43, 179-194, 2013, B.J. Schoenfeld, Fig. 1.

KEY POINT

Numerous intracellular signaling pathways have been identified in skeletal muscle including PI3K/Akt, MAPK, phosphatidic acid, AMPK, and calcium-dependent pathways. The serine/threonine kinase mTOR has been shown to be critical to mechanically induced hypertrophic adaptation.

PI3K/Akt Pathway

The phosphatidylinositol 3-kinase (PI3K)/Akt pathway is considered a master network for regulating skeletal muscle growth (82, 339, 761). Akt, also known as protein kinase B (PKB), acts as a molecular upstream nodal point that functions both as an effector of anabolic signaling and a dominant inhibitor

of catabolic signals (771). Multiple isoforms of Akt have been identified in skeletal muscle (Akt1, Akt2, Akt3), and each has a distinct physiological role. Of these isoforms, Akt1 appears to be most responsive to mechanical stimuli (856). Early research indicated that high mechanical intensities were required to activate Akt; however, subsequent studies demonstrate evidence to the contrary (856).

A primary means by which Akt carries out its actions is by signaling mTOR, which has been shown to be critical to hypertrophic adaptations induced by mechanical loading. mTOR, named because the pharmacological agent rapamycin antagonizes its growth-promoting effects, exists in two functionally distinct signaling complexes: mTORC1 and mTORC2. Only mTORC1 is inhibited by rapamycin, and thus mTOR's hypertrophic regulatory actions are believed to be carried

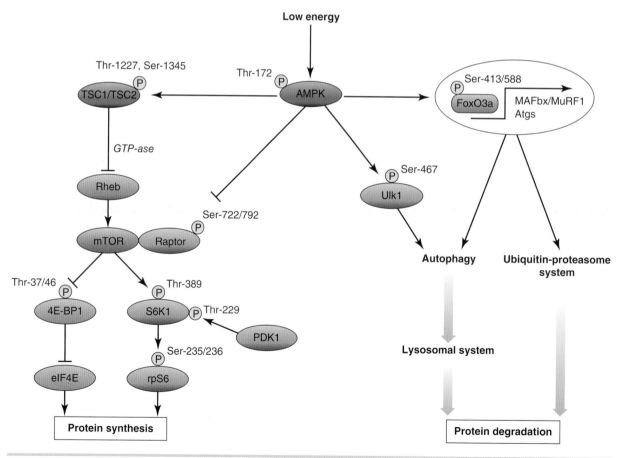

FIGURE 2.3 Primary proteolytic pathways.

Reprinted, by permission, from A.M.J. Sanches et al., 2012, "The role of AMP-activated protein kinase in the coordination of skeletal muscle turnover and energy homeostasis," *American Journal of Physiology–Cell Physiology* 303(5): C475-C485.

out primarily through this complex. Once activated, mTOR exerts its effects by turning on various downstream anabolic effectors. A primary target of mTOR is p70^{S6K}, which plays an important role in the initiation of mRNA translation (259). mTOR also exerts anabolic effects by inhibiting eukaryotic initiation factor 4E-binding protein 1 (eIF4EB1), a negative regulator of the eIF4E protein that is a potent mediator of protein translation (250).

Signaling through PI3K/Akt also regulates mTOR-independent growth regulatory molecules to directly inhibit catabolic processes. For one, Akt phosphorylates FOXO proteins—a subgroup of the Forkhead family of transcription factors that encourage atrophy—thereby inducing their translocation from the nucleus to the cytoplasm (259, 289). The cytoplasmic sequestration of FOXO proteins, in turn, blocks upregulation of the ubiquitin ligases MuRF-1 and atrogin-1 (also called MAFbx) and thus helps to lessen muscle protein breakdown. Indeed, activation of Akt was found to be sufficient to impair atrophy-associated increases in MuRF-1 and atogin-1 transcription via FOXO phosphorylation (250). Akt also suppresses the activation of glycogen synthase kinase 3 beta (GSK3β), which blocks protein translation initiated by the eIF2B protein (250, 551). As opposed to mTORC1, which regulates the translation of a small subset of mRNAs, eIF2B is believed to control the translation initiation of virtually all mRNAs, and thus acts to regulate global rates of protein synthesis (259). Thus, the anticatabolic actions of PI3K/Akt may indirectly provide an even more potent stimulus for growth than its anabolic effects.

The hypertrophic properties of PI3K/Akt are incontrovertible. Induction of the pathway has been shown to mediate protein translation both in vitro and in vivo, as well as promote myoblast differentiation (250). However, recent research indicates that PI3K/Akt activation is not obligatory for increases in muscle hypertrophy (797). Resistance exercise activates p70^{S6K} in humans via an Akt-independent pathway (201, 459, 754). Moreover, mTOR can be activated via a variety of intracellular signals other than PI3K/Akt, indicating that the pathways influencing growth are complex and diverse.

MAPK Pathways

Mitogen-activated protein kinase (MAPK) is a primary regulator of gene expression, redox status, and metabolism (393). With respect to exercise-induced muscle growth, MAPK is believed to link cellular stress with an adaptive response in myofibers, modulating their growth and differentiation (631). Three distinct MAPK signaling modules are associated with compensatory hypertrophic adaptations: ERK1/2, p38 MAPK, and JNK. Activation of these modules depends on the type, duration, and intensity of the stimulus.

ERK1/2 is upregulated by both aerobic endurance and resistance training, and the magnitude of its phosphorylation correlates with the intensity of exercise (393). Studies investigating the role of ERK1/2 in the regulation of muscle mass have been somewhat conflicting. On one hand, there is evidence that it mediates satellite proliferation and induces muscle protein synthesis; on the other hand, some studies show opposite effects (202). That said, early signaling of mTORC1 likely occurs through activation of the ERK/TSC2 pathway (501). Whereas Akt and ERK1/2 both stimulate mTOR to a similar extent, their combined effects lead to an even greater stimulation compared to either alone (833). Moreover, the two pathways appear to be synergistic to satellite cell function; ERK1/2 stimulates cell proliferation, and PI3K facilitates differentiation (272).

Activation of p38 MAPK occurs primarily following aerobic endurance exercise. Four p38 isoforms have been identified (p38α, p38β, p38δ, and p38γ). Of these isoforms, p38γ is specific to muscle tissue, whereas p38α and p38β are expressed throughout the body; p38δ does not appear to be involved with muscular actions. p38γ is preferentially upregulated in slow-twitch fibers while remaining largely inactive in fast-twitch fibers (226). Moreover, a loss of p38γ in rat and mouse models is associated with a decrease in slow-twitch fiber size and no change in fast-twitch fibers (226). There is evidence that p38 may regulate hypertrophy by stimulating Notch signaling, which has been deemed essential for the activation, proliferation, and progression of myogenic satellite cells necessary for muscle regeneration and repair (97).

Of all the MAPK modules, JNK appears to be the most sensitive to mechanical tension, and it is particularly responsive to eccentric actions. Contraction-induced phosphorylation of JNK correlates with a rapid rise in mRNA of transcription factors that mediate cell proliferation and DNA repair (45, 46), indicating a role in muscle regeneration following intense exercise. Moreover, JNK phosphorylation displays a linear increase with heightened levels of contractile force (393). However, the specific role of JNK in exercise-induced muscle hypertrophy remains undetermined. In fact, some studies suggest that its inhibition actually enhances muscle protein accretion (97).

The interplay between the MAPK modules and their potential hypertrophic synergism with one another has yet to be established. In response to synergist ablation of the rat gastrocnemius, p38α MAPK phosphorylation occurred early following overload and remained elevated in both slow-twitch soleus and fast-twitch plantaris muscles over the ensuing 24-hour study period. Conversely, ERK2 and JNK phosphorylation increased transiently postablation; levels returned to that of sham-operated controls (placebo-controlled surgical interventions) by 24 hours. The implications of these findings are not clear at present.

Calcium-Dependent Pathways

Intracellular calcium plays an important role in signal transduction in a variety of cell types, including skeletal muscle (135). An increase in myoelectrical activity substantially elevates calcium levels within myofibers, and this alteration is considered to be a primary mediator of skeletal muscle gene expression (135). Various calcium-dependent pathways have been implicated in the control of skeletal muscle mass. Calcineurin, a calcium-regulated phosphatase, is believed to have a particularly important role in muscular adaptations. Cal-

cineurin is activated by a sustained increase in intracellular calcium levels. Once aroused, it acts on various downstream anabolic effectors, including myocyte-enhancing factor 2 (MEF2), GATA transcription factors, and nuclear factor of activated T cells (NFAT) (490). Calcineurin has been shown to promote hypertrophy in all fiber types, whereas its inhibition prevents growth even when muscles were subjected to overload (192, 193). Early evidence suggested that, along with PI3K/Akt signaling, activation of calcineurin was required for IGF-1–mediated hypertrophic adaptations (326). It was hypothesized that these effects were expressed via activation of NFAT, which in turn mediated the signaling of transcriptional regulators such as proliferator-activated receptor gamma coactivator 1-alpha (PGC1α) and striated muscle activator of Rho signaling (STARS) (446, 456). However, subsequent research challenged these findings: studies indicated that calcineurin in muscle was primarily responsible for producing a shift toward a slower phenotype (521, 739). When considering the body of literature as a whole, evidence suggests both correlative and causal links between calcineurin and muscle fiber size, especially in slow-twitch fibers (326). That said, muscle growth does not appear to be dependent on calcineurin activity (62), and the role (if any) that the enzyme plays in the hypertrophic response to exercise overload is unclear.

The calcium-calmodulin-dependent kinases (i.e., CaMKII and CaMKIV) also have a prominent role in muscle plasticity. CaMKII and CaMKIV have multiple isoforms that detect and respond to calcium signals via multiple downstream targets (135). CaMKII is activated by both acute and long-duration exercise, indicating that it mediates muscle growth as well as mitochondrial biogenesis (135). Interestingly, increases in one of the CaMKII isoforms (CaMKIIγ) occurs during muscle atrophy, leading to the possibility that it is upregulated as a compensatory response to counter the wasting process (135).

Phosphatidic Acid Pathway

Phosphatidic acid (PA) is a lipid second messenger that regulates a diverse array of cellular processes including muscle growth. The activation of PA is mediated via several classes of enzymes. In particular, it is synthesized by phospholipase D1 (PLD1), which hydrolyzes phosphatidylcholine into PA and choline. Once activated, PA exerts effects on both protein synthesis and proteolysis. This is principally accomplished by its binding to mTOR and then activating p70^{S6K} activity (681, 856). PA also can phosphorylate p70^{S6K} in an mTOR- independent manner, presenting yet another path whereby mechanical stimuli may directly drive anabolic processes (414). In addition, overexpression of PLD1 is associated with a decrease in catabolic factors such as FOXO3, atrogin-1, and MuRF-1 (260). Suppression of these atrophy-related genes is believed to be due to Akt phosphorylation and subsequent activation of mTORC2. Thus, PLD1 carries out anabolic and anticatabolic actions through varied intracellular mechanisms.

PA is highly sensitive to mechanical stimulation. Both ex vivo passive stretches (i.e., stretches performed on a muscle removed from the body) and in vivo eccentric actions (i.e., actions of a muscle that is intact in the body) were found to increase PA and mTOR signaling (260). Moreover, administration of 1-butanol—a PLD antagonist—blunts both PA synthesis and mTOR signaling (315). In combination, these data indicate that PLD-derived PA is integrally involved in the mechanical activation of mTOR (260). It should be noted that PA can be synthesized by alternative enzymes, and there is some evidence that its activation by diacylglycerol kinase may play a role in its hypertrophic effects as well.

AMPK Pathway

The trimeric enzyme 5'-AMP-activated protein kinase (AMPK) plays a key role in the regulation of cellular energy homeostasis. AMPK acts as a cellular energy sensor; its activation is stimulated by an increase in the AMP/ATP ratio (259). As such, conditions that elicit substantial intracellular energy stress—including exercise—cause an increase in AMPK. Once activated, AMPK suppresses energy-intensive anabolic processes such as protein synthesis and amplifies catabolic processes including protein breakdown (259).

Because of its inherent actions, AMPK is theorized to be involved in the maintenance of skeletal muscle mass. This contention is supported by evidence showing that knockout (inactivation) of AMPK in animal models causes hypertrophy both in vitro and in vivo (259). Alternatively, activation of AMPK by AICAR—an AMPK agonist—promotes myotube atrophy, whereas its suppression counteracts the atrophic response (259). Taken together, these findings indicate that AMPK regulates muscle hypertrophy by modulating both protein synthesis and proteolysis.

The precise mechanisms by which AMPK carries out its actions are still being elucidated. Proteolytic effects of AMPK appear to be related at least in part to its influence over atrogin-1. Protein degradation induced by AMPK agonists (AICAR and metformin) has been found to correlate with atrogin-1 expression, whereas another AMPK antagonist (Compound C) blocks such expression. Evidence shows that these actions may involve an AMPK-induced increase in FOXO transcription factors, thereby stimulating myofibrillar protein degradation via atrogin-1 expression (517). AMPK has also been shown to induce protein degradation via activation of *autophagy* (regulated cell degradation) (259), although it remains to be determined whether this mechanism plays a role in skeletal muscle following mechanical overload. Other research indicates that AMPK reduces cell differentiation of myoblasts and thus negatively affects hypertrophic adaptations without necessarily accelerating protein degradation (784).

In addition to the catabolic actions of AMPK, compelling evidence suggests that it suppresses the rate of protein synthesis. It is theorized that this negative influence is mediated at least in part by antagonizing the anabolic effects of mTOR, either by direct phosphorylation of mTOR, indirect phosphorylation of the tuberous sclerosis complex (TSC), or both, which has the effect of inhibiting the Ras homolog enriched in brain (RHEB) (500, 717).

Another potential means whereby AMPK is theorized to negatively affect muscle protein synthesis is the inhibition of translation elongation and the indirect suppression of the anabolic effector eIF3F (259). Thus, there are multiple potential mechanisms for AMPK-mediated regulation of protein synthesis.

A number of studies lend support to the theory that AMPK plays a role in the muscular adaptations in response to regimented exercise training. AMPK activation shows a strong inverse correlation with the magnitude of muscle hypertrophy following chronic overload (762). In addition, AMPK inhibition is associated with an accelerated growth response to mechanical overload, whereas its activation attenuates hypertrophy (259). However, other research calls into question the extent to which AMPK regulates exercise-induced hypertrophy. In humans, mTOR signaling and muscle protein synthetic rate are elevated following resistance exercise despite concomitant activation of AMPK (188). This indicates that, in the very least, the activation of AMPK is not sufficient to completely blunt growth. Moreover, growth in mice lacking the primary upstream kinase for AMPK was not enhanced following functional overload, casting uncertainty about the importance of AMPK in muscular adaptations to mechanical loading (474).

Metabolic Stress

Although the importance of mechanical tension in promoting muscle growth is indisputable, there is compelling evidence that other factors also play a role in the hypertrophic process. One such factor proposed to be of particular relevance to exercise-induced anabolism is *metabolic stress* (626, 668, 705). Simply stated, metabolic stress is an exercise-induced accumulation of metabolites, particularly lactate, inorganic phosphate, and H+ (732, 758). Several researchers have claimed that metabolite buildup may have an even greater impact on muscle hypertrophy than high force development (685), although other investigators dispute this assertion (222).

Metabolic stress is maximized during exercise that relies heavily on anaerobic glycolysis for energy production. Anaerobic glycolysis is dominant during exercise lasting from about

KEY POINT

There is compelling evidence that metabolic stress associated with resistance training can promote increases in muscle hypertrophy.

15 to 120 sec, and corresponding metabolite accumulation causes peripherally (as opposed to centrally) induced fatigue (i.e., fatigue related to metabolic or biochemical changes, or both, as opposed to reductions in neural drive) (620). Research shows that performing 1 set of 12 repetitions to failure (with a total time under tension of 37±3 sec) elevates muscle lactate levels to 91 mmol/kg (dry weight), and values increase to 118 mmol/kg after 3 sets (443). In contrast, minimal metabolite buildup is seen in protocols involving very heavy loading (≥90% of 1RM) because the short training durations involved (generally <10 sec per set) primarily tap the phosphagen system for energy provision. In addition, muscle oxygenation is compromised during resistance training that relies on fast glycolysis. The persistent compression of circulatory flow throughout a longer-duration set results in acute hypoxia, thereby heightening metabolite buildup (740). The combination of these factors causes the rapid accumulation of intramuscular metabolites along with a concomitant decrease in pH levels (731).

Typical bodybuilding routines are intended to capitalize on the growth-promoting effects of metabolic stress at the expense of higher intensities of load (232, 656). These routines, which involve performing multiple sets of 8 to 12 repetitions per set with relatively short interset rest intervals (402), have been found to increase metabolic stress to a much greater degree than higher-intensity regimens typically employed by powerlifters (385-387). It is well documented that despite regular training at moderate intensities of load, bodybuilders display hypermuscular physiques and levels of lean body mass at least as great as, if not greater than, those achieved by powerlifters (232, 352). Indeed, there is evidence that bodybuilding-type routines produce superior hypertrophic increases compared to higher-load powerlifting-style routines (136, 461, 648), although findings are not consistent across all trials when equating for volume load (119, 661).

A number of factors are theorized to mediate hypertrophic adaptations from exercise-induced metabolic stress, including increased fiber recruitment, myokine production alterations, cell swelling, accumulation of reactive oxygen species (ROS), and elevated systemic hormone production (261, 262, 533, 737). What follows is a discussion of how these factors are thought to drive anabolism (figure 2.4).

Fiber Recruitment

As discussed in chapter 1, muscle fiber recruitment is carried out in an orderly fashion whereby low-threshold motor units are recruited first and then higher-threshold motor units are progressively recruited to sustain muscle contraction depending on force demands (301). Although heavy loading activates the full spectrum of fiber types, research indicates that metabolic stress increases the recruitment of higher-threshold motor units even when lifting light loads. Studies show that as fatigue increases during sustained submaximal exercise, recruitment thresholds correspondingly decrease (321, 638, 801). Accordingly, activation of fast-twitch fibers is high provided a set is carried out to the point of muscular failure. Studies employing EMG (737, 738), glycogen depletion (332), and organic phosphate splitting (731, 732) have all demonstrated increased fast-twitch fiber recruitment in BFR training, causing some researchers to speculate that this is the primary factor by which occlusion mediates anabolism (426, 488).

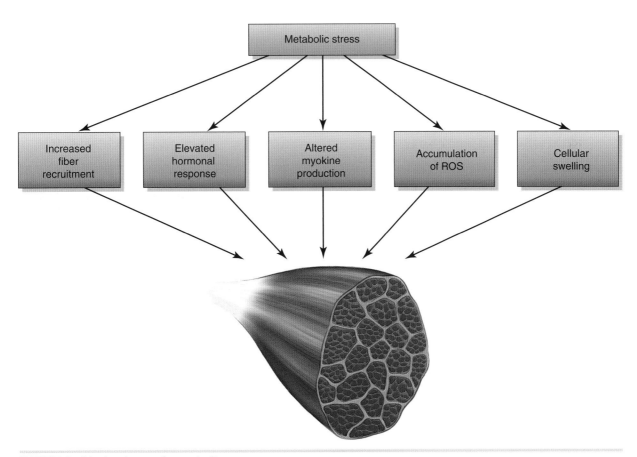

FIGURE 2.4 Mechanisms of metabolic stress.

With kind permission from Springer Science+Business Media: *Sport Medicine*, "Potential mechanisms for a role of metabolic stress in hypertrophic adaptations to resistance training," 43, 179-194, 2013, B.J. Schoenfeld, Fig. 2.

RESEARCH FINDINGS
BLOOD FLOW RESTRICTION

The impact of metabolic stress on hypertrophic adaptations is exemplified by *blood flow restriction* (BFR) training studies. BFR training involves restricting venous inflow via the use of a pressure cuff while training (figure 2.5) with light weights (generally equating to <40% of 1RM), thereby heightening ischemia in the muscle as it contracts.

The prevailing body of literature shows that BFR training stimulates anabolic signaling and muscle protein synthesis (233) and markedly increases muscle growth (427) despite employing loads often considered too low to promote significant hypertrophy (119, 392).

It has been speculated that metabolic stress is the driving force behind BFR-induced muscle hypertrophy. Significant metabolite buildup has been noted during such training (425), pointing to an association between metabolic stress and muscle growth. In further support of this contention, significant increases in cross-sectional area of the thigh muscle were found in college-aged males after 3 weeks of walking with BFR of the legs (8). Given that healthy young subjects generally do not gain muscle from performing low-intensity aerobic exercise, the study provides strong evidence that factors other than mechanical tension were responsible for hypertrophic adaptations. Indeed, increases in muscle cross-sectional area were found to be significantly correlated with the changes in inorganic phosphate ($r = .876$) and intramuscular pH ($r = .601$) during BFR training carried out at 20% of 1RM. This indicates that metabolic stress generated during resistance exercise is a key regulator of muscle growth (735).

FIGURE 2.5　A blood flow restriction implement on an arm.

Studies investigating resistance training under conditions of hypoxia provide further evidence for a correlation between metabolic stress and muscle growth. Kon and colleagues (377) found that breathing 13% oxygen during a multiset, low-load (~50% of 1RM) protocol with fairly short interset rest intervals (~1 min) significantly heightened blood lactate levels compared to the same routine performed under normoxic conditions. Similarly, Nishimura and colleagues (533) reported significantly greater increases in elbow flexor cross-sectional area when 4 sets of 10 repetitions at 70% of 1RM were performed under conditions of acute hypoxia versus normoxia. Mechanistic actions responsible for the enhanced hypertrophic response to hypoxic training have yet to be determined, but increased metabolite accumulation is suspected to play a role in the process (674).

The precise mechanisms whereby metabolic stress augments fast-twitch fiber recruitment are not entirely clear. It has been hypothesized that H+ accumulation plays a substantial role by inhibiting contractility in working fibers and thus promoting the recruitment of additional high-threshold motor units (173, 495, 738). MacDougall and colleagues (443) proposed that fatigue during single-set training to failure is due to a combination of acidosis and PCr depletion, whereas acidosis is more likely the cause in multiset resistance exercise.

Although it would seem that increased fiber recruitment is at least partly responsible for the increases in hypertrophy associated with metabolic stress, it appears that other factors likely play a role as well. Suga and colleagues (732) demonstrated that only 31% of subjects displayed recruitment of fast-twitch fibers during occlusion training at 20% of 1RM compared with 70% of subjects who performed nonoccluded training at 65% of 1RM. Considering that BFR at this intensity (20% of 1RM) has been shown to increase muscle growth to an extent similar to, or greater than, high-intensity resistance training (409, 850), the anabolic effects logically cannot be solely a function of equal fiber recruitment. These findings are further supported by research showing significantly higher EMG amplitudes when traditional training is carried out at 80% of 1RM compared to occluded training at 20% of 1RM, indicating reduced muscle activation at the lower intensity (450). Recent studies investigating heavy- versus light-load training also show significantly greater muscle activation during the higher-intensity bout despite an apparently much greater metabolite accumulation during the light-load condition (21, 157, 660).

Myokine Production

Metabolic stress may influence growth by upregulating anabolic myokines or downregulating catabolic myokines, or both (654). Although there is a logical basis for this claim, research on the topic is equivocal. Takarada and colleagues (737) demonstrated a gradual increase in IL-6 following multiple sets of knee extensions with BFR compared to volume-matched exercise without occlusion; levels remained elevated 24 hours postexercise. The effect size was small, however, and the absolute amount of the increase was only 1/4 that reported for heavy-load eccentric exercise. Fujita and colleagues (236) found that 6 days of leg extensor occlusion training increased thigh cross-sectional area by 2.4% without any changes noted in IL-6 levels. Similarly, other studies showed that IL-6 levels

remained unchanged following BFR training protocols known to elevate metabolic stress (5, 233). The totality of these findings would seem to refute a role for IL-6 in hypertrophy induced by metabolic stress. The correlation between metabolic stress and other local growth factors has not been well studied, precluding the ability to draw conclusions regarding their potential relevance.

Evidence suggests that metabolic stress may influence muscle growth by downregulating local catabolic factors. Kawada and Ishii (354) reported significantly decreased MSTN levels in the plantaris muscle of Wistar rats following BFR exercise versus a sham-operated control group. Conversely, no differences in MSTN gene expression were seen in humans 3 hours after low-intensity exercise with and without occlusion (189). Another human trial showed that although BFR had no effect on MSTN, it downregulated several important proteolytic transcripts (FOXO3A, atrogin-1, and MuRF-1) 8 hours after exercise compared to a nonoccluded control group (451). In a study of physically active males, Laurentino and colleagues (409) investigated the effects of BFR on chronic MSTN levels following 8 weeks of training. Results showed a significant 45% reduction in MSTN gene expression with BFR compared to a nonsignificant reduction when performing low-intensity exercise without occlusion. The conflicting nature of these findings makes it difficult to formulate conclusions about whether hypertrophic adaptations from metabolic stress are related to alterations in myokine production.

Cell Swelling

Another mechanism purported to mediate hypertrophy via metabolic stress is an increase in intracellular hydration (i.e., *cell swelling*). Cell swelling is thought to serve as a physiological regulator of cell function (292, 293). A large body of evidence demonstrates that an increase in the hydration status of a cell concomitantly increases protein synthesis and decreases protein breakdown. These findings have been shown in a wide variety of cell types including osteocytes, breast cells, hepatocytes, and muscle fibers (405).

Current theory suggests that an increase in cellular hydration causes pressure against the cytoskeleton and cell membrane, which is perceived as a threat to the cell's integrity. In response, the cell upregulates an anabolic signaling cascade that ultimately leads to reinforcement of its ultrastructure (406, 656). Signaling appears to be mediated via integrin-associated volume osmosensors within cells (430). These sensors turn on anabolic protein-kinase transduction pathways, which are thought to be mediated by local growth factors (142, 403). PI3K appears to be an important signaling component in modulating amino acid transport in muscle as a result of increased cellular hydration (430). Research suggests that anabolic effects are also carried out in an mTOR-independent fashion (647), with evidence of direct regulation by MAPK modules (216, 646). Moreover, swelling of myofibers may trigger the proliferation of satellite cells and promote their fusion to the affected fibers (168), providing an impetus for further growth.

Evidence is lacking as to whether cell swelling resulting from exercise-induced metabolic stress promotes hypertrophy. However, a sound rationale can be made for such an effect. Resistance exercise acutely alters intra- and extracellular water balance (699), and the extent of alterations depends on the type of exercise and the intensity of training. Cell swelling is thought to be heightened by resistance training that generates high amounts of lactic acid via the osmolytic properties of lactate (230, 698), although some research refutes this hypothesis (781). Intramuscular lactate accumulation activates volume regulatory mechanisms; the effects are seemingly amplified by the associated increased acidosis (405). Fast-twitch fibers are thought to be especially sensitive to osmotic changes, presumably because they contain a high concentration of aquaporin-4 (AQP4) water transport channels (230). Considering that fast-twitch fibers have been shown to have the greatest growth potential (382), an increased swelling in these fibers could conceivably enhance their adaptation in a meaningful way.

Systemic Hormone Production

It has been posited that acute postexercise elevations in anabolic hormones resulting from metabolite accumulation during resistance training may augment the hypertrophic response. In particular, exercise-induced metabolic stress is strongly associated with a spike in postworkout growth hormone levels (261-263, 273, 579, 736, 737). Although transient, the magnitude of these elevations is sizable. One study reported a 10-fold increase in GH levels with BFR training over and above that seen with similar-intensity nonoccluded exercise (237); another showed that postworkout increases reached 290-fold over baseline (737). Postexercise elevations are thought to be mediated by a heightened accumulation of lactate or H+ (261, 273). People who lack *myophosphorylase*, a glycolytic enzyme responsible for breaking down glycogen and thus inducing lactate production, demonstrate an attenuated postexercise growth hormone response (252), providing strong evidence for a link between lactate production and GH release. A metabolite-induced decrease in pH also may augment GH release via chemoreflex stimulation regulated by intramuscular metaboreceptors and group III and IV afferents (425, 796).

Given that GH is known to potentiate IGF-1 secretion, it seems logical that metabolite accumulation would be associated with increased postexercise IGF-1 levels as well. This has been borne out to some extent by studies showing significantly greater IGF-1 elevations following the performance of metabolically fatiguing routines (385, 386, 633), although other research has failed to find such an association (388). Moreover, several (6, 237, 736), but not all, (189) studies have reported acute increases in postexercise IGF-1 levels following BFR training, which suggests that the results were mediated by metabolic stress. Importantly, the body of research is specific to the circulating IGF-1 isoform, and findings cannot necessarily be extrapolated to intramuscular effects.

The effect of metabolic stress on acute testosterone elevations remains unknown. Lu and colleagues (431) reported that exercise-induced lactate production correlated with increases in testosterone during a bout of high-intensity swimming in Sprague-Dawley rats. In a second component of the study, direct infusion of lactate into rat testes was found to cause a dose-dependent elevation in testosterone levels. On the other hand, controlled research in humans has produced disparate findings. Although some studies show higher postexercise testosterone release following metabolically fatiguing protocols compared with those that do not cause significant metabolite buildup (108, 263, 273, 471, 701), others show no significant differences (385, 605, 731). In addition, a majority of BFR studies have failed to find significantly higher acute testosterone elevations despite high levels of metabolites (237, 605, 796), casting doubt as to whether the hormone is affected by metabolite accumulation. Inconsistencies between studies may be related to demographic factors such as sex, age, and training experience, and nutritional status also has been shown to affect testosterone release (391). As noted in chapter 1, whether transient postexercise hormonal spikes have an effect on hypertrophic adaptations remains questionable. If there is such an effect, it would seem to be of small consequence.

Muscle Damage

Intense exercise, particularly when a person is unaccustomed to it, can cause damage to

RESEARCH FINDINGS

CONCLUSIONS ABOUT THE HYPERTROPHIC ROLE OF METABOLIC STRESS

Strong evidence exists that exercise-induced metabolic stress contributes to the hypertrophic response. What remains to be determined is whether these effects are additive to the stimulus from mechanical forces or perhaps redundant provided a given loading threshold is achieved. A problem in trying to draw inferences from experimental training designs is that mechanical tension and metabolic stress occur in tandem, confounding the ability to tease out the effects of one from the other. This can result in misinterpreting metabolic factors as causal for growth when mechanical factors are, in fact, responsible, or vice versa.

The ability to draw a cause–effect relationship between metabolic stress and hypertrophy is further confounded by the fact that the exercise-induced buildup of metabolites generally occurs in tandem with damage to myofibers. Given the commonly held belief that damaging exercise mediates anabolism (657), it is difficult to tease out the effects of one variable from the other with respect to hypertrophic adaptations. Research showing that blood flow restriction training increases muscle growth without significant damage to fibers suggests that the hypertrophic effects of metabolite accumulation are indeed separate from myodamage (428), although conflicting evidence on the topic renders a definitive conclusion premature (815).

Finally and importantly, the mechanisms responsible for any anabolic effects of metabolic stress have not been fully elucidated. Although increased muscle fiber recruitment appears to play a role, it seems unlikely that recruitment solely accounts for any or all of the hypertrophic benefits associated with metabolite accumulation. Rather, evidence suggests that the combined integration of multiple local and perhaps systemic factors contributes to growth in a direct or permissive manner, or both (825). The fact that studies to date have been primarily carried out in untrained subjects leaves open the prospect that mechanisms may differ based on training experience.

skeletal muscle (146, 195, 397). This phenomenon, commonly known as *exercise-induced muscle damage* (EIMD), can be specific to just a few macromolecules of tissue or manifest as large tears in the sarcolemma, basal lamina, and supportive connective tissue, as well as injury to contractile elements and the cytoskeleton (figure 2.6) (791). The severity of EIMD depends on factors such as the type, intensity, and total duration of training (448).

EIMD is highly influenced by the type of muscular action. Although concentric and isometric exercise can bring about EIMD, eccentric actions have by far the greatest impact on its manifestation (144, 245). Eccentrically induced EIMD is more prevalent in fast-twitch than in slow-twitch fibers (792). Possible reasons include a reduced oxidative capacity, higher levels of tension generated during training, and structural differences between fiber phenotypes (593).

Damage from eccentric actions are attributed to mechanical disruption of the acto-myosin bonds rather than ATP-dependent detachment, thereby placing a greater strain on the involved machinery in comparison to concentric and isometric actions (204). Studies show that the weakest sarcomeres reside in different aspects of each myofibril, leading to speculation that the associated nonuniform lengthening results in a shearing of myofibrils. This sets off a chain of events beginning with a deformation of T-tubules and a corresponding disruption of calcium homeostasis that mediates the secretion of the calcium-activated neutral proteases (such as calpain) involved in further degradation of structural muscle proteins (24, 65). There is evidence of a dose–response relationship, whereby higher exercise volumes correlate with a greater degree of myodamage (537). Symptoms of EIMD include decreased force-producing capacity, increased musculoskeletal stiffness and swelling, delayed-onset muscle soreness (DOMS), and a heightened physiological stress response typified by an elevated heart rate response to submaximal exercise and heightened lactate production (751).

EIMD decreases when a person performs the same exercise consistently, a phenomenon commonly known as the *repeated bout effect* (477). Several factors are thought to be responsible for this effect, including an adaptive strengthening of connective tissue, increased efficiency in the recruitment of motor units, enhanced synchronization of motor units, a more even distribution of the workload among fibers, and a greater contribution of muscle synergists (94, 751). The effects of the repeated bout effect can last for several months, even in the absence of eccentric training during this period. Evidence that the upper-extremity muscles have a greater predisposition to EIMD than the leg muscles suggests a protective benefit in muscles that are frequently used during everyday activities (133).

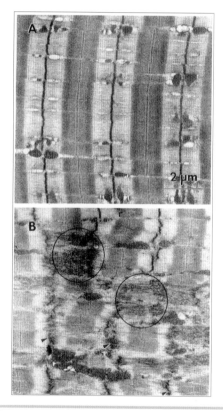

FIGURE 2.6 Sarcomere disruption following eccentric contractions. *(a)* Sarcomeres from normal muscle show excellent alignment and regular banding patterns; *(b)* sarcomeres from muscle exposed to eccentric contractions show regions of Z-disc streaming and frank sarcomere disruption next to sarcomeres that appear normal.

Reprinted, by permission, from R.L. Lieber, T.M. Woodburn, and J. Friden, 1991, "Muscle damage induced by eccentric contractions of 25% strain," *Journal of Applied Physiology* 70(6): 2498-2507.

CHALLENGES TO THE EIMD HYPOTHESIS

As discussed, muscles become increasingly less susceptible to damage with recurring exercise—a function of the repeated bout effect. This phenomenon would seem to rule out any involvement of EIMD in the hypertrophic response of those who are well trained (537). However, there is evidence that myodamage is indeed present in trained lifters, albeit to a lesser extent than in novices. Gibala and colleagues (246) recruited 6 resistance-trained men to perform 8 sets of 8 repetitions at a load equivalent to 80% of 1RM. The researchers employed a unilateral protocol whereby one arm performed only concentric actions while the other arm performed only eccentric actions. Muscle biopsies taken 21 hours after the exercise bout showed a significantly greater disruption in fibers from the eccentrically trained arms versus the concentrically trained arms. These findings underscore the fact that the repeated bout effect only attenuates the magnitude of muscle damage as opposed to preventing its occurrence, and leaves open the possibility that EIMD may contribute to hypertrophy in well-trained people.

Some researchers have questioned whether EIMD confers any anabolic effects, based on research showing marked hypertrophy from low-intensity BFR training with ostensibly minimal tissue damage (6, 737). The BFR technique combines light loads (20% to 50% of 1RM) with occlusion via pressure cuff to impede venous return without obstructing arterial inflow. Regular performance of BFR induces marked hypertrophy, often similar to what is observed with the use of heavy loads. Given the light loads employed, it is hypothesized that BFR confers these hypertrophic benefits while minimizing disruption of myofibers. However, muscle damage is a known consequence of reperfusion subsequent to ischemia (224, 267). Takarada and colleagues (737) demonstrated that although markers of muscle damage were attenuated after BFR training, there was evidence of fine microdamage within myofibers, leaving open the possibility that damage may have contributed to the results. Moreover, it remains possible that hypertrophy would have been enhanced to an even greater extent had EIMD been heightened in the BFR group. Markers of muscle damage following BFR have been demonstrated elsewhere, including lengthy decrements in maximal voluntary contraction, heightened delayed-onset muscle soreness, and elevated sarcolemmal permeability (815).

Some investigators have questioned whether EIMD mediates hypertrophic adaptations based on research showing that downhill running can induce significant damage to muscle tissue without corresponding growth (94). This observation, however, fails to take into account the unique molecular responses associated with aerobic versus resistance exercise. The two types of training activate and suppress distinctly different subsets of genes and cellular signaling pathways (295), thereby bringing about divergent muscular adaptations. It also should be noted that damage elicited by aerobic training manifests differently from that elicited by resistance exercise. Peak creatine kinase activity is noted approximately 12 to 24 hours after downhill running, whereas that associated with resistance training is not evident until about 48 hours after the training bout and can peak 4 to 6 days postworkout (672). In addition, downhill running is associated with peak creatine kinase levels of between 100 to 600 IU, whereas those of resistance range from 2,000 to 10,000 IU (145). The implications of these variances remain to be established. Moreover, creatine kinase levels do not necessarily reflect the degree or time course of myodamage (146), calling into question their practical relevance with respect to exercise training. What can be inferred from aerobic training data is that muscle damage by itself is not sufficient to induce significant muscle growth. Thus, if EIMD does play a role in compensatory hypertrophy, it can do so only in the presence of resistance-based mechanical overload.

Although EIMD can be deleterious from a performance standpoint, some researchers have speculated that the associated increases in inflammation and protein turnover are necessary for muscle growth (208, 816). The rationale is based on the hypothesis that structural alterations associated with damage influence gene expression in a manner that strengthens the affected tissue, thereby serving to protect the muscle against further injury (57). Substantial evidence links muscle damage with factors involved in the hypertrophic response to exercise.

Despite the sound theoretical basis, however, there is a dearth of research directly investigating the causal relationship between EIMD and muscle growth. Komulainen and colleagues (376) exposed the tibialis anterior muscles of anesthetized Wistar rats to repeated concentric or eccentric muscle actions. The eccentric muscle actions produced massive injury to the muscle; beta-glucuronidase activity (a measure of myodamage) showed a 7.1-fold increase from baseline. Alternatively, concentric muscle actions resulted in a modest 2.6-fold increase in beta-glucuronidase activity, indicating that the damage was relatively minor. Similar increases in muscle cross-sectional area were noted in both groups, suggesting a threshold for EIMD-induced growth beyond which myodamage provides no additional beneficial hypertrophic effects. The study is confounded by evaluating polar-extreme levels of damage. Whether a dose–response relationship exists between hypertrophy and moderate levels of EIMD, therefore, cannot be determined. Moreover, the severe damage experienced in the eccentric muscle actions may have been so excessive that it negatively affected remodeling. The ability to draw inferences from this study is thus limited.

In a human trial on the topic, Flann and colleagues (219) randomly assigned 14 young, healthy men and women into one of two groups: (1) a control group that engaged in eccentric cycle ergometry at a "somewhat hard" level (gauged by a rating of perceived exertion scale; training was performed 3 times per week for 20 minutes over an 8-week period), and (2) a pretrained group that carried out the identical protocol to the control group, except that it included a 3-week ramp-up period during which subjects performed exercise at a low intensity to gradually acclimate their muscles to the training stimulus. At the study's end, similar increases in muscle girth were found between the groups. Although these results are intriguing, the study had numerous methodological limitations including the use of untrained subjects, unequal training duration between the groups, and a small sample size that compromised statistical power. In addition, the pretrained group did show evidence of myodamage as assessed by elevated creatine kinase levels, although the extent was significantly less than that noted in the control group. This raises the possibility that the magnitude of damage sustained by those who were pretrained was adequate to maximize any added hypertrophic adaptations. Alternatively, it remains conceivable that EIMD incurred during training by the untrained subjects exceeded the body's reparative capabilities, ultimately mitigating growth by impairing the ability to train with proper intensity and delaying supercompensatory adaptations.

The regeneration and repair of muscle tissue following EIMD is carried out by novel transcriptional programs that are associated with or promoted by inflammatory processes, satellite cell activity, IGF-1 production, and cell swelling (446). Following is an overview of factors hypothesized to promote an EIMD-induced hypertrophic response.

KEY POINT

Research suggests that EIMD can enhance muscular adaptations, although excessive damage has a negative effect on muscle development. It remains to be determined the extent to which these mechanisms are synergistic and whether an optimal combination exists to maximize the hypertrophic response to resistance training.

Inflammatory Processes

The body's response to EIMD can be equated to its response to infection (656). After a damaging exercise bout, neutrophils migrate to the injury site while agents are released by affected fibers that attract macrophages to the region as well (475). This sets off a cascade of events in which inflammatory cells then secrete other substances to facilitate the repair and regeneration of damaged muscle. Inflammatory processes resulting from EIMD can have either a beneficial or deleterious effect on muscular function depending on the magnitude of the response, previous exposure to the applied stimulus, and injury-specific interactions between the muscle and inflammatory cells (764).

Neutrophils are more abundant in the human body than any other type of white blood cell. In addition to possessing phagocytic capabilities, neutrophils release proteases that aid in breaking down cellular debris from EIMD. They also secrete cytolytic and cytotoxic substances that can exacerbate damage to injured muscle and inflict damage to healthy neighboring tissues (764). Hence, their primary role in skeletal muscle is likely confined to myolysis and other facets associated with the removal of cellular debris as opposed to the regeneration of contractile tissue.

Despite a lack of evidence directly linking neutrophils to hypertrophy, it is conceivable that they may mediate anabolism by signaling other inflammatory cells necessary for muscle remodeling. One such possibility is reactive oxygen species (ROS) (779), which have been shown to mediate intracellular signaling in response to intense physical activity (258, 340, 341, 574, 760). Neutrophils are associated with the production of numerous ROS variants, including hydrogen peroxide, superoxide, hydroxyl radical, and hypochlorous acid (372). ROS are associated with hypertrophy of both smooth muscle and cardiac muscle (734), and some speculate that anabolic effects extend to skeletal muscle as well (737). In support of this hypothesis, transgenic mice displaying suppressed levels of selenoproteins (a class of proteins that act as powerful antioxidants) had 50% more muscle mass following synergist ablation compared to wild-type controls (313). These findings suggest that redox-sensitive signaling pathways may enhance exercise-induced muscular adaptations.

ROS have been shown to mediate anabolism via activation of the MAPK pathway. The treatment of C2 myoblasts with an ROS variant heightens MAPK signaling, and the temporal response varies between MAPK subfamilies (ERK1/2, JNK, and p38 MAPK) (357). Given that eccentric exercise is associated with greater MAPK activation compared to concentric or isometric actions (446, 454), it is conceivable that ROS production contributes to this stimulus. There also is evidence that ROS enhance growth processes by amplifying IGF-1 signaling. In vitro ROS treatment of mouse C2C12 myocytes significantly increased phosphorylation of the IGF-1 receptor, whereas phosphorylation was markedly suppressed with antioxidant provision (283). These findings suggest a crucial role for ROS in the biological actions of IGF-1.

Interestingly, there is evidence that ROS interfere with the signaling of various serine/threonine phosphatases, such as calcineurin. ROS activity impairs calcineurin activation by blocking its calmodulin-binding domain (128). Calcineurin is thought to be involved in both skeletal muscle growth (193, 490) and fiber phenotype transformation (560), and thus its inhibition may be detrimental to anabolism. Moreover, some studies have failed to demonstrate that ROS are in fact activated in response to EIMD (644). When considering the body of literature as a whole, any anabolic effects of ROS are likely dependent on exercise mode (i.e., anaerobic versus aerobic), the species of ROS produced, and perhaps other factors.

In contrast to neutrophils, research indicates a potential role for macrophages in regenerative processes following EIMD (764), and some researchers even speculate that they are necessary for muscle growth (372). Macrophages appear to exert anabolic effects by secreting local growth factors associated with inflammatory processes. It was originally thought that myodamage directly led to the production of pro-inflammatory myokines (99, 565). Although this would seem to have a logical basis, more recent research indicates that such myokine production may be largely independent of EIMD. A study by Toft and colleagues (770) showed that IL-6 levels were only modestly elevated relative to increases in creatine kinase following 60 minutes of eccentric cycle ergometry exercise, suggesting a weak association between EIMD and IL-6 production. These results are consistent with those of others showing poor correlation in the time course of IL-6 and creatine kinase appearance (164). The totality of findings has led to the supposition that IL-6 release is predominantly a function of muscle contraction. Mechanistically, some researchers have hypothesized that this facilitates the mobilization of substrate from fuel depots so that glucose homeostasis is maintained during intense exercise (214).

It is important to note that only IL-6 and IL-8 have been shown to be released from skeletal muscle in the absence of damaging exercise (129). Many other myokines may play a role in the hypertrophic response to EIMD. Systemic IL-15 levels and IL-15 mRNA in skeletal muscle are markedly elevated after eccentric (but not concentric) exercise, giving credence to the notion that elevations are contingent on damage to fibers (100, 616). Some studies show that IL-15 directly regulates hypertrophy by increasing muscle protein synthesis and reducing proteolysis in differentiated myotubes (530, 596), although these findings recently have been challenged (583). There also is evidence that fibroblast growth factors (FGFs)—powerful proliferative agents involved in hypertrophic processes—are preferentially upregulated following eccentric exercise. Research indicates that FGFs are secreted from damaged fibers (142) and that their time course of release parallels the increased creatine kinase levels associated with EIMD (143). These findings lend mechanistic support to the hypothesis that damaging exercise promotes an anabolic stimulus.

Satellite Cell Activity

A large body of evidence links EIMD with satellite cell activity (179, 634, 671). Damaged myofibers must rapidly acquire additional myonuclei to aid in tissue repair and regeneration or otherwise face cell death. Satellite cells facilitate these means by proliferating and fusing to damaged fibers. Because satellite cells tend to populate under the myoneural junction (308, 696), it is speculated that they may be further stimulated by activation from motor neurons innervating damaged fibers, enhancing the regenerative response (791). It has been hypothesized that under certain conditions stimulated satellite cells fuse to each other to form new myofibers (60), but evidence as to how this relates to traditional resistance training practices is currently lacking.

Initial signaling to activate satellite cells following EIMD is purported to originate from muscle-derived nitric oxide, potentially in combination with the release of HGF (11, 748, 764). The process appears to be controlled at least to some extent by the cyclooxygenase (COX)-2 pathway, which is considered necessary for maximizing exercise-induced hypertrophic adaptations (710). COX-2 acts to promote the synthesis of prostaglandins believed to stimulate satellite cell proliferation, differentiation, and fusion (86). Research shows an enhanced myogenic response when inflammatory cells are abundant and a blunted response in their absence (86), suggesting that inflammatory processes subsequent to damaging exercise are critical to remodeling. The hypertrophic importance of COX-2 is further supported by research investigating the effects of COX-inhibiting nonsteroidal anti-inflammatory drugs (NSAIDs) on the postexercise satellite cell response (55). A majority of studies show decreased postexercise satellite cell activity when NSAIDs are administered (86, 87, 445, 491), which would conceivably limit long-term muscle growth, although these findings are not universal (564). It is important to point out that mechanical stimuli alone can instigate satellite cell proliferation and

EFFECT OF NSAIDS ON MUSCLE HYPERTROPHY

Nonsteroidal anti-inflammatory drugs (NSAIDs) are a class of analgesics commonly used to relieve the pain and swelling associated with delayed-onset muscle soreness. NSAIDs are thought to promote pain-reducing effects by inhibiting the activity of cyclooxygenase (COX), a family of enzymes that catalyze the conversion of arachidonic acid to pro-inflammatory prostanoids (109, 787). Thirty million people are estimated to take NSAIDS on a daily basis (63), and their use is especially widespread among those who participate in intense exercise programs (806).

An often overlooked issue with NSAID consumption in combination with resistance training, however, is the potential interference with muscular adaptations. In addition to the effects of NSAIDs on pain sensation, prostanoids also are purported to stimulate the upstream regulators of protein synthesis including PI3K and extracellular signal-regulated kinases (235, 555, 621). Moreover, there is evidence that prostanoids are intricately involved in enhancing satellite cell proliferation, differentiation, and fusion (85), thereby facilitating greater muscle protein accretion (317). These data provide compelling evidence that COX enzymes are important and perhaps even necessary for maximizing resistance training–induced muscle hypertrophy (709).

Despite a seemingly logical basis for COX-mediated hypertrophic effects, acute studies on the use of NSAIDs do not seem to show a detrimental impact on postexercise protein synthesis. Although NSAID administration in animal trials following chronic overload has consistently found impairments in protein metabolism (555, 621, 786), only one human trial showed a blunting of protein synthesis (774); several others failed to note a deleterious effect (103, 492, 570). Discrepancies between findings may be related to methodological variances, physiological differences between species, or differences in the mechanisms of the NSAIDs used (i.e., selective versus nonselective COX inhibitors).

On the other hand, the body of literature strongly suggests that NSAID usage interferes with satellite cell function. This has been shown in vitro (486, 554) as well as in vivo in both animal (85, 87) and human trials (445, 491). It has been proposed that hypertrophy is limited by a myonuclear domain ceiling, estimated at approximately 2,000 μm^2; beyond this ceiling, additional nuclei must be derived from satellite cells for further increases in hypertrophy to occur (573). Therefore, a blunting of satellite cell function would seemingly limit a person's hypertrophic potential by restricting the satellite cell pool.

How the acute data play out over the long term is not clear. Results from studies that have directly investigated the effects of NSAIDs on hypertrophy are conflicting. Consistent with the research on protein synthesis, animal studies indicate that NSAID administration markedly reduces overload-induced muscle growth (87, 539, 709). Alternatively, human trials have either failed to demonstrate hypertrophic impairments (394, 569) or showed a positive effect from NSAID use during regimented resistance training (776). When attempting to reconcile differences between studies, it is possible that NSAIDs reduce protein breakdown to a similar or even greater degree than they suppress protein synthesis, thus resulting in a nonnegative protein balance. Rodent studies lend support to this hypothesis (621). The fact that the study showing increased hypertrophy from the use of NSAIDs (776) was carried out in elderly adults (60 to 85 years of age) raises the possibility that positive benefits were due to a suppression of chronic inflammation, which has been shown to impair anabolism and accelerate proteolysis (618). It is also conceivable that the extent of hypertrophy in human trials was below the subjects' myonuclear domain ceiling. This would seemingly explain why animal models using techniques designed to promote extreme rates of hypertrophy (i.e., synergist ablation, chronic stretch) far beyond that of traditional resistance training in humans show substantial hypertrophic impairment, because a robust satellite cell pool would be required for continued muscle growth.

In summary, evidence indicates that the occasional use of NSAIDs will not impair muscle hypertrophy. Whether chronic NSAID administration is detrimental to muscle growth remains undetermined and likely is population specific: those with chronic low-grade inflammation might benefit from their usage, whereas healthy, well-trained people could see long-term impairments.

differentiation even without appreciable damage to skeletal muscle (526, 805). Hence, it is not clear whether the effects of EIMD are additive or redundant with respect to maximizing muscle protein accretion.

IGF-1 Production

There is evidence that EIMD potentiates IGF-1 production and, thus, given the anabolic functions of this hormone, may enhance muscle growth. McKay and colleagues (479) studied the effects of performing a series of 300 lengthening knee extension contractions on all three IGF-1 isoforms in untrained young men. The results showed a significant increase in *MGF* mRNA 24 hours postexercise. Intriguingly, expression of both *IGF-1Ea* and *IGF-1Eb* mRNA were not elevated until 72 hours after training. The early-phase activation of MGF as a result of the damaging protocol suggests that this IGF-1 isoform is preferentially involved in the repair and remodeling process following EIMD. Similarly, Bamman and colleagues (53) evaluated the effects of 8 sets of 8 eccentric versus concentric actions on muscle IGF-1 mRNA concentration. The eccentric exercise resulted in a significant 62% increase in IGF-1 mRNA concentrations as opposed to a non-significant increase from concentric exercise. In addition, eccentric exercise caused a reduction of IGFBP-4 mRNA—a strong inhibitor of IGF-1—by 57%, whereas the concentric condition showed only modest changes in the levels of this protein. Importantly, results were positively correlated with markers of muscle damage, suggesting that the IGF-1 system is involved in the repair process.

The association between EIMD and IGF-1 upregulation has not been universally confirmed in the literature. Garma and colleagues (241) compared the acute anabolic response of volume-equated bouts of eccentric, concentric, and isometric exercise in rodents. Results showed similar effects on cell signaling independent of the type of muscle action; no significant differences were seen in IGF-1 mRNA levels, and pre- to postexercise increases were actually greatest in the isometric condition. The reason for these conflicting findings is not readily evident and likely relates to methodological differences in the studies.

Cell Swelling

As discussed earlier in the section on metabolic stress, cell swelling has been shown to positively regulate anabolic and anticatabolic processes. Specifically, increases in cellular hydration are associated with an increase in muscle protein synthesis and a concomitant decrease in proteolysis. The inflammatory response that accompanies damaging exercise involves a buildup of fluid and plasma proteins within damaged muscle. Depending on the extent of damage, the amount of accumulated fluid can exceed the capacity of the lymphatic drainage system, which leads to tissue swelling (268, 475, 593). Trauma to capillaries may increase the magnitude of edema (146). Swelling associated with an acute bout of eccentric elbow flexion exercise in untrained subjects produced an increase in arm circumference of as much as 9%, and values remained elevated for up to 9 d (323). Similarly, Nosaka and Clarkson (538) found that edema increased arm circumference by as much as 1.7 inches (4.3 cm) after unaccustomed eccentric exercise, and swelling was evident in all subjects by 3 days after performance. Although swelling is diminished over time with regimented exercise via the repeated bout effect, substantial edema can persist even in well-trained subjects for at least 48 hours postworkout (322).

Whether the swelling associated with EIMD contributes to myofiber hypertrophy is unknown. Confounding factors make this an extremely difficult topic to study directly. There is some evidence that the use of NSAIDs, which blunt the inflammatory response and hence moderate the extent of cell swelling, impairs the increase in muscle protein synthesis normally associated with resistance exercise (555, 621, 774). It is feasible that deleterious effects on anabolism may be related to a decrease in cell swelling. However, these findings do not imply a cause–effect relationship between increased cellular hydration and muscle protein accretion; factors such as impaired satellite cell and macrophage activity may also be responsible for any negative effects. Moreover, other studies have failed to show an impaired muscle protein synthetic response following NSAID administration (103, 492), further clouding the ability to draw conclusions on the topic.

CONCLUSIONS ABOUT THE HYPERTROPHIC ROLE OF MUSCLE DAMAGE

A sound theoretical rationale exists for how EIMD may contribute to the accretion of muscle proteins. Although exercise-induced hypertrophy can apparently occur without significant myodamage (832), evidence implies that microtrauma enhances the adaptive response or at least initiates the signaling pathways that mediate anabolism. That said, a cause–effect relationship between EIMD and hypertrophy has yet to be established, and if such a relationship does exist, the degree of damage necessary to maximize muscle growth remains to be determined. Research does suggest a threshold for a hypertrophic stimulus, beyond which additional myodamage confers no further benefits and may in fact interfere with growth-related processes. There is clear evidence that excessive EIMD reduces a muscle's force-producing capacity. This in turn interferes with the ability to train at a high level, which impedes muscle development. Moreover, although training in the early recovery phase of EIMD does not seem to exacerbate muscle damage, it may interfere with the recovery process (395, 537). Taken as a whole, current research indicates that a protocol that elicits a moderate amount of damage would be most appropriate for maximizing the hypertrophic response. Considering that a ceiling effect slows the rate of hypertrophy as one gains training experience, EIMD may be particularly relevant to the anabolic response in well-trained people.

TAKE-HOME POINTS

- Numerous intracellular signaling pathways have been identified in skeletal muscle including PI3K/Akt, MAPK, phosphatidic acid, AMPK, and calcium-dependent pathways. The serine/threonine kinase mTOR has been shown to be critical to mechanically induced hypertrophic adaptations.

- Mechanical tension appears to be the most important factor in training-induced muscle hypertrophy. Mechanosensors are sensitive to both the magnitude and duration of loading, and these stimuli can directly mediate intracellular signaling to bring about hypertrophic adaptations.

- There is compelling evidence that the metabolic stress associated with resistance training promotes increases in muscle protein accretion. Hypothesized factors involved in the process include increased fiber recruitment, heightened myokine production, cell swelling, and systemic hormonal alterations.

- Research suggests that EIMD can enhance muscular adaptations, although excessive damage has a negative effect on muscle development. Hypothesized factors involved in the process include the initiation of inflammatory processes, increased satellite cell activity, the mediation of IGF-1 production, and cell swelling. The extent to which these mechanisms are synergistic, and whether an optimal combination exists to maximize the hypertrophic response to resistance training, remains to be determined.

Role of Resistance Training Variables in Hypertrophy

3

A number of research-based methods exist for examining the muscular response to mechanical stimuli. For example, synergist ablation of the gastrocnemius muscle results in the soleus and plantaris muscles being forced to carry out plantar flexion. The heightened load on these muscles results in increases in muscle cross-sectional area of 30% to 50% within several weeks postsurgery. Neuromuscular electrical stimulation also is frequently used to promote hypertrophy in animal models. This technique, which involves stimulating muscles with high-frequency electrical impulses (levels above 60 Hz), produces significant gains in muscle mass in just a few sessions. In humans, however, resistance training is the primary means for increasing muscle growth.

Resistance training programs are a composite of *program design variables* that include volume, frequency, load, exercise selection, type of muscle action, rest interval length, repetition duration, exercise order, range of motion, and intensity of effort. These variables can be manipulated to stimulate the neuromuscular system, and they do so in different ways. Consistent with the *SAID principle* (specific adaptations to imposed demands), the way such stimuli are applied influences phenotypic adaptations. This chapter provides an overview of each variable with respect to how its manipulation affects the hypertrophic response to resistance training.

Volume

Volume refers to the amount of exercise performed over a period of time. Volume is often expressed as the number of repetitions completed in a resistance training bout (sets × repetitions). However, this value does not take into account the amount of load lifted. Thus, a more appropriate term to reflect the total work completed is *volume load*, which is the product of sets × repetitions × load. Although an increase in training frequency can create the largest increase in weekly volume load provided volume per session is kept static, an increase in the number of sets performed (and thus total repetitions) in a training bout can also substantially increase training volume (298).

Research provides compelling evidence that higher-volume loads are necessary to maximize anabolism. Terzis and colleagues (755) showed that phosphorylation of p70[S6K] and ribosomal protein S6 increases 30 min following resistance training in a volume-dependent manner. The fact that it did not reach a plateau in the volumes studied suggests that higher volumes might have led to even greater increases. Intriguingly, the study found similar elevations in mTOR independent of training volume, suggesting that increased training volumes may augment S6 phosphorylation via alternative anabolic pathways, anticatabolic pathways, or a combination of the two. Burd and colleagues (104) found significantly greater increases in muscle protein synthesis 5 hours after 3 sets of knee extension exercises versus a single set (3.1- vs. 2.3-fold, respectively). Moreover, muscle protein synthesis in the 3-set condition remained significantly elevated (by 2.3-fold) at 29 hours postworkout, whereas levels in the 1-set condition had returned to baseline. In contrast to the Terzis and colleagues study, however, phosphorylation of S6 was similar between the 1- and 3-set conditions. The combined findings from these studies indicate that multiple-set protocols in resistance training programs have greater positive effects on intracellular signaling and muscle protein synthesis than single-set protocols.

The prevailing body of evidence from longitudinal studies is consistent with evidence from studies of acute data. A clear dose–response relationship was noted between volume and hypertrophy—that is, higher volumes correlate to greater hypertrophic adaptations, at least up to a certain point. A meta-analysis encompassing eight studies and 277 subjects found a 40% greater effect size from the performance of multiple- versus single-set protocols (396). Consistent with a dose–response relationship, effect sizes for hypertrophy tended to parallel increases in the number of sets performed up to a maximum of 6 sets (0.24 for 1 set, 0.34 for 2 or 3 sets, and 0.44 for 4 to 6 sets). Importantly, every study included in the analysis showed an effect size superiority for multiple- versus single-set training, indicating meaningful differences between protocols.

A systematic review by Wernbom and colleagues (814) showed that the cross-sectional area of the elbow flexors increased from 0.15% per day when 7 through 38 repetitions were performed per session to 0.26% per day when 42 through 66 repetitions were performed per session. The rate of increase diminished to 0.18% per day with volumes in the range of 74 through 120 repetitions per session, suggesting that very high volumes impair the hypertrophic response, perhaps by causing an overtrained state. With respect to total sets, hypertrophic increases peaked between 4 and 6 sets (0.24% increase in cross-sectional area per day); lesser responses were noted

from the performance of 3 to 3.5 sets and ≥9 sets (0.17% and 0.18% increase per day, respectively). With respect to the quadriceps, the findings were similar across a wide spectrum of clusters; 0.12% to 0.13% increases in cross-sectional area per day were seen from the performance of 21 through 100+ repetitions per session. The only exception was in the cluster of 66 through 90 repetitions per day, in which cross-sectional area increases were on the order of 0.08% per day. Analysis of the optimal number of sets showed a benefit to higher volumes, and the greatest response was seen in studies incorporating ≥10 sets. Importantly, the vast majority of these studies were carried out in untrained subjects, thereby limiting the ability to generalize to trained lifters.

KEY POINT

Multiset protocols favoring high volumes of resistance training optimize the hypertrophic response. To avoid overtraining, people should increase volume progressively over the course of a training cycle and integrate periods of reduced training volume on a regular basis to facilitate the recovery process.

In a comprehensive long-term study on the topic, Radaelli and colleagues (599) compared muscle thickness of the upper extremities following 6 months of resistance training using 1, 3, or 5 sets per exercise. Training was carried out 3 days per week using loads equating to 8- to 12RM. Results showed a clear and marked positive relationship between volume and muscle growth. Effect sizes for the elbow flexors were trivial for the 1-set group (0.10), moderate for the 3-set group (0.73), and large for the 5-set group (1.10). Changes in muscle thickness in the elbow extensors were even more dependent on higher levels of volume; only trivial effect sizes were seen for both the 1- and 3-set groups (0.05), whereas the effect size was large for the 5-set group (2.33). Because hypertrophic increases did not plateau at the 5-set condition, it is possible that higher volumes would have resulted in yet further increases in muscle size.

Research shows that hypertrophic advantages from higher training volumes are associated with an augmented satellite cell response. Hanssen and colleagues (286) reported a greater increase in the number of satellite cells in the quadriceps femoris after 11 weeks of performing 3 sets compared to 1 set of lower-body exercises. However, no significant differences were seen in the upper-body musculature, suggesting an enhanced effect

of volume on the leg muscles. These findings are consistent with previous work showing significantly greater hypertrophy from a multiple- versus single-set protocol in the lower body (11% vs. 7%, respectively), whereas no significant differences were noted in the upper-body musculature (624). Both studies were carried out with untrained subjects, so whether discrepancies persist in those with considerable lifting experience remains unclear.

Table 3.1 summarizes the research related to volume and muscle hypertrophy.

TABLE 3.1 Summary of Hypertrophy Training Studies Investigating Training Volume

Study	Subjects	Design	Study duration	Hypertrophy measurement	Findings
Bottaro et al. (90)	30 untrained young men	Random assignment to a resistance training protocol in which one group performed 3 sets of knee extension exercises and 1 set of elbow flexion exercises while the other group performed 3 sets of elbow flexion exercises and 1 set of knee extension exercises. All subjects performed 8- to 12RM of each exercise twice per week.	12 weeks	Ultrasound	No significant differences in muscle thickness between conditions
Cannon and Marino (122)	31 untrained young and elderly women	Random assignment to a resistance training protocol of either 1 or 3 sets per exercise. Exercise consisted of bilateral knee extensions and knee curls for 10 reps at an intensity of 50% to 75% of 1RM. Training was carried out 3 days per week.	10 weeks	MRI	No significant differences in muscle volume between conditions
Correa et al. (159)	35 untrained postmenopausal women	Random assignment to a resistance training protocol of either 1 or 3 sets per exercise. All subjects performed 8 exercises targeting the entire body at 15RM.	12 weeks	Ultrasound	No significant differences in muscle volume between conditions
Galvao et al. (239)	28 untrained elderly men and women	Random assignment to a resistance training protocol of either 1 or 3 sets per exercise. All subjects performed 7 exercises targeting the entire body at 8RM. Training was carried out twice weekly.	20 weeks	DXA	No significant differences in lean body mass between conditions
Marzolini et al. (457)	53 untrained elderly men and women with coronary artery disease	Random assignment to a resistance training protocol of either 1 or 3 sets per exercise. All subjects performed 10 exercises targeting the entire body for 10 to 15 reps.	24 weeks	DXA	Markedly greater increases in lean body mass, lean arm mass, and lean leg mass for the high-volume condition

(continued)

Table 3.1 *(continued)*

Study	Subjects	Design	Study duration	Hypertrophy measurement	Findings
McBride et al. (468)	28 untrained young men and women	Random assignment to a resistance training protocol consisting of 5 exercises including the biceps curl, leg press, chest fly, sit-up, and back extension. One group performed a single set of each of these exercises, while the other group performed 6 sets for the biceps curl and leg press and 3 sets for all other exercises. All subjects performed 6- to 15RM of the exercises twice weekly.	12 weeks	DXA	No significant differences in lean body mass between conditions
Mitchell et al. (496)	18 untrained young men	Random assignment to perform 2 of 3 unilateral knee extension protocols: 3 sets at 30% of 1RM; 3 sets at 80% of 1RM; 1 set at 80% of 1RM. Each participant trained both legs and was thus assigned to 2 of the 3 possible training conditions. Training was carried out 3 days per week.	10 weeks	MRI	No statistically significant differences in quadriceps hypertrophy between conditions, although the high-volume condition experienced more than double the absolute growth of the low-volume condition.
Munn et al. (513)	115 untrained young men and women	Random assignment to a resistance training protocol of 1 or 3 sets per exercise in either a slow or fast fashion. Training was carried out using elbow flexion exercises at 6- to 8RM for 3 days per week.	6 weeks	Skinfold and circumference measurements	No significant differences in lean mass between conditions
Oshowski et al. (553)	27 resistance-trained young men	Random assignment to a resistance training protocol of 1, 2, or 4 sets per exercise. All subjects performed a 4-day split-body routine working each of the major muscle groups with multiple exercises in a session at 7- to 12RM.	10 weeks	Ultrasound	No significant differences in muscle thickness between conditions
Radaelli et al. (597)	20 untrained elderly women	Random assignment to a resistance training protocol of either 1 or 3 sets per exercise. All subjects performed 10 exercises targeting the entire body at 10- to 20RM. Training was carried out twice weekly.	13 weeks	Ultrasound	No significant differences in muscle thickness between conditions
Radaelli et al. (599)	48 recreationally trained young men	Random assignment to a resistance training protocol of 1, 3, or 5 sets per exercise. All subjects performed 8- to 12RM for multiple exercises for the entire body. Training was carried out 3 days per week.	6 months	Ultrasound	Significantly greater increases in elbow flexor muscle thickness for the 5-set condition compared to the other two conditions. Only the 3- and 5-set groups significantly increased elbow flexor muscle thickness from baseline. Significantly greater increases in elbow extensor muscle thickness in the 5-set condition compared with the other two conditions. Only the 5-set group significantly increased elbow extensor thickness from baseline.

Study	Subjects	Design	Study duration	Hypertrophy measurement	Findings
Radaelli et al. (600)	27 untrained elderly women	Random assignment to a resistance training protocol of either 1 or 3 sets per exercise. All subjects performed 10 exercises targeting the entire body at 10- to 20RM. Training was carried out twice weekly.	6 weeks	Ultrasound	No significant differences in muscle thickness between conditions
Radaelli et al. (598)	20 untrained elderly women	Random assignment to a resistance training protocol of either 1 or 3 sets per exercise. All subjects performed 10 exercises targeting the entire body at 6- to 20RM. Training was carried out twice weekly.	20 weeks	Ultrasound	Significantly greater increases in quadriceps thickness for the high-volume group
Rhea et al. (611)	18 resistance-trained young men	Random assignment to a resistance training protocol of either 1 or 3 sets per exercise. All subjects performed 4- to 10RM on the bench press and leg press. Subjects also performed an additional set of multiple exercises considered unrelated to the bench press or leg press. Training was carried out 3 days per week.	12 weeks	BodPod	No significant differences in lean body mass between conditions
Ribeiro et al. (612)	30 untrained elderly women	Random assignment to a resistance training protocol consisting of 8 exercises for the total body performed either 1 or 3 days per week. All subjects performed 10-15 repetitions.	12 weeks	DXA	No significant differences in lean body mass between conditions
Ronnestad et al. (624)	21 untrained young men	Random assignment to a resistance training protocol in which one group performed 3 sets of upper-body exercises and 1 set of lower-body exercises, while the other group performed 3 sets of lower-body exercises and 1 set of upper-body exercises. Training consisted of 8 exercises for the entire body performed at 7- to 10RM and carried out 3 days per week.	11 weeks	MRI	Significantly greater increases in thigh muscle cross-sectional area for the higher-volume condition
Sooneste et al. (712)	8 untrained young men	Within-subject crossover in which all subjects performed a 2-day-per-week resistance training protocol of preacher curls so that one arm used 3 sets in a session and the other arm used a single set in the following session. Training was performed at 80% of 1RM and carried out 2 days per week.	12 weeks	MRI	Significantly greater increases in upper-arm cross-sectional area for the high-volume condition
Starkey et al. (722)	48 untrained mixed-aged men and women	Random assignment to a resistance training protocol of knee flexions and extensions performed either 1 or 3 days per week. All subjects performed 8 to 12 reps for 3 days per week.	14 weeks	Ultrasound	No significant differences in the thickness of the anterior or posterior thigh muscles between conditions, although only the high-volume group significantly increased hypertrophy of the vastus medialis relative to control

Abbreviations: RM = repetition maximum; DXA = dual X-ray absorptiometry; MRI = magnetic resonance imaging.

VOLUME

Evidence for a dose–response relationship between volume and hypertrophy is compelling: higher training volumes are clearly and positively associated with greater muscular gains. Based on the findings of Wernbom and colleagues (814), multiset routines totaling 40 to 70 repetitions per muscle group per session can be considered a general guideline for those with limited training experience. More advanced lifters seem to require greater volumes to maximize muscle protein accretion, perhaps double that of untrained people. Given that consistently employing high volumes over time hastens the onset of overtraining, periodizing programming by progressively increasing volume over the course of a training cycle appears beneficial. Moreover, periods of reduced training volume should be integrated on a regular basis to facilitate the recovery process.

Although the evidence for a dose–response relationship is compelling, there is undoubtedly a limit above which additional volume confers no additional hypertrophic benefits. A number of bodily systems, including metabolic, hormonal, nervous, and muscular, are sensitive to the magnitude of training volume (390), and overstressing these systems is bound to have negative consequences. The relationship between volume and hypertrophy is hypothesized to follow an inverted-U curve, whereby muscle accretion peaks at a given volume load and, beyond this point, further increases in volume can actually impair muscular gains (figure 3.1) (298). It is important to note that the threshold for volume-related hypertrophic benefits varies based on genetics (see chapter 5); lifestyle-related factors such as nutritional status, daily stress levels, and sleep patterns also play a role in individual responses. Some authors have posited that well-trained people require a particularly high training volume (>10 sets) to induce maximal hypertrophy (571). Although this hypothesis has a logical basis, the paucity of data on the topic in trained lifters precludes the ability to draw definitive conclusions.

Frequency

Frequency of training pertains to the number of exercise sessions performed in a given period

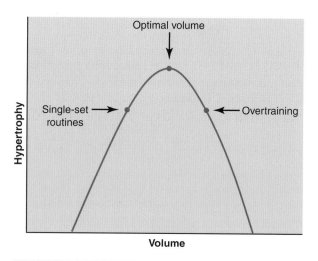

FIGURE 3.1 Dose response for the effects of volume on hypertrophy.

of time, generally a week (656). Perhaps more important to hypertrophic outcomes, frequency also includes the number of times a muscle group is worked over the course of a week. With respect to hypertrophy training, frequency can be varied to manipulate training volume. Neuromuscular factors limit how much volume can be incorporated into a single training session; beyond a given threshold, the quality of training begins to degrade. Studies show superior neuromuscular adaptations, hormonal markers for recovery, strength improvement, and gains in lean body mass in those performing volume-equated programs with higher frequencies and less volume per session (298). Thus, distributing volume per muscle group over more frequent bouts can be an effective strategy for maintaining weekly volume with less fatigue per session.

Hypertrophy-oriented routines generally involve a high volume of work per muscle group in a session but relatively infrequent training of each muscle group. To best carry out this strategy, people often follow a *split-body routine* in which they perform multiple exercises for a specific muscle group in one training session. In comparison to a total-body routine, split routines allow total weekly training volume to be maintained or increased with fewer sets performed per training session and greater recovery afforded between sessions (361). Moreover, performing multiple exercises for a muscle group in the same bout heightens metabolic stress and thus may enhance anabolism (656). A survey of competitive male bodybuilders revealed that more than 2/3 trained each muscle group only once per week, and none reported working a muscle group more than twice weekly; every respondent reported using a split-body routine (270).

KEY POINT

Split routines allow for a greater volume of work per muscle group per session, potentially enhancing muscular adaptations via the dose–response relationship between volume and hypertrophy.

General hypertrophy training guidelines recommend allowing at least 48 hours between resistance bouts for the same muscle group (656). It has been surmised that training before muscle protein synthesis has fully run its course—which lasts up to approximately 48 hours postexercise—impairs muscle protein accretion (442). Research in rodents shows that myogenic responses are attenuated when recovery occurs less than 48 hours after

the previous resistance bout (271). Moreover, total RNA has been shown to be elevated in humans 72 hours after a bout of maximal isometric electrical contractions (77). Because the majority of skeletal muscle RNA is ribosomal, these findings suggest that a cell's potential for protein synthesis remains heightened even beyond the 2-day time point.

The extent of muscle damage also mitigates training frequency. Metabolically fatigued muscle fibers display a greater membrane permeability consequent to an increase in free calcium ions, leading to the activation of potassium channels and proteolytic enzymes. Performing a multiset, high-volume routine consistent with hypertrophy training protocols may thus require at least 48 to 72 hours of rest between workouts for the same muscle group to ensure adequate repair, recovery, and adaptation (395, 444).

Research examining the effects of frequency on long-term hypertrophic adaptations in humans is limited. A systematic review by Wernbom and colleagues (814) determined that although novice lifters benefit from training muscle groups up to 4 days a week, those with more experience realize optimal gains with a weekly frequency of 2 or 3 days. There was insufficient data for determining whether higher frequencies would be beneficial in a well-trained population. Importantly, the analysis did not account for greater volumes associated with higher training frequencies, thereby confounding the ability to draw conclusions on the specific impact of varying the number of weekly training sessions.

Only a handful of studies have examined training frequency when volumes are equated. Ribeiro and colleagues (614) investigated a group of 10 competitive male bodybuilders who were randomly assigned to perform a split-body resistance training program either 4 or 6 times per week. Training for each exercise involved 4 sets that descended from 12RM to 6RM in a pyramid fashion (i.e., 12-, 10-, 8-, and 6RMs on successive sets, respectively). Volume was equated between the groups, in that those training 4 times a week trained more muscle groups in a session than did those training 6 times a week. Nutritional intake was strictly controlled; meals were individually prepared for each subject daily. After 4 weeks, similar increases in fat-free mass were noted in both groups. These results indicate that, with respect to increases in lean mass, spreading out the training load over the course of a week is as effective as performing a greater per-session volume. The 90-minute training sessions with higher per-session training volumes did not seem to compromise muscle growth compared to more frequent 60-minute sessions. Findings need to be interpreted with caution given the study's small sample size and short duration. Moreover, because each muscle group was trained twice weekly, the findings cannot be extrapolated to the effects of working individual muscles with different frequencies.

Benton and colleagues (69) compared body composition changes in untrained middle-aged women performing either a total-body or split-body routine on a volume-equated basis. Those in the total-body group worked each muscle group 3 days a week; those in the split-body group worked each muscle group twice weekly. After 8 weeks, similar increases were seen in lean mass in both groups. These findings indicate that 2 and 3-day-a-week frequencies are equally effective for increasing muscle development in the early stages of training. In contrast, McLester and colleagues (480) evaluated body composition changes between training 1 and 3 days a week on a volume-equated basis in resistance-trained men. After 12 weeks, the 3-day-a-week group displayed markedly greater increases in fat-free mass than those training once weekly, suggesting that a greater training frequency enhances muscle development. However, findings were limited by the use of indirect hypertrophy measures (i.e., skinfolds). In addition, the weekly volume was low compared to typical bodybuilding routines, (i.e., subjects performed only 3 weekly sets per muscle group).

In a study from my lab that compared muscular adaptations in a split- versus total-body routine in well-trained men (666), participants were pair-matched according to baseline strength and then randomly assigned to a split-body routine, in which multiple exercises were performed for a specific muscle group in a session with only one muscle group trained per bout, or a total-body routine in which 1 exercise was performed per muscle group in a session and all muscle groups were trained in each bout ($n = 10$). After 8 weeks, the group performing total-body workouts showed greater gains in both the upper- and lower-extremity muscles compared to those performing the split protocol. These findings indicate a benefit to greater frequencies of training for muscle groups, at least in the short term. An interesting point to consider here is that 16 of the 19 subjects reported regularly training each muscle once per week using a split routine prior to participating in the study. This raises the possibility that the novelty factor of a new stimulus may have positively influenced the results in the total-body training group.

A popular strategy to increase volume by manipulating training frequency is to split up a workout by performing multiple sessions in a day (often morning and evening). This strategy, called a *double-split routine*, is commonly used by bodybuilders to allow for high weekly training volumes while maintaining optimal mental and physical abilities during training. A study by Häkkinen and Kallinen (274) lends support to the value of double splits for hypertrophy training. Employing a crossover design, female athletes performed 2 training blocks lasting 3 weeks each. The athletes trained once a day during the first block and twice a day during the second block. The training volume was the same for each block, and training occurred 3 days per week. Results showed greater increases in muscle cross-sectional area when the athletes performed 2 sessions per day rather than when they performed all sets in a single bout. Conversely, Hartmann and colleagues (291) found that once-daily training produced slightly greater cross-sectional area increases compared to twice-daily splits in a group of nationally competitive male weightlifters over a 3-week period, although the differences were not statistically significant. Both of these studies were of very short duration, limiting the ability to draw practical conclusions on the topic. The conflicting results leave open the possibility that double-split routines are a viable option for hypertrophy training provided that the person can fit such an approach into his or her daily schedule.

Table 3.2 provides a summary of the research related to training frequency and muscle hypertrophy.

TABLE 3.2   Summary of Hypertrophy Training Studies Investigating Training Frequency

Study	Subjects	Design	Study duration	Volume equated?	Hypertrophy measurement	Findings
Arazi and Asadi (41)	39 untrained young men	Random assignment to a resistance training protocol of 12 exercises targeting the entire body divided into a 1-, 2-, or 3-day-per-week schedule. All subjects trained at 60% to 80% of 1RM.	8 weeks	Yes	Circumference measurements	No significant differences in arm or thigh girth between conditions
Benton et al. (69)	21 untrained middle-aged women	Random assignment to resistance training either 3 nonconsecutive days per week using a total-body protocol of 3 sets of 8 exercises or 4 consecutive days per week using an alternating split-body protocol of 3 sets of 6 upper-body exercises or 6 sets of 3 lower-body exercises. All subjects performed 8 to 12 reps at 50% to 80% of 1RM.	8 weeks	Yes	BodPod	No significant differences in lean body mass between conditions
Calder et al. (115)	30 untrained young women	Random assignment to either a total-body group performing 4 upper-body exercises and 3 lower-body exercises twice a week or a split-body group performing the lower-body exercises on separate days from the upper-body exercises so that training was carried out over 4 weekly sessions. All subjects performed 5 sets of 6- to 12RM to concentric muscle failure.	20 weeks	Yes	DXA	No significant differences in lean mass between groups
Candow and Burke (120)	29 untrained middle-aged men and women	Random assignment to 9 resistance training exercises for the total body either 2 times per week performing 3 sets of 10 reps or 3 times per week performing 2 sets of 10 reps.	6 weeks	Yes	DXA	No significant differences in lean body mass between conditions
Carneiro et al. (124)	53 untrained elderly women	Random assignment to a total-body resistance training protocol performed either twice or thrice each week. All subjects performed a single set of 10 to 15 reps for 8 exercises per session.	12 weeks	No	DXA	No significant differences in skeletal muscle mass between groups

(continued)

Table 3.2 *(continued)*

Study	Subjects	Design	Study duration	Volume equated?	Hypertrophy measurement	Findings
Gentil et al. (244)	30 untrained young men	Random assignment to 8 upper-body resistance training exercises performed either in a single session once per week or split into 2 sessions of 4 exercises performed twice per week. Training consisted of 3 sets at 8- to 12RM.	10 weeks	Yes	Ultrasound	No significant differences in elbow flexor thickness between groups
Hakkinen et al. (274)	10 resistance-trained young women	Within-subject crossover in which all subjects performed a resistance training protocol as a single session 3.5 days per week and then with the training volume split into twice-daily training sessions for a total of 7 weekly sessions.	3 weeks	Yes	Ultrasound	Greater increases in quadriceps thickness in the higher-frequency condition
Hartman et al. (291)	10 elite-level male weightlifters	Random assignment to an Olympic weightlifting protocol performed either as a single session 4 days per week or split into twice-daily training sessions separated by 3 hours for a total of 8 weekly sessions. Loads were 80% to 95% of 1RM.	3 weeks	Yes	Ultrasound	No significant differences in thickness of the quadriceps femoris between conditions
McLester et al. (480)	25 recreationally trained young men and women	Random assignment to resistance training either 1 day per week of 3 sets to failure or 3 days per week of 1 set to failure. All subjects performed 9 exercises for the total body.	12 weeks	Yes	Skinfold technique and circumference measurements	Nonsignificant trend for greater increases in lean body mass in the higher-frequency condition
Ribeiro et al. (614)	10 elite male bodybuilders	Random assignment to either a 4- or 6-day-per-week split-body resistance training routine. Subjects performed the same 23 exercises the same number of times per week. The distribution of exercises was more concentrated in the 4-day-per-week condition. The protocol involved 6- to 12RM for all exercises except those for the calves and abdominals, which were performed at 15- to 20RM.	4 weeks	Yes	DXA	No significant differences in lean mass between conditions
Schoenfeld et al. (666)	19 resistance-trained young men	Random assignment to resistance training either 1 day per week using a split-body routine or 3 days per week using a total-body routine. All subjects performed 8 to 12 reps of 7 exercises for the entire body.	8 weeks	Yes	Ultrasound	Significantly greater increases in elbow flexor muscle thickness and a trend for greater increases in vastus lateralis thickness for the greater-frequency, total-body condition

Abbreviations: RM = repetition maximum; DXA = dual X-ray absorptiometry.

PRACTICAL APPLICATIONS

FREQUENCY

Modulating training frequency is an effective strategy to manipulate volume loads. There appears to be a benefit to higher training frequencies, at least over short-term training protocols. Thus, total-body routines represent an attractive option for maximizing training frequency for each muscle group. However, split routines allow for a greater volume of work per muscle group per session, potentially enhancing muscular adaptations via the dose–response relationship between volume and hypertrophy. A case can be made for periodizing frequency over time, altering the number of times a muscle group is trained weekly in accordance with individual response. This can be accomplished by alternating total-body and split routines (e.g., progressing from a cycle of 3 weekly sessions to 4 weekly sessions the next cycle, and then culminating in a cycle of 6 weekly sessions). In this way, the lifter can maximize hypertrophy while reducing the potential for overtraining.

Load

The load lifted is widely considered one of the most important factors in the hypertrophic response to resistance training. *Intensity of load* refers to the percentage of 1RM employed in a given exercise. For example, if someone has a maximal bench press of 100 lb (45.5 kg) and performs a set with 80 lb (36.4 kg), then the intensity of load would be expressed as 80% of 1RM.

Intensity of load is often categorized into loading zones that correspond to repetition ranges. Typically, repetition ranges are classified as heavy (1- to 5RM), medium (6- to 12RM), and light (15+RM) (656). Although formulas have been designed to estimate repetitions at a given percentage of 1RM, at best they can provide only a crude approximation of the relationship between repetitions and the percentage of 1RM. The combination of genetic factors (e.g., muscle fiber typing, internal moment arm length), physiological factors (e.g., buffering capacity), and exercise types (e.g., upper body versus lower body, single joint versus multijoint; see chapters 5 and 6 for more detail) affect the generalizability of values. Hoeger and colleagues (310) found that a load of 80% of 1RM corresponded to a 10RM in the bench press, lat pulldown, and knee extension; however, this intensity of load varied from 6RM for the leg curl and

7- to 8RM for the arm curl, to 15RM for the leg press. Moreover, the accuracy of these formulas declines substantially as loads become progressively lighter. To this end, another study showed that, for individual subjects, repetitions to failure in the leg press ranged between 7 and 24 at 75% of 1RM, whereas the disparity widened to 30 to 71 at 30% of 1RM (660).

In a systematic review, Wernbom and colleagues (814) concluded that maximal hypertrophy is achieved through the use of a medium-repetition range, a claim that has been echoed by other researchers (390, 656). This hypothesis is primarily based on an extrapolation of mechanistic factors associated with the hypertrophic response to resistance training.

Heavy loading is generally believed to promote neural adaptations and to have lesser effects on hypertrophy (327). High intensities of load (>85% of 1RM) naturally result in high levels of mechanical tension on muscles. However, because the duration of a heavy set is short (<15 seconds), energy during such training is primarily derived from the ATP-PC system and little contribution occurs from fast glycolysis. Thus, metabolite accumulation is relatively low, which is supported by research showing that peripheral fatigue induced via metabolic stress was significantly reduced when training in a low-repetition range (5 repetitions per set) compared to sets carried out in a medium-repetition range (10 repetitions per set) (620).

At the other end of the loading zone continuum, light-load training is associated with high amounts of metabolic stress. Sets of ≥15 repetitions generally last 45 seconds or more, requiring the majority of energy production to be derived from the fast glycolytic system. This results in a substantial buildup of metabolites and acidosis, and generates a significant muscle pump. However, it has been theorized that the forces required to lift light loads are insufficient to recruit the highest-threshold motor units (660), which would mitigate hypertrophic gains.

Training in a medium-repetition range is purported to provide an optimal combination of mechanical tension and metabolic stress for maximizing hypertrophic adaptations. Loads during such training are heavy enough to recruit the majority of fibers in the target musculature and to maintain their stimulation over a sufficient period of time. Moreover, sets generally last between 20 and 40 seconds, requiring a substantial contribution from fast glycolysis and correspondingly generating high levels of metabolic stress (194). Because of these factors, medium loading is often referred to as the *hypertrophy range*.

KEY POINT

Training across a wide spectrum of repetition ranges (1 to 20+) is recommended to maximize all possible avenues for the complete development of the whole muscle. However, there is some merit to focusing on a medium-repetition range (6- to 12RM), which may provide an optimal combination of mechanical tension and metabolic stress.

Despite having a sound logical basis, the concept of an optimal hypertrophy range has come under scrutiny. With respect to muscle recruitment, fast-twitch fibers begin to be activated when force exceeds 20% of maximal voluntary isometric contraction, and activation of the full motor unit pool occurs at approximately 80% of maximal voluntary isometric contraction (256, 756). Recruitment during traditional resistance training under dynamic conditions is less clear. Tesch and colleagues (756) employed glycogen depletion analysis to evaluate recruitment during dynamic knee extension performance at loads of 30%, 45%, and 60% of 1RM. Results showed that Type IIa fibers began to be recruited at 30% of 1RM, and about half of these fibers showed glycogen loss as the load approached 50% of 1RM. However, the Type IIax and IIx fibers were activated only when the load reached 60% of 1RM. The study was limited by the fact that sets were not carried out to muscular failure. Research has shown a corresponding increase in EMG amplitude during fatiguing contractions, ostensibly as a result of an increased contribution of higher-threshold motor units recruited to maintain force output (718). It has therefore been postulated that training to the point of concentric muscular failure, regardless of the magnitude of load, ultimately results in the recruitment of the full spectrum of available motor units (107, 126). However, although acknowledging that motor unit activity does increase with fatigue, others claim that lifting very heavy loads results in specific recruitment patterns that are not attainable with light-load training (390).

My lab carried out two experiments to determine the minimum threshold for activating all available fibers in working muscle. The first study evaluated muscle activation in the quadriceps and hamstrings during performance of the leg press at 75% of 1RM versus 30% of 1RM (660). Both mean and peak muscle activation were markedly greater during the heavy-load condition compared to the light-load condition (by 57% and 29%, respectively). Importantly, not a single subject displayed equal or greater activation during low-load training. A follow-up study using an identical research design investigated muscle activation at 80% of 1RM versus 50% of 1RM in the bench press (653). Although peak EMG amplitude was similar between conditions, mean activation and the area under the curve were significantly greater when training with heavy loads. The combined findings of these studies indicate that intensities above 50% are needed for fully activating the entire motor unit pool. However, recall from chapter 1 that recruitment is but one component for maximizing muscle development; once recruited, the fiber must be stimulated for a sufficient period of time (i.e., time under load). To put things into context, training at a higher percentage of 1RM creates more recruitment and stimulation of higher-threshold motor units upon initiation of a set and trains muscle at an earlier point than when using light loads (298). Alternatively, training with light loads maintains tension in the lower-threshold motor units for an extended period. This could be particularly important in optimizing the development of the Type I fibers that are highly fatigue resistant. Indeed, an emerging body of research shows that Type I fiber hypertrophy is significantly greater when training with low loads than when training with high loads (523-525).

The authors of several animal studies have investigated the acute molecular responses to training at various intensities of load. Using an in situ model, Martineau and Gardiner (454) subjected rat plantaris muscles to peak concentric, eccentric, and isometric actions via electrical stimulation. Results showed tension-dependent phosphorylation of JNK and ERK1/2, and higher mechanical tension resulted in progressively greater phosphorylation. This suggests that peak tension is a better predictor of MAPK phosphorylation than either time under tension or rate of tension development. Follow-up work by the same laboratory revealed a linear relationship between time under tension and signaling of JNK, whereas the rate of tension change showed no effect, highlighting the importance of time under tension in anabolic signaling (455). Taken together, these findings point to the importance of overall training volume for maximizing the acute molecular responses related to skeletal muscle hypertrophy irrespective of loading intensity.

Human data provide further insight into the process. Hulmi and colleagues (327) found that early-phase postexercise MAPK and $p70^{S6K}$ phosphorylation responses were significantly

greater following 5 sets of leg press exercises at 10RM compared to 15 sets at 1RM. Taylor and colleagues (749) demonstrated that the ERK1/2 pathway was similarly activated at the upper and lower limits of the medium-repetition range (85% vs. 65% of 1RM), but a strong trend was seen for greater circulating IGF-1 release at the higher intensity of load. Popov and colleagues (589) displayed diverse responses in anabolic signaling and myogenic gene expression following resistance exercise performed at 74% versus 54% of 1RM. With respect to muscle protein synthesis, increases in heavy-load and moderate-load training are similar in the initial hours following resistance training on a volume-equated basis (399). In contrast, muscle protein synthesis appears to be blunted at lower intensities of load (<60% of 1RM) when training is not carried out to failure (399). On the other hand, Burd and colleagues (105) reported that muscle protein synthesis over 24 hours was actually greater when training to failure at 30% of 1RM compared to 90% of 1RM. Considering the body of acute data as a whole, findings suggest a robust acute response to resistance training regardless of intensity of load, provided training is carried out to muscular failure and, in the case of heavy loading, volume is equated. However, the responses are complex and suggest a synergism to training across loading zones.

A number of studies have attempted to compare muscular adaptations as a result of loading zones over time. Those investigating heavy versus medium loading have generally favored the hypertrophy range when volume was not equated between groups. Choi and colleagues (136) randomly assigned 11 young men to either a bulk-up protocol of 9 sets of knee extensions at 40% to 80% of 1RM with 30 seconds of rest between sets or a power-up protocol consisting of 5 sets at 90% of 1RM with 3 minutes of rest between sets. After 8 weeks, the results showed significantly greater increases in quadriceps hypertrophy for the bulk-up group. Masuda and colleagues (461) reported similar findings when employing an identical protocol. Alternatively, studies that equated volume between heavy- and medium-load training have failed to demonstrate superiority for the hypertrophy range (119, 134). All of the aforementioned studies used untrained subjects, limiting the ability to generalize findings to trained lifters.

My lab (661) investigated heavy versus moderate loading in 20 well-trained men who were randomly assigned to one of two groups: a hypertrophy group that performed a body-building-style routine, or a strength group that performed a powerlifting-style routine. The hypertrophy group protocol was a split routine in which each muscle was worked once per week with 3 exercises per session, performing 3 sets of 10 repetitions and resting 90 seconds between sets. The strength group protocol was a total-body routine in which each muscle was worked 3 times per week with one exercise per session, performing 7 sets of 3 repetitions and resting 3 minutes between sets. Volume load was equated so that subjects in both groups lifted approximately the same amount of weight per week. All sets were performed to the point of momentary concentric muscular failure. After 8 weeks, subjects in both groups significantly increased biceps muscle thickness, and no differences were seen between groups. Subjects in both groups also significantly increased 1RM strength, but the strength group had greater increases in the bench press and showed a trend for greater increases in the squat. From a hypertrophy-training standpoint, these results suggest that hypertrophy is similar along a continuum of 3 to 10 repetitions as long as equal volumes are performed, but that maximizing strength requires lifting very heavy weights.

It should be noted that that per-session training time in the strength group was 70 minutes, whereas that in the hypertrophy group was 17

PRACTICAL APPLICATIONS

LOAD

Hypertrophy can be achieved in all loading zones. Low-load training emphasizes metabolic stress and promotes the greatest increases in local muscular endurance, whereas low-repetition, high-load training requires high mechanical tension and enhances the ability to lift heavier loads as a result of greater neural adaptations. There appears to be a fiber type–specific response in which heavy-load training produces greater cross-sectional area increases in Type II fibers and light loads have a preferential effect on Type I hypertrophy. Thus, if the primary goal is maximizing hypertrophy without regard to strength-related factors, then training across a wide spectrum of repetition ranges (1 through 20+) is recommended to exploit all possible avenues for the complete development of the whole muscle. There is merit to focusing on a medium-repetition range (6- to 12RM), because it provides high levels of mechanical tension sufficient to stimulate the full array of fiber types while allowing for sufficient training volumes. Incorporating heavy loading (1- to 5RM) enhances strength, which ultimately allows the use of heavier loads during medium-repetition lifting. Additionally, light-load training should be included both to ensure the optimal development of Type I fibers and to improve the buffering capacity of muscle so that additional repetitions can be performed at a given medium intensity of load.

On the other hand, if the goal is to promote hypertrophy to maximize strength, there appears little reason to employ loads less than approximately 70% of 1RM. The compelling body of research indicates the presence of a strength–endurance continuum, in which lighter loads promote the ability to carry out submaximal resistive efforts at the expense of maximal force production (119). Increases in Type I fiber hypertrophy, as would be expected when training with low loads, have limited transfer to strength-related improvements.

minutes. So, from a time-efficiency standpoint, the bodybuilding-type training produced similar hypertrophy (as well as nearly similar strength increases) in about 1/4 of the time that the powerlifting-type training did. In fact, time constraints associated with the strength group allowed for only three major body areas to be worked in the study: chest (using upper-body pushing exercises), back (using upper-body pulling exercises), and thighs. The efficiency of the hypertrophy group would have allowed for additional volume in the muscle groups trained or the inclusion of exercises for other muscle groups, or both. Working specific muscles (and aspects of muscles), such as the middle and posterior deltoids, the hamstrings, and the calves, alone would have benefited overall muscle hypertrophy. Moreover, exit interviews revealed that those in the strength group felt overtaxed by the end of the study. Almost all complained of sore joints and general fatigue, and the two dropouts from this group were because of joint-related injury. These results indicate that although mechanistically heavy and moderately heavy weights appear to promote similar hypertrophic responses when volumes are equated, from an application standpoint, it simply is not practical to constantly lift heavy loads at the high volumes needed for maximizing muscle growth.

With respect to high-repetition training, research shows that muscle hypertrophy is diminished when loads higher than 60% of 1RM are not carried out to a point that approaches muscular failure. This was clearly demonstrated in a study by Holm and colleagues (311), in which subjects performed 8 repetitions of knee extensions on one leg and 36 repetitions of knee extensions on the other leg. In the light-load condition, subjects performed 1 repetition every 5th second for 3 minutes, thereby reducing the effects of fatigue; training in the heavy-load condition was carried out in a traditional fashion. Ten sets were performed each session, and training occurred 3 days a week. After 12 weeks, muscle cross-sectional area was 3-fold greater in the group that performed heavy-load training. These findings correlate with acute data showing an attenuation of muscle protein synthesis when training substantially short of failure at intensities of load below 60% of 1RM (399).

Research investigating the hypertrophic effects of light-load training to muscular failure has produced conflicting findings. A recent meta-analysis (662) sought to provide clarity on the topic by evaluating hypertrophic adaptations in randomized experimental trials that compared resistance training at ≥65% of 1RM to that at ≤60% of 1RM; both conditions were carried out to failure. Nine studies encompassing 251 subjects met inclusion criteria. Meta-analytic data showed a trend for greater growth in the heavier-load condition, but results were not statistically different. A review of the results of the individual studies revealed that three found a significant advantage for high-load training (119, 311, 670), and six showed no significant differences between low-load and high-load training (412, 496, 543, 588, 743, 744). An important caveat is that two of the six studies that failed to show significant differences demonstrated clear relative hypertrophic advantages for higher-load training, and cross-sectional area increases of 34% to 150% (588, 744). All of these studies were carried out with untrained subjects, thereby limiting the generalizability of the findings.

Subsequently, my lab carried out a longitudinal study (665) that compared muscular adaptations in low-load versus high-load training in resistance-trained subjects. Eighteen young men with an average of more than 3 years resistance training experience were randomly assigned to perform either a medium-repetition (8- to 12RM) or a high-repetition (25- to 35RM) routine. All other variables were rigidly controlled, and subjects performed 3 sets of 7 exercises for the upper and lower body on 3 nonconsecutive days a week. After 8 weeks, both groups significantly increased thickness of the biceps brachii, triceps brachii, and quadriceps femoris, but no statistical differences were noted between groups. Consistent with the concept of a strength–endurance continuum, gains in maximal muscle strength were markedly higher in the medium-repetition group, and improvements in local muscular endurance were significantly greater in the high-repetition group.

Table 3.3 provides a summary of the research related to intensity of load and muscle hypertrophy.

TABLE 3.3 Summary of Hypertrophy Training Studies Investigating Training Load

Study	Subjects	Design	Study duration	Volume equated?	Hypertrophy measurement	Findings
Campos et al. (119)	32 untrained young men	Random assignment to high-intensity (3- to 5RM), intermediate-intensity (9- to 11RM), or low-intensity (20- to 28RM) exercise. Exercise consisted of 2 to 4 sets of squat, leg press, and knee extensions, performed 3 days per week. Tempo was consistent between conditions.	8 weeks	Yes	Muscle biopsy	Significant increases in CSA for high-intensity exercise; no significant increase in CSA for low-intensity exercise. Significantly greater increases in muscle strength for high- vs. low-intensity group.
Holm et al. (311)	11 untrained young men	Random, counterbalanced performance of 10 sets of unilateral knee extensions, training one leg at 70% of 1RM and the contralateral leg at 15.5% of 1RM, performed 3 days per week.	12 weeks	Yes	MRI	Significantly greater increases in quadriceps CSA for high- vs. low-load exercise
Leger et al. (412)	24 untrained middle-aged men	Random assignment to either low-intensity (3- to 5RM) or high-intensity (20- to 28RM) exercise. Exercise consisted of 2 to 4 sets of squats, leg presses, and knee extensions, performed 3 days per week.	8 weeks	Yes	CT	No differences in CSA between low- and high-intensity exercise
Mitchell et al. (496)	18 untrained young men	Random assignment to perform 2 of 3 unilateral knee extension protocols: 3 sets at 30% of 1RM, 3 sets at 80% of 1RM, and 1 set at 80% of 1RM. Tempo was consistent between conditions. Training was carried out 3 days per week.	10 weeks	No	MRI, muscle biopsy	No differences in CSA between low- and high-intensity exercise. Significantly greater strength gains in high- vs. low-load group.
Ogasawara et al. (543)	9 untrained young men	Nonrandomized crossover design to perform 4 sets of bench press exercises at 75% of 1RM. Training was carried out 3 days per week. Tempo was consistent between conditions. After a 12-month washout period, the same protocol was performed at 30% of 1RM.	6 weeks	No	MRI	No differences in CSA between low- and high-intensity exercise. Significantly greater increases in strength favoring high over low load.
Popov et al. (588)	18 untrained young men	Random assignment to either high-intensity (80% of MVC) or low-intensity (50% of MVC) exercise without relaxation. Exercise consisted of leg press exercises performed 3 days per week. Tempo was consistent between conditions.	8 weeks	No	MRI	No differences in CSA or strength between groups
Schoenfeld et al. (665)	18 well-trained young men	Random assignment to a resistance training protocol of either 8- to 12RM or 25- to 35RM. All subjects performed 3 sets of 7 exercises. Training was carried out 3 days per week for 8 weeks.	8 weeks	No	Ultrasound	No significant differences in thickness of the biceps, triceps, or quadriceps between conditions

Study	Subjects		Study duration	Volume equated?	Hypertrophy measurement	Findings
Schuenke et al. (670)	34 untrained young women	Random assignment to moderate intensity (80% to 85% of 1RM) at a tempo of 1 to 2 seconds, low intensity (~40% to 60% of 1RM) at a tempo of 1 to 2 seconds, or slow speed (~40% to 60% of 1RM) at a tempo of 10 seconds concentric and 4 seconds eccentric. Exercise consisted of 3 sets of squats, leg presses, and knee extensions, performed 2 or 3 days per week for 6 weeks.	6 weeks	No	Muscle biopsy	Significant increases in CSA for high-intensity exercise; no significant increase in CSA for low-intensity exercise.
Tanimoto and Ishii (743)	24 untrained young men	Random assignment to 50% of 1RM with a 6-second tempo and no relaxation phase between reps, 80% of 1RM with a 2-second tempo and 1 second of relaxation between reps, or 50% of 1RM with a 2-second tempo and 1 second of relaxation between reps. Exercise consisted of 3 sets of knee extensions performed 3 days per week for 12 weeks.	12 weeks	No	MRI	No differences in CSA or strength between low- and high-intensity exercise
Tanimoto et al. (744)	36 untrained young men (12 served as nonexercising controls)	Random assignment to either ~55% of 1RM with a 6-second tempo and no relaxation phase between reps or 80% to 90% of 1RM with a 2-second tempo and 1 second of relaxation between reps. Exercise consisted of 3 sets of squats, chest presses, lat pulldowns, abdominal bends, and back extensions, performed 2 days per week.	13 weeks	No	B-mode ultrasound	No differences in CSA or strength between low- and high-intensity exercise
Van Roie et al. (783)	56 untrained elderly adults	Random assignment of leg press and knee extension training at high load (2 × 10 to 15 reps at 80% of 1RM), low load (1 × 80 to 100 reps at 20% of 1RM), or low-load+ (1 × 60 reps at 20% of 1RM, followed by 1 × 10 to 20 reps at 40% of 1RM). Tempo was consistent between conditions.	12 weeks	No	CT	No differences in muscle volume between groups. Greater increases in strength for high- and low- vs. low-load conditions.
Weiss et al. (811)	44 untrained young men	Random assignment to high-load (3- to 5RM), moderate-load (13- to 15RM), or light-load (23 to 25RM) resistance training. Exercise consisted of 3 sets of squats performed 3 days per week.	7 weeks	No	B-mode ultrasound	No significant differences in muscle thickness between conditions

Abbreviations: RM = repetition maximum; CSA = cross-sectional area; CT = computerized tomography; MRI = magnetic resonance imaging.

"Muscular adaptations in low- versus high-load resistance training: A meta-analysis," pp. 1-10, B.J. Schoenfeld, J.M. Wilson, R.P. Lowery, and J.W. Krieger, *European Journal of Sport Science*, 2014, Taylor and Francis, adapted by permission of Taylor and Francis (Taylor & Francis Ltd, http://www.tandfonline.com).

Exercise Selection

The human body is designed to carry out movement in three-dimensional space. Muscle architecture is intricately arranged to accomplish complex movement patterns efficiently and effectively. Therefore, varying exercise parameters (i.e., angle of pull, plane of movement, position of extremities) can preferentially target aspects of the musculature, as well as make synergists and stabilizers more or less active (656). Thus, choice of exercise may contribute to the degree of selective hypertrophy of specific muscles (278).

Numerous muscles have common origins, but their fibers diverge to insert at different attachment sites. These different heads provide greater leverage for carrying out multiplanar movement. A classic example is the deltoid muscle: the anterior deltoid performs shoulder flexion, the middle deltoid performs abduction, and the posterior deltoid performs horizontal abduction. Other examples are the pectoralis major (clavicular and sternal heads), biceps brachii (short and long heads), and gastrocnemius (medial and lateral heads). Moreover, the direction of the fibers in a given muscle allow for greater or lesser leverage in a given movement. The trapezius, for example, is subdivided so that the upper aspect elevates the scapula, the middle aspect abducts the scapula, and the lower aspect depresses the scapula (423).

Evidence suggests that it is possible to target not only different aspects of a muscle but also portions of a given muscle fiber as a result of *fiber partitioning*. The partitioning hypothesis is based on research showing that the arrangement of individual muscles is more complex than simply a bundle of fibers attaching at aponeuroses, tendons, or bones with a single muscle nerve innervation (203). Rather, many muscles are segmented into distinct compartments, and these compartments are innervated by their own neural branches. Muscles such as the sartorius, gracilis, semitendinosus,

PRACTICAL APPLICATIONS

EXERCISE SELECTION

Architectural variances of individual muscles lend support to the notion of the need to adopt a multiplanar, multiangled approach to hypertrophy training using a variety of exercises. Moreover, evidence suggests that frequent exercise rotation is warranted to fully stimulate all fibers within a muscle and thus maximize the hypertrophic response.

As mentioned in chapter 1, neural mechanisms are primarily responsible for increases in strength during the early stages of resistance training. Thus, lifters in the initial training phase should focus on acquiring the necessary motor learning and control to effectively carry out exercise performance. Simplification and repetition are important in this context. Performing the same movements over and over ingrains motor patterns so that proper technique becomes second nature. For those who have difficulty with coordination, reducing degrees of freedom with machine-based training can be an effective means to enhance neural development. They can then progress to more complex variations in three-dimensional space.

A variety of exercises should be employed over the course of a periodized training program to maximize whole-body muscle hypertrophy. This should include the liberal use of free-form exercises (i.e., free weights and cables) that maximize the contribution of stabilizer muscles, as well as machine-based movements that target specific muscles or portions thereof. Similarly, both multi- and single-joint exercises should be included in a hypertrophy-specific routine to maximize muscular growth.

and biceps femoris contain subdivisions of individual fibers that are innervated by separate motor neurons (824, 836). Moreover, the sartorius and gracilis, among other muscles, are actually composed of relatively short, in-series fibers that terminate intrafascicularly, refuting the supposition that myofibers always span the entire origin to insertion (304).

Muscular partitions may have functional or task-oriented roles; that is, different portions of one muscle may be called into play depending on the task-relevant demands of the situation (203). This is exemplified in the biceps brachii, in which both the long and short heads have architectural compartments that are innervated by private branches of the primary neurons (676). Research indicates that fibers in the lateral portion of the long head of the muscle are recruited for elbow flexion, fibers in the medial aspect are recruited for supination, and fibers that are centrally located are recruited for nonlinear combinations of flexion and supination (752, 753). Moreover, the short head demonstrates greater activity in the latter part of an arm curl (i.e., greater elbow flexion), whereas the long head is more active in the early phase of movement (98). These findings lend support to the notion that a variety of exercises will ensure the complete stimulation of all fibers.

Although evidence that varying exercises enhances muscle activation is compelling, the extent to which selective activation of a given portion of a muscle enhances its site-specific hypertrophic response remains to be determined. A large body of research shows that muscle hypertrophy occurs in a nonuniform fashion, in terms of preferential growth of both individual muscles in a muscle group and different regions within the same muscle. For example, multiple studies have shown that knee extension exercises result in a heterogeneous hypertrophic response in which certain areas of the quadriceps femoris show greater hypertrophy than others (278, 320, 520). Similar nonuniform growth has been demonstrated in the triceps brachii following regimented elbow extension exercises (802, 803).

Some evidence suggests that regional hypertrophy is specific to the site of muscle activation. Using magnetic resonance imaging technology, Wakahara and colleagues (802) determined muscle activation in a group of subjects performing 5 sets of 8 repetitions of the lying triceps extension exercise. Another group of subjects then underwent a 12-week supervised exercise program employing the same variables used in the acute activation study. Results showed that the extent of hypertrophy in the triceps was specific to the region of activation. Follow-up work by the same lab showed a similar outcome from the close-grip bench press exercise; triceps hypertrophy correlated to the site of activation, but occurred in a different region of the muscle compared to the previous study (803). To the contrary, other research shows that regional differences in quadriceps femoris hypertrophy following regimented resistance training are a function of muscle oxygenation status during exercise as opposed to neuromuscular activity (499).

KEY POINT

Once people have learned the movement patterns of basic resistance training exercises, they should use a variety of exercises to maximize whole-body muscle hypertrophy. This should include free-form as well as machine-based exercises. Similarly, both multi- and single-joint exercises should be included in hypertrophy-specific routines to maximize muscular growth.

Fonseca and colleagues (223) demonstrated the importance of varying exercise selection in a study in which they compared muscular adaptations following performance of the Smith machine squat with a volume-equated combination of the Smith machine squat, leg press, lunge, and deadlift. Results showed that the varied exercise routine produced more uniform muscle hypertrophy of all four quadriceps muscles compared to performing the Smith machine squat alone. In fact, the Smith machine squat failed to significantly increase cross-sectional area in the vastus medialis and rectus femoris muscles. It is interesting to speculate whether hypertrophic results would have been enhanced even further if more targeted single-joint exercises, such as the knee extension, were included in the varied routine.

Although the growth-related benefits of training variety are clear, the concept should not be taken to an extreme. When exercise variation occurs too frequently, a person may spend too much time developing motor skills with suboptimal loads, which compromises the hypertrophic response (298). This is particularly important during the initial stages of training in which improvements in strength are largely related to an improved neuromuscular response (see chapter 1). During this motor learning period, the number of exercises in a program should be limited so that neural patterns become ingrained into the subconscious. On the other hand, trained lifters can be more liberal in varying exercise selection; their neural patterns are much more entrenched, and depending on the complexity of the exercise, coordinated movements are maintained even after a lengthy period without training. Moreover, significant transfer of training from exercise variations (i.e., back squat to front squat) facilitates the retention of neural patterns over time.

Table 3.4 provides a summary of the research related to exercise selection and muscle hypertrophy.

Type of Muscle Action

Mechanosensors are sensitive not only to the magnitude and duration of stimulation, but also to the type of imposed action. As discussed in chapter 1, the three basic types of muscle actions are concentric, eccentric, and isometric. Mechanistically, there is a logical basis for speculation that eccentric actions produce the greatest anabolic response, and research often focuses on this type of muscle action. Eccentric strength is approximately 20% to 50% greater than concentric strength (53) and allows heavier loading during exercise. Moreover, forces generated during eccentric training are 45% higher than those generated during concentric training (343) and approximately double that of isometric contractions (656). The greater mechanical tension per active fiber is thought to be due to a reversal of the size principle of recruitment, which states that Type II fibers are selectively recruited at the expense of Type I fibers (684, 738). Evidence for preferential Type II recruitment has been noted during plantar flexion, as has derecruitment of the slow-twitch soleus muscle and the corresponding increase in activity of the gastrocnemius during the eccentric component of movement (518). These findings are consistent with EMG data indicating selective recruitment of a small number of motor units during eccentric hamstring exercise, including additional recruitment of previously inactive motor units (476). However, other research shows that

TABLE 3.4 Summary of Hypertrophy Training Studies Investigating Exercise Selection

Study	Subjects	Design	Study duration	Volume equated?	Hypertrophy measurement	Findings
Fonseca et al. (223)	49 untrained young men	Random assignment to a resistance training protocol involving performance of the Smith machine squat or a combination of the Smith machine squat, leg press, lunge, and deadlift. All subjects performed the routine twice per week at 6- to 10RM for each exercise.	12 weeks	Yes	MRI	Greater hypertrophy of the vastus medialis and rectus femoris muscles in the varied-exercise condition

Abbreviation: MRI = magnetic resonance imaging.

Type I and Type II fibers are equally glycogen depleted following eccentric exercise, suggesting no preferential recruitment of high-threshold motor units (750).

Hypertrophic advantages of eccentric exercise are also thought to be related to muscle damage (657). Although concentric and isometric exercise can induce muscle damage, the extent of damage is heightened during eccentric actions. This is believed to be due to greater force demands on fewer active fibers, which are prone to tear when attempting to resist lengthening. Because the weakest sarcomeres are located at different regions of each myofibril, it is hypothesized that the associated nonuniform lengthening causes a shearing of myofibrils. This deforms membranes, particularly T-tubules, leading to a disturbance of calcium homeostasis that further damages muscle tissue by eliciting the release of the calcium-activated neutral proteases involved in degrading Z-line proteins (24, 65).

A number of researchers have investigated the acute signaling response to modes of contractions. Franchi and colleagues found that eccentric training preferentially upregulated early MAPK activation (p38 MAPK, ERK1/2, p90[RSK]) compared to concentric training, but neither mode affected Akt/mTOR or inflammatory signaling 30 minutes after exercise (228). Eliasson and colleagues (201) found that maximal eccentric actions (4 sets of 6 repetitions) significantly increased early-phase (2 hours) phosphorylation of p70[S6K] and the ribosomal protein S6, whereas the same number of maximal concentric actions showed no effect on phosphorylation of these signaling molecules. Consistent with the study by Franchi and colleagues, neither contraction mode produced significant increases in Akt or mTOR, suggesting that eccentric actions activate p70[S6K] via an Akt-independent pathway. In addition, eccentric exercise was shown to promote significantly greater upregulation of STARS mRNA compared to concentric exercise (10-fold vs. 3-fold, respectively) as well as greater expression of downstream serum response factor (SFR) target genes (798). These findings suggest that eccentric exercise preferentially modulates the transcription of specific myofibrillar genes associated with adaptation to resistance exer-

cise, possibly as a mechanism to protect against contractile-induced muscle damage.

Research investigating the effect of contraction modes on muscle protein synthesis has produced disparate results. Several studies have failed to demonstrate any differences in either mixed muscle (246, 575) or myofibrillar (166) muscle protein synthesis after submaximal eccentric or concentric resistance exercise. Conversely, Moore and colleagues (507) reported a more rapid rise in myofibrillar muscle protein synthesis following 6 sets of 10 work-matched maximal eccentric versus concentric knee extension repetitions. The discrepancies between findings suggest that although muscle protein synthesis is similar in all contraction modes during submaximal exercise, maximal eccentric actions enhance the accretion of muscle proteins.

KEY POINT

Concentric and eccentric muscle actions appear to recruit muscle fibers in different orders, result in different signaling responses, and produce distinct morphological adaptations in muscle fibers and fascicles. Therefore, both concentric and eccentric actions should be incorporated during training.

Longitudinal studies provide limited evidence of a hypertrophic advantage from eccentric actions. In a meta-analysis encompassing 73 subjects from three studies meeting inclusion criteria, Roig and colleagues (622) found significantly greater increases in muscle hypertrophy following eccentric versus concentric resistance training protocols. Moreover, the researchers reported that two of the three studies not included in the analysis underscored the superiority of eccentric exercise in maximizing growth. That said, several studies have failed to demonstrate a hypertrophic superiority from eccentric actions (15, 114, 228, 508), and some research actually shows greater growth-related benefits to performing concentric training (464). Contradictions in the data are likely due at least in part to volume-related differences in the studies—that is, higher loads used during eccentric exercise resulted in an overall greater volume load. It is conceivable that the addition of supramaximal eccentric actions to a training program may enhance hypertrophic adaptations (650). This strategy can be achieved by performing an eccentric set or two of a given exercise with a load of approximately 120% to 140% of 1RM, and having a spotter assist in returning the weight concentrically.

One thing that is quite clear from the literature is that concentric and eccentric actions produce distinct morphological adaptations at the fiber and fascicle levels. Franchi and colleagues (228) found that eccentric training produced significantly greater increases in fascicle length compared to concentric training (12% vs. 5%, respectively), whereas concentric actions produced significantly greater increases in pennation angle (+30% vs. +5%). These findings are consistent with those of other research on the topic (606, 683) and

indicate a predisposition toward in-series hypertrophy following eccentric exercise. Interestingly, fascicle length changes seem to be specific to the initial stages of resistance training; increases abate after 5 weeks of consistent training (80).

Contraction modes also display region-specific effects on hypertrophy; eccentric actions show preferential growth in the distal aspect of the vastus lateralis (8% eccentric vs. 2% concentric), and concentric actions target the midportion of the muscle (7% eccentric vs. 11% concentric) (228). It is speculated that site-specific hypertrophy might be related to regional muscle damage along the length of the fiber and consequently nonuniform changes in muscle activation (297).

Table 3.5 provides a summary of the research related to type of muscle action and muscle hypertrophy.

TABLE 3.5 **Summary of Hypertrophy Training Studies Investigating Type of Muscle Action**

Study	Subjects	Design	Study duration	Mode	Hypertrophy measurement	Findings
Ben-Sira et al. (68)	48 untrained young women	Random assignment to a resistance training protocol of eccentric-only, concentric-only, mixed eccentric and concentric, or supramaximal eccentric actions for the knee extensors. The mixed-condition group performed 3 sets of 10 reps at 65% of concentric 1RM; the supramaximal eccentric group performed 3 sets of 5 reps at 130% of concentric 1RM; the concentric-only and eccentric-only groups performed 3 sets of 10 reps for these actions at 65% of concentric 1RM. Training was carried out twice per week.	8 weeks	Knee extension machine	Circumference measurement	No significant differences in thigh girth between conditions
Blazevich et al. (80)	21 untrained young men and women	Random assignment to a resistance training protocol of either eccentric or concentric actions for the knee extensors. All subjects performed 4 to 6 sets of 6 maximal reps. Training was carried out 3 days per week.	10 weeks	Isokinetic dynamometer	MRI and ultrasound	No significant differences in quadriceps hypertrophy between conditions

Study	Subjects	Design	Study duration	Mode	Hypertrophy measurement	Findings
Cadore et al. (113)	22 recreationally trained young men and women	Random assignment to a resistance training protocol of either eccentric or concentric actions for the knee extensors. All subjects performed 2 to 5 sets of 8 to 10 maximal reps. Training was carried out twice weekly.	6 weeks	Isokinetic dynamometer	Ultrasound	No significant differences in muscle thickness between conditions
Farup et al. (212)	22 untrained young men	Within-subject design in which subjects performed concentric actions of the knee extensors with one leg and eccentric actions with the other leg. All subjects performed 6 to 12 sets of 6- to 15RM. Eccentric actions were performed at 120% of concentric 1RM. Training was carried out 3 days per week.	12 weeks	Knee extension machine	MRI	No significant differences in quadriceps hypertrophy between conditions
Farup et al. (211)	22 untrained young men	Within-subject design in which subjects performed concentric actions of the knee extensors with one leg and eccentric actions with the other leg. All subjects performed 6 to 12 sets of 6- to 15RM. Eccentric actions were performed at 120% of concentric 1RM. Training was carried out 3 days per week.	12 weeks	Knee extension machine	Muscle biopsy	Significantly greater increases in Type II fiber CSA for the concentric condition
Farthing and Chilibeck (209)	36 untrained young men and women	Within-subject design in which subjects performed concentric actions of the elbow flexors with one arm and eccentric actions with the other arm. Subjects were randomly assign to perform the actions at either a fast or slow speed. All subjects performed 2 to 6 sets of 8 maximal reps. Training was carried out 3 days per week.	8 weeks	Isokinetic dynamometer	Ultrasound	Greater increase in muscle thickness for the eccentric condition
Franchi et al. (228)	12 untrained young men	Random assignment to a resistance training protocol of either eccentric or concentric actions of the lower-limb extensors. All subjects performed 4 sets of 8- to 10RM. Eccentric actions were performed at 120% of concentric 1RM. Concentric actions were performed for 2 seconds; eccentric actions, for 3 seconds. Training was carried out 3 days per week.	10 weeks	Leg press machine	MRI	No significant differences in thigh hypertrophy between conditions
Higbie et al. (307)	54 untrained young women	Random assignment to a resistance training protocol of either eccentric or concentric actions for the knee extensors. All subjects performed 3 sets of 10 maximal reps. Training was carried out 3 days per week.	10 weeks	Isokinetic dynamometer	MRI	Significantly greater increases in quadriceps muscle hypertrophy for the eccentric condition

(continued)

Table 3.5 *(continued)*

Study	Subjects	Design	Study duration	Mode	Hypertrophy measurement	Findings
Horto-bagyi et al. (318)	21 untrained young men	Random assignment to a resistance training protocol of either eccentric or concentric actions for the knee extensors. All subjects performed 4 to 6 sets of 8 to 12 maximal reps. Training was carried out 3 days per week.	12 weeks	Isokinetic dynamo-meter	Biopsy	Significantly greater increase in Type II fiber hypertrophy of the quadriceps for the eccentric condition
Horto-bagyi et al. (319)	48 untrained young men and women	Random assignment to a resistance training protocol of either eccentric or concentric actions for the knee extensors. All subjects performed 4 to 6 sets of 8 to 12 maximal reps. Training was carried out 3 days per week.	12 weeks	Isokinetic dynamo-meter	Biopsy	Significantly greater increase in quadri-ceps hypertrophy of all fiber types for the eccentric condition
Jones and Ruther-ford (343)	12 untrained young men and women	Within-subject design in which subjects performed concentric actions of the knee extensors with one leg and eccentric actions with the other leg. All subjects performed 4 sets of 6 maximal reps. Eccentric actions were performed at 145% of concentric 1RM. Train-ing was carried out 3 days per week.	12 weeks	Variable resistance knee extension machine	CT	No significant dif-ferences in thigh hypertrophy between conditions
Kim et al. (368)	13 young men and women (training status not disclosed)	Random assignment to a resistance training protocol of either eccentric or concentric actions for the shoulder abduc-tors. All subjects performed 4 to 6 sets of 6 to 8 maximal reps. Training was carried out 3 days per week.	8 weeks	Isokinetic dynamo-meter	Ultrasound	No significant differ-ences in hypertrophy of the supraspinatus between conditions
Komi and Buskirk (375)	31 untrained young men	Random assignment to a resistance training protocol of either eccentric or concentric actions of the forearm flexors. Training was carried out 4 days per week.	7 weeks	Isokinetic dynamo-meter	Circumfer-ence meas-urements	Greater increases in upper-arm girth for the eccentric condi-tion
Mayhew et al. (464)	20 untrained young men and women	Random assignment to a resistance training protocol of either eccentric or concentric actions for the knee extensors. Concentric actions were per-formed at an intensity of 90% of maximal concentric power, whereas eccentric actions were performed at the same relative power level. Training was car-ried out 3 days per week.	4 weeks	Isokinetic dynamo-meter	Biopsy	Greater increases in Type II quadriceps fiber area for the con-centric condition

Study	Subjects	Design	Study duration	Mode	Hypertrophy measurement	Findings
Moore et al. (506)	9 untrained young men	Within-subject design in which subjects performed concentric actions of the elbow flexors with one arm and eccentric actions with the other arm. All subjects performed 2 to 6 sets of 10 maximal reps. Training was carried out twice per week.	9 weeks	Isokinetic dynamometer	CT	No significant differences in hypertrophy of the elbow flexors between conditions
Nickols-Richardson et al. (528)	70 untrained young women	Random assignment to a resistance training protocol of either eccentric or concentric actions for the limbs. All subjects performed 5 sets of 6 maximal reps. Training was carried out 3 days per week.	5 months	Isokinetic dynamometer	DXA	No significant differences in fat-free soft tissue mass between conditions
Reeves et al. (606)	19 untrained elderly men and women	Random assignment to a resistance training protocol of either eccentric or mixed (eccentric and concentric) actions for the lower body. The mixed condition was performed for 2 sets of 10 reps with a load of ~80% of the mixed-action 5RM. The eccentric-only condition was performed for 2 sets of 10 reps with a load of ~80% of the eccentric 5RM. Training was carried out 3 days per week.	14 weeks	Knee extension and leg press machines	Ultrasound	No significant differences in vastus lateralis thickness between conditions
Seger et al. (677)	10 untrained young men	Within-subject design in which subjects performed concentric actions of the knee extensors with one leg and eccentric actions with the other leg. All subjects performed 4 sets of 10 maximal reps. Training was carried out 3 days per week.	10 weeks	Isokinetic dynamometer	MRI	Greater increases in whole quadriceps muscle hypertrophy distally for the eccentric condition
Smith and Rutherford (705)	10 untrained young men and women	Within-subject design in which subjects performed concentric actions of the knee extensors with one leg and eccentric actions with the other leg. All subjects performed 4 sets of 10 maximal reps. Eccentric actions were performed at 135% of concentric 1RM. Training was carried out 3 days per week.	20 weeks	Knee extension machine	CT	No significant differences in quadriceps hypertrophy between groups

(continued)

Table 3.5 *(continued)*

Study	Subjects	Design	Study duration	Mode	Hypertrophy measurement	Findings
Vikne et al. (793)	17 resistance-trained young men	Random assignment to a resistance training protocol of either eccentric or concentric actions for the elbow flexors. Training was divided between maximum and medium days. Those in the maximum training group performed 3 to 5 sets of 4- to 8RM; those in the medium training group performed 3 or 4 sets of the same repetition scheme but with lighter loads. Concentric actions were performed explosively, whereas eccentric actions were performed in 3 to 4 sec. Training was carried out 2 or 3 days per week.	12 weeks	Specially designed cable pulley apparatus	CT scan and biopsy	Significantly greater increases in whole muscle CSA of the upper arm for the eccentric condition. Greater increases in Type I and Type II fiber area for the eccentric condition.

Abbreviations: RM = repetition maximum; CSA = cross-sectional area; CT = computerized tomography; MRI = magnetic resonance imaging; DXA = dual X-ray absorptiometry.

PRACTICAL APPLICATIONS

TYPE OF MUSCLE ACTION

Both concentric and eccentric actions should be included in hypertrophy-oriented training programs. These actions appear to complement each other from a growth standpoint. There is a lack of research investigating whether isometric actions provide an additive hypertrophic benefit when combined with dynamic concentric and eccentric training.

Rest Interval Length

The time taken between sets is referred to as the *rest interval*, or *rest period*. Rest intervals can be classified into three broad categories: short (30 seconds or less), moderate (60 to 90 seconds), and long (3 minutes or more) (656). Research demonstrates that rest interval length has distinct effects on the acute response to resistance training, and these responses have been hypothesized to affect chronic hypertrophic adaptations.

Short rest intervals have been shown to markedly increase metabolite accumulation. Ratamess and colleagues (603) found that 30-second rest intervals reduced training volume by more than 50% over the course of 5 sets at 10RM, and marked decreases in load were seen in each subsequent set. Thus, metabolic enhancement is achieved at the expense of reduced mechanical tension, resulting in the need to progressively reduce the amount of loading over subsequent sets to sustain performance in a given repetition range.

Long rest intervals provide a sustained ability to maintain mechanical tension throughout each successive set. Strength capacity has been shown to be largely preserved over 3 sets with rest intervals of 3 minutes or more (383, 603). However, metabolite accumulation diminishes with increasing rest between sets, particularly with respect to lactic acid buildup (4).

Moderate rest periods are believed to provide an ideal compromise between metabolic stress and mechanical tension. A hypertrophy-type workout in which people rested 90 seconds between sets showed significantly greater increases in blood lactate concentration and reductions in pH compared to a strength-type workout with 5 minutes of rest between sets (527). With respect to the effect on loading, Medeiros and colleagues (485) found that using 60 second rest intervals required a reduction of 5% to 10% in each successive set to allow for the maintenance of 8- to 12RM loads in resistance-trained subjects. Because moderate rest intervals induce a favorable metabolic environment without substantially compromising mechanical forces, a rest interval of 60 to 90 seconds is generally prescribed for maximizing hypertrophy.

Despite the commonly accepted belief that hypertrophy-oriented routines benefit from moderate rest between sets, only a handful of studies have directly investigated the effect of rest intervals on muscle growth over time. In a crossover design, Ahtiainen and colleagues (20) assessed the hypertrophic impact in well-trained men of taking 2-minute versus 5-minute rest intervals while performing volume-matched work bouts of lower-body resistance exercise. Training was carried out over two separate 3-month periods, in which subjects rested 2 minutes in one of the periods and 5 minutes in the other. No significant differences in muscle cross-sectional areas were seen between conditions. The study had several strengths including a randomized crossover design (which substantially increases statistical power), the inclusion of trained subjects, and the use of magnetic resonance imaging to measure muscle growth. The primary issue with the study is that the 2-minute rest period is longer than what is generally advised for hypertrophy-type training. Specifically, the impact on metabolic stress diminishes with longer rest periods, and in fact, blood lactate levels were not significantly different between the groups in the study, which may have compromised anabolic signaling.

Buresh and colleagues (108) carried out a study in which 12 untrained people performed their workout with either 1 or 2.5 minutes of rest between sets. This study showed that longer interset rest intervals produced superior hypertrophy in the arms and a trend for greater growth in the legs compared to training with shorter rest intervals. Although the results may seem compelling, it should be noted that muscle cross-sectional area was determined by anthropometric means (i.e., surface measurements), which can be quite unreliable and thus compromise accuracy. Further confounding matters is the small number of subjects (only 6 in each group) and the fact that subjects were not resistance trained.

KEY POINT

Although rest periods of 60 to 90 seconds induce a favorable metabolic environment for achieving hypertrophy, research indicates that resting at least 2 minutes between sets provides a hypertrophic advantage compared to shorter rest periods because of the ability to maintain greater volume load.

In a novel research design, DeSouza and colleagues (172) randomized 20 resistance-trained men to either a group that used a constant rest interval or a group that used descending rest intervals. All of the men began by performing 3 sets of 10 to 12 repetitions with 2 minutes of rest for the first 2 weeks. Thereafter, the length of the rest interval progressively decreased to 30 seconds in the descending rest interval group over an ensuing 6-week period, whereas that of the constant rest interval group remained the same. After 8 weeks, both groups had significantly increased hypertrophy of the upper and lower extremities; no significant differences were noted in rest interval conditions despite a reduction in training volume for the descending group. A follow-up study using essentially the same protocol but with subjects receiving creatine supplementation again found no significant hypertrophic differences between constant and descending rest intervals (715). Interestingly, effect sizes were substantially greater

for descending versus constant rest intervals in the cross-sectional area of both the upper arm (2.53 vs. 1.11, respectively) and thigh (3.23 vs. 2.02, respectively).

My lab recently carried out a study investigating the impact of short versus long rest intervals on hypertrophy (651). Subjects were randomized to perform multiple sets of 7 exercises for the major muscle groups of the upper and lower body with either 1 or 3 minutes of rest between sets. After 8 weeks, the longer rest condition produced greater increases in the anterior thigh muscles, and a strong trend for greater increases was noted in the triceps brachii. Beneficial effects of longer rest periods on hypertrophy were attributed to the ability to maintain a higher volume load over the course of the study.

Table 3.6 provides a summary of the research related to rest interval length and muscle hypertrophy.

Repetition Duration

Repetition duration represents the sum of the concentric, eccentric, and isometric components of a repetition, and is predicated on the tempo at which the repetition is performed (548). *Tempo* is often expressed as a three-digit arrangement in which the first number is the time (in seconds) to complete the concentric action, the second number is the isometric transition phase between concentric and eccentric actions, and the third number is the time to complete the eccentric action (548). For example, a tempo of 2-0-3 would indicate a repetition taking 2 seconds on the concentric action, not pausing at the top of the movement, and then taking 3 seconds to perform the eccentric action. In the preceding example, the repetition duration would be 5 seconds.

To a certain degree, tempo can be volitionally manipulated. The extent depends on two factors: the intensity of load and the accumulated fatigue. Heavier loads take longer to lift; the closer the load is to the person's 1RM, the slower the concentric action will be, even when the intent is to move the weight as quickly as possible. Moreover, the onset of

TABLE 3.6 Summary of Hypertrophy Training Studies Investigating Rest Interval Length

Study	Subjects	Design	Study duration	Volume equated?	Hypertrophy measurement	Findings
Ahtiainen et al. (20)	13 resistance-trained young men	Within-subject crossover design in which all subjects performed a resistance training protocol with either 2 or 5 minutes of rest between sets. Training consisted of a multiset split-body routine of 8 to 12 reps carried out 4 days per week.	12 weeks	Yes	MRI	No significant differences seen in muscle CSA between groups
Buresh et al. (108)	12 untrained young men	Randomized assignment to a resistance training protocol with either 1 or 2.5 minutes of rest between sets. Training consisted of a multiset split-body routine of 8 to 11 reps carried out 4 days per week.	10 weeks	Yes	Hydrostatic weighing and circumference measurements	Significantly greater increases in arm CSA and a trend for greater increases in thigh CSA for the longer rest interval condition
Schoenfeld et al. (651)	21 resistance-trained young men	Randomized assignment to a resistance training protocol with either 1 or 3 minutes of rest between sets. Training consisted of 7 exercises for the total body of 8 to 12 reps carried out 3 days per week.	8 weeks	Yes	Ultrasound	Significantly greater increases in anterior thigh muscle thickness and a trend for greater increases in the triceps brachii thickness for the longer rest interval condition
Villanueva et al. (794)	22 untrained elderly men	Randomized assignment to a resistance training protocol with either 1 or 4 minutes of rest between sets. Training consisted of 2 or 3 sets of 4 to 6 reps carried out 3 days per week.	8 weeks	Yes	DXA	Significantly greater increases in lean body mass for the shorter rest interval condition

Abbreviations: RM = repetition maximum; CSA = cross-sectional area; MRI = magnetic resonance imaging; DXA = dual X-ray absorptiometry.

fatigue causes velocity to decrease because of the inability of working fibers to maintain force output. The capacity to lift even very light loads is curtailed when repetitions approach failure. In one study the first three concentric repetitions of a 5RM bench press took approximately 1.2 to 1.6 seconds to complete, whereas the fourth and fifth repetitions took 2.5 to 3.3 seconds, respectively (503). These results were seen despite the fact that subjects attempted to lift explosively on all repetitions.

The use of loads of ≤80% of 1RM allows lifters to vary concentric lifting cadence; lighter loads enhance this ability. Given that eccentric strength is approximately 20% to 50% greater than concentric strength (53), the velocity of eccentric actions can be altered at loads in excess of concentric 1RM. Some have speculated that intentionally extending the duration of repetitions leads to a superior hypertrophic response as a result of the longer time under load (359).

A recent systematic review and meta-analysis examined whether alterations in repetition duration affect the hypertrophic response to resistance training (664). Studies met inclusion criteria if they were randomized trials that directly compared training tempos in dynamic exercise using both concentric and eccentric repetitions carried out to momentary muscular failure. Eight studies met the inclusion criteria, comprising a total of 204 subjects. Repetition duration was stratified into four groups: fast/heavy (sets of 6 to 12 repetitions with a total repetition duration of 0.5 to 4 seconds), fast/light (sets of 20 to 30 with a total repetition duration of 0.5 to 4 seconds), medium (sets of 6 to 12 with a total repetition duration of 4 to 8 seconds), or light (sets of 6 to 12 with a total repetition duration of >8 seconds). Results of the meta-analysis showed no significant differences in muscle hypertrophy in the training durations evaluated. When considering just the studies that employed traditional dynamic constant external resistance (i.e., isotonic) training, it can be inferred that there are no discernable differences in hypertrophy using durations up to 6 seconds.

Subanalysis of data indicated that superslow training is likely detrimental to maximizing hypertrophy. Keogh and colleagues (359) assessed muscle activation in a group of trained lifters during the bench press under a variety of training conditions, including a very slow tempo and a traditional tempo. Those in the slow lifting condition used a repetition duration of 10 seconds (5 seconds for both concentric and eccentric actions), whereas those in the traditional training condition attempted to lift the load as fast as possible. Each condition was carried out to the point of concentric muscular failure. In comparison to the slow tempo, mean EMG activity of the pectoralis major during traditional lifting was markedly higher on the concentric portion of the movement (by ~18%, 19%, and 12% for the first, middle, and last repetition, respectively). During eccentric actions, the activation advantage for training at a traditional versus a slow tempo increased to 32%, 36%, and 36% in the first, middle, and last repetition, respectively. These findings provide evidence that volitionally slowing the tempo during a repetition is suboptimal for maximally activating the target muscle.

In the only study to date that directly evaluated muscle hypertrophy subsequent to superslow versus traditional training, Schuenke and colleagues (670) randomized untrained young females to perform multiple sets of the squat, leg press, and knee extension 2 or 3 days a week for 6 weeks. The superslow group carried out repetitions using a 14 second duration (10 seconds concentric, 4 seconds eccentric); the traditional training

KEY POINT

Current evidence suggests that little difference exists in muscle hypertrophy when training at isotonic repetition durations from 0.5 to 6 seconds. Training at very slow volitional durations (>10 seconds per repetition) appears to produce inferior increases in muscle growth.

PRACTICAL APPLICATIONS

REPETITION DURATION

Current evidence suggests little difference in muscle hypertrophy when training with isotonic repetition durations ranging from 0.5 to 6 seconds to muscular failure. Thus, it would seem that a fairly wide range of repetition durations can be used if the primary goal is to maximize muscle growth. Research is limited on the topic, making it difficult to draw concrete conclusions. Concentric and eccentric tempos of 1 to 3 seconds can be considered viable options. On the other hand, training at very slow volitional durations (>10 seconds per repetition) appears to produce inferior increases in muscle growth, although a lack of controlled studies on the topic makes it difficult to draw definitive conclusions. It is conceivable that combining different repetition durations could enhance the hypertrophic response to resistance training, although this hypothesis requires further study.

group employed a tempo of 1 to 2 seconds on both concentric and eccentric actions. Both groups performed 6- to 10RM per set, but the loading when training in superslow fashion was much lighter than when using a traditional tempo (~40% to 60% of 1RM vs. ~80% to 85% of 1RM, respectively) to allow maintenance of the target repetition range. Poststudy increases in Type IIa and Type IIx fibers were substantially greater using a traditional tempo (~33% and 37%, respectively) versus superslow training (~12% and 19%, respectively). In addition, there was a distinctly greater decrease in total Type IIx fiber area in the traditional group compared to the superslow group (~39% vs. 28%, respectively), along with a correspondingly greater increase in total Type IIa fiber area (~30% vs. 11%, respectively). This implies that lifting at a volitionally very slow cadence does not stimulate the highest-threshold motor units. Follow-up work from the same lab found that satellite cell content was significantly greater after traditional compared to superslow training across fiber types (303).

With respect to the individual muscle actions, some investigators have postulated that intentionally slowing concentric velocity reduces the momentum during a repetition, thereby heightening the tension on a muscle (822). Hypothetically, increased mechanical tension could positively mediate intracellular anabolic signaling, promoting a greater hypertrophic response. It has been shown, however, that the effects of momentum are inconsequential in a concentric movement of 2 seconds versus 10 seconds when the load is kept constant (342). A potential downside of lifting very quickly is a reduction in metabolic stress. Performing the concentric phase of a repetition at 2 seconds resulted in a greater lactate accumulation compared to an explosive concentric contraction despite an equated volume and lower power in the slower cadence (eccentric repetitions were standardized at 2 seconds (465). The residual effects of this observation on hypertrophy are not clear.

Nogueira and colleagues (534) found that performing concentric actions explosively

with a 1-second concentric repetition produced greater increases in muscle thickness compared to performing the repetitions at 2 to 3 seconds. A limitation of the study was that both groups used light loads (40% to 60% of 1RM), and sets were terminated well short of muscular failure. Thus, the design would have provided a bias to the 1-second condition because faster velocities promote greater recruitment and stimulation of higher-threshold motor units in the absence of fatigue (718).

Some have theorized that performing eccentric actions at higher velocities enhances anabolism as a result of increased tension on muscle during high-speed lengthening. Roschel and colleagues (627) found similar activation of Akt, mTOR, and p70[S6K] following 5 sets of 8 eccentric repetitions at a slow (20° per second) versus fast (210° per second) velocity, suggesting that the velocity of eccentric actions does not influence intracellular anabolic signaling. Several studies have shown a benefit to faster eccentric actions. Shepstone and colleagues (684) reported a trend for greater increases in muscle cross-sectional area of the elbow flexors with faster eccentric repetitions (210° per second vs. 20° per second) and Farthing and Chilibeck (209) demonstrated that fast (180° per second) eccentric actions produced greater increases in muscle thickness as compared to both slow (30° per second) and fast concentric actions, but not slow eccentric actions. It should be noted that all of these studies used isokinetic dynamometry, and the results therefore cannot necessarily be generalized to traditional isotonic training methods using coupled concentric and eccentric actions.

Some evidence suggests that the isometric component at the bottom phase of movement should be minimized to maintain constant tension on the target muscle. Tanimoto and Ishii (743) found that untrained young men performing 12 weeks of knee extensions using a 3-0-3-0 cadence (no rest between eccentric and concentric repetitions) experienced a similar hypertrophic response as men using a 1-1-1-0 cadence (relaxing for 1 second after each eccentric component). These results were seen despite the use of substantially heavier loads in the faster versus slower cadence conditions (~80% vs. ~50% of 1 RM, respectively). On the surface it is tempting to speculate that the lack of a relaxation phase in the slow cadence condition positively mediated results, perhaps via effects associated with increased ischemia and hypoxia. However, the fact that other aspects of the study were not controlled (i.e., concentric and eccentric tempo, intensity of load) clouds the ability to draw firm conclusions on the topic.

Table 3.7 provides a summary of the research related to repetition duration and muscle hypertrophy.

Exercise Order

Current resistance training guidelines prescribe placing large-muscle, multijoint exercises early in a workout, and placing small-muscle, single-joint movements later (29). These recommendations are based on the premise that the performance of multijoint exercises is impaired when the smaller secondary synergists are prefatigued by prior single-joint exercises. For example, performance of the arm curl would fatigue the biceps brachii, thereby impeding the ability to overload the larger latissimus dorsi muscle during subsequent performance of the lat pulldown.

Despite wide acceptance that exercise order should proceed from large- to small-muscle groups, research is equivocal on the topic. Acute studies show that performance, as determined by the number of repetitions performed, is compromised in exercises per-

formed toward the end of a session regardless of the size of the muscle trained (692). However, given the heavier loads used during multijoint movements, the absolute magnitude of the decreases are generally greater in these exercises when they are performed after those involving small-muscle groups. Thus, volume load tends to be better preserved when large-muscle exercises are placed early in the training bout.

KEY POINT

Despite widespread belief that exercise order should proceed from large- to small-muscle groups, the benefit has not been demonstrated in controlled research studies.

Several studies have attempted to directly quantify the effects of exercise order on muscle hypertrophy. Simao and colleagues (691) investigated the performance of upper-body exercises when progressing from large to small muscle groups compared to small to large muscle groups in untrained men. Exercises included the bench press, lat pulldown, triceps extension, and arm curl. Training was carried out twice per week for 12 weeks. Muscle thickness of the triceps brachii increased only in the group that performed small-muscle-group exercises first, although differences in the thickness of the biceps were similar on an absolute basis. The same lab replicated this basic study design and similarly found greater increases in triceps thickness when the

PRACTICAL APPLICATIONS

EXERCISE ORDER

Evidence indicates a hypertrophic benefit for muscles worked first in a resistance training bout. Therefore, exercise order should be prioritized so that lagging muscles are trained earlier on in the session. In this way the person expends the greatest energy and focus on the sets of most importance. Whether the muscle group is large or small is of secondary concern.

TABLE 3.7 Summary of Hypertrophy Training Studies Investigating Repetition Duration

Study	Subjects	Design	Repetition duration	Study duration	Hypertrophy measurement	Findings
Claflin et al. (141)	63 untrained young and old men and women	Random assignment to a resistance training protocol at either a high velocity (hip 250° to 350° per second, knee 100 to 160° per second) or low velocity (hip 30° to 90° per second, knee 20° to 40° per second). All subjects performed 2 sets of 10 reps with a 3rd set that induced failure using between 5 and 15 reps. Training was carried out 3 days per week.	0.5 to 0.66 seconds vs. 1 to 2 seconds vs. 2 to 6 seconds vs. 4 to 8 seconds	14 weeks	Biopsy	No effect of training on Type I fibers; 8.2% increase in Type II fibers irrespective of tempo
Keeler et al. (356)	14 untrained young and middle-aged women	Random assignment to either superslow or traditional Nautilus resistance training protocol. Subjects performed 1 set of 8- to 12RM for 8 exercises targeting the entire body. Training was carried out 3 days per week.	6 seconds vs. 15 seconds	10 weeks	BodPod	No significant differences in body composition
Munn et al. (513)	115 untrained young men and women	Random assignment to a resistance training protocol of 1 or 3 sets of elbow flexion exercise in either a slow or fast fashion. Training was at 6- to 8RM for 3 days per week.	2 seconds vs. 6 seconds	6 weeks	Skinfold and circumference measurements	No significant differences in lean mass between conditions
Neils et al. (522)	16 untrained young men and women	Random assignment to a protocol of either superslow at 50% of 1RM or traditional resistance training at 80% of 1RM. All subjects performed 1 set of 6- to 8RM for 7 exercises targeting the entire body. Training was carried out 3 days per week.	6 seconds vs. 15 seconds	8 weeks	DXA	No significant differences in body composition between conditions
Nogueira et al. (534)	20 untrained elderly men	Random assignment to an equal work output resistance training protocol in which concentric actions were performed either as fast as possible or at a cadence of 2 to 3 seconds. All subjects performed 3 sets of 8 reps of 7 exercises targeting the entire body. Loads were 40% to 60% of 1RM, and eccentric tempo was 2 to 3 seconds for both conditions. Training was carried out twice weekly.	3 to 4 seconds vs. 4 to 6 seconds	10 weeks	Ultrasound	Significantly greater increases in thickness of the biceps brachii for the fast condition

(continued)

Table 3.7 *(continued)*

Study	Subjects	Design	Repetition duration	Study duration	Hypertrophy measurement	Findings
Rana et al. (601)	34 untrained young women	Random assignment to a resistance training protocol of moderate intensity (80% to 85% of 1RM) at a tempo of 1 to 2 seconds, low intensity (~40% to 60% of 1RM) at a tempo of 1 to 2 seconds, or slow speed (~40% to 60% of 1RM) at a tempo of 10 seconds concentric and 4 seconds eccentric. All subjects performed 3 sets of 6- to 10RM of 3 lower-body exercises. Training was carried out 2 or 3 days per week.	2 to 4 seconds vs. 14 seconds	6 weeks	BodPod	No significant differences in FFM between conditions
Schuenke et al. (670)	34 untrained young women	Random assignment to a resistance training protocol of moderate intensity (80% to 85% of 1RM) at a tempo of 1 to 2 seconds, low intensity (~40% to 60% of 1RM) at a tempo of 1 to 2 seconds, or slow speed (~40% to 60% of 1RM) at a tempo of 10 seconds concentric and 4 seconds eccentric. All subjects performed 3 sets of 6- to 10RM of 3 lower-body exercises. Training was carried out 2 or 3 days per week.	2 to 4 seconds vs. 14 seconds	6 weeks	Biopsy	Significantly greater increases in CSA for the faster condition
Tanimoto and Ishii (743)	24 untrained young men	Random assignment to 50% of 1RM with a 6-second tempo and no relaxing phase between reps, ~80% of 1RM with a 2-second tempo and 1 second of relaxation between reps, or ~50% of 1RM with a 2-second tempo and 1 second of relaxation between reps. All subjects performed 3 sets at 8RM (807) of knee extension exercises. Training was carried out 3 days per week.	2 seconds vs. 6 seconds	12 weeks	MRI	No significant differences in muscle CSA between conditions
Tanimoto et al. (744)	36 untrained young men	Random assignment to ~55% to 60% of 1RM with a 6-second tempo and no relaxing phase between reps or ~80% to 90% of 1RM with a 2-second tempo and 1 second of relaxation between reps. All subjects performed 3 sets at 8RM of 5 exercises targeting the entire body. Training was carried out twice weekly.	2 seconds vs. 6 seconds	13 weeks	Ultrasound	No significant differences in muscle thickness between conditions

Study	Subjects	Design	Repetition duration	Study duration	Hypertrophy measurement	Findings
Watanabe et al. (807)	40 untrained elderly men and women	Random assignment to a resistance training protocol of a 6-second tempo and no relaxing phase between reps or a 2-second tempo and 1 second of relaxation between reps. All subjects performed 3 sets of 8 reps at 50% of 1RM of knee extension and knee flexion exercises. Training was carried out twice weekly.	2 seconds vs. 6 seconds		Ultrasound	Significantly greater quadriceps thickness for the slow condition
Watanabe et al. (808)	18 untrained elderly men and women	Random assignment to a resistance training protocol of a 6-second tempo and no relaxing phase between reps or a 2-second tempo and 1 second of relaxation between reps. All subjects performed 3 sets of 13 reps at 30% of 1RM of knee extension exercises. Training was carried out twice weekly.	2 seconds vs. 6 seconds	12 weeks	MRI	Significantly greater increases in quadriceps hypertrophy for the slow condition
Young and Bilby (852)	18 untrained young men	Random assignment to a resistance training protocol of either fast concentric contractions or slow controlled movements. All subjects performed 4 sets at 8- to 12RM of the barbell half-squat exercise. Training was carried out 3 days per week.	2 seconds vs. 4 to 6 seconds	7.5 weeks	Ultrasound	No significant differences in muscle thickness between conditions

Abbreviations: RM = repetition maximum; DXA = dual X-ray absorptiometry; MRI = magnetic resonance imaging; CSA = cross-sectional area; FFM = fat-free mass.

With kind permission from Springer Science+Business Media: *Sports Medicine*, "Effect of repetition duration during resistance training on muscle hypertrophy: A systematic review and meta-analysis," 45(4): 575-585, 2015, B.J. Schoenfeld, D.I. Ogborn, and J.W. Krieger, figure 1.

order of exercises progressed from small- to large-muscle groups (720). Although these findings might seem to indicate a benefit to performing smaller-muscle-group exercises first, it should be noted that hypertrophy of the larger muscles was not assessed in either study. It is possible, if not likely, that whichever muscles were worked earlier in the session hypertrophied to a greater extent than those performed toward the end of the bout. This suggests a benefit to prioritizing exercise order so that lagging muscles are worked at the onset of a workout.

It has been postulated that lower-body exercise should precede upper-body exercise. This is based on the hypothesis that lower-body exercise causes a hypoperfusion that compromises the delivery of anabolic hormones to the upper-body musculature when performed after arm training (821). Ronnestad and colleagues (625) found that hypertrophy of the elbow flexors was magnified when training of these muscles was preceded by lower-body exercise, ostensibly as a result of an increase in postexercise hormonal elevations. These results were in contrast to those of West and colleagues (818), who showed that performing lower-body exercise after arm training did not amplify elbow flexor hypertrophy. The disparate findings between these studies seemingly lend credence to a hypertrophic advantage of performing lower-body exercise prior to upper-body exercise. However, West and colleagues (821) demonstrated that delivery of testosterone, GH, and IGF-1 to the elbow flexors was not influenced by exercise order. Moreover, the impact of acute systemic fluctuations is of questionable significance and likely has, at best, a small impact on the hypertrophic response (see chapter 2).

Table 3.8 provides a summary of the research related to exercise order and muscle hypertrophy.

Range of Motion

Basic principles of structural anatomy and kinesiology dictate that muscles have greater contributions at different joint angles for given exercises. For example, there is evidence that the quadriceps muscles are differentially activated during knee extensions: the vastus lateralis is maximally activated during the first 60° of range of motion (ROM), whereas the

TABLE 3.8   Summary of Hypertrophy Training Studies Investigating Exercise Order

Study	Subjects	Design	Study duration	Hypertrophy measurement	Findings
Fisher et al. (218)	39 resistance-trained young men and women	Random assignment to a resistance training protocol in which exercises were performed either from compound to single joint or rotating between a single joint exercise followed by a compound exercise. All subjects performed a single set at a moderate intensity of load to muscular failure. Training was carried out 2 days per week.	12 weeks	BodPod	No significant differences in lean body mass between conditions
Simao et al. (691)	31 recreationally trained young men	Random assignment to a resistance training protocol in which exercise order either began with large- and progressed to small-muscle-group exercises or began with small- and progressed to large-muscle-group exercises. The protocol consisted of 2 to 4 sets of 4 upper-body exercises: 2 compound movements and 2 single-joint movements were carried out twice per week. Intensity of load was periodized from light to heavy each month over the course of the study, descending from 12- to 15RM to 3- to 5RM.	12 weeks	Ultrasound	No significant differences in thickness of the biceps or triceps between conditions
Spineti et al. (720)	30 recreationally trained young men	Random assignment to a resistance training protocol in which exercise order either began with large- and progressed to small-muscle-group exercises or began with small- and progressed to large-muscle-group exercises. The protocol consisted of 2 to 4 sets of 4 upper-body exercises: 2 compound movements and 2 single-joint movements were carried out twice per week. Intensity of load was carried out in an undulating periodized fashion alternating between light (12- to 15RM), moderate (8- to 10RM), and heavy (3- to 5RM).	12 weeks	Ultrasound	No significant differences in thickness of the biceps or triceps between conditions

PRACTICAL APPLICATIONS
RANGE OF MOTION

Maximal muscle development requires training through a complete ROM. Thus, full ROM movements should form the basis of a hypertrophy-oriented program. The stretched position appears particularly important to elicit hypertrophic gains. That said, integrating some partial-range movements may enhance hypertrophy.

vastus medialis is maximally activated during the final 60° of ROM (688). Similar findings have been reported during the arm curl: the short head appears to be more active in the latter phase of the movement (i.e., greater elbow flexion), whereas the long head is more active in the early phase (98).

When comparing partial and complete ROMs, the body of literature shows a clear hypertrophic benefit to training through a full ROM. This has been displayed in both upper- and lower-body muscles using a variety of exercises. Pinto and colleagues (581) showed that full ROM training of the elbow flexors (0 to 130° of flexion) produced greater increases in muscle thickness compared to partial-range training (50 to 100° of flexion). The difference in effect size strongly favored the full ROM condition (1.09 vs. 0.57, respectively), indicating that the magnitude of variance was meaningful. Similarly, McMahon and colleagues (482) showed that although knee extension at full ROM (0 to 90°) and partial ROM (0 to 50°) both increased quadriceps muscle cross-sectional area, the magnitude of hypertrophy was significantly greater at 75% of femur length in the full-range condition. Interestingly, Bloomquist and colleagues (81) showed that deep squats (0 to 120° of knee flexion) promoted increases in cross-sectional area across the entire frontal thigh musculature, whereas shallow squats (0 to 60° of knee flexion) elicited significant growth only in the two most proximal sites. Furthermore, the overall change in cross-sectional area was greater at all measured sites in the deep squat group.

There is evidence that training at longer muscle lengths (i.e., when the muscle is in a stretched position) promotes greater hyper-

KEY POINT

Muscles are activated differently throughout the range of motion. Full ROM movements should therefore form the basis of a hypertrophy training program.

trophic adaptations than training at shorter muscle lengths. McMahon and colleagues (481) compared the hypertrophic response to knee extensions at shortened (0 to 50° of knee flexion) or lengthened (40 to 90° of knee flexion) positions. Results showed significantly greater increases in distal cross-sectional area of the quadriceps (53% vs. 18%) as well as fascicle length (29% vs. 14%) in favor of the long- versus short-length training, respectively. Moreover, IGF-1 levels were significantly greater following long- versus short-length training (31% vs. 7%, respectively), suggesting that exercise at long muscle lengths induces greater metabolic and mechanical stress. Other research also shows a clear hypertrophic advantage to training at longer muscle lengths during knee extension exercises (535). The combination of findings indicates that stretched muscle is in an optimal position for hypertrophy.

Table 3.9 provides a summary of the research related to ROM and muscle hypertrophy.

Intensity of Effort

The effort exerted during resistance training, often referred to as *intensity of effor*t, can influence exercise-induced hypertrophy. Intensity of effort is generally gauged by the proximity to muscular failure, which is defined as the point during a set at which muscles can no longer

TABLE 3.9 **Summary of Hypertrophy Training Studies Investigating Range of Motion**

Study	Subjects	Design	Study duration	RM equated?	Hypertrophy measurement	Findings
Bloom-quist et al. (81)	24 untrained young males	Random assignment to squat training performed as either a deep squat (0 to 120° of knee flexion) or shallow squat (0 to 60° of knee flexion). All subjects performed 3 to 5 sets of 6 to 10 reps for 3 days per week.	12 weeks	Yes	MRI and DXA	Significantly greater increases in frontal thigh CSA and greater absolute gains in lean mass for the 0 to 120° condition
McMa-hon et al. (482)	26 recreation-ally active young men and women	Random assignment to lower-body training performed either as a full ROM (0 to 90° of knee flexion) or partial ROM (0 to 50° of knee flexion). All subjects per-formed 3 sets at 80% of 1RM for 3 days per week.	8 weeks	Yes	Ultrasound	Significantly greater increases in vastus lateralis CSA for the full ROM condition
Pinto et al. (581)	40 untrained young males	Random assignment to elbow flexion exercises with either a full ROM (0 to 130°) or partial ROM (50 to 100°). All subjects performed 2 to 4 sets of 8- to 20RM twice per week.	10 weeks	Yes	Ultrasound	No significant differ-ences between con-ditions

Abbreviations: RM = repetition maximum; MRI = magnetic resonance imaging; DXA = dual X-ray absorptiometry; ROM = range of motion; CSA = cross-sectional area.

produce the force necessary for concentrically lifting a given load (656). Although the merits of training to failure are still a matter of debate, it is commonly believed that the practice is necessary to maximize the hypertrophic response (106, 829).

The primary rationale for training to failure is to maximize motor unit recruitment (829), which is a requisite for achieving maximal protein accretion across all fiber types. Evidence supporting this position is lacking, however. It has been demonstrated that fatiguing contractions result in a corresponding increase in surface EMG activity, presumably as a result of the increased contribution of high-threshold motor units to maintain force output as lower-threshold motor units fatigue (718). However, surface EMG is not necessarily specific to recruitment; increases in amplitude can be due to a number of other factors including rate coding, synchronization, muscle fiber propagation velocity, and intracellular action potentials (64, 183).

The extent of motor unit activation likely depends on the magnitude of load. During heavy-load training, the highest-threshold motor units are recruited almost immediately, whereas

KEY POINT

Evidence that training to failure maximizes motor unit recruitment is lacking, although other benefits of training to failure have been shown.

during lighter-load training, the recruitment of these motor units is delayed. The point at which complete motor unit activation occurs is not clear, but recent work from our lab suggests that it is in excess of 50% of 1RM during multijoint upper-body exercise as determined by surface EMG (653). Research does seem to indicate that the stimulation of higher-threshold motor units is enhanced when training is performed to muscular failure with light loads (718). Thus, a high intensity of effort becomes increasingly important as the intensity of loading is reduced. That said, there is evidence that muscle activity plateaus 3 to 5 repetitions from failure with a resistance equating to approximately 15RM (733). It should be noted that muscle activation as determined by surface EMG is primarily a combination of recruitment and rate coding, but can involve other factors as well. Thus, the implications of these findings must be considered accordingly.

Training to failure may also enhance hypertrophy by increasing metabolic stress. Continuing to train under conditions of anaerobic glycolysis heightens the buildup of metabolites, which theoretically augments postexercise anabolism. Moreover, the continued compression of vessels induces greater acute hypoxia in the working muscles, which may further contribute to hypertrophic adaptations (674).

Few researchers have attempted to investigate the effects of failure training on hypertrophic adaptations in a controlled fashion. Goto and colleagues (262) compared hypertrophic adaptations between two groups of recreationally trained men performing 3 to 5 sets of 10 repetitions with an interset rest period of 60 seconds. One group performed repetitions continuously to failure, and the other group took a 30-second rest period at the midpoint of each set. After 12 weeks, muscle cross-sectional area was markedly greater in the group that carried out training to failure compared to the group that did not. Although these results are intriguing, the style of training does not replicate a traditional nonfailure approach in which sets are stopped just short of all-out effort. At most, the study shows that stopping well short of failure attenuates hypertrophic adaptations. Conversely, Sampson and Groeller (642) found no differences in untrained people between training to failure at

85% of 1RM and stopping 2 repetitions short of failure at this intensity of load. This suggests that failure might be less important when training with heavy loads. The study was confounded by the fact that the nonfailure group performed a single set to failure at the end of each week to determine loading for the subsequent week. It is not clear whether this factor influenced results. A recent study by Giessing and colleagues (247) revealed that well-trained subjects gained significantly greater lean mass when training to muscular failure at 80% of 1RM than when using a self-determined termination of a set at 60% of 1RM. Limitations of the study include the use of a single-set training protocol, which as previously discussed is suboptimal for maximal hypertrophic gains, and different intensities of load between conditions.

Although training to failure may enhance the hypertrophic stimulus, there is evidence that it also increases the potential for overtraining and psychological burnout (231). Izquierdo and colleagues (338) reported reductions in resting IGF-1 concentrations and a blunting of resting testosterone levels in a group of physically active men when failure training was consistently employed over the course of a 16-week resistance training protocol. Such hormonal alterations are consistent with chronic overtraining, suggesting a detrimental effect of repeatedly working to the point of failure.

Table 3.10 provides a summary of the research related to intensity of effort and muscle hypertrophy.

TABLE 3.10 **Summary of Hypertrophy Training Studies Investigating Intensity of Effort**

Study	Subjects	Design	Study duration	Hypertrophy measurement	Findings
Giessing et al. (247)	79 resistance-trained men and women	Random assignment to a resistance training protocol involving either training to self-selected RM at 60% of 1RM or training to momentary muscular failure at 80% of 1RM. All subjects performed a single set of 8 exercises for the entire body. Training was carried out 3 days per week.	10 weeks	BIA	Greater increases in lean mass for the training to fatigue condition

(continued)

Table 3.10 *(continued)*

Study	Subjects	Design	Study duration	Hypertrophy measurement	Findings
Goto et al. (262)	26 untrained young men	Random assignment to perform either 3 to 5 sets of 10RM or the same routine with a 30-second rest at the midpoint of each set so that failure was not induced. All groups performed 2 upper-body exercises and 1 lower-body exercise twice per week.	12 weeks	MRI	Significantly greater increases in quadriceps CSA for the training to fatigue condition
Sampson and Groeller (642)	28 untrained young men	Random assignment to perform resisted elbow flexion under one of three conditions: a control condition that performed both concentric and eccentric components at a speed of 2 seconds; a rapid shortening condition that performed maximal acceleration during the concentric action followed by a 2-second eccentric action; or a stretch–shortening group that performed both eccentric and concentric components with maximal acceleration. The control group trained to failure; the other two groups did not. Training consisted of 4 sets at 85% of 1RM performed 3 days per week.	12 weeks	MRI	No significant differences in elbow flexor CSA between groups
Schott et al. (667)	7 untrained young men and women	Within-subject design in which subjects performed either an intermittent isometric knee extension protocol consisting of 4 sets of 10 reps lasting 3 seconds with a 2-second rest between reps and a 2-minute rest between sets or a continuous protocol of 4 sets of isometric actions lasting 30 seconds with a 1-minute rest between sets. Training was carried out 3 days per week.	14 weeks	CT	Greater increases in quadriceps hypertrophy for the training to fatigue condition

Abbreviations: BIA = bioelectrical impedance analysis; RM = repetition maximum; CSA = cross-sectional area; CT = computerized tomography; MRI = magnetic resonance imaging.

PRACTICAL APPLICATIONS

INTENSITY OF EFFORT

The literature suggests a benefit to performing at least some sets to failure in a hypertrophy-oriented program. This seems to be particularly important when employing high-repetition training because of the relationship between the proximity to failure and muscle activation during light-load training. However, persistently training to failure increases the potential for nonfunctional overreaching and perhaps overtraining. The best approach is to periodize the use and frequency of failure training to maximize muscular adaptations while avoiding an overtrained state. An example would be performing an initial cycle in which all sets are stopped a repetition or two short of failure, followed by taking the last set of each exercise to failure, and then culminating in a brief cycle in which the majority of sets are carried out to failure.

TAKE-HOME POINTS

- Multiset protocols favoring high volumes of resistance training optimize the hypertrophic response. As a general guideline, beginners should perform approximately 40 to 70 repetitions per muscle group per session; more advanced lifters may need double this amount. To avoid overtraining, volume should be progressively increased over the course of a training cycle; periods of reduced training volume should be integrated on a regular basis to facilitate the recovery process.

- Higher training frequencies appear to confer benefits, at least over short-term training protocols. However, split routines allow for a greater volume of work per muscle group per session, potentially enhancing muscular adaptations via the dose–response relationship between volume and hypertrophy. It may be beneficial to periodize frequency over time, altering the number of times a muscle group is trained weekly in accordance with individual response.

- Training across a wide spectrum of repetition ranges (1 to 20+) is recommended to ensure the complete development of the whole muscle. There is merit to focusing on a medium-repetition range (6- to 12RM) and devoting specific training cycles to lower- and higher-repetition training.

- Once facility has been established with the basic movement patterns, a variety of exercises should be employed over the course of a periodized training program to maximize whole-body muscle hypertrophy. This should include the liberal use of free-form (i.e., free weights and cables) and machine-based exercises. Similarly, both multi- and single-joint exercises should be included in a hypertrophy-specific routine to maximize muscular growth.

- Both concentric and eccentric actions should be incorporated during training. Evidence of the benefits of combining isometric actions with dynamic actions is lacking at this time. The addition of supramaximal eccentric loading may enhance the hypertrophic response.

- An optimal rest interval for hypertrophy training does not appear to exist. Research indicates that resting at least 2 minutes between sets provides a hypertrophic advantage over resting for shorter periods. Including training cycles that limit rest periods to 60 to 90 seconds may allow a lifter to take advantage of any additive effects of metabolic stress, if they exist.

- Current evidence suggests little difference in muscle hypertrophy when training with isotonic repetition durations ranging from 0.5 to 6 seconds to muscular failure. Thus, it would seem that a fairly wide range of repetition durations can be employed if the primary goal is to maximize muscle growth. Training at very slow volitional durations (>10 sec per repetition) appears to be suboptimal for increasing muscle size and thus should be avoided. Combining repetition durations could conceivably enhance the hypertrophic response to resistance training.

- Evidence indicates a hypertrophic benefit for muscles worked first in a resistance training bout. Therefore, lagging muscles should be trained earlier in the session.

- Full ROM movements should form the basis of a hypertrophy-oriented program. Integrating some partial-range movements may enhance hypertrophy.
- Hypertrophy-oriented programs should include sets taken to muscular failure as well as those that are terminated short of an all-out effort. The use of failure training should be periodized to maximize muscular adaptations while avoiding an overtrained state.

Role of Aerobic Training in Hypertrophy

4

It is commonly thought that aerobic endurance exercise produces little to no increase in muscle hypertrophy. This belief is consistent with evidence showing that aerobic-type exercise mediates catabolic pathways, whereas anaerobic exercise mediates anabolic pathways. Atherton and colleagues (47) conducted pioneering work to elucidate differences in the intracellular signaling response between the two types of exercises. Using an ex vivo model, they electrically stimulated isolated rat muscles with either intermittent high-frequency bursts to simulate resistance-type training or continuous low-frequency activation to simulate aerobic-type training. Postintervention analysis revealed that AMPK phosphorylation in the low-frequency condition increased approximately 2-fold immediately and 3 hours poststimulation, whereas phosphorylation was suppressed in the high-frequency condition over the same period. Conversely, phosphorylation of Akt was a mirror image of AMPK results: markedly greater phosphorylation was seen in the high-frequency condition. Recall from chapter 2 that AMPK acts as an energy sensor to turn on catabolic signaling cascades, whereas Akt promotes the intracellular signaling responses associated with anabolism. These findings led to the *AMPK–Akt switch* hypothesis (see figure 4.1), which states that aerobic and anaerobic exercise produce opposing signaling responses and thus are incompatible for optimizing muscular adaptations (47).

Subsequent research, however, indicates that the concept of a switch that regulates anabolic and catabolic signaling pathways is at best overly simplistic and ultimately somewhat misleading. Considerable overlap has been shown to exist between candidate genes involved in aerobic and strength phenotypes, indicating that the two muscle traits are not at opposite ends of the molecular spectrum (765). In fact, multiple studies have shown increased mTOR activation following aerobic endurance exercise (71, 458, 460), whereas resistance training has consistently been found to increase the levels of AMPK (149, 188, 380, 797). To this end, research shows that of 263 genes analyzed in the resting state, only 21 were differently expressed in aerobic endurance–trained athletes and strength-trained athletes (724).

This chapter addresses how aerobic endurance exercise affects muscle growth. The topic is addressed both when aerobic exercise is performed in isolation and when it is combined with resistance exercise (i.e., concurrent training).

Hypertrophic Effects From Aerobic-Only Training

Contrary to popular belief, a majority of studies show that aerobic training can promote a hypertrophic response in untrained subjects.

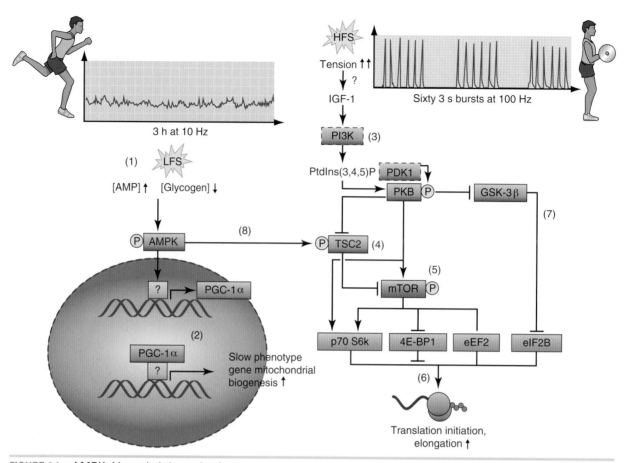

FIGURE 4.1   AMPK-Akt switch hypothesis.

Republished with permission of FASEB, from *FASEB Journal,* "Selective activation of AMPK-PGC-1a or PKB-TSC2-mTOR signaling can explain specific adaptive responses to endurance or resistance training-like electrical muscle stimulation," Philip J. Atherton, John A. Babraj, Kenneth Smith, Jaipaul Singh, Michael J. Rennie, and Henning Wackerhage, 10.1096/fj.04-2179fje, 2005; permission conveyed through Copyright Clearance Center, Inc.

Reported short-term (12 weeks) gains in skeletal muscle mass from aerobic training are similar to those seen in some resistance training protocols, and findings are demonstrated across a spectrum of age ranges in both men and women (379). The following mechanisms have been proposed to account for aerobic exercise–induced muscle growth (379), but the specific roles of these factors and their interactions have yet to be determined:

- Increased insulin-mediated anabolic signaling
- Increased muscle protein synthetic response to nutrition and insulin
- Increased basal postabsorptive muscle protein synthesis
- Increased amino acid delivery
- Increased blood flow and skeletal muscle perfusion

- Decreased myostatin
- Decreased chronic inflammation
- Decreased FOXO signaling
- Decreased protein and DNA damage
- Increased mitochondrial proliferation and dynamics
- Increased mitochondrial energetics (e.g., decreased ROS and increased ATP)

Although most studies have evaluated the muscular adaptations associated with lower-body aerobic training, there is evidence that hypertrophy can be achieved from upper-body arm cycle ergometry as well (778). The extent of hypertrophic adaptations is contingent on intensity, frequency, volume, and mode, as well as additional factors. The following sections present the specifics of each of these factors.

Intensity

The body of literature indicates that high intensities are necessary for achieving significant muscle growth from aerobic training. Decreases in muscle cross-sectional area of approximately 20% have been noted in both Type I and Type II fibers after 13 weeks of marathon run training. This shows that low-intensity exercise is not beneficial to hypertrophy and, in fact, seems to be detrimental when carried out over long durations (773). Although the precise aerobic intensity threshold necessary to elicit hypertrophic adaptations seems to depend on the person's level of conditioning, current research suggests that at least some of the training should be carried out at a minimum of 80% of heart rate reserve (HRR). Training with brief high-intensity intervals (85% of $\dot{V}O_2$peak) interspersed with recovery was shown to increase thigh muscle cross-sectional area by 24% in middle-aged people with type 2 diabetes, indicating a potential dose–response relationship between hypertrophy and aerobic intensity.

KEY POINT

Aerobic exercise can promote increases in muscle hypertrophy in untrained people, but intensity needs to be high—likely 80% of HRR or more.

Volume and Frequency

Volume and frequency of aerobic training also seem to play a role in the hypertrophic response to aerobic training, a conclusion supported in the literature. Harber and colleagues (288) found that untrained elderly men achieved levels of hypertrophy similar to those of their younger counterparts following 12 weeks of cycle ergometry training despite completing approximately half of the total mechanical workload. These findings indicate that longer periods of sedentarism reduce the total volume necessary for increasing muscle mass, which lends credence to the hypothesis that reviving muscle lost over time is easier to

achieve than increasing levels that are close to baseline. Thus, higher aerobic training volumes would seemingly be required in untrained younger people to promote an adaptive response.

The impact of volume may be at least in part frequency dependent. Schwartz and colleagues (673) compared body composition changes in younger versus older men in response to a 6-month aerobic endurance protocol. Each session lasted 45 minutes, and training occurred 5 days per week. Intensity was progressively increased so that participants ultimately worked at 85% of heart rate reserve over the last 2 months of the study. Results showed that only the older men increased muscle mass; no muscular changes were seen in the younger men. The researchers noted that attendance of the younger subjects was significantly less than that of their older counterparts, implying a hypertrophic benefit to greater aerobic training frequency. Notably, it is impossible to tease out the effects of frequency from volume in this study. Whether simply performing longer durations during a single session would confer similar benefits to spreading out frequency over the course of a week is as yet undetermined.

Mode

What, if any, impact the modality of aerobic training has on hypertrophic adaptations is unclear. The vast majority of studies on the topic to date have involved cycling exercise, and most of these trials have shown increased muscle protein accretion with consistent training. Studies using noncycling activities have produced mixed results. The previously mentioned study by Schwartz and colleagues (673) found increased muscle mass in elderly but not young male subjects following 6 months of a walk/jog/run protocol. In a study of elderly women, Sipila and Suominen (697) showed that a combination of step aerobics and track walking at intensities up to 80% of HRR did not significantly increase muscle cross-sectional area after 18 weeks of training. These findings suggest that it may be more difficult to promote a hypertrophic effect from ambulatory aerobic exercise, perhaps because such activity is performed more often in daily life. Jubrias and colleagues (345) reported no muscle cross-sectional area changes in elderly men and women following a 24-week stair climbing and kayaking-type aerobic exercise protocol performed with progressively increased intensity up to 85% of HRR.

Table 4.1 provides a summary of the research related to aerobic training and muscle hypertrophy.

TABLE 4.1 Summary of Research Related to Aerobic Training and Muscle Hypertrophy

Study	Subjects	Aerobic modality	Study duration	Frequency	Training duration	Intensity	Hypertrophy measurement	Findings
Farup et al. (210)	7 young women	Cycling	10 weeks	3 days per week	30 to 45 minutes	60% to 90% of watt max	Ultrasound	No significant change in muscle mass
Harber et al. (287)	7 elderly women	Cycling	12 weeks	3 or 4 days per week	20 to 45 minutes	60% to 80% of HRR	MRI	12% increase in quadriceps volume from baseline
Harber et al. (288)	13 young women and elderly men	Cycling	12 weeks	3 or 4 days per week	20 to 45 minutes	60% to 80% of HRR	MRI	6% increase in quadriceps volume for elderly men; 7% increase in quadriceps volume for young women
Hudel-maier et al. (325)	19 middle-aged women	Cycling	12 weeks	3 days per week	50 minutes	55% to 85% of MHR	MRI	4% to 5% increase in quadriceps CSA from baseline
Izquierdo et al. (336)	10 elderly men	Cycling	16 weeks	2 days per week	30 to 40 minutes	70% to 90% of MHR	Ultrasound	4% increase in quadriceps CSA from baseline
Izquierdo et al. (337)	11 middle-aged men	Cycling	16 weeks	2 days per week	30 to 40 minutes	70% to 90% of MHR	Ultrasound	10% increase in quadriceps CSA from baseline
Jubrias et al. (345)	40 elderly men and women	Single-leg press and kay-aking	6 months	3 days per week	40 minutes	80% to 85% of HRR	MRI	No significant change in muscle mass
Konopka et al. (378)	9 elderly women	Cycling	12 weeks	3 or 4 days per week	20 to 45 minutes	60% to 80% of HRR	MRI	11% increase in quadriceps CSA from baseline
Lovell et al. (429)	12 elderly men	Cycling	16 weeks	3 days per week	30 to 45 minutes	50% to 70% of $\dot{V}O_2$max	DXA	4% increase in leg muscle mass from baseline

Study	Subjects	Aerobic modality	Study duration	Frequency	Training duration	Intensity	Hypertrophy measurement	Findings
McPhee et al. (483)	28 young women	Cycling	6 weeks	3 days per week	45 minutes (continuous and interval)	75% to 90% of MHR	MRI	7% increase in quadriceps volume from baseline
Schwartz et al. (673)	28 young and elderly men	Walk/jog	6 months	5 days per week	45 minutes	50% to 85% of HRR	CT	9% increase in thigh muscle CSA for elderly subjects from baseline; no significant change for young subjects
Short et al. (686)	65 young, middle-aged, and elderly men	Cycling	16 weeks	3 or 4 days per week	20 to 40 minutes	70% to 80% of MHR	CT	No significant change in muscle mass
Sillanpaa et al. (689)	15 middle-aged women	Cycling	21 weeks	2 days per week	30 to 90 minutes	Steady pace performed under aerobic threshold alternated every other session with intensities varying from under aerobic threshold to over anaerobic threshold	DXA	2.5% increase in lean leg mass from baseline
Sipila and Suominen (697)	12 elderly women	Walk and step aerobics	18 weeks	3 days per week	60 minutes	50% to 80% of HRR	CT	No significant change in muscle mass

Abbreviations: HRR = heart rate reserve; MRI = magnetic resonance imaging; MHR = maximum heart rate; DXA = dual X-ray absorptiometry; CT = computerized tomography.

Adapted from Konopka et al. (379).

Other Factors

Although evidence seems to indicate that aerobic training can induce growth in sedentary people, increases in whole-muscle hypertrophy do not necessarily reflect what is occurring at the fiber level. Consistent with its endurance-oriented nature, aerobic-type training appears to produce hypertrophic changes specific to Type I fibers. Harber and colleagues (287) found that Type I cross-sectional area increased by approximately 16% in a group of untrained elderly women following 12 weeks

PRACTICAL APPLICATIONS

INTENSITY, FREQUENCY, VOLUME, AND MODE OF AEROBIC TRAINING

Aerobic exercise can increase hypertrophy in sedentary people, primarily in Type I muscle fibers. The extent of hypertrophic increases depends on the level of sedentarism; greater gains are seen in the elderly than in the young. Intensities of ≥80% of HRR are generally needed to elicit significant muscular growth. Although definitive evidence regarding the effects of aerobic volume on hypertrophy is lacking, research indicates that longer periods of sedentarism reduce the total weekly duration required to promote the accretion of lean mass. With respect to the modality of exercise, cycling appears to have the greatest hypertrophic benefit, although the paucity of studies on alternative modalities makes it difficult to draw firm conclusions on this variable. Importantly, muscular gains are limited to the early phases after initiating a regimented aerobic exercise program. Results plateau in a relatively short time, and evidence suggests that persistent aerobic training can actually have a detrimental impact on Type II fiber hypertrophy.

of cycle ergometry training; no change was noted in Type IIa fibers. A follow-up study employing a similar protocol in younger and older men showed that 12 weeks of cycle ergometry produced an increase in Type I fiber cross-sectional area of approximately 20% (288). Type IIa fiber diameter actually decreased in younger subjects, although not significantly, whereas that of the older subjects remained relatively constant. These findings imply that aerobic exercise may have a detrimental effect on hypertrophy of the faster fiber types. However, other studies show beneficial effects of aerobic training on Type II fiber cross-sectional area in both older (132, 152) and younger (32) subjects. The cause of the discrepancies in findings between studies are not clear.

Evidence also suggests that an increase in mitochondrial proteins is responsible for at least some of the increased fiber growth associated with aerobic endurance training (433). A number of studies have reported that aerobic exercise increases only basal mitochondrial protein synthesis and has no effect on myofibrillar protein synthesis (185, 257, 312, 828). However, recent work by Di Donato and colleagues (180) showed that both mitochondrial and myofibrillar protein

fractions were elevated following an acute bout of high-intensity (90% of maximal heart rate) and low-intensity (66% of maximal heart rate) aerobic exercise. Interestingly, only the high-intensity condition showed sustained muscle protein synthesis elevations at 24 to 28 hours postexercise recovery. Based on these acute results, it would seem that sarcoplasmic proteins account for a considerable portion of aerobic-induced hypertrophic adaptations. Given evidence that the growth of a given muscle fiber is achieved at the expense of its aerobic endurance capacity (784), the accretion of mitochondrial proteins seems to have a negative impact on the ability to maximize gains in contractile proteins.

An important limitation of current research is that the time course of hypertrophic adaptations during aerobic training has not been well investigated. In those who are sedentary, virtually any training stimulus—including aerobic exercise—is sufficient to overload muscle. This necessarily results in an adaptive response that promotes tissue remodeling. However, the intensity of aerobic training is not sufficient to progressively overload muscle in a manner that promotes further adaptations over time. Thus, it stands to reason that the body would quickly plateau after an initial increase in muscle size.

Early-phase increases in aerobic-induced hypertrophy may be in part due to quantitative or qualitative mitochondrial adaptations, or both. Inactivity induces negative alterations in mitochondrial morphology, and these effects are exacerbated by prolonged sedentarism (147). Mitochondrial dysfunction is associated with increased activation of AMPK and subsequent stimulation of protein degradation, ultimately causing atrophy (259). As previously mentioned, aerobic training enhances mitochondrial protein fractions, which would confer a positive effect on anabolic processes. It therefore is conceivable that early-phase hypertrophy in aerobic training is due to restoring normal mitochondrial function and perhaps improving these measures above baseline.

Although aerobic exercise can positively affect muscle mass in the untrained, compelling evidence indicates that it is suboptimal for promoting muscle growth in physically active people. For those who are sedentary, virtually any stimulus challenges the neuromuscular system and thus leads to an accretion of muscle proteins. Adaptations in these early stages are therefore more indicative of the novelty of the exercise bout as opposed to an increased potential for chronic adaptation. On the other hand, well-trained people have already adapted to lower-level stresses, and it therefore remains highly dubious whether aerobic training would provide enough of a stimulus for further muscular adaptation. In trained lifters, the mechanical strain associated with aerobic endurance exercise does not rise to the level necessary for mechanotransducers to switch on mTORC1 signaling (797). Indeed, aerobic endurance athletes display slight increases in Type I fiber size while showing a reduction in hypertrophy of Type II fibers (198). Even very intense aerobic exercise does not seem to confer a beneficial hypertrophic effect in those who are highly physically active. This was demonstrated by the fact that 6 weeks of high-intensity interval training resulted in a significant decrease in Type II fiber cross-sectional area in a group of well-trained distance runners (373).

In summary, muscular adaptations to aerobic training exist on a continuum, and

hypertrophic responses ultimately depend on a variety of individual and environmental factors. Although between-study comparisons suggest that early-phase gains in muscle mass are similar between aerobic and resistance training protocols (238), within-study results indicate a clear hypertrophic advantage to resistance training. Pooled data from studies directly comparing hypertrophy in the two types of exercise show a strong overall mean effect size for resistance training (0.92), whereas aerobic training produced a weak overall effect (0.27); these differences were statistically significant (831). Moreover, increases in muscle size following aerobic training are not well correlated with increased force capacity, indicating that hypertrophic adaptations are not entirely functional (433).

Concurrent Training

Aerobic exercise is often performed in combination with resistance training for accelerating fat loss, enhancing sport performance, or both. This strategy, called *concurrent training*, has been shown to have a positive effect on weight management (10). However, evidence suggests that the addition of aerobic exercise to a regimented resistance training program may compromise muscle growth. Negative hypertrophic effects from concurrent training have been attributed to a phenomenon known as *chronic interference* (figure 4.2), the hypothesis for which alleges that trained muscle cannot simultaneously adapt optimally morphologically or metabolically to both strength and aerobic endurance training (831). Like the AMPK–Akt switch hypothesis, the chronic interference hypothesis states that these competing adaptations produce divergent intracellular signaling responses that mitigate muscular gains.

Despite the logical basis for the chronic interference theory, the effect of the phenomenon in humans when performing traditional training protocols is unclear. Although some studies show that combining aerobic and resistance exercise impedes anabolic signaling (150, 151), others have

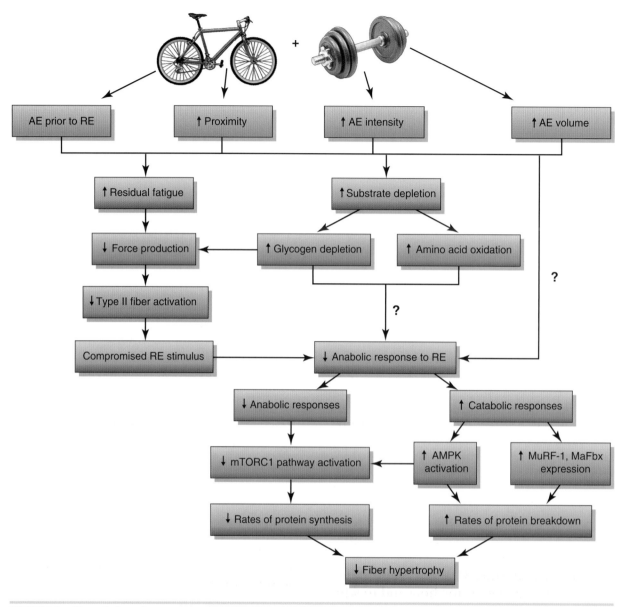

FIGURE 4.2 Chronic interference hypothesis. AE = aerobic exercise; RE = resistance exercise.

With kind permission from Springer Science+Business Media: *Sports Medicine*, "Interference between concurrent resistance and endurance exercise: Molecular bases and the role of individual training variables," 44(6): 743-762, 2014, J.J.I. Fyfe, D.J. Bishop, and N.K. Stepto, figure 2.

failed to note any negative consequences (39). There is even evidence that concurrent training heightens mTOR and p70[S6K] to a greater extent than resistance training alone does (432). Moreover, studies show no deleterious effects of concurrent training on muscle protein synthesis (127, 185). Discrepancies in the findings may be related to a number of factors. Importantly, the time course of evaluation in the current literature was generally limited to several hours postexercise and thus

does not provide a complete snapshot of the adaptive response, which can last in excess of 24 hours. Furthermore, these findings are specific to acute bouts of exercise, whereas any interference would seemingly manifest over a period of weeks or months.

It is conceivable that concurrent training negatively affects growth in other ways. For one, acute factors associated with aerobic training may interfere with resistance training capacity. Specifically, aerobic exercise can cause residual fatigue, substrate depletion, or both, which ultimately impairs the quality of the resistance training bout (238). Muscular adaptations are predicated on the capacity to train with an intensity of effort that sufficiently stimulates myofiber growth. If this ability is compromised, muscular gains necessarily suffer.

Another potential issue with concurrent training is an increased potential for overtraining. When the volume or intensity of training exceeds the body's ability to recover, physiological systems are disrupted. The stress of adding aerobic exercise to an intense hypertrophy-oriented resistance training program can overtax recuperative abilities, leading to an overtrained state. The interference effects of aerobic exercise associated with overtraining may be mediated by a catabolic hormonal environment and chronic muscle glycogen depletion (493).

Long-term training studies investigating muscular adaptations to concurrent training have produced conflicting findings. When considering the body of literature as a whole, evidence suggests that aerobic exercise blunts the hypertrophic response to resistance training. A meta-analysis by Wilson and colleagues (831) revealed that effect size for muscular gains was reduced by almost 50% in those who solely lifted weights when aerobic endurance training was added to the mix. However, multiple factors ultimately determine how and to what extent aerobic training influences the adaptations associated with resistance training. In particular, the manipulation of aerobic exercise intensity, volume and frequency, mode, and scheduling is paramount in creating the response. The following sections provide an overview of these variables and their reputed effects on resistance training–induced hypertrophy.

KEY POINT

Evidence suggests that, over time, aerobic exercise blunts the hypertrophic response to resistance training.

Intensity

Research directly assessing the hypertrophy-related effects of aerobic endurance exercise intensities during concurrent training is lacking. Evidence suggests that high-intensity sprint cycle interval training is more detrimental to intracellular anabolic signaling than moderate-intensity steady-state cycling is (150, 151). Moreover, the post-endurance-exercise activity of negative regulators of muscle protein synthesis (including AMPK and eIF4EB1) are elevated in an intensity-dependent fashion. In addition, one of the two catalytic isoforms of AMPK (AMPKα1)—which has been shown to selectively inhibit mTORC1—may be preferentially activated by higher, but not lower, aerobic intensities (238). The apparently greater interference associated with high-intensity training suggests that lower-intensity exercise may be preferable if the goal is to maximize hypertrophy during concurrent training. However, caution must be used when extrapolating conclusions from nonmatched studies and isolated signaling data, particularly given the general lack of correlation between acute molecular events and chronic hypertrophy in untrained subjects (12).

Long-term studies on muscular adaptations associated with varying aerobic intensities are similarly scarce. Silva and colleagues (690) randomly assigned 44 young women to one of four groups:

1. Concurrent resistance and continuous running training
2. Concurrent resistance and interval running training
3. Concurrent resistance and continuous cycle ergometer training
4. Resistance training only

Results showed that all groups significantly increased measures of maximal strength and local muscular endurance, and no differences between the groups were seen. Muscle hypertrophy was not assessed, however, precluding any conclusions as to any effects of intensity on growth. Overall, the paucity of direct evidence makes it impossible to draw any definitive conclusions as to what, if any, effects aerobic intensity has on hypertrophy during concurrent training.

Volume and Frequency

Volume may have the biggest impact on the hypertrophic interference associated with concurrent training, potentially related to overtraining symptoms induced by a catabolic hormonal environment and chronic muscle glycogen depletion (493). This contention is supported by research showing attenuations in maximal strength with frequencies of more than 3 sessions per week but not less than 2 sessions per week (238). Pooled data from Wilson and colleagues (831) revealed a significant negative correlation between muscle hypertrophy and the volume (duration and frequency) of aerobic exercise during concurrent training. With respect to the specific components of volume, inverse correlations were especially strong for the duration of exercise ($r = .75$), whereas frequency displayed a relatively weak correlation ($r = .26$).

The effect of varying aerobic frequencies on muscular adaptations was directly studied in the context of a concurrent training program (344). Subjects performed a 3-day-a-week resistance protocol and supplemented it with 0, 1, or 3 days of aerobic endurance training. Results showed an inverse dose–response relationship between increases in limb girth and aerobic frequency (4.3%, 2.8%, and 1% for the 0-, 1-, and 3-day-a-week conditions). These findings indicate that the frequency of aerobic endurance training should remain low if muscle hypertrophy is the primary desired outcome.

KEY POINT

If hypertrophy is the desired outcome, the frequency of aerobic endurance training should remain low and a lengthy intervening recovery period should be inserted between aerobic and resistance bouts. Perhaps even better, the two should be performed on separate days.

Mode

Although aerobic exercise can be carried out using a variety of modalities, running and cycling have primarily been studied in the context of concurrent training. The meta-analysis by Wilson and colleagues (831) revealed that running had a particularly negative effect on the hypertrophic adaptations associated with resistance training, whereas cycling did not appear to cause a significant detriment. The authors speculated that running-related impairments on muscle growth could be related to excessive muscle damage caused by its high eccentric component. Conceivably, this could inhibit recuperative abilities and thus blunt the postexercise adaptive response. Alternatively, they proposed that cycling has greater biomechanical similarities to multijoint free weight exercise compared to running and therefore may have provided a greater transfer of training. Counterintuitively, Panissa and colleagues (556) reported that high-intensity aerobic cycling negatively affected strength to a greater degree than high-intensity treadmill running when performed immediately prior to a resistance training bout. Over time, this would likely have a detrimental impact on hypertrophy as a result of chronic reductions in mechanical tension.

Scheduling

Depending on the scope of the training program, aerobic endurance exercise can be performed either in the same session with resistance training or on alternate days. Several studies have examined how the order of aerobic and resistance exercise performed in the same session affects intracellular signaling responses. Coffey and colleagues (151) investigated the acute effects of a combined session of knee extension resistance exercise and moderate-intensity cycling. Cycling before resistance exercise resulted in a heightened phosphorylation of Akt but a reduction in IGF-1 mRNA; alternatively, reversing the order of performance elevated concentrations of MuRF-1 mRNA. Follow-up work by the same lab revealed that performing a high-intensity sprint cycling bout prior to knee extensions blunted phosphorylation of p70^{S6K} compared to performing resistance exercise first (150). Moreover, the upregulation of translation initiation via the PI3K/Akt signaling pathway may be altered when resistance training is performed after glycogen depleting aerobic exercise (160). Combined, these findings suggest greater interference when aerobic exercise precedes a resistance bout.

Data on the long-term effects of the order of same-day concurrent training on muscular adaptations are limited. Multiple studies show that strength gains are similar regardless of the sequence of training (138, 153, 264). Hence, mechanical tension does not appear to be compromised by the order of performance. From a hypertrophy standpoint, Cadore and colleagues (113) found similar increases in

RESEARCH FINDINGS

CONCURRENT TRAINING

Research indicates that concurrent training can have a negative impact on hypertrophic adaptations. Mitigating aerobic volume, intensity, or both reduces the potential for any negative consequences associated with the strategy. Non-weight-bearing aerobic activities such as cycling appear to attenuate deleterious effects compared to running, although some evidence is contradictory. There is an absence of research on the effects of cross-training on various modalities in the context of a regimented resistance training program. Whether such variation would enhance or hinder results remains speculative.

The majority of concurrent training studies have been carried out with untrained subjects, making it difficult to extrapolate conclusions to physically active people. The few studies that have employed subjects experienced in exercise training indicate greater interference in those who are well trained. Kraemer and colleagues (389) investigated the compatibility of aerobic and resistance exercise in a group of army recruits involved in standard military training for at least 3 days per week for 2 years before the onset of the study. Subjects were randomly assigned to perform aerobic endurance exercise, resistance exercise, or concurrent training. The aerobic endurance protocol consisted of a combination of steady-state and high-intensity interval training. After 12 weeks, subjects in the resistance-only group displayed increases in Type I, Type IIa, and Type IIc fiber diameters, whereas those in the concurrent group showed significant increases only in Type IIa fibers. Bell and colleagues (66) found similar results in a group of physically active university students, at least some of whom had experience in strength and aerobic endurance training. Subjects performed 12 weeks of cycle ergometry, resistance training, or a combination of both modalities. Results showed that resistance training only increased both Type I and Type II fiber cross-sectional area, whereas concurrent training produced increases only in Type II fibers. Moreover, the magnitude of Type II fiber hypertrophy was markedly greater in the resistance-only group compared to those who performed concurrent training (28% vs. 14%, respectively). Taken together, these findings suggest that concurrent training may be particularly detrimental to those with training experience.

Consideration also must be given to the relatively short duration of most concurrent training studies. Hickson (306) found no evidence of interference in a combined aerobic and resistance protocol until the 8th week of training. This finding indicates that negative effects on hypertrophy may not manifest for months, but ultimately long-term increases in muscle size would be compromised.

upper- and lower-body muscle thickness independent of whether aerobic or resistance training was performed first in a session. Similarly, Davitt and colleagues (170) found that changes in body composition were unaffected by aerobic endurance exercise either before or after resistance training. These studies seem to cast doubt on the importance of training sequence as a variable during concurrent training.

That said, the effects of order may be intensity dependent. Higher-intensity aerobic endurance exercise impedes subsequent force production, whereas lower-intensity continuous aerobic exercise tends to have less of an effect on residual fatigue (238). Both high-intensity cycling and treadmill exercise were shown to negatively affect the maximum number of repetitions and total session volume of a resistance training protocol performed after the aerobic bout (556). Interestingly, the extent of interference was highest after cycling compared to running. Residual fatigue from previous aerobic training also negatively affects the volume of work performed during subsequent resistance training (238). Given the well-established dose–response relationship between volume and muscular adaptations, such reductions in total work may impede hypertrophy over time.

Taking the body of literature on the topic into account, interference appears to be best minimized by either inserting a lengthy intervening recovery period between aerobic and resistance bouts or, perhaps even better, performing them on separate days. Indeed, Wilson and colleagues (831) found a trend for greater hypertrophy when aerobic and resistance exercise were performed on separate days as opposed to in the same session (effect size of 1.05 vs. 0.8, respectively).

Interestingly, performing an acute resistance training bout 6 hours after aerobic-oriented cycle ergometry was shown to elicit greater mTOR and p70[S6K] phosphorylation compared to performing resistance training alone (432). This suggests that the aerobic bout actually potentiated anabolic signaling. The practical implications of these findings are undetermined.

TAKE-HOME POINTS

- Aerobic exercise can promote increases in muscle hypertrophy in untrained people, and gains are primarily limited to Type I fibers. The extent of hypertrophic adaptations is contingent on intensity, volume, frequency, and mode of training, as well as the person's level of deconditioning.

- Aerobic intensities of >80% of HRR are generally required to promote gains in muscle mass in untrained people.

- Although highly deconditioned people can experience hypertrophic increases with relatively low volumes of aerobic training, those who are more active require higher training volumes.

- Evidence suggests that cycling exercise may be more conducive to increasing muscle mass than walking, running, or jogging, possibly because ambulatory activities are performed more often in daily life.

- Concurrent training can interfere with hypertrophic adaptations. Higher aerobic volumes appear particularly detrimental in this regard, although the effect of high aerobic intensities is not well elucidated.

- The negative effects of concurrent training are best minimized by either inserting a lengthy intervening recovery period between aerobic and resistance bouts or, perhaps even better, performing them on separate days.

Factors in Maximal Hypertrophic Development

A number of population-specific factors affect skeletal muscle mass and the hypertrophic response to resistance exercise. Of particular note in this regard are genetics, age, sex, and training experience. This chapter provides an overview of these factors and their effects on the ability to increase muscle size.

Genetics

A theoretical upper limit to muscle fiber size exists, which is ultimately determined by a person's genotype and phenotype. *Genotype* can be broadly defined as the genetic makeup of an organism; *phenotype* refers to how genotypes are expressed. In short, genetically coded information (genotype) is interpreted by the body's cellular machinery to produce the physical properties of the muscle (phenotype). With respect to hypertrophy, someone may have the genetic makeup to become an elite bodybuilder, for example, but if he or she never engages in a regimented resistance training program, that genotype will not be expressed to bring about a championship-caliber physique.

The manifestation of muscle genotype and phenotype has been extensively researched. Twin studies show that up to 90% of the variance in baseline muscle mass is hereditary (282), and stark interindividual hypertrophic differences are seen in response to a resistance training program. In a study of over 500 subjects, Hubal and colleagues (324) demonstrated highly dissimilar responses in both men and women to 12 weeks of progressive resistance training of the elbow flexors. Some subjects increased biceps brachii cross-sectional area by up to 59%, while others showed little to no muscular gains. Similarly, in a cluster analysis, Bamman and colleagues (56) categorized a group of young and old men and women based on their response to 16 weeks of multiset progressive lower-body resistance exercise: The top quartile increased muscle cross-sectional area by 58%, and the bottom quartile showed no mean gains; the balance of the group showed a moderate response with an increase of 28%. These findings have led to classifying subjects as *responders* and *nonresponders* to resistance exercise, thereby highlighting the role of genetics in muscle development. The body of evidence suggests that genetics contributes less to muscular phenotype with advancing age (725).

KEY POINT

A variety of genetic factors influence hypertrophic potential, and this influence declines with advancing age.

An array of hereditary factors are believed to influence hypertrophic potential. Pioneering multidisciplinary work published in a large exercise genomics study titled *"Functional Single Nucleotide Polymorphisms Associated With*

Human Muscle Size and Strength" (FAMuSS) identified 17 genes believed to explain some of the variances in interindividual muscular adaptations (568). One such gene, bone morphogenetic protein 2 (BMP2), is believed to be especially relevant to hypertrophic outcomes. Devaney and colleagues (178) found that polymorphisms of the BMP2 gene were responsible for differences in muscular adaptations to intense exercise. Specifically, young males with the CC genotype displayed greater gains in muscle mass following 12 weeks of progressive resistance training than did those carrying the A allele (a form of a gene). BMP2 was estimated to explain 3.9% of the trait variation.

The extent of hypertrophy also has been genetically linked to several growth and inflammatory factors. The ability to induce gene expression of MGF, the local form of IGF-1, appears to be particularly important in this regard. Bamman and colleagues (56) found that MGF was differentially expressed across a varied group of men and women: extreme hypertrophic responders displayed a robust increase in MGF mRNA, whereas nonresponders experienced only a nonsignificant trend for an increase. Interestingly, genetic differences in the expression of the IGF-1Ea isoform did not have an effect on gains in muscle mass, although other studies suggest a possible role (568). With respect to inflammatory factors, research has focused on interleukin-15 (IL-15), a myokine that has shown to be anabolic in both in vitro and animal models. Riechman and colleagues (616) reported that a polymorphism in the IL-15 gene explained a significant proportion of the hypertrophic variation in a group of 153 young men and women following 10 weeks of heavy resistance training. However, a larger trial found associations between IL-15 and baseline muscle size but no correlation in muscular adaptations to regimented resistance training (582). Findings from the latter study are consistent with recent research showing that IL-15 promotes changes more indicative of an oxidative phenotype as opposed to regulating increases in muscle mass in humans (583).

There is compelling evidence that individual variances in satellite cell response play a role in a person's hypertrophic potential. A cluster analysis of 66 untrained men and women found that extreme hypertrophic responders to resistance exercise had a greater population of satellite cells at baseline and were better able to expand the available satellite cell pool during training than could modest responders and nonresponders (574). Moreover, the extreme responders were most adept at incorporating new nuclei in existing myofibers. These findings are in line with recent research showing that the acute satellite cell response to a bout of resistance training is predictive of long-term hypertrophic outcomes (67).

Emerging research indicates that micro RNAs (miRNAs) may play a significant role in the interindividual response to resistance exercise. Micro RNAs are short, noncoding RNA molecules capable of altering the translation of protein-coding genes (169). To date, hundreds of miRNAs have been identified, and many are known to be responsive to extracellular stimuli, such as physical exercise, and thereby regulate muscle phenotype (70, 169). Davidsen and colleagues (169) found a moderate correlation between resistance training–induced muscle growth and changes in the quantity of miRNAs. Specifically, low responders presented a downregulation of miR-378, -26a, and -29a, and an upregulation of miR-451; these changes were linked to a suppression of mTOR signaling. The collective findings suggest a hereditary link between certain miRNAs and human skeletal muscle hypertrophy.

Muscle morphology is another potential candidate for genetic differences in the hypertrophic response to resistance training. Cadaver studies show significant interindividual differences in fiber number between individuals (9). By the age of 24 weeks, fiber numbers remain constant; further increases in growth are attributed to hypertrophy as opposed to hyperplasia (725). Logically, a greater number of fibers would be advantageous to increasing muscle size. Research lends support to this hypothesis, and a moderate correlation has been noted between fiber number and whole-muscle cross-sectional area. Moreover, a group of male bodybuilders and age-matched controls showed that those with the largest biceps brachii had a larger number of fibers in this muscle (441).

Differences in muscle fiber type may also play a role in the phenotypic response to resistance training. Approximately 45% of the variance in fiber type is thought to be associated with genetic factors (694). Substantial heterogeneity exists in fiber type percentages between individuals; approximately 25% have either less than 35% or more than 65% Type I fibers in the vastus lateralis muscle (694). Moreover, dominance of a given fiber type in a given muscle is not necessarily indicative of whole-body fiber type proportions; those with a high percentage of Type I fibers in one muscle could have a high percentage of Type II fibers in another muscle. The prospect that variances in fiber type percentage could be responsible for differential hypertrophic adaptations seems to have a logical basis. Fast-twitch fibers grow about 50% more than their slow-twitch counterparts following resistance training, although a high degree of interindividual variability is seen with respect to the extent of hypertrophic adaptation (382). Anecdotally, athletes with higher percentages of Type II fibers are more muscular in appearance than those dominant in Type I fibers. Interestingly, however, a recent cluster analysis revealed that the degree of hypertrophy in response to regimented resistance training did not differ on the basis of pretraining percentages of Type I and Type II myofibers (56).

Although it is tempting to look at genes in isolation, it is likely that interactions of multiple genetic loci (the specific location of a gene, DNA sequence, or position on a chromosome) ultimately determine a person's genetic capacity (568). The hypertrophic impact of a single genetic influence tends to be fairly modest, but the combination of variances can have a profound effect on phenotype. Moreover, the term *nonresponder* is somewhat of a misnomer. Although approximately 25% of subjects show little to no growth following a research-based resistance training protocol (56), this does not necessarily imply that these people are incapable of increasing muscle mass. The duration of most resistance training studies is relatively short, usually a few months. Anecdotally, the overwhelming majority of those who train consistently for long periods ultimately gain significant muscle mass, albeit less than "responders" do. In addition, just because a person fails to respond to one training protocol does not mean that he or she will not respond to an alternative protocol. For example, it has been postulated that a fiber type–specific approach to training may enhance the genetic capacity to hypertrophy. Specifically, people dominant in Type I fibers may obtain superior results from training with lighter loads, whereas those dominant in Type II fibers would be best served by employing heavy loads (217). This hypothesis warrants further investigation. Moreover, some people respond better to lower training volumes and frequencies (574), suggesting that genetic limitations can be surmounted, at least in part, by manipulating both of these variables over time.

KEY POINT

Although the terms *responders* and *non-responders* have been proposed in the literature, even nonresponders can increase muscle mass over baseline levels. They may require longer periods of consistent training and alternative training strategies to gain additional hypertrophy.

It should be noted that the genetic predisposition to hypertrophic gains can be specific to a given muscle. A common complaint from those who resistance train is the difficulty in bringing up a lagging muscle group. Indeed, observations from studies carried out in my lab routinely see one subject showing significant increases in quadriceps growth with little to no growth in the elbow flexors and another subject displaying the opposite growth pattern. Again, this does not necessarily reflect an inability to increase muscle size in the lagging muscle, but rather the need to employ alternative training strategies to spur additional hypertrophy.

Age

The aging process is associated with alterations in both the quantity and quality of muscle. Human muscle mass reaches peak levels between the ages of 20 and 40 (112). Thereafter, the body loses approximately 0.5% of its muscle mass per year during the fourth decade of life, increasing to 1% to 2% annually after the age of 50 and then accelerating to 3% annually after the age of 60 (figure 5.1) (809, 854). This age-related loss of muscle tissue has been termed *sarcopenia*. Sedentary people show larger rates of decline than those who are active, although leisure time physical activity has only minor effects on tempering muscle loss (809). Sarcopenic changes have been attributed to reduced rates of basal, postabsorptive myofibrillar muscle protein synthesis, elevated proteolysis, or both, but more recent findings suggest that basal skeletal muscle net protein balance is not compromised with aging in healthy people (93). Alternatively, it has been postulated the chronic systemic inflammation may compromise muscle protein metabolism in frail elderly (93). Various disease states and lifestyle factors are known to exacerbate the rate of muscle wasting with age.

Sarcopenia is characterized not only by fiber atrophy, but also by widened sarcoplasmic spaces and Z-band and myofibrillar disruption (695). These negative effects are seen in both Type I and Type II fibers, but they are most pronounced in the fast-twitch variety. There is evidence that Type II fibers actually undergo *apoptosis* (programmed cell death as part of normal growth, development, or aging). The number of these fibers decreases from 60% in sedentary young men to less than 30% in people over the age of 80 (207). Autopsy results show that the quadriceps muscles in the elderly are 18% smaller than those in younger people, and the total fiber number is 25% lower; a reduction of approximately 110,000 fibers is attributed to the aging process (420). Other research indicates a significant decline in the number of myofibers regardless of fiber type between the sixth and eighth decades of life (421). In addition, an alteration in the chemical and physical properties of skeletal muscle proteins occurs, which includes reduced contractile, mitochondrial, and enzyme protein synthetic rates; altered expression and posttranslational modifications to muscle proteins; reduced maximal voluntary muscle strength; and reduced muscle strength per unit of muscle mass and muscle power (849). These changes are apparently mediated, at least in part, by a chronic decrease in circulating levels of testosterone, GH, and IGF-1 (111).

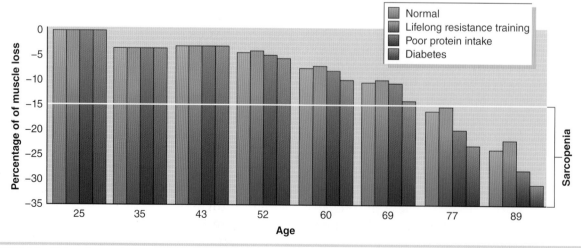

FIGURE 5.1 Rate of muscle mass loss with age.

Data from Buford et al. (102).

Satellite cell content is also altered as one ages, particularly in Type II muscle fibers. The number of satellite cells per Type II fiber has been shown to be markedly lower in the elderly than in the young, as are the number of satellite cells relative to total nuclei (790). A number of other studies support these findings (347, 609), although some have failed to show significant differences in satellite cell populations (629). Null findings have been attributed to a lack of muscle fiber type–specific data (790). Taken as a whole, the body of evidence strongly indicates that the age-related atrophy of Type II fibers is associated with a fiber type–specific decline in satellite cell content, which would likely accelerate the extent of sarcopenic changes.

Regular resistance training can attenuate muscle loss in the elderly and, depending on genetic, environmental, and training-related factors, even produce increases in lean mass above that in sedentary younger people. However, the hypertrophic potential is blunted with advancing age. This anabolic insensitivity is reflected in the acute response to resistance training. Kumar and colleagues (399) found that phosphorylation of p70^{S6K} and eIF4EB1 at 60% to 90% of 1RM was diminished in older men following multiple sets of unilateral knee extension and flexion exercises at 60% to 90% of 1RM. Moreover, p70^{S6K} phosphorylation was uncoupled with the rate of muscle protein synthesis at 1 to 2 hours postexercise in elderly subjects, but not in the young. Other studies show similar findings (234, 399, 812). The totality of evidence indicates an age-induced anabolic resistance of intracellular signaling and muscle protein synthesis to resistance exercise.

Most longitudinal research studies support the notion of a diminished hypertrophic response to resistance exercise in the elderly (382, 487, 510, 813), although some studies show no age-related differences in muscle protein accretion (275, 630). Moreover, a substantially greater percentage of elderly are deemed nonresponders to resistance exercise compared to young subjects (56). The underlying reasons for the age-related impairment of muscular adaptations are not clear, but it could be due to a combination of anabolic resistance, chronic low-grade systemic inflammation, compromised satellite cell function, and perhaps other factors. That said, elderly people can and do see robust muscle growth after performing regimented progressive resistance training protocols. Hypertrophic gains in excess of 20% are routinely seen in this population, and increases are noted in both Type I and Type II muscle fibers (56). Even the very elderly (≥75 years of age) respond favorably to resistance training; increases in cross-sectional area of 1.5% to 15.6% have been reported in the literature (726). Meta-analytic data indicate that higher training volumes become increasingly beneficial to maximize muscle mass as we age (572).

KEY POINT

After age 40, the body loses progressively more muscle mass per year. Regular resistance training can reduce this loss. Although the elderly do have a diminished hypertrophic response, they can gain muscle mass; however, a greater weekly training dose appears necessary to maintain the gains.

Research by Bickel and colleagues (76) indicates that elderly people need a greater weekly minimum training dose to maintain muscle once they have achieved a given level of hypertrophy from resistance training. Seventy young (20 to 35 years of age) and old (60 to 75 years of age) participants performed a 3-day-per-week resistance training program for 16 weeks. Following training, the subjects were randomly assigned to a detraining protocol involving no exercise, a maintenance protocol that was 1/3 that of the original program, or a maintenance protocol that was 1/9 that of the original. As expected, progressive resistance training resulted in significant hypertrophic increases in both the young and the old. However, although the two maintenance protocols were sufficient for preserving hypertrophy in the young, the elderly in both maintenance groups showed significant reductions in muscle size.

Sex

Substantial sex-based differences exist in the maintenance and hypertrophy of skeletal muscle tissue. On average, women have less muscle mass than men from both an absolute and relative standpoint. These discrepancies become evident during puberty and persist through old age.

It is believed that sexual dimorphism is highly influenced by hormonal variances between the sexes. Testosterone levels in men are approximately 10 times higher than those in women. As discussed in chapter 1, testosterone is a highly anabolic hormone that exerts its actions by increasing myofibrillar protein synthesis and decreasing muscle protein breakdown (780, 860). Theoretically, low circulating testosterone levels in women would reduce the potential to substantially increase muscle mass. However, attenuations in anabolism from a lack of testosterone appear to be at least partially offset by higher estrogen levels. The anabolic effects of estrogen are attributed to reductions in muscle protein breakdown, a hypothesis supported by research showing that hormone replacement therapy counteracts the upregulation of the ubiquitin–proteasome system in menopausal women (587). There also is evidence that estrogen positively modulates myogenic gene expression following resistance training, indicating a potential role in enhancing sensitivity to anabolic stimuli (182).

On a relative basis, men and women experience similar increases in muscle hypertrophy following regimented resistance training (7, 324, 382). However, these results must be understood in the context that women start off with less muscle mass at baseline, thus biasing increases in their favor. From an absolute standpoint, hypertrophic gains are significantly greater in men than in women. Ivey and colleagues (333) found that men increased muscle volume approximately twice as much as women following 9 weeks of unilateral knee extension exercises. In a study of elite bodybuilders, biceps brachii cross-sectional area was two times larger in male than in female competitors (26). These sex-based differences were primarily attributed to greater absolute mean Type II fiber areas in male bodybuilders. Males also had a greater total number of muscle fibers, a finding that has been reported in other studies as well (639). So although women can build appreciable muscle from regimented resistance exercise, their hypertrophic potential is somewhat less on average than men.

KEY POINT

Although men and women experience similar relative increases in muscle hypertrophy following regimented resistance training, from an absolute standpoint, men can obtain significantly greater absolute gains, which is largely attributed to their higher testosterone levels.

Aging appears to have a particularly detrimental effect on muscle mass in women (figure 5.2). Despite higher resting protein synthetic rates in the postmenopausal period, elderly women experience an accelerated loss of muscle resulting from increased rates of proteolysis, a phenomenon partly attributed to decreased estrogen production (284). Moreover, the anabolic response to protein feeding is blunted to a greater degree in older women (702). In addition, the hypertrophic response to resistance training is impaired in elderly women (54, 382), as are postexercise elevations in muscle protein synthesis (704). Taken together, these findings indicate that postmenopausal reductions in estrogen in women have a more detrimental impact on muscle mass than decreased testosterone levels associated with aging in men.

Despite these obstacles, elderly women can significantly increase fundamental muscle mass with regimented resistance exercise (131, 547, 807). Training-induced increases in hypertrophy have been correlated with reductions in primary inflammatory markers

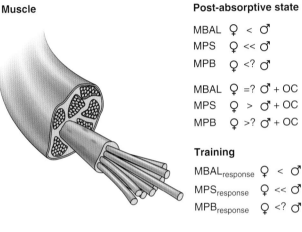

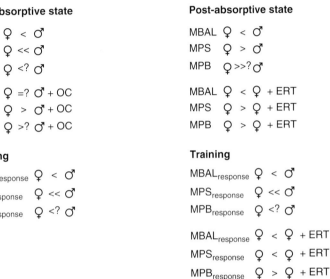

FIGURE 5.2 Effect of menopause on hypertrophic development. MBAL = muscle protein balance; MPS = muscle protein synthesis; MPB = muscle protein breakdown.

Reprinted, by permission, from M. Hansen and M. Kjaer, 2014, "Influence of sex and estrogen on musculotendinous protein turnover at rest and after exercise," *Exercise in Sport Science Review* 42(4): 183-192.

such as C-reactive protein (CRP) and tumor necrosis factor-alpha (TNF-α) (547). Whether a cause–effect relationship exists is not clear, but these correlations raise the possibility that chronic inflammation is particularly detrimental to older women in their ability to build muscle.

Training Status

The vast majority of resistance training studies are carried out in untrained people. This is generally a function of convenience because the pool of untrained subjects is larger than the pool of resistance-trained subjects. However, the hypertrophic response of trained subjects is substantially different than that of their untrained counterparts (571), thereby limiting the generalizability of such studies outside of the initial stages of training.

Differences in the hypertrophic potential between trained and untrained people can be attributed to the *ceiling effect*, or *window of adaptation* (figure 5.3). During the initial stages of training, the neuromuscular system is deconditioned and responds to virtually any stimulus because the ceiling for growth is high. Even steady-state cardiorespiratory exercise has been shown to produce hypertrophic increases in those who were previously sedentary (379). As people become resistance trained and move closer to their genetic ceiling, however, it becomes progressively more difficult to increase muscular size (i.e., the window of adaptation becomes smaller). Theoretically, an excess of muscle mass would be energetically and kinetically inefficient, and thus the human body limits the amount of lean tissue that can be gained. In support of this hypothesis, research shows that the extent of hypertrophic gains is relatively small (~3% to 7%) in highly competitive bodybuilders over 5 months of resistance training, suggesting these people are at the upper limits of their genetic ceilings (28).

Alterations in anabolic intracellular signaling have been demonstrated between trained and untrained subjects in both animal and human models. Ogasawara and colleagues (545) exposed male rats to maximal isometric contractions via percutaneous electrical stimulation of the gastrocnemius muscle every other day for either 1 bout, 12 bouts, or 18 bouts. Those in a detraining group performed 12 bouts, detrained for 12 days, and then were subjected to an additional exercise session prior to being sacrificed. Phosphorylation of p70[S6K], ribosomal protein S6, and p90[RSK] were elevated in the group that performed 1 bout, but repeated exercise bouts suppressed phosphorylation levels. This indicates that anabolic signaling becomes desensitized to resistance training when it is performed consistently over time. In a human study, Coffey and colleagues (149) investigated the effects of multiple sets of maximal isokinetic knee extensions in well-trained cyclists versus competitive powerlifters. Postexercise biopsy results showed that AMPK was significantly elevated in the aerobic endurance–trained subjects, but not the strength-trained subjects. Moreover, p70[S6K] and S6 ribosomal protein

phosphorylation was markedly elevated in the aerobic endurance–trained subjects, but not strength-trained subjects. Similarly, Wilkinson and colleagues (828) found that the duration of elevations in Akt and p70[S6K] phosphorylation was attenuated, and the levels of S6 phosphorylation remained similar to resting levels after 10 weeks of resistance training. These results are consistent with research showing that genes involved in cellular hypertrophy are suppressed following a regimented resistance training protocol (516).

Similar to the findings of acute signaling studies, there is evidence that the muscle protein synthetic response to resistance exercise is blunted in well-trained people. Whereas muscle protein synthesis remains elevated in the untrained state for approximately 48 to 72 hours (494, 575), research indicates that the time course is truncated in trained subjects (their levels return to baseline within 36 hours) (442, 741). It should be noted, however, that substantial individual variation exists in this response, and elevations in muscle protein synthesis in some trained subjects can persist up to 48 hours and perhaps longer postexercise (442). The attenuated muscle protein synthesis duration following regimented training may be related at least in part to the protective response of the repeated bout effect. Given that well-trained people have conditioned their muscles to the stress of resistance exercise, the associated tissue breakdown is reduced and thus there is less need for remodeling.

It should be noted that the ceiling effect is an abstract concept. Although a theoretical

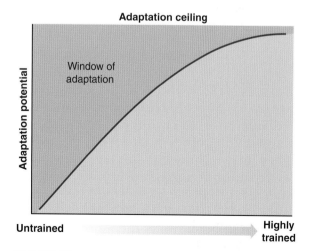

FIGURE 5.3 The ceiling effect, or window of adaptation.

KEY POINT

As people become resistance trained and move closer to their genetic ceiling, it becomes progressively more difficult to increase muscular size. Meaningful hypertrophic responses can be gained by precise manipulation of program variables, including strategic brief periods of deloading to restore the anabolic responsiveness of trained muscle.

ceiling does exist, people never actually realize their full genetic potential. The ability to further increase muscle mass is always present. Indeed, muscular gains can be made even at very advanced levels, albeit at a much slower pace than during the initial stages of training. Numerous research studies show that those with considerable training experience do build appreciable muscle when a novel stimulus is applied (20, 661, 665). The results of Alway and colleagues (28) showing modest muscle growth in competitive bodybuilders indicate that the precise manipulation of program variables becomes increasingly important to elicit a meaningful hypertrophic response as people approach their genetic ceiling. Moreover, there is evidence that integrating brief periods of detraining can restore the anabolic responsiveness of trained muscle (545). It is therefore possible that bodybuilders in the Alway and colleagues (28) study might have improved their hypertrophic response by periodizing volume and intensity over the course of the training cycle to include deload periods that facilitate remodeling and rejuvenation.

TAKE-HOME POINTS

- There is a large genetic component in the individual hypertrophic response. A wide array of genes has been identified as playing a role in the ability to gain muscle. It is likely that interactions of multiple genetic loci ultimately determine a person's genetic potential to gain muscle. Hereditary differences in muscle morphology also are believed to govern the extent of a person's muscle-building capacity. Although the terms *responders* and *nonresponders* have been proposed in the literature, these classifications are overly simplistic; virtually everyone can increase muscle mass over baseline levels with consistent resistance training.

- Biological aging has a marked effect on muscle mass. Peak mass is achieved between the third and fifth decades of life, after which a gradual, progressive loss of muscle ensues (i.e., sarcopenia). An age-related reduction in anabolic hormones and satellite cell function are believed to be largely responsible for sarcopenic changes. Chronic low-grade inflammation also appears to play a role in the process. Regular resistance exercise can help abate age-related muscle loss and even produce hypertrophic increases above that in sedentary younger people. However, hypertrophic potential diminishes with advancing age, and evidence indicates that elderly people need a greater weekly minimum training dose to maintain muscle once they have achieved a given level of hypertrophy.

- The ability to build muscle differs between the sexes. Although women realize approximately equal relative muscle growth compared to men following regimented resistance training, men gain significantly more muscle on an absolute basis. These differences are attributed, at least in part, to variances in circulating testosterone. Women tend to experience a greater age-related muscle loss than men, conceivably mediated by postmenopausal reductions in estrogen levels.

- Hypertrophic capacity progressively diminishes as people become more trained. This is attributed to a ceiling effect in which alterations in anabolic intracellular signaling impair the ability to accrete muscle proteins with consistent participation in a resistance training program. However, although a theoretical ceiling does exist, people never actually realize their full genetic potential; the ability to further increase muscle mass is always present.

Program Design for Maximal Hypertrophy

This chapter builds on the information from previous chapters to explore the practical application of the science of hypertrophy training. Considerations for exercise selection are discussed from a biomechanical standpoint with a focus on how movements can be synergistically varied to ensure complete muscular development. A discussion of program design follows that details the nuances of manipulating program variables over the course of a periodized training cycle to maximize the hypertrophic response. Numerous examples are provided throughout the chapter to illustrate the practical application of relevant concepts. It is important to understand that these examples represent the art of program design and are for illustrative purposes only. While paying proper attention to underlying scientific principles, lifters should harness their personal experience in conjunction with their own needs and abilities to formulate a strategic plan. This is the essence of an evidence-based approach to training.

Biomechanics

Biomechanics is the study of how internal and external forces affect the living body; particular attention is given to the musculoskeletal system. A variety of biomechanical factors must be taken into account when choosing exercises for a hypertrophy-oriented program. These include the length–tension relationship, training angle, plane of movement, spacing of hands and feet, and exercise type, which are addressed in this section. The ensuing section, Exercise Selection Strategies, explores how to apply these factors to resistance training program design to maximize hypertrophy.

KEY POINT

Length–tension relationship, training angle, plane of movement, spacing of hands and feet, and exercise type can all be carefully manipulated in program design to maximize hypertrophy.

Length–Tension Relationship

The capacity of a muscle fiber to produce force is predicated on the position of the actin and myosin filaments in its sarcomeres. This phenomenon, known as the *length–tension relationship* (figure 6.1), can be harnessed to target muscles or portions thereof by making them more or less active during exercise. Two primary strategies are applicable here: active insufficiency and passive tension. *Active insufficiency* refers to when a two-joint muscle is shortened at one joint while a muscular action is initiated at the other joint. Because a muscle loses the ability to shorten when its attachments are close together, it is in a functionally disadvantageous position on the length–tension curve, resulting in a diminished capacity to produce force. For example, in the flexed position of the biceps curl, the biceps brachii's origin at the scapula and insertions below the elbow are brought closer together, and the bicep's ability to produce force is limited. Alternatively, *passive tension* refers to when a two-joint muscle is elongated at one joint while carrying out dynamic movement at the other joint. This produces a favorable length–tension relationship, enhancing the muscle's ability to produce force. For example, the long head of the triceps brachii crosses both the shoulder and elbow joints, carrying out shoulder flexion and elbow extension at these joints, respectively. Because the muscle is shortened during shoulder extension, it is lengthened during shoulder flexion. Thus, performing an exercise in which the shoulder joint is flexed (such as the overhead triceps extension) places the muscle in a position of stretch while carrying out its action at the elbow and consequently allows for greater force production.

Training Angle

Muscle fibers contract optimally when placed in direct opposition to gravity along the direction of the fiber. Changing the angle of training at which a muscle is worked best targets the full spectrum of its fibers, allowing for more symmetrical muscular development. Thus, the orientation of fibers in a given muscle must be considered when selecting exercises.

Movement Plane

The human body is designed to move in three-dimensional space. To account for this capability, the body can be segmented into sections in terms of three anatomical planes (figure 6.2): *sagittal*, which divides the body into left and right halves and encompasses flexion and extension; *frontal* (i.e., coronal), which divides the body into front and back sections and includes abduction, adduction, elevation, depression, inversion, eversion, and lateral flexion; and *transverse*, which divides the body into top and bottom portions and includes horizontal adduction, horizontal abduction, rotation, pronation, and supination. Note that although these planes are rigidly defined, diagonal movement in all planes is possible depending on the task requirement and individual mobility.

To carry out movement efficiently and effectively, the musculoskeletal system summons muscles based on the directional require-

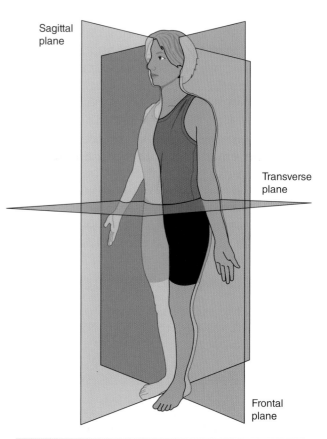

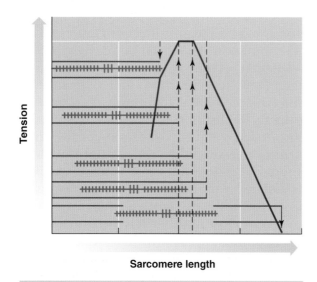

FIGURE 6.1 The length–tension relationship.

FIGURE 6.2 The planes of movement.

ments of the task. As such, muscular activation changes based on the plane of movement in which the body is worked. The application of training in various planes to maximize muscular development depends on the degrees of freedom of the joint. Joints that have multiple degrees of freedom (e.g., ball-and-socket joints) benefit from multiplanar training, whereas those with a single degree of freedom (e.g., hinge joints) do not.

Spacing of Hands and Feet

The positioning of the extremities can alter muscle activation patterns. The orientation of fibers within a given muscle ultimately dictates the extent to which changes in hand and foot spacing influence activation. The effects of such alterations tend to be rather subtle, but nevertheless can be sufficient to promote meaningful differences in muscle development.

Exercise Type

Multijoint exercises involve the dynamic activation of numerous muscles while statically engaging many stabilizers. Moreover, because loading is dispersed over multiple joints and muscles, heavy weights can be employed to maximize mechanical tension without creating undue joint stress. Hence, multijoint exercises provide an effective means to train the entire body efficiently. However, they are limited because some muscles make a greater contribution to movement than others do. Single-joint exercises afford the ability to directly target individual muscles and elicit unique neuromuscular activation patterns that enhance overall muscular development (35). The torque-angle curves of single-joint exercises must be taken into account in program design. Contreras and colleagues (155) employed biomechanical modeling to propose a three-part torque-angle classification system for single-joint exercises:

1. Long-length accentuated force exercises create maximal torque while the prime movers are stretched (e.g., chest fly; figure 6.3a).

2. Short-length accentuated force exercises create maximal torque while the prime movers are shortened (e.g., hip thrust; figure 6.3b).

3. Mid-length accentuated force exercises create maximal torque while the prime movers are between the extremes (e.g., 45° back extension; figure 6.3c).

a

b

c

FIGURE 6.3 Exercises typifying a torque-angle classification system for single-joint exercises: *(a)* chest fly—maximal torque while the prime movers are stretched; *(b)* hip thrust—maximal torque while the prime movers are shortened; and *(c)* 45° back extension—maximal torque while the prime movers are between the extremes.

ATTENTIONAL FOCUS AND MUSCLE HYPERTROPHY

Attentional focus is a well-recognized aspect of motor learning, and its use has important implications for muscular hypertrophy. Operationally defined from a resistance training standpoint, *attentional focus* refers to what a person thinks about during each repetition. Two primary types of attentional focus have been recognized in the literature: internal and external. An *internal focus* involves thinking about bodily movements during performance, whereas an *external focus* involves thinking about the outcomes of movements.

The majority of research supports adopting an external focus of attention when carrying out performance-oriented tasks. A recent comprehensive review of the literature found superior effects from using an external versus an internal focus in more than 90% of studies that examined performance-oriented outcomes (840). The performance-based superiority of an external focus during resistance training is thought to be due to an enhanced economy of movement associated with greater force production and reduced muscular activity (452). It is important to note, however, that improvements in performance-related measures do not necessarily equate to maximal increases in muscle hypertrophy. A case can be made that an internal focus is a better approach when the goal is to maximize muscle development.

Employing a hypertrophy-oriented internal focus of attention is consistent with the long-standing bodybuilding axiom of making a mind–muscle connection. Simply stated, this strategy involves visualizing the target muscle during the course of a lift and willfully directing neural drive to that muscle. When properly executed, the approach theoretically allows for increased stimulation of the target muscle while reducing the involvement of other synergists.

Although no research to date has been carried out to investigate whether long-term changes in muscle mass result from attentional strategies, indirect evidence seems to support a hypertrophic benefit when using an internal focus. Numerous studies have found that activation of a given muscle was enhanced by using an internal focus of attention. Snyder and Leech (706) demonstrated that subjects were able to significantly increase EMG activity in the latissimus dorsi by directing their focus to this muscle during the lat pulldown exercise. A follow-up study by the same lab showed that the pectoralis major and triceps could be individually targeted after subjects were instructed to visualize those muscles during performance of the bench press at 50% of 1RM (707). Interestingly, the magnitude of the effect was substantially reduced when the load was increased to 80% of 1RM. This may be due to increased force demands when training with heavier loads, thereby altering the ability to focus on the muscle being worked. The implication is that the hypertrophy-related benefits of using an internal focus may be attenuated or annulled when training with very heavy loads. That said, the ability to increase muscle activation through an internal focus has been shown in other muscles as well, including the abdominals (95, 163, 351), gluteus maximus (419), and elbow flexors (452, 785). The findings provide strong support for using an internal focus to target a given muscle.

The logical question is whether increasing activation of a muscle translates into greater muscle growth. Although definitive conclusions cannot be drawn, some research suggests that this is indeed the case. Wakahara and colleagues (802) carried out a two-part experiment to investigate the topic. In the first part of the experiment, muscle activation was assessed by T2-weighted magnetic resonance imaging during 5 sets of 8 repetitions of the lying triceps extension in 12 untrained men. The results showed that activation of the triceps brachii was significantly higher in the proximal and midaspects of the muscle versus the distal portion. In the second part of the study, 12 additional subjects performed the same routine used in part 1 of the study for 3 days per week over 12 weeks. At the study's conclusion, increases in muscle cross-sectional area corresponded to the specific regions most activated during exercise performance. A follow-up study by the same lab reported similar findings using alternative exercises for the triceps brachii (803).

The findings of increased muscle activation combined with those showing site-specific hypertrophy in the region of activation seem to suggest that an internal attentional focus is the best approach for maximizing muscle development. Although many gym-derived tenets of bodybuilding are of questionable practice, claims of the hypertrophic benefit of developing a mind–muscle connection and employing it during exercise performance seem to have merit.

Exercise Selection Strategies

Selecting the appropriate exercises is an important factor for maximizing whole-body muscle hypertrophy. For example, certain muscles have multiple attachments that improve leverage for movement patterns. Moreover, myofibers are often subdivided into neuromuscular compartments, each of which is innervated by its own nerve branch (824, 836). These inter- and intramuscular architectural variances reinforce the need to adopt a multiplanar, multiangled approach to hypertrophy-oriented training using a variety of exercises. Maximal hypertrophy can be achieved only by systematically varying the exercise performed and fully working all aspects of the targeted musculature. This section explains how to employ these strategies to maximize hypertrophy in each of the major muscle groups.

KEY POINT

Maximal hypertrophy can be achieved only by systematically varying the exercise performed and fully working all aspects of the targeted musculature, varying the angles and planes involved, and using both multijoint and single-joint exercises.

Back

The back muscles benefit from being trained in all three planes of movement. The frontal and sagittal planes, in particular, should be exploited to optimize muscular development. The latissimus dorsi (lats) are maximally stimulated by humeral adduction carried out in the frontal plane. The pull-up and lat pulldown exercises using a pronated grip are excellent for targeting the lats (435, 851). Grip widths in these movements show minor differences in muscle activation, but varying these positions from shoulder-width to twice shoulder-width distance may help to fully stimulate the musculature (33).

The midback muscles (middle trapezius and rhomboids) are best targeted using sagittal plane exercises (e.g., bent-over row and seated row). A neutral grip reduces biceps brachii activation, which seemingly allows the back musculature to carry out a greater amount of work. Despite a logical basis, there does not appear to be any added benefit to actively retracting the scapulae during rowing movements (413).

Single-joint shoulder extension exercises in the sagittal plane such as the pullover are often recommended for lat development. There is evidence that muscle activation in the pullover significantly favors the pectoralis major more than the lats, and the level of activation depends on the external force lever arm produced (453). However, the pullover exerts a great stretch in the lats at the start position, which may accentuate growth via increased myodamage. Therefore, the pullover with a focus on accentuating the beginning phase of the movement can be a useful addition to a hypertrophy-oriented routine.

Chest

The pectoralis major is maximally activated in the transverse plane using horizontal adduction movements. Both multijoint exercises (horizontal, incline, and decline bench press) and single-joint exercises (horizontal, incline, and decline chest fly) are viable choices to develop the chest musculature. Pressing movements allow for the use of heavier loads, and the chest fly provides greater isolation of the target muscles at the exclusion of assistors

(346). A combination of both types of exercises conceivably maximizes the hypertrophic response, although evidence for this hypothesis is lacking.

The pectorals can benefit from the use of a variety of training angles. The sternal head is best targeted during supine exercises (figure 6.4a) and decline exercises (figure 6.4b) (249), whereas the clavicular head is more aligned with gravitational forces when the torso is inclined (figure 6.4c) (777). Hand spacing also influences pectoral muscle activation. A narrow grip elicits greater activation of the clavicular head (58). This is likely due to the fact that a narrow grip brings the elbows close to the torso, which makes the exercise a sagittal plane shoulder flexion movement. Single-joint overhead shoulder extension exercises such as the dumbbell pullover (figure

FIGURE 6.4 Exercises that target the pectorals from a variety of training angles: *(a)* flat bench press, *(b)* decline bench press, *(c)* incline bench press, *(d)* dumbbell pullover.

6.4*d*) substantially activate the sternal head of the pectoralis major (453), making it a viable addition to a comprehensive training program.

Torque angle during chest training also must be considered with respect to the modality of exercise. Barbell and dumbbell exercises heavily load the pectoralis major in the early phase of movement, but the musculature becomes increasingly unloaded at the finish position. Conversely, cable pulleys and many machines allow for a more constant muscular tension through the ROM, which enhances metabolic stress in the pectorals. Thus, employing a variety of modalities would seemingly benefit hypertrophic adaptations. The addition of bands or chains can help to balance out the strength curve in free weight exercises, potentially enhancing their effectiveness (110, 240).

Shoulder

The deltoids are partitioned into three distinct heads that function in each of the cardinal planes: the anterior head is a shoulder flexor and thus is targeted with sagittal plane movements (e.g., front raise); the middle head is an abductor and thus is targeted with frontal plane movements (e.g., lateral raise); and the posterior head is a horizontal abductor and thus is targeted with transverse plane movements (e.g., reverse shoulder fly, bent-over lateral raise) (91).

Shoulder rotation also must be considered when working the deltoids. The shoulder press, a frontal plane exercise, is generally thought to target the middle head of the deltoid. However, because the shoulder joint is externally rotated during performance, the anterior head is placed in a position to directly oppose gravity and thereby receives the majority of stimulation; the middle and posterior heads are substantially less active (91). Internal shoulder rotation is needed to place the middle head in a position to directly oppose gravity, which is naturally accomplished in the wide-grip upright row (466, 649). Similarly, an internally rotated shoulder (i.e., pinky up) should be maintained during the lateral raise for optimal stimulation of the middle deltoid.

An externally rotated shoulder position during horizontal abduction exercise is best for targeting the posterior deltoid (655).

Upper Arm

The elbow is a hinge joint and thus moves in only one plane (sagittal). The muscles acting at the elbow are heavily involved in multijoint upper-body exercises such as presses, pull-ups, and rows. However, both the elbow flexors and the elbow extensors contain *biarticular* (crossing two joints) muscles. The length–tension relationship of these muscles is therefore suboptimal during multijoint exercises. Accordingly, targeted single-joint exercises afford the potential for stronger muscular contractions and thus greater growth.

With respect to the elbow flexors, the biceps brachii crosses both the shoulder and elbow joints. The long head, in particular, acts as a shoulder flexor (418), which makes it maximally active in exercises in which the humerus is extended behind the body (e.g., incline biceps curl; figure 6.5*a*). The long head also functions as a humeral abductor. The short head, therefore, can be targeted by performing exercises in which the humerus is abducted to 90° because the long head is actively insufficient in this position (269). Considering that the biceps are powerful radioulnar supinators, performing exercises with the hands neutral (e.g., hammer curl; figure 6.5*b*) or pronated (e.g., reverse curl; figure 6.5*c*) renders the biceps actively insufficient, thereby progressively increasing the work of the brachioradialis and brachialis muscles, respectively.

With respect to the elbow extensors, the long head of the triceps brachii has an optimal length–tension relationship when the shoulder is flexed to about 180° (411), meaning that this aspect of the musculature is most active during exercises in which the humerus is held overhead (e.g., overhead triceps extension). Conversely, the medial and lateral heads are more active during movements such as the triceps pushdown, in which the humerus is held at the sides (803). This renders the long head less active so that the other heads carry out a greater amount of work.

FIGURE 6.5 Exercises to target the elbow flexors: *(a)* incline biceps curl, *(b)* hammer curl, *(c)* reverse curl.

Hip

The gluteals make up the primary muscle group of the hip and include the gluteus maximus, gluteus medius, and gluteus minimus. The gluteals function in all three planes of movement, but particularly in the transverse and frontal planes. Sagittal plane multijoint exercises for the lower body, such as the squat, lunge, and leg press, heavily involve the gluteus maximus. A wide stance increases activation of the gluteus maximus (532, 557),

and greatest muscle activity occurs at 140% of shoulder width (472). However, maximal hip extension torque in these exercises occurs when the hip is flexed; torque progressively decreases during extension and is minimal at the finish of movement. This is counter to maximal activation of the gluteus maximus, which occurs at the end range of hip extension (837). Indeed, EMG data show that the hip thrust produces significantly greater activation of the gluteus maximus compared to the squat (156). Moreover, gluteus maximus activity is diminished during combined hip and knee extension, although activation of the three *vasti* muscles (vastus lateralis, vastus intermedius, and vastus medialis) of the quadriceps is enhanced (843). Therefore, multijoint lower-body movements might be best for inducing muscle damage in the gluteus maximus because peak activation occurs in the lengthened position, whereas an exercise such as the hip thrust is best for optimizing mechanical tension.

Single-joint hip extension exercises should also be incorporated for maximal development of the gluteus maximus. It is best to include a combination of all three lengths of accentuated force movements to cover the spectrum of mechanisms governing hypertrophy.

The primary action of the gluteus medius and gluteus minimus is to abduct the thigh. Frontal plane abduction movements, such as the cable hip side raise, are therefore needed to target these muscles. These muscles also benefit from active external rotation during movement (116).

Anterior Thigh

The quadriceps are primary knee extensors and thus benefit from both multijoint and single-joint lower-body movements. Multijoint lower-body movements (e.g., the squat) have been found to elicit greater activation in the vasti muscles, whereas the knee extension targets the rectus femoris (196, 205). These findings are consistent with research showing that multijoint lower-body exercise maximally activates the quadriceps during deep knee flexion, whereas activation in open-chain knee extension is greatest during full extension (826). This suggests a synergy between movements that warrants combining exercises to achieve peak activation at varying muscle lengths. In addition, rotating multijoint exercises over the course of a training cycle promotes more symmetrical quadriceps development compared to performing the same movement on a volume-equated basis (223).

Stance width during multijoint lower-body exercise does not appear to affect muscular activity in the quadriceps (472), nor does alter-

ing foot position (i.e., tibial rotation) from 30° inward rotation to 80° outward rotation (328, 532). On the other hand, there is evidence that foot position influences quadriceps activity in open-chain single-joint exercise, and that an externally rotated position elicits greater activation of the rectus femoris (688). However, given that extreme rotation of the tibia can change normal patella tracking and potentially cause undesirable varus or valgus moments, the practical value of altering foot positions in an attempt to target aspects of the quadriceps remains questionable.

Posterior Thigh

The hamstrings are a biarticular muscle complex. The semimembranosus, semitendinosus, and long head of the biceps femoris carry out both hip extension and knee flexion; the short head of the biceps femoris crosses only the knee joint and thus is purely a knee flexor. Contrary to popular belief, the hamstrings are only moderately active during multijoint lower-body exercise, producing approximately half the amount of EMG activity as single-joint exercise (826, 838). This is consistent with the fact that when the hamstrings are shortening at the hip, they are lengthening at the knee, and vice versa. Their length thus remains fairly constant throughout performance, thereby limiting force output.

Single-joint exercises are required to fully stimulate the hamstrings. Exercises that involve hip extension (e.g., stiff-leg deadlift, good morning) and those that involve knee flexion (e.g., lying leg curl) are viable choices. Zebis and colleagues (859) found that the Romanian deadlift (a hip extension movement) targets the semitendinosus, whereas the lying leg curl (a knee flexion exercise) targets the biceps femoris. Moreover, there is evidence that knee flexion exercise produces greater activation of the lower aspect of the hamstrings (663). Thus, both types of movements should be included for optimal muscular development. The individual hamstring muscles can be further targeted by altering foot position during both hip extension and knee flexion exercise. Internally rotating the foot targets the semitendinosus and semimembranosus, and external rotation favors the biceps femoris (438).

Lower Leg

The gastrocnemius and soleus (collectively known as the *triceps surae*) are the primary plantar flexors of the ankle joint and comprise the bulk of the muscular mass in the calf region. The gastrocnemius is a biarticular muscle that originates at the distal femur and fuses with the Achilles tendon to insert at the calcaneus. At the ankle, the gastrocnemius acts as a plantar flexor, whereas at the knee, it assists the hamstrings in flexion. Thus, straight-leg (knee) plantar flexion exercises (e.g., standing calf raise) place the gastrocnemius under maximal stretch and maximize force output (296). Alternatively, bent-leg (knee) plantar flexion exercises (e.g., seated calf raise) render the gastrocnemius actively insufficient and allow the uniarticular soleus to take over a majority of the work (296). There also is evidence that foot position can influence calf muscle activation: turning the feet inward targets the lateral head of the gastrocnemius, whereas turning the feet outward targets the medial head (617), although the overall effect of this strategy on muscular activity is relatively modest and of questionable practical meaningfulness.

Periodization

Hypertrophy-oriented resistance training program design is thought to benefit from a periodized approach (298). Simply stated, the goal of periodization is to optimize a given fitness component over a period of time. This is accomplished by manipulating program variables to create consistent improvement in the target outcome without plateau or regression.

Periodization is based on Selye's general adaptation syndrome (GAS) theory, which proposes that the body undergoes a three-stage reaction to stress: alarm, resistance, and exhaustion (figure 6.6) (678). An applied example of the GAS theory is the body's response to a virus. Initially, exposure to the virus causes an alarm reaction in which the immune system mobilizes to counteract the stressor. If the immune defense is sufficiently strong, the virus is quelled and the body becomes resistant to subsequent exposure. However, if the virus overwhelms the immune response, health continues to decline, leading to severe illness or even death.

Given that intense physical activity is a potent stressor, the GAS theory is applicable to exercise. Performance of rigorous resistance training initiates an alarm response in which the body increases protein synthesis

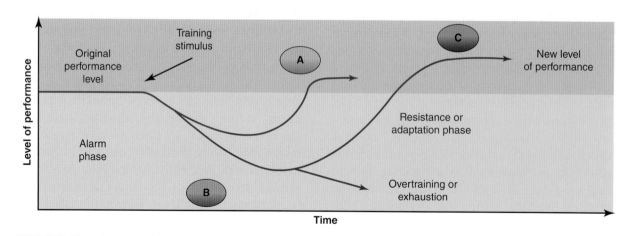

FIGURE 6.6 Illustration of Selye's general adaptation syndrome theory. A = typical training; B = overtraining; C = overreaching or supercompensation.

Adapted, by permission, from A.C. Fry, 1998, The role of training intensity in resistance exercise overtraining and overreaching. In *Overtraining in sport,* edited by R.B. Kreider, A.C. Fry, and M.L. O'Toole (Champaign, IL: Human Kinetics), 114.

and other anabolic processes. Under ideal circumstances, the exercise stress is sufficient to cause a supercompensatory response that leads to greater muscle protein accretion. If the applied stress does not progressively challenge the neuromuscular system sufficiently, a plateau ensues and no further increases in growth occur. Alternatively, if the stress is repeatedly too great for the body, the response is maladaptive, leading to an overtrained state. To avoid overtraining and ensure ongoing increases in growth, lifters must periodize their exercise programs over time (51, 858).

Periodization Models

An array of periodization models have been proposed to maximize muscular adaptations to resistance training. Of these models, three have been studied with respect to their effects on muscle hypertrophy: traditional linear periodization, nonlinear (undulating) periodization, and reverse periodization. This section provides an overview of the research on each of these models.

It should be noted that periodization is a concept, not a defined system of training. Thus, there are virtually unlimited ways to structure a periodized program based on a person's unique needs and abilities. Given that all training variables can be manipulated, and given the plethora of possible combinations of manipulation, the ability to draw practical inferences from research is limited. So although periodization appears to maximize hypertrophy, multiple approaches remain viable options.

Traditional Linear Periodization

The origins of periodization can be traced back to the 1950s. Matveyev is widely credited with developing the *traditional linear periodization model* to prepare athletes for Olympic competition (727). The linear model has three basic phases: the *macrocycle*, which encompasses an entire training period generally ranging from 6 months to several years; the *mesocycle*, which splits the macrocycle into at least two subdivisions lasting from several weeks to months; and the *microcycle*, which further subdivides the mesocycle into weekly phases focused on

daily training variations. In the classic linear model, intensity and volume are inversely structured so that mesocycles progress from periods of high volume and low intensity to periods of low volume and high intensity. A typical three-phase linear mesocycle begins with a hypertrophy or muscle endurance phase in which intensities of load are 60% to 75% of 1RM (10 to 20 repetitions). Next is a strength phase in which loading intensities range from 80% to 90% of 1RM (4 to 8 repetitions). The final mesocycle focuses on strength and power by increasing intensities even further, approaching or exceeding 95% of 1RM (2 to 5 repetitions). Each increase in intensity is met with a corresponding reduction in training volume to accommodate the greater stress on the neuromuscular system. Ultimately, the person peaks at the end of the final mesocycle so that the training outcomes transfer to competition.

Several studies have been carried out to determine whether periodizing a resistance training program enhances muscle growth. In their pioneering work, Stone and colleagues (729) found that a periodized program increased lean body mass (as determined by hydrostatic weighing) to a significantly greater extent than a nonperiodized routine did. Unfortunately, the values for each group were not published, thereby precluding the ability to assess the magnitude of differences in the protocols. In a subsequent study, Baker and colleagues (52) failed to detect any significant differences in lean body mass between periodized and nonperiodized models; another study (502) showed greater absolute differences in favor of periodized training, but values did not rise to statistical significance. It should be noted that the two latter studies used the skinfold technique to evaluate body composition, which is of questionable accuracy for assessing relatively small changes in lean mass over short periods. So although there is some direct evidence to support the use of periodization in a hypertrophy-oriented program, the research at this point remains equivocal, precluding the ability to form definitive conclusions on the topic. That said, considerable evidence shows that periodization elicits greater gains in strength than nonperiodized approaches do (17, 502, 540, 728, 830). Given that mechanical tension is a primary driving force for muscle protein accretion (656), a case can be made that greater increases in strength alone would facilitate superior hypertrophic gains over time.

Table 6.1 provides a summary of the research related to periodized versus nonperiodized programs.

TABLE 6.1 Summary of Hypertrophy Training Studies Investigating Periodized Versus Nonperiodized Programs

Study	Subjects	Design	Study duration	Hypertrophy measurement	Findings
Baker et al. (52)	22 resistance-trained young men	Random assignment to a linear periodized, undulating periodized, or nonperiodized split-body resistance training protocol. The linear protocol progressively increased load from 10- to 3RM; the undulating protocol rotated every other week between 3- and 10RM; the nonperiodized protocol performed 6RM every session. All subjects performed multiple sets of multiple exercises each session. Training was carried out 3 days per week.	12 weeks	Skinfold technique	No significant differences in lean mass between conditions
Monteiro et al. (502)	27 resistance-trained young men	Random assignment to a linear periodized, undulating periodized, or nonperiodized split-body resistance training protocol. Those in the linear protocol progressively increased load from 12- to 15RM to 4- to 5RM; those in the undulating protocol rotated between 4- and 15RM over each microcycle; and those in the nonperiodized protocol performed 8- to 10RM every session. Multiple sets were performed for 13 exercises. Training was carried out 4 days per week.	12 weeks	Skinfold technique	No significant differences in lean mass between conditions, although the nonperiodized group lost lean mass while the periodized groups showed slight gains
Stone et al. (729)	20 young men (training status not disclosed)	Random assignment to either a periodized or a nonperiodized split-body resistance training protocol. The periodized group trained with 5 sets of 10 reps in weeks 1 through 3, 5 sets of 5 reps in week 4, 3 sets of 3 reps in week 5, and 3 sets of 2 reps in week 6; the nonperiodized group performed 3 sets of 6 reps each session. All subjects performed 6 multijoint exercises over the course of 3 weekly training sessions.	6 weeks	Underwater weighing	Significantly greater increases in lean body mass for the periodized condition

Study	Subjects	Design	Study duration	Hypertrophy measurement	Findings
Souza et al. (714)	31 recreationally active young men	Random assignment to a linear periodized, undulating periodized, or nonperiodized lower-body resistance training protocol. Those in the linear protocol performed 12RM in weeks 1 through 4 and 8RM in weeks 5 and 6; those in the undulating protocol rotated between 12- and 8RM in weeks 1 through 4 and then 6- to 10RM in weeks 5 and 6; those in the nonperiodized protocol performed 8RM every session. Multiple sets were performed for two exercises. Training was carried out 2 days per week.	6 weeks	MRI	No significant differences in quadriceps CSA between conditions

Abbreviations: RM = repetition maximum; MRI = magnetic resonance imaging; CSA = cross-sectional area.

Nonlinear (Undulating) Periodization

A number of variations to the original periodization model have been proposed to enhance results. One of the most popular is the concept of *nonlinear periodization*, often referred to as *undulating periodization*, which was first introduced into the literature by Poliquin (586). Nonlinear periodization is thought to address inherent issues with the traditional model—namely, that progressive increases in load intensity do not allow sufficient time for regeneration, thus placing undue stress on the body over extended periods and increasing the potential for overtraining (586). Moreover, the hypertrophic gains obtained during the early phases of training are not well maintained because volume—a primary driver of hypertrophy—is progressively decreased over the latter phases of the linear macrocycle. To account for these drawbacks, nonlinear periodized programs vary volume and intensity in an undulatory manner. The phases are therefore much shorter in the nonlinear approach. Poliquin (586) originally proposed alternating phases of accumulation and intensification on a biweekly basis to optimize a given fitness outcome without overtaxing bodily systems. A popular modification to this approach is the *daily undulating periodization* (DUP) model. Typically, DUP involves alternating heavy-, moderate-, and light-load sessions over the course of a week.

A number of studies have been carried out to directly compare the hypertrophic adaptations of volume-equated linear and nonlinear periodization models (52, 171, 290, 374, 502, 592, 693, 714); see table 6.2 for a summary. Of these studies, only one reported significant differences in the models; the nonlinear approach produced superior increases in the thickness of the elbow flexors and elbow extensors in untrained young men (693). Taking the body of literature as a whole, both linear and nonlinear models seem to be equally viable options for promoting increases in muscle growth.

Reverse Periodization

Another variation of the traditional periodization model specifically designed to maximize hypertrophy is *reverse periodization*. As previously mentioned, the traditional linear model involves progressive reductions in training volume to account for corresponding increases in load. Considering the strong dose–response relationship between volume and hypertrophy, this seemingly is counterproductive for maximizing muscle mass in the peak phase of the macrocycle. Reverse periodization addresses this issue by placing a hypertrophy mesocycle at the end of the

TABLE 6.2 Summary of Hypertrophy Training Studies Investigating Linear Versus Nonlinear Periodization

Study	Subjects	Design	Study duration	Hypertrophy measurement	Findings
Baker et al. (52)	22 resistance-trained young men	Random assignment to a linear periodized, undulating periodized, or nonperiodized total-body resistance training protocol. Those in the linear protocol progressively increased load from 10- to 3RM; those in the undulating protocol rotated every other week between 3- and 10RM; those in the nonperiodized protocol performed 6RM every session. All subjects performed multiple sets of multiple exercises each session. Training was carried out 3 days per week.	12 weeks	Skinfold technique	No significant differences in lean mass between conditions
de Lima et al. (171)	28 untrained young women	Random assignment to either a linear or undulating periodized resistance training program. The linear protocol increased load each week for 4 weeks from 30- to 25- to 20- to 15RM and then repeated this sequence for the balance of the study; the undulating protocol alternated weekly between 25- and 30RM and 15- and 20RM. Multiple sets were performed for 16 exercises in split-body fashion. Training was carried out 4 days per week.	12 weeks	Skinfold	No significant differences in lean mass between conditions
Harries et al. (290)	26 recreationally trained adolescent males	Quasi-experimental random assignment to either a linear or undulating periodized resistance training program. The linear protocol progressively increased load each week; the undulating protocol varied between a higher- and lower-repetition day each week. Multiple exercises were performed, but only the squat and bench press were periodized. All training was carried out twice per week.	12 weeks	BIA	No significant differences in skeletal muscle mass between conditions
Kok et al. (374)	20 untrained young women	Random assignment to either a linear or undulating periodized resistance training program. The linear protocol progressively increased load every 3 weeks from 10- to 6- to 3RM; the undulating protocol varied loading each week from 10- to 6- to 3RM and then repeated this cycle over the course of the study. Three sets were performed for 10 exercises carried out 3 days per week.	9 weeks	Ultrasound	No significant differences in quadriceps femoris thickness between conditions

Study	Subjects	Design	Study duration	Hypertrophy measurement	Findings
Monteiro et al. (502)	27 resistance-trained young men	Random assignment to a linear periodized, undulating periodized, or nonperiodized split-body resistance training protocol. Those in the linear protocol progressively increased load from 12- to 15RM to 4- to 5RM; those in the undulating protocol rotated between 4- and 15RM over each microcycle; those in the nonperiodized protocol performed 8- to 10RM every session. Multiple sets were performed for 13 exercises. Training was carried out 4 days per week.	12 weeks	Skinfold technique	No significant differences in lean mass between conditions, although the nonperiodized group lost lean mass, while the periodized groups showed slight gains
Prestes et al. (592)	40 resistance-trained young men	Random assignment to either a linear or undulating periodized resistance training program. The linear protocol increased load each week for 4 weeks from 12- to 10- to 8- to 6RM and then repeated this sequence for the balance of the study; the undulating protocol alternated weekly between 10- to 12RM and 6- to 8RM. All subjects performed 3 sets of multiple exercises carried out 4 days per week.	12 weeks	Skinfold technique	No significant differences in lean mass between conditions
Simao et al. (693)	30 recreationally trained young men	Random assignment to either a linear or undulating periodized resistance training program. The linear protocol focused on local muscular endurance the first 4 weeks (2 × 12RM), hypertrophy the next 4 weeks (3 × 8RM), and strength the final 4 weeks (4 × 3RM); the undulating protocol varied these components every 2 weeks for 6 weeks and then repeated this schedule the next 6 weeks. All subjects performed multiple sets of 4 upper-body exercises.	12 weeks	Ultrasound	No significant differences in thickness of the biceps or triceps were noted between conditions, but only the undulating group showed significant increases from baseline in these measures.
Souza et al. (714)	31 recreationally active young men	Random assignment to a linear periodized, undulating periodized, or nonperiodized lower-body resistance training protocol. Those in the linear protocol performed 12RM in weeks 1 through 4 and 8RM in weeks 5 and 6; those in the undulating protocol rotated between 12 and 8 reps in weeks 1 through 4 and then between 6 and 10 reps in weeks 5 and 6; those in the nonperiodized protocol performed 8RM every session. Multiple sets were performed for 2 exercises. Training was carried out 2 days per week.	6 weeks	MRI	No significant differences in quadriceps CSA between conditions

Abbreviations: BIA = bioelectrical impedance analysis; RM = repetition maximum; CSA = cross-sectional area; MRI = magnetic resonance imaging.

macrocycle so that volume is high at the point at which a peak is desired.

Research comparing the hypertrophic adaptations of linear and reverse linear models is sparse (see table 6.3). In one of the few controlled studies on the topic, Prestes and colleagues (591) randomized a group of young women experienced in resistance training to perform either a traditional periodized program in which loads were progressively increased from 12- to 14RM to 4- to 6RM or a program in which the progression was reversed (from 4- to 6RM to 12- to 14RM). Both groups performed 3 sets of multiple exercises for the whole body, and training occurred 3 days per week over 12 weeks. Body composition as assessed by the skinfold method showed that subjects in the linear periodized group significantly increased fat-free mass by approximately 7%, whereas those in the reverse linear periodized group had nonsignificant increases of approximately 4%. Although these results are intriguing and somewhat counterintuitive, the use of skinfolds limits the ability to

draw any definitive conclusions about the difference in hypertrophic effects of the two periodization models.

Deloading Periods

The accretion of muscle proteins requires that the body be repeatedly challenged beyond its present state over time. However, persistently overtaxing the body's resources with excessive training and insufficient recovery ultimately leads to an *overtrained state* (i.e., the exhaustion phase of GAS). The upshot is an increase in the expression of catabolic proteins (atrogin-1) and a reduction in anabolic factors (MyoD, myogenin, and IGF-1), and a corresponding decrease in muscle cross-sectional area (25). There is evidence that such negative complications can be avoided by taking breaks from training. Animal research shows that chronic resistance training suppresses the phosphorylation of intracellular anabolic signaling, but signaling is restored after a brief period of detraining (545). Ogasawara and colleagues (544) demonstrated that taking a 3-week break from training at the midpoint of a 15-week resistance training program did not interfere with muscular adaptations. Follow-up work from the same lab found that repeated 3-week detraining and 6-week retraining cycles produced improvements in muscle cross-sectional area that were similar to those resulting from a continuous resistance training over a 6-month period (546).

KEY POINT

Both linear and nonlinear models of periodization seem to be equally viable for maximizing hypertrophy. Despite a logical basis, reverse periodization has not been shown to be more effective, but more research is needed to draw definitive conclusions.

TABLE 6.3 **Summary of Hypertrophy Training Studies Investigating Linear Versus Reverse Linear Periodization**

Study	Subjects	Design	Study duration	Hypertrophy measurement	Findings
Prestes et al. (591)	20 resistance-trained young women	Random assignment to either a linear periodization protocol beginning with 12- to 14RM and progressively increasing loads to finish with 4- to 6RM or a reverse linear protocol beginning with 4- to 6RM and progressively decreasing loads to finish with 12- to 14RM. All subjects performed 3 sets of 8 or 9 exercises 3 days per week.	12 weeks	Skinfold measurements	Greater increases in fat-free mass with linear periodization

Rather than taking time off from training, people may be able to enhance muscular adaptations via a *deloading period*—that is, systematically reducing training intensity or volume, or both. When properly executed, deloading promotes restoration and rejuvenation in a manner that facilitates continued progress (84). Unfortunately, no studies to date have attempted to quantify the extent of reductions in either volume or intensity (or both) to best promote hypertrophic gains. A 3:1 ratio (in weeks) of training and deloading is often recommended as a starting point. Modifications should then be made depending on the needs and abilities of the individual.

Periodizing Intensity of Load

As previously explained, sessions can be partitioned into loading zones encompassing heavy loads (1- to 5RM), moderate loads (8- to 12RM), and light loads (20+RM). A periodized approach to this variable can be carried out using either a linear or undulating model.

Table 6.4 illustrates a strategy for varying loads across a 3-day-per-week undulating program in which all muscles are trained in a session. Table 6.5 expands on the undulating program to a 4-day up per/lower split. Note that in this scenario all loading ranges are trained over the course of 10 days as opposed to 1 week in the 3-day full-body program.

TABLE 6.4 Sample 3-Day Undulating Periodized Program

Exercise	Sets	Repetitions	Rest interval
Monday (heavy)			
Bench press	4 or 5	3 to 5	3 minutes
Bent barbell row	4 or 5	3 to 5	3 minutes
Military press	4 or 5	3 to 5	3 minutes
Squat	4 or 5	3 to 5	3 minutes
Romanian deadlift	4 or 5	3 to 5	3 minutes
Wednesday (moderate)			
Incline press	3 or 4	8 to 12	2 minutes
Lat pulldown	3 or 4	8 to 12	2 minutes
Upright row	3 or 4	8 to 12	2 minutes
EZ curl	2 or 3	8 to 12	2 minutes
Overhead triceps extension	2 or 3	8 to 12	2 minutes
Leg press	3 or 4	8 to 12	2 minutes
Seated leg curl	3 or 4	8 to 12	2 minutes
Standing calf raise	2 or 3	8 to 12	2 minutes
Kneeling abdominal cable crunch	2 or 3	8 to 12	2 minutes
Friday (light)			
Dumbbell incline fly	2 or 3	15 to 25	30 to 60 seconds
Seated cable row	2 or 3	15 to 25	30 to 60 seconds
Machine lateral raise	2 or 3	15 to 25	30 to 60 seconds
Dumbbell hammer curl	2 or 3	15 to 25	30 to 60 seconds
Cable pushdown	2 or 3	15 to 25	30 to 60 seconds
Knee extension	2 or 3	15 to 25	30 to 60 seconds
Hyperextension	2 or 3	15 to 25	30 to 60 seconds
Seated calf raise	2 or 3	15 to 25	30 to 60 seconds
Reverse crunch	2 or 3	15 to 25	30 to 60 seconds

Concepts adapted from B.J. Schoenfeld, 2013, *The M.A.X. muscle plan* (Champaign, IL: Human Kinetics).

TABLE 6.5 Sample 4-Day Undulating Periodized Program

Exercise	Sets	Repetitions	Rest interval
Week 1			
Monday (heavy lower)			
Squat	5 or 6	3 to 5	3 minutes
Deadlift	5 or 6	3 to 5	3 minutes
Leg press	5 or 6	3 to 5	3 minutes
Glute to ham raise	5 or 6	3 to 5	3 minutes
Tuesday (heavy upper)			
Bench press	5 or 6	3 to 5	2 minutes
Weighted pull-up	5 or 6	3 to 5	2 minutes
Standing push-press	5 or 6	3 to 5	2 minutes
Barbell bent row	5 or 6	3 to 5	2 minutes
Thursday (moderate lower)			
Front squat	3 or 4	8 to 12	2 minutes
Bulgarian split squat	3 or 4	8 to 12	2 minutes
Barbell hip thrust	3 or 4	8 to 12	2 minutes
Romanian deadlift	3 or 4	8 to 12	2 minutes
Lying leg curl	3 or 4	8 to 12	2 minutes
Standing calf raise	3 or 4	8 to 12	2 minutes
Friday (moderate upper)			
Incline press	3 or 4	8 to 12	2 minutes
Flat dumbbell fly	3 or 4	8 to 12	2 minutes
Lat pulldown	3 or 4	8 to 12	2 minutes
One-arm dumbbell row	3 or 4	8 to 12	2 minutes
Military press	3 or 4	8 to 12	2 minutes
Machine lateral raise	3 or 4	8 to 12	2 minutes
Cable abdominal crunch	3 or 4	8 to 12	2 minutes
Week 2			
Monday (light lower)			
Dumbbell lunge	2 or 3	15 to 25	30 to 60 seconds
Knee extension	2 or 3	15 to 25	30 to 60 seconds
Cable glute hip extension	2 or 3	15 to 25	30 to 60 seconds
Seated leg curl	2 or 3	15 to 25	30 to 60 seconds
Reverse hyperextension	2 or 3	15 to 25	30 to 60 seconds
Seated calf raise	2 or 3	15 to 25	30 to 60 seconds
Tuesday (light upper)			
Hammer chest press	2 or 3	15 to 25	30 to 60 seconds
Cable fly	2 or 3	15 to 25	30 to 60 seconds
Cross cable pulldown	2 or 3	15 to 25	30 to 60 seconds
Seated pulley row	2 or 3	15 to 25	30 to 60 seconds
Dumbbell seated shoulder press	2 or 3	15 to 25	30 to 60 seconds
Dumbbell rear deltoid raise	2 or 3	15 to 25	30 to 60 seconds
Reverse crunch	2 or 3	15 to 25	30 to 60 seconds

Concepts adapted from B.J. Schoenfeld, 2013, *The M.A.X. muscle plan* (Champaign, IL: Human Kinetics).

Table 6.6 illustrates a modified linear approach to varied loading for hypertrophy. The length of each mesocycle is generally between 1 and 3 months, but it can be shorter or longer depending on the person's goals and abilities. Note that the hypertrophy mesocycle is at the end of the macrocycle so that growth peaks at this time.

TABLE 6.6 Sample Modified Linear Periodized Program for Loading

Exercise	Sets	Repetitions	Rest interval
Strength phase			
Microcycle 1: total body program, 3 weeks of training 3 days per week			
Monday, Wednesday, Friday			
Bench press	3	4 to 5	3 minutes
Barbell bent reverse row	3	4 to 5	3 minutes
Standing military press	3	4 to 5	3 minutes
Barbell squat	3	4 to 5	3 minutes
Deadlift	3	4 to 5	3 minutes
Microcycle 2 (deload): 1 week of training 2 days per week			
Monday, Thursday			
Incline chest fly	3	15 to 20	2 minutes
Front lat pulldown	3	15 to 20	2 minutes
Barbell upright row	3	15 to 20	2 minutes
Bulgarian squat	3	15 to 20	2 minutes
Lying hamstring curl	3	15 to 20	2 minutes
Standing calf raise	3	15 to 20	2 minutes
Microcycle 3: upper/lower split body, 3 weeks of training 4 days per week			
Monday, Thursday			
Barbell chest press	4 or 5	3 to 5	3 minutes
Incline dumbbell fly press	3	6 to 8	2 minutes
Barbell reverse row	4 or 5	3 to 5	3 minutes
Lat pulldown	3	6 to 8	2 minutes
Standing military press	4 or 5	3 to 5	3 minutes
Dumbbell lateral raise	3	6 to 8	2 minutes
Tuesday, Friday			
Squat	4 or 5	3 to 5	3 minutes
Deadlift	4 or 5	3 to 5	3 minutes
Good morning	3	6 to 8	2 minutes
Lying hamstring curl	3	6 to 8	2 minutes
Standing calf raise	3	6 to 8	2 minutes
Metabolic phase			
Microcycle 1: total body program, 3 weeks of training 3 days per week			
Monday, Wednesday, Friday			
Incline dumbbell chest press	3	15 to 25	30 to 60 seconds
One-arm dumbbell row	3	15 to 25	30 to 60 seconds
Dumbbell shoulder press	3	15 to 25	30 to 60 seconds

(continued)

Table 6.6 (*continued*)

Exercise	Sets	Repetitions	Rest interval
Microcycle 1: total body program, 3 weeks of training 3 days per week			
Monday, Wednesday, Friday			
Seated dumbbell curl	3	15 to 25	30 to 60 seconds
Dumbbell overhead triceps extension	3	15 to 25	30 to 60 seconds
Leg press	3	15 to 25	30 to 60 seconds
Lying hamstring curl	3	15 to 25	30 to 60 seconds
Standing calf raise	3	15 to 25	30 to 60 seconds
Microcycle 2 (deload): 1 week of training 2 days per week			
Monday, Thursday			
Incline chest fly	3	15 to 20	2 minutes
Front lat pulldown	3	15 to 20	2 minutes
Barbell upright row	3	15 to 20	2 minutes
Bulgarian squat	3	15 to 20	2 minutes
Lying hamstring curl	3	15 to 20	2 minutes
Standing calf raise	3	15 to 20	2 minutes
Hypertrophy phase			
Microcycle 1: total body program, 3 weeks of training 3 days per week			
Monday			
Dumbbell chest press	3 or 4	6 to 12	2 minutes
Seated pulley row	3 or 4	6 to 12	2 minutes
Military press	3 or 4	6 to 12	2 minutes
Incline dumbbell curl	2 or 3	6 to 12	2 minutes
Triceps pushdown	2 or 3	6 to 12	2 minutes
Front squat	3 or 4	6 to 12	2 minutes
Seated hamstring curl	3 or 4	6 to 12	2 minutes
Standing calf raise	3 or 4	6 to 12	2 minutes
Wednesday			
Incline barbell chest press	3 or 4	6 to 12	2 minutes
Lat pulldown	3 or 4	6 to 12	2 minutes
Cable lateral raise	3 or 4	6 to 12	2 minutes
Hammer curl	2 or 3	6 to 12	2 minutes
Lying triceps extension	2 or 3	6 to 12	2 minutes
Hack squat	3 or 4	6 to 12	2 minutes
Romanian deadlift	3 or 4	6 to 12	2 minutes
Seated calf raise	3 or 4	6 to 12	2 minutes
Friday			
Cable chest fly	3 or 4	6 to 12	2 minutes
One-arm dumbbell row	3 or 4	6 to 12	2 minutes
Rear delt raise	3 or 4	6 to 12	2 minutes
EZ curl	2 or 3	6 to 12	2 minutes
Overhead triceps extension	2 or 3	6 to 12	2 minutes
Leg press	3 or 4	6 to 12	2 minutes
Lying leg curl	3 or 4	6 to 12	2 minutes
Toe press	3 or 4	6 to 12	2 minutes

Exercise	Sets	Repetitions	Rest interval
Microcycle 2: (deload): 1 week of training 2 days per week			
Monday, Thursday			
Incline chest fly	3	15 to 20	2 minutes
Front lat pulldown	3	15 to 20	2 minutes
Barbell upright row	3	15 to 20	2 minutes
Bulgarian squat	3	15 to 20	2 minutes
Lying hamstring curl	3	15 to 20	2 minutes
Standing calf raise	3	15 to 20	2 minutes
Microcycle 3: upper/lower split body, 3 weeks of training 4 days per week			
Monday			
Barbell flat press	3 or 4	6 to 12	2 minutes
Incline dumbbell fly	3 or 4	6 to 12	2 minutes
Reverse lat pulldown	3 or 4	6 to 12	2 minutes
Seated wide grip cable row	3 or 4	6 to 12	2 minutes
Dumbbell shoulder press	3 or 4	6 to 12	2 minutes
Cable lateral raise	3 or 4	6 to 12	2 minutes
Barbell curl	3 or 4	6 to 12	2 minutes
Overhead dumbbell triceps extension	3 or 4	6 to 12	2 minutes
Tuesday			
Barbell split squat	3 or 4	6 to 12	2 minutes
Knee extension	3 or 4	6 to 12	2 minutes
Stiff-legged deadlift	3 or 4	6 to 12	2 minutes
Lying leg curl	3 or 4	6 to 12	2 minutes
Standing calf raise	3 or 4	6 to 12	2 minutes
Seated calf raise	3 or 4	6 to 12	2 minutes
Cable kneeling twisting rope crunch	3 or 4	6 to 12	2 minutes
Thursday			
Incline machine press	3 or 4	6 to 12	2 minutes
Pec deck	3 or 4	6 to 12	2 minutes
Chin-up	3 or 4	6 to 12	2 minutes
One-arm dumbbell row	3 or 4	6 to 12	2 minutes
Dumbbell shoulder press	3 or 4	6 to 12	2 minutes
Kneeling cable reverse fly	3 or 4	6 to 12	2 minutes
Dumbbell biceps curl	2 or 3	6 to 12	2 minutes
Dumbbell triceps kickback	2 or 3	6 to 12	2 minutes
Friday			
Leg press	3 or 4	6 to 12	2 minutes
Dumbbell side lunge	3 or 4	6 to 12	2 minutes
Hyperextension	3 or 4	6 to 12	2 minutes
Seated leg curl	3 or 4	6 to 12	2 minutes
Seated calf raise	3 or 4	6 to 12	2 minutes
Toe press	3 or 4	6 to 12	2 minutes
Reverse crunch	3 or 4	6 to 12	2 minutes

(continued)

Table 6.6 *(continued)*

Exercise	Sets	Repetitions	Rest interval
Microcycle 4: (deload): 1 week of training 2 days per week			
Monday, Thursday			
Incline chest fly	3	15 to 20	2 minutes
Front lat pulldown	3	15 to 20	2 minutes
Barbell upright row	3	15 to 20	2 minutes
Bulgarian squat	3	15 to 20	2 minutes
Lying hamstring curl	3	15 to 20	2 minutes
Standing calf raise	3	15 to 20	2 minutes
Microcycle 5: 3-way split-body, 3 weeks of training 6 days per week			
Monday, Friday			
Lat pulldown	3 or 4	6 to 12	2 minutes
One-arm dumbbell row	3 or 4	6 to 12	2 minutes
Dumbbell pullover	3 or 4	6 to 12	2 minutes
Incline barbell press	3 or 4	6 to 12	2 minutes
Decline dumbbell press	3 or 4	6 to 12	2 minutes
Cable fly	3 or 4	6 to 12	2 minutes
Barbell abdominal rollout	3 or 4	6 to 12	2 minutes
Twisting crunch	3 or 4	6 to 12	2 minutes
Tuesday, Saturday			
Barbell back squat	3 or 4	6 to 12	2 minutes
Dumbbell lunge	3 or 4	6 to 12	2 minutes
Knee extension	3 or 4	6 to 12	2 minutes
Hip thrust	3 or 4	6 to 12	2 minutes
Barbell stiff-legged deadlift	3 or 4	6 to 12	2 minutes
Leg curl	3 or 4	6 to 12	2 minutes
Standing calf raise	3 or 4	6 to 12	2 minutes
Seated calf raise	3 or 4	6 to 12	2 minutes
Wednesday, Sunday			
Barbell military press	3 or 4	6 to 12	2 minutes
Machine lateral raise	3 or 4	6 to 12	2 minutes
Machine rear delt fly	3 or 4	6 to 12	2 minutes
Cable overhead triceps extension	2 or 3	6 to 12	2 minutes
Hammer curl	2 or 3	6 to 12	2 minutes
Lying triceps extension	2 or 3	6 to 12	2 minutes
Concentration curl	2 or 3	6 to 12	2 minutes
Cable triceps kickback	2 or 3	6 to 12	2 minutes
Dumbbell incline curl	2 or 3	6 to 12	2 minutes
Microcycle 6 (active recovery): 1 week of light recreational activity only			

Concepts adapted from B.J. Schoenfeld, 2013, *The M.A.X. muscle plan* (Champaign, IL: Human Kinetics).

Figure 6.7 shows how a step-loading approach can be employed in the context of a linear model. Step loading involves a progressive increase in intensity of load over a period of weekly microcycles followed by a deloading period of substantially reduced intensity. This structure creates a wavelike loading pattern that allows the use of a broad spectrum of repetitions within a target repetition range while reducing the potential for overtraining. The example in figure 6.7 is specific to a hypertrophy mesocycle, but the concept is applicable to any loading zone.

Periodizing Volume and Frequency

A clear dose–response relationship has been found between volume and hypertrophy; higher training volumes correlate with greater muscle protein accretion, at least up to a given threshold. However, consistently training with high volumes will inevitably overtax recuperative abilities, leading to an overtrained state. Excessive volume has been shown to have a greater propensity for resulting in overtraining than consistently training at very high intensities. A logical solution is to increase training volume progressively over the course of a training cycle.

The hypertrophy phase in table 6.6 illustrates a strategy for systematically increasing volume across a training cycle. This strategy can be used in both linear and undulating models. Microcycle 1 shows a 3-day-per-week routine in which all major muscles are trained in each workout session. In this scheme training would generally be carried out on nonconsecutive days (e.g., Mondays, Wednesdays, and Fridays); the other days are reserved for recovery. Microcycle 3 increases frequency to 4 days per week employing an upper-body/lower-body split routine. This type of routine is often carried out on a 2-on/1-off, 2-on/2-off basis (e.g., training on Mondays, Tuesdays, Thursdays, and Fridays). Although training volume remains the same on a per-session basis, total weekly volume is greater because of the higher frequency of training. Microcycle 5 increases frequency to 6 days per week employing a traditional bodybuilding-style split routine. Typically training in this type of protocol is carried on a 3-on/1-off basis (e.g., training on Mondays, Tuesdays, Wednesdays, Fridays, Saturdays, and Sundays). Again, the per-session training volume remains constant, as with the previous protocols, but weekly volume is further increased as a result of more frequent training.

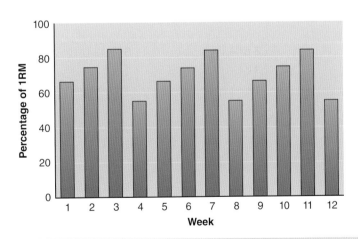

FIGURE 6.7   The wavelike loading pattern of step loading in a hypertrophy mesocycle.

TAKE-HOME POINTS

- A number of biomechanical considerations need to be taken into account when selecting exercises for a hypertrophy-oriented program. These include length–tension relationship, training angle, plane of movement, spacing of hands and feet, and exercise type.

- The application of biomechanical principles to exercise selection is specific to a given muscle, its architecture, and the joint at which it originates. Combining exercises based on applied anatomy and kinesiology is essential to ensure the complete development of the major musculature.

- Hypertrophy-oriented training programs should be periodized to promote continued gains while reducing the risk of overtraining. A number of periodized models can be employed to maximize muscle mass, including linear, undulating, and reverse linear approaches. Research has not shown any model to be superior over another, and each can thus be considered a viable strategy in program design. Importantly, periodization is a general concept, not a rigid training system; thus, the implementation of the models should be adapted based on the needs and abilities of the lifter.

- Deload periods of reduced intensity, volume, or both, should be integrated into periodized programs to facilitate rejuvenation and recovery. A 3:1 ratio (in weeks) of training and deloading is a good guideline to use as a starting point. Modifications should then be made depending on individual response.

Nutrition for Hypertrophy

Proper nutrition is essential to maximizing muscle growth. This chapter focuses on the aspects of nutrition as they pertain to muscle hypertrophy; any discussion about fat loss is restricted to how it relates to the regulation of skeletal muscle mass. Moreover, the discussion is specific to healthy people; dietary intake in those with morbidities is not addressed, nor are the implications of diet on general health and wellness.

The chapter assumes a general understanding of nutritional biochemistry. Although basic principles are presented to provide appropriate context, a detailed exploration of the nuances of the topic is beyond the scope of this book. Those interested in exploring its intricacies further are referred to the excellent resource *Advanced Nutrition and Human Metabolism*, by Gropper and Smith.

Energy Balance

Energy balance, the net result between energy intake and energy expenditure, has a profound effect on the capacity to build muscle. Molecular signaling is altered during short-term energy deficits to favor catabolism over anabolism. Studies show that caloric restriction induces a decrease in both Akt phosphorylation and muscle protein synthesis, leading to activation of the FOXO family of transcription factors and upregulation of atrogin-1 and MuRF-1 expression (562). Moreover, nutrient deprivation activates AMPK and NAD-dependent deacetylases, such as sirtuin

1, which in turn blunt mTOR phosphorylation (478). Because AMPK concurrently impairs translational processes while heightening high-oxidative gene expression and proteolysis, a caloric deficit would induce a high rate of protein turnover that would limit increases in myofiber size (784).

Eucaloric conditions (i.e., an equal caloric intake and energy expenditure; also called *energy balance* or *caloric balance*) are suboptimal for inducing muscle growth as well. During periods of energy balance, the recurrent catabolism of proteins occurring in bodily organs and vital tissues is replenished in the postabsorptive state via amino acids derived predominantly from skeletal muscle (478). Although resistance training counteracts these losses, the anabolic response is nevertheless blunted, which compromises hypertrophic growth.

Alternatively, a positive energy balance alone is a potent stimulator of anabolism, even in the absence of resistance exercise training, provided that the intake of dietary protein is adequate (140). Combining resistance training with an energy surplus enhances the anabolic effect: gains in fat-free mass increase from 38% to 46% of the total weight gain achieved by sedentary subjects to as much as 100% in trained subjects (242).

The amount of lean tissue gains associated with a combined energy surplus and resistance varies with training status. Rozenek and colleagues (632) reported that untrained subjects gained approximately 3 kg (6.6 lb) in 8 weeks when resistance training was combined with an energy surplus of approximately 2,000 kcal/day; a control group consuming a eucaloric diet did not significantly increase body mass. Virtually the entire amount of weight gain in the group consuming an energy surplus was attributed to the accretion of fat-free mass. In a study of elite athletes, Garthe and colleagues (242) randomized subjects to a diet designed to provide a surplus of approximately 500 kcal/day or an *ad libitum* intake (however much the person wants to consume). All subjects participated in the same 4-day-per-week hypertrophy-type resistance training program, which was carried out over a period of 8 to 12 weeks. Results showed a greater increase in fat-free mass in favor of those in a caloric surplus versus those at maintenance (1.7 vs. 1.2 kg, or 3.7 vs. 2.6 lb, respectively), although the results did not reach statistical significance. Interestingly, the differences in fat-free mass between the groups was specific to the lower-body musculature, where a significant advantage was noted for those in an energy surplus. Greater increases in fat-free mass associated with the energy surplus were accompanied by an increased fat deposition compared to the eucaloric condition (1.1 vs. 0.2 kg, or 2.4 vs. 0.4 lb, respectively). Thus, well-trained people appear to use less of the surplus for lean tissue–building purposes; a higher amount goes toward adipose tissue. It is not clear what, if any, effect an even greater energy surplus would have had on body composition changes.

Beyond a certain point, overconsumption of energy has a negative impact on muscle growth. When macronutrient intake exceeds

KEY POINT

To a degree, combining resistance training with a positive energy balance increases the anabolic effect; untrained people experience large gains in fat-free mass. Well-trained people use less of the energy surplus for lean tissue building and should therefore aim for a lower positive energy balance.

bodily requirements to maintain homeostasis and energy production for cellular processes, skeletal muscle can ultimately become resistant to insulin. This occurs via a dysregulation of the insulin signaling pathway and leads to protein catabolism (478). Relatively untrained subjects can benefit from a substantial energy surplus (~2,000 kcal/d); in this population, body mass gains are predominantly achieved by increasing fat-free mass at the expense of body fat. In well-trained subjects, evidence suggests that a positive energy balance of 500 to 1,000 kcal/day is preferable for increasing fat-free mass (242). The discrepancy between populations can be attributed to the fact that untrained subjects have a higher hypertrophic potential and faster rate of growth than trained subjects do, which accommodates more energy and substrate for building new tissue.

Macronutrient Intake

In addition to energy balance, the consumption of macronutrients (protein, carbohydrate, and lipid) is also of great importance from a nutritional standpoint. Each macronutrient is discussed in this section in terms of its relevance to muscle hypertrophy, along with practical recommendations for intake.

Protein

Dietary protein provides 4 kcal of energy per g and comprises chains of *amino acids* (nitrogenous substances containing both amino and acid groups). Over 300 amino acids have been identified in nature, but only 20 of them serve as the building blocks of bodily proteins. The anabolic effects of nutrition are primarily driven by the transfer and incorporation of amino acids obtained from dietary protein sources into bodily tissues (49). Because of variations in their side chains, the biochemical properties and functions of amino acids differ substantially (839).

Amino acids can be classified as *essential* (indispensable) or *nonessential* (dispensable). Essential amino acids (EAAs) cannot be synthesized adequately to support the body's needs and thus must be provided through the diet. Nonessential amino acids, on the other hand, can be synthesized by the body. Deprivation of even a single EAA impairs the synthesis of virtually all cellular proteins via an inhibition of the initiation phase of mRNA translation (220). Certain amino acids are classified as *conditionally essential* if they are required in the diet when amino acid use is greater than its rate of synthesis (839). Importantly, all 20 amino acids are necessary for proper cell function and growth. Table 7.1 lists the essential, nonessential, and conditionally essential amino acids.

An increase in plasma and myocellular amino acids above fasting levels initiates an anabolic response characterized by robust elevations in muscle protein synthesis. Under resting conditions this response is very transient; maximal stimulation of muscle protein synthesis occurs approximately 2 hours after amino acid ingestion and then rapidly returns to postabsorptive levels (561). Thus, muscles are receptive to the anabolic effects for a relatively short period of time in the nonexercised state.

Effect on Performance

Exercise potentiates the anabolic effect of protein intake, heightening both the magnitude and duration of the response (49). After a brief latency period, dramatic increases in muscle protein synthesis are seen between 45 and 150 min postworkout, and elevations are sustained for up to 4 hours in the fasted state (49). Despite this exercise-induced increase in muscle protein synthesis, postexercise net protein balance remains negative in the absence of nutrient consumption (220). Provision of EAAs rapidly reverses this process so that protein balance becomes positive, and anabolic sensitivity is sustained for longer than 24 hours (49).

The essential amino acid leucine, one of the *branched-chain amino acids* (BCAAs), is believed to be particularly important to the regulation of muscle mass. Leucine has been shown to stimulate muscle protein synthesis both in vitro and in vivo. The mechanism of action appears to be the result of an enhanced translation initiation mediated by increased mTOR phosphorylation (561, 839). This contention is supported by findings that activation of mTOR is relatively unaffected by the other two BCAAs, valine and isoleucine (839). Leucine also has a positive effect on protein balance by attenuating muscle protein breakdown via the inhibition of autophagy (839). The influence of leucine is limited to the activation of muscle protein synthesis, not the duration; sustaining elevated muscle protein synthesis levels appears to rely on sufficient intake of the other EAAs, especially the BCAAs (578).

Some researchers have proposed the concept of a *leucine threshold* (also termed *leucine trigger*); they postulate that a certain concentration

TABLE 7.1 **Essential, Nonessential, and Conditionally Essential Amino Acids**

Essential amino acids	Nonessential amino acids
Histidine	Alanine
Isoleucine	Arginine*
Leucine	Asparagine*
Lysine	Aspartic acid
Methionine	Cysteine
Phenylalanine	Glutamic acid
Threonine	Glutamine*
Tryptophan	Glycine*
Valine	Proline*
	Serine*
	Tyrosine*

*Conditionally essential amino acids.

of leucine in the blood must be reached to maximally trigger muscle protein synthesis (294). Research shows that a 2 g oral dose of leucine (equating to approximately 20 g of a high-quality protein such as whey or egg) is necessary to attain the threshold in young, healthy people (505), although variations in body size would seemingly mitigate this amount. Leucine requirements are heightened in the elderly. The aging process results in desensitization of muscles to EAAs (i.e., an anabolic resistance), whereby older people require larger per-meal doses than their younger counterparts (190). Mechanistically, this is thought to be due to a dysregulation of mTORC1 signaling (see chapter 2), which in turn necessitates a higher leucinemia to trigger elevations in muscle protein synthesis (577). Katsanos and colleagues (353) found that 6.7 g of EAAs—an amount shown to be sufficient to elicit a marked anabolic response in young people—was insufficient to elevate muscle protein synthesis above rest in an elderly group; only after supplementation with 1.7 to 2.8 g of leucine did a robust increase occur. The findings suggest that older people require approximately double the amount of leucine per serving that younger people require to reach the leucine threshold.

It should be noted that the dose–response anabolic effects of leucine are maxed out once the threshold is attained; increasing intake beyond this point has no additional effect on muscle protein synthesis either at rest or following resistance exercise (561). Moreover, longitudinal studies in animal models have failed to show increased protein accretion from leucine supplementation in the absence of other amino acids (197, 436). This raises the possibility that supplementation of leucine alone results in an EAA imbalance that impairs transcriptional or translational function, or both. Alternatively, although leucine supplementation triggers the activation of muscle protein synthesis, the duration may not be sufficient to produce substantial synthesis of contractile elements. Either way, the findings reinforce the need for adequate consumption of the full complement of EAAs in promoting muscular development.

Requirements

The accretion of lean mass depends on meeting daily dietary protein needs. The RDA for protein is 0.8 g/kg of body mass. This recommendation is based on the premise that such an amount is sufficient for 98% of healthy adults to remain in a nonnegative nitrogen balance. However, the RDA, although adequate for those who are largely sedentary, cannot be generalized to a resistance-trained population. For one, the maintenance of nitrogen balance indicates that day-to-day protein losses are offset by the synthesis of new bodily proteins; gaining muscle requires a positive nitrogen balance (i.e., protein synthesis exceeds degradation over time). Moreover, intense exercise substantially increases protein turnover, heightening the need for additional substrate. In addition, the nitrogen balance technique has serious technical drawbacks that can result in lower-than-optimal protein requirements (578). Considering the totality of these factors, the protein needs of those seeking to maximize muscle size are substantially higher than those listed in the RDA guidelines.

KEY POINT

It is important to ingest protein, and especially leucine, after resistance exercise to sustain muscle protein synthesis postworkout. Those seeking to maximize muscle size need substantially more protein than the RDA guidelines propose. Older adults require more protein than younger adults do to build appreciable muscle.

A number of studies have been carried out to determine protein requirements for those involved in resistance training. Lemon and colleagues (415) found that novice bodybuilders in the early phase of intense training required approximately 1.6 to 1.7 g/kg/day—approximately double the RDA. Similar findings have been reported by other researchers (745). This increased protein requirement is necessary to offset the oxidation of amino acids during exercise as well as to supply substrate for lean tissue accretion and the repair of exercise-induced muscle damage (118). The dose–response relationship between protein intake and hypertrophy appears to top out at approximately 2.0 g/kg/day (118); consuming substantially larger amounts of dietary protein does not result in further increases in lean tissue mass. There is even some evidence that protein requirements actually decrease in well-trained people. Moore and colleagues (504) found that heavy resistance exercise reduced whole-body leucine turnover in previously untrained young men; an intake of approximately 1.4 g/kg/day was adequate to maintain a positive nitrogen balance over 12 weeks of training. The findings suggest that regimented resistance training causes the body to become more efficient at using available amino acids for lean tissue synthesis, thereby mitigating the need for higher protein intakes.

Optimal total daily protein intake depends on both energy balance status and body composition. Phillips and Van Loon (578) estimated that a protein intake of up to 2.7 g/kg/day was needed during hypoenergetic periods to avoid lean tissue losses. Helms and colleagues (300) made similar recommendations, suggesting an intake of up to 3.1 g/kg/day of fat-free mass in lean, calorically restricted people. It has been theorized that the higher protein dosage in this population promotes phosphorylation of PBK/Akt and FOXO proteins, suppressing the proteolytic factors associated with caloric restriction and thus enhancing lean tissue preservation (478).

Quality

Protein quality also must be taken into consideration with respect to the accretion of skeletal muscle mass. The quality of a protein is primarily a function of its composition of EAAs, in terms of both quantity and proportion. A *complete protein* contains a full complement of all nine EAAs in the approximate amounts needed to support lean tissue maintenance. Alternatively, proteins low in one or more of the EAAs are considered *incomplete proteins*. With the exception of gel-

atin, all animal-based proteins are complete proteins. Vegetable-based proteins, on the other hand, lack various EAAs, which makes them incomplete.

A number of indices are used to assess the quality of protein sources (see table 7.2). The protein digestibility–corrected amino acid score (PDCAA) is perhaps the most widely used index; a score of 1.0 indicates that the protein is of high quality. PDCAA scores for whey, casein, and soy are all >1.0, implying that there is no difference in their effects on protein accretion. Comparative studies of isolated proteins indicate that this is not the case. Wilkinson and colleagues (827) demonstrated that the postexercise ingestion of a serving of skim milk containing 18 g of protein stimulated muscle protein synthesis to a greater extent than an isonitrogenous, isoenergetic serving of soy. Follow-up work by Tang and colleagues (742) showed that 10 g of EAAs provided by whey hydrolysate (a *fast-acting protein*) promoted markedly greater increases in mixed muscle protein synthesis after both rest and exercise compared to soy protein isolate and casein (*slow-acting proteins*). It is speculated that the fast-digesting nature of whey is responsible for this enhanced anabolic response. Theoretically, the rapid assimilation of leucine into circulation following whey consumption triggers anabolic processes to a greater extent than the slower assimilation of leucine following soy and casein consumption (578). Emerging evidence indicates the potential superiority of a blend of rapidly and slowly absorbed proteins compared to a fast-acting protein alone. Specifically, it is theorized that the addition of casein to a serving of whey results in a slower but more prolonged *aminoacidemia* (heightened amount of amino acids in the blood), which leads to higher nitrogen retention and less oxidation and therefore a prolonged muscle protein synthetic response (607). To generalize, high-quality fast-digesting proteins robustly stimulate muscle protein synthesis during the first 3 hours after consumption, whereas slow-digesting proteins exert a more graded stimulatory effect over 6 to 8 hours (181).

TABLE 7.2 Proteins and Their Respective Qualitative Scores on Commonly Used Measurement Scales

Protein source	PDCAAS	BV	PER
Casein	1.00	77	2.5
Whey	1.00	104	3.2
Egg	1.00	100	3.9
Soy	1.00	74	2.2
Beef	0.92	80	2.9
Black beans	0.75	—	—
Peanuts	0.52	—	1.8
Wheat gluten	0.25	64	0.8

PDCAAS = protein digestibility–corrected amino acid score; BV = biological value; PER = protein efficiency ratio.
Data from Hoffman and Falvo 2004.

PRACTICAL APPLICATIONS

METHODS FOR ASSESSING PROTEIN QUALITY

Several methods have been developed to determine the quality of protein in a given food. These include the protein digestibility–corrected amino acid score (PDCAAS), protein efficiency ratio (PER), chemical score (CS), biological value (BV), and net protein utilization (NPU). Each method uses its own criteria for assessing protein quality, which is ultimately a function of a food's essential amino acid composition and the digestibility and bioavailability of its amino acids (64 5). For example, the CS method analyzes the content of each essential amino acid in a food, which is then divided by the content of the same amino acid in egg protein (considered to have a CS of 100). Somewhat similarly, the PDCAAS method is based on a comparison of the EAA content of a test protein with that of a reference EAA profile, but, as the name implies, it also takes into account the effects of digestion. The PER method takes a completely different approach; it measures weight gain in young rats that are fed a test protein as compared to every gram of consumed protein. Alternatively, both the BV and NPU methods are based on nitrogen balance: BV measures the nitrogen retained in the body and divides it by the total amount of nitrogen absorbed from dietary protein, whereas NPU simply compares the amount of protein consumed to the amount stored.

Given the inherent differences in the protein quality measured, the methods can result in large discrepancies in the reported quality of protein-containing foods. Determining which single method is the best is difficult, but a case can be made that the PDCAAS and BV methods are the most relevant to human growth because they take protein digestibility into account. That said, because each method has drawbacks, the best approach to assessing protein quality is to take multiple measures—particularly PDCAAS and BV—into account.

Caution must be exercised when attempting to draw practical conclusions from the findings. Given that that the aforementioned studies measured muscle protein synthesis over short periods, they do not reflect the extended anabolic impact of protein consumption following an exercise bout. There is little evidence that consuming specific protein sources has a tangible impact on hypertrophic outcomes for those who consume adequate quantities of animal-based foods. Vegans have to be more cognizant of protein quality. Because vegetable proteins are largely incomplete, vegans must focus on eating the right combination of foods to ensure the adequate consumption of EAAs. For example, grains are limited in lysine and threonine, and legumes are low in methionine. Combining the two offsets the deficits, thereby helping to prevent a deficiency. Note that these foods do not have to be eaten in the same meal; they just need to be included in the diet on a regular basis.

Table 7.3 provides a summary of the protein intake recommendations to maximize hypertrophy.

Carbohydrate

Carbohydrates are plant-based compounds that, similar to dietary protein, also provide 4 kcal/g of energy. In broad terms, carbohydrates can be classified as either *simple* (monosaccharides and disaccharides composed of one or two sugar molecules, respectively) or *polysaccharides* (containing many sugar molecules). To be used by the body, carbohydrates must be broken down into monosaccharides, of

which there are three types: glucose, fructose, and galactose. These monosaccharides are then used as immediate sources of energy or stored for future use.

Carbohydrate is not essential in the diet because the body can manufacture the glucose needed by tissues through gluconeogenesis. Amino acids and the glycerol portion of triglycerides serve as substrate for glucose production, particularly in the absence of dietary carbohydrate. Nevertheless, there is a sound logical basis for including carbohydrate-rich foods in the diet when the goal is maximal hypertrophy.

First and foremost, as much as 80% of ATP production during moderate-repetition resistance training is derived from glycolysis (402). Substantial reductions in muscle glycogen therefore limit ATP regeneration during resistance exercise, leading to an inability to sustain muscular contractility at high force outputs. In addition, a distinct pool of glycogen is localized in close contact with key proteins involved in calcium release from the sarcoplasmic reticulum; a decrease in these stores is believed to hasten the onset of muscular fatigue via an inhibition of calcium release (552). Because of glycogen's importance as both a substrate and mediator of intracellular calcium, multiple studies have shown performance decrements in low-glycogen states. Leveritt and Abernethy (417) found that muscle glycogen depletion significantly decreased the number of repetitions performed in 3 sets of squats at 80% of 1RM. Similar impairments in anaerobic performance have been noted as a result of following a low-carbohydrate diet (408). Reduced glycogen levels also have been reported to diminish isometric strength performance (302) and augment exercise-induced muscle weakness (853). Low glycogen levels can be particularly problematic during higher-volume routines, because the resulting fatigue is associated with reduced energy production from glycogenolysis (700, 810).

Effect on Performance

Although dietary carbohydrate has been shown to enhance exercise performance, only

TABLE 7.3 Macronutrient Recommendations for Maximizing Hypertrophy

Macronutrient	Recommended intake
Protein	1.7–2.0 g/kg/day
Carbohydrate	≥3 g/kg/day
Dietary fat	≥1 g/kg/day ≥1.6 and 1.1 g/day* of omega-3 fatty acids for men and women, respectively

*An absolute amount, not relative to body weight.

moderate amounts appear to be required to achieve beneficial effects. Mitchell and colleagues (498) found that a diet consisting of 65% carbohydrate had no greater effect on the amount of work performed during 15 sets of 15RM lower-body exercise compared to a 40% carbohydrate diet. Similarly, a low-carbohydrate diet (25% of total calories) was shown to significantly reduce time to exhaustion during supramaximal exercise, but a high-carbohydrate diet (70% of total calories) did not improve performance compared to a control diet of 50% carbohydrate (422). In contrast, Paoli and colleagues (558) reported that following a *ketogenic diet* (a diet containing less than 50 g of carbohydrate daily) for 30 days did not negatively affect anaerobic performance in a group of elite gymnasts. It is possible that these subjects became keto adapted and therefore were better able to sustain muscular function during intense exercise. A confounding factor is that subjects in the keto group consumed substantially higher amounts of dietary protein than did subjects in the control group (201 vs. 84 g, respectively). Accordingly, those in the keto group lost more body fat and retained more lean mass, which may have helped to nullify any performance decrements over time.

Glycogen also may have a direct influence on muscle hypertrophy by mediating intracellular signaling. These actions are presumably carried out via regulatory effects on AMPK. As discussed in chapter 2, AMPK acts as a cellular energy sensor that facilitates energy availability. This is accomplished by inhibiting energy-consuming processes including the phosphorylation of mTORC1, as well as amplifying catabolic processes such as glycol-ysis, beta-oxidation, and protein degradation (259). Glycogen has been shown to suppress purified AMPK in cell-free assays (467), and glycogen depletion correlates with heightened AMPK activity in humans in vivo (835). Moreover, ketogenic diets impair mTOR signaling in rats, which is theorized to explain its antiepileptic actions (841).

Evidence suggests that low glycogen levels alter exercise-induced intracellular signaling. Creer and colleagues (160) randomized trained aerobic endurance athletes to perform 3 sets of 10 repetitions of knee extensions with a load equating to 70% of 1RM after following either a low-carbohydrate diet (2% of total calories) or a high-carbohydrate diet (77% of total calories). Muscle glycogen content was markedly lower in the low- compared to high-carbohydrate condition (~174 vs. ~591 mmol/kg dry weight). Early-phase Akt phosphorylation was significantly elevated only in the presence of high glycogen stores; phosphorylation of mTOR mimicked the Akt response, although the ERK1/2 pathway was relatively unaffected by muscle glycogen content status. Glycogen inhibition also has been shown to impede $p70^{S6K}$ activation, inhibit translation, and decrease the number of mRNA of genes responsible for regulating muscle growth (139, 175). Conversely, Camera and colleagues (117) reported that glycogen levels had no effect on anabolic signaling or muscle protein synthetic responses during the early postworkout recovery period following performance of a multiset lower-body resistance training protocol. A plausible explanation for contradictions between studies is not yet clear.

Research also shows that carbohydrate intake influences hormone production. Testosterone concentrations were consistently higher in healthy males following 10 days of high-carbohydrate compared to low-carbohydrate consumption (468 vs. 371 ng/dL, respectively), despite the fact that the diets were equal in total calories and fat (34). These changes were paralleled by lower cortisol concentrations in high- versus low-carbohydrate intake. Similar findings are seen when carbohydrate restriction is combined with vigorous exercise. Lane and colleagues (404)

KEY POINT

A moderate amount of dietary carbohydrate is needed for enhancing exercise performance. It is unclear how much carbohydrate intake is needed for maximizing exercise-induced muscle hypertrophy, but 3 g/kg/day is a reasonable starting point.

reported significant decreases of over 40% in the free-testosterone-to-cortisol ratio in a group of athletes consuming 30% of calories from carbohydrate following 3 consecutive days of intense training; no alterations were seen in a comparative group of athletes who consumed 60% of total calories as carbohydrate. Whether such alterations in hormone production negatively affect muscular adaptations is unknown.

Despite a compelling basis for the notion that carbohydrate is important for building muscle, few longitudinal studies have compared hypertrophic adaptations in low- versus high-carbohydrate diets. In a recent study, Wilson and colleagues (personal correspondence) were the first to investigate the topic in a controlled fashion. Subjects were randomized to follow either a ketogenic (5% carbohydrate) or Western (55% carbohydrate) diet; protein intake was equated between groups. Regimented resistance exercise was carried out 3 times per week, employing a combination bodybuilding- and strength-type training program. After 8 weeks, lean body mass was greater in the group following the Western diet. However, retesting of lean body mass subsequent to a 1-week carb-up period in the ketogenic group showed that the observed hypertrophic advantages of the Western diet disappeared. These findings indicate that muscle protein accretion was similar regardless of the amount of carbohydrate intake; any differences are seemingly the result of glycogen-induced intracellular water variances. Further study is needed for getting a better perspective on how varying carbohydrate intake affects exercise-induced muscle hypertrophy.

Requirements

Based on current evidence, no definitive conclusions can be made for ideal carbohydrate intake from the standpoint of maximizing hypertrophic gains. Slater and Phillips (700) proposed an intake of 4 to 7 g/kg/day for strength-type athletes, including bodybuilders. Although this recommendation is reasonable, its basis is somewhat arbitrary and does not take into account large interindividual variations with respect to dietary response. The use of carbohydrate as a fuel source both at rest and during exercise of various intensities varies by as much as 4-fold among athletes; it is influenced by a diverse array of factors including muscle fiber composition, diet, age, training, glycogen levels, and genetics (299). At the very least, it would seem prudent to consume enough carbohydrate to maintain fully-stocked glycogen stores. The amount needed to accomplish this task varies based on a number of factors (e.g., body size, source of carbohydrate, volume of exercise), but a minimum intake of approximately 3 g/kg/day would seem to be sufficient. Additional carbohydrate intake should then be considered in the context of individual preference and response to training.

Table 7.3 provides a summary of the recommended intake of carbohydrate to maximize hypertrophy.

Dietary Fat

Fat, also known as *lipid*, is an essential nutrient that plays a vital role in many bodily functions. These functions include cushioning the internal organs for protection; aiding in the absorption of vitamins; and facilitating the production of cell membranes, hormones, and prostaglandins. At 9 kcal/g, fat provides more than twice the energy per unit as protein or carbohydrate.

Dietary fat is classified into two basic categories: *saturated fatty acids* (SFAs), which have a hydrogen atom on both sides of every carbon atom (i.e., the carbons are saturated with hydrogens), and *unsaturated fatty acids*, which contain one or more double bonds in their carbon chain. Fats with one double bond are called *monounsaturated fatty acids* (MUFAs), of which oleate is the most common. Fats with two or more double bonds are called *polyunsaturated fatty acids* (PUFAs). There are two primary classes of PUFAs: omega-6 linoleate (also called *omega-6* or n-6 *fatty acids*) and omega-3 alpha-linolenate (also called *omega-3* or n-3 *fatty acids*). Because of an absence of certain enzymes, these fats cannot be manufactured by the human body and are therefore an essential component in food.

Further subclassification of fats can be made based on the length of their carbon chains. The chains range between 4 and 24 carbon atoms, and hydrogen atoms surround the carbon atoms. Fatty acids with chains of 4 to 6 carbons are called *short-chain fatty acids*; those with chains of 8 to 12 carbons are called *medium-chain fatty acids*, and whose with more than 12 carbons are called *long-chain fatty acids*.

Effect on Performance

Dietary fat consumption has little if any effect on resistance performance. As previously noted, resistance training derives energy primarily from anaerobic processes. Glycolysis, particularly fast glycolysis, is the primary energy system driving moderate-repetition, multiset protocols (402). Although intramuscular triglyceride does provide an additional fuel source during heavy resistance training (206), the contribution of fat is not a limiting factor in anaerobic exercise capacity.

Fat consumption has been shown to have an impact on testosterone concentrations. Testosterone is derived from cholesterol, a lipid. Accordingly, low-fat diets are associated with a modest reduction in testosterone production (186, 279). The relationship between dietary fat and hormone production is complex, however, and is interrelated with energy intake, macronutrient ratios, and perhaps even the types of dietary fats consumed (799). Moreover, very high-fat meals actually have been shown to suppress testosterone concentrations (800). There appears to be an upper and lower threshold for dietary fat intake to optimize testosterone production, above or below which hormone production may be impaired (641). What, if any, effect these modest alterations in testosterone levels within a normal physiological range have on hypertrophy remains uncertain at this time.

Evidence shows that the type of dietary fat consumed has a direct influence on body composition. Rosqvist and colleagues (628) demonstrated that overfeeding young men and women of normal weight foods high in *n*-6 fatty acids caused an increase in lean tissue mass approximately 3-fold compared

to comparable overfeeding with saturated fats. It is conceivable that results were related to differential effects on cell membrane fluidity between the types of fats consumed. Specifically, PUFAs have been shown to enhance the fluidity of the membrane, whereas SFAs have the opposite effect (514). Cell membranes serve a critical role in regulating the passage of nutrients, hormones, and chemical signals into and out of cells. When membranes harden, they are desensitized to external stimuli, inhibiting cellular processes including protein synthesis. Alternatively, cell membranes that are more fluid have an increased permeability, allowing substances and secondary messenger molecules associated with protein synthesis to readily penetrate the cytoplasm (711). This provides a physiological basis for a beneficial impact of PUFAs on muscle protein synthesis, compared to the negative effects of excess SFAs, which reduce the fluidity of the cell membrane (88).

The *n*-3 fatty acids are believed to have a particularly important role in protein metabolism. A number of studies show that *n*-3 fatty acid supplementation results in greater accretion of muscle proteins compared to other types of fats in both animals (72, 248) and humans (536, 635, 703). These effects may be in part regulated by *n*-3 fatty acid–mediated increases in cell membrane fluidity (23), which facilitates an enhanced mTOR/p70^{S6K} signaling response (703). Additional benefits may be attributed to reductions in protein breakdown associated with the inhibition of the ubiquitin–proteasome pathway (823), which theoretically would lead to a greater accretion of muscle proteins. Although these findings are intriguing, the aforementioned studies were not carried out in conjunction with a structured resistance training protocol. It therefore remains speculative as to what, if any, effects *n*-3 fatty acids have for those seeking to maximize hypertrophic adaptations.

Requirements

Similar to carbohydrate intake, no concrete guidelines can be given as to the amount of dietary fat needed to maximize muscle growth. As a general rule, fat intake should comprise

KEY POINT

Polyunsaturated fatty acids (PUFAs) are conceivably important for enhancing muscle protein synthesis and should be prioritized over saturated fatty acids (SFAs). A minimum of 1 g/kg/day of dietary fat appears sufficient to prevent hormonal alterations.

the balance of calories after accounting for the consumption of protein and carbohydrate. Given a caloric surplus, there is no problem meeting basic needs for dietary lipids. Based on limited data, a minimum of 1 g/kg/day appears sufficient to prevent hormonal alterations. It would seem prudent to focus on obtaining the majority of fat calories from unsaturated sources. The PUFAs, in particular, are essential not only to proper biological function, but seemingly to maximize muscle protein accretion.

Recommendations for dietary fat intake to maximize hypertrophy are shown in table 7.3.

Feeding Frequency

The frequency of nutrient consumption can influence muscle protein accretion. Given evidence of a leucine threshold, a case can be made for consuming multiple protein-rich meals throughout the day. Studies show dose-dependent and saturable effects at 10 g of EAAs, which is equivalent to approximately 20 g of a high-quality protein source (49). This is consistent with the "muscle full" concept: that muscle protein synthesis becomes unresponsive to any further increases in intake once the saturable level is reached (48). Cir-

KEY POINT

It is hypothesized that consuming protein every few hours throughout the day optimizes muscle protein accretion by continually elevating levels of muscle protein synthesis and attenuating muscle protein breakdown.

culating amino acids are then shunted to fuel other protein-requiring processes, to suppress proteolysis, or toward oxidation (177). With muscle full status, myofibrillar muscle protein synthesis is stimulated within 1 hour, but the stimulation returns to baseline within 3 hours despite sustained elevations in amino acid availability (181). Hence, it is hypothesized that consuming protein every few hours throughout the day optimizes muscle protein accretion by continually elevating levels of muscle protein synthesis and attenuating muscle protein breakdown (50, 700).

Support for frequent feedings was provided by Areta and colleagues (42), who investigated the effects of various distributions of protein consumption on anabolic responses. Twenty-four well-trained men were randomized to consume 80 g of whey protein as either a pulse feeding (8 × 10 g every 1.5 hours), an intermediate feeding (4 × 20 g every 3 hours), or a bolus feeding (2 × 40 g every 6 hours) during 12 hours of recovery after a resistance training bout. Results showed that the intermediate feeding condition was superior to either the pulse or bolus feeding condition for stimulating muscle protein synthesis over the recovery period. The findings are consistent with the leucine threshold concept. The 20 g of whey provided in the intermittent feeding condition was sufficient to hit the threshold, and more frequent feedings at this saturable amount seemingly kept muscle protein synthesis elevated throughout the day. Alternatively, the pulse feeding of 10 g was insufficient to trigger leucine's maximal effects, whereas the bolus feeding was not provided frequently enough to sustain muscle protein synthesis elevations. Several issues with this study hinder the ability to extrapolate findings in practice. Although the provision of only a fast-acting protein (whey) provides the necessary control to tease out confounding effects from other nutrients, it has little relevance to real-life eating patterns. Consumption of a mixed meal increases transit time through the gut, which would necessarily require higher protein intakes to provide a leucine trigger and then release the remaining amino acids slowly over the succeeding 5 hours. Moreover, the 80 g dose of total daily protein provided to subjects is far below that needed by most people to maintain a nonnegative protein balance.

A recent study by Mamerow and colleagues (449) provides additional insight into the topic. In a randomized crossover design, 8 healthy subjects followed isoenergetic and isonitrogenous diets at breakfast, lunch, and dinner for two separate 7-day periods. During one condition, protein was distributed approximately evenly throughout each meal; in the other, it was skewed so that almost 2/3 of the daily protein dose was consumed at dinner. Protein intake was sufficient for maximal anabolism, amounting to 1.6 g/kg/day. All meals were individually prepared by the research staff. Consistent with the findings of Areta and colleagues, results showed that muscle protein synthesis was approximately 25% greater when protein intake was evenly distributed compared to a skewed distribution.

Several longitudinal studies have investigated the effects of protein intake frequency on body composition in conjunction with mixed meals. In a 2-week intervention on elderly women, Arnal and colleagues (43) demonstrated that protein pulse feeding (women consumed 79% of total daily protein in a single feeding of ~52g) resulted in a greater retention of fat-free mass compared to a condition in which protein feedings were equally spread over the course of 4 daily meals. Alternatively, a follow-up study by the same researchers using an almost identical nutritional protocol found no difference between pulse- and spread-feeding frequencies in a group of young women (44). These findings are consistent with those of Adechian and colleagues (16), who reported no differences in body composition between protein pulse feeding (80% protein in one meal) and spread feeding (4 equally spaced portions of protein) in a group of young obese women. The discrepancies in studies can seemingly be attributed to the age-related differences in the subjects. As previously mentioned, the aging process desensitizes muscle to protein feedings, resulting in a greater per-meal requirement to hit the leucine threshold. It is estimated that elderly people require high-quality protein in a dose of approximately 40 g for a maximal anabolic response; younger people require approximately half this amount (834, 845). The spread-feeding group in the study of elderly subjects consumed approximately 26 g of protein per meal (43), which would put them far below the leucine threshold during each feeding. The pulse-feeding group, on the other hand, would have hit the leucine threshold in the 80% protein meal, which may have been sufficient to promote a superior anabolic effect. In the studies of young subjects (16, 44), the spread-feeding group consumed >20 g per serving, thus exceeding the leucine threshold. A limitation of these studies is that subjects did not perform resistance exercise, thereby impeding generalizability to those seeking to maximize hypertrophy.

Nutrient Timing

Nutrient timing is a strategy to optimize the adaptive response to exercise. The postexercise

---

PRACTICAL APPLICATIONS

EATING FREQUENCY FOR HYPERTROPHY

Given that the anabolic effect of a protein-rich meal lasts approximately 5 to 6 hours (410), it is reasonable to conclude that young people should consume three meals, spread throughout the day, containing at least 10 g of EAAs to optimize muscle growth. This frequency pattern ensures that the body remains in anabolism over the course of the day and takes full advantage of the >24-hour sensitizing effect of resistance training on skeletal muscle (49). Elderly people may require up to double this amount.

period is often considered the most critical part of nutrient timing from a muscle-building standpoint. This is based on the premise of an *anabolic window of opportunity*, whereby the provision of nutrients within approximately 1 hour of the completion of exercise enhances the hypertrophic response to the bout (360). According to nutrient timing theory, delaying consumption outside of this limited window has negative repercussions on muscle growth. Some researchers have even postulated that the timing of nutrient consumption is of greater importance to body composition than absolute daily nutrient consumption (121).

Protein is clearly the critical nutrient for optimizing the hypertrophic response. As previously noted, anabolism is primarily mediated by EAAs, with minimal contribution from nonessential amino acids (89, 767). It has been proposed that consumption of carbohydrate potentiates the anabolic effects of postexercise protein intake, thereby increasing muscle protein accretion (334).

The basis for nutrient timing is well founded. Intense exercise causes the depletion of a substantial proportion of stored fuels (including glycogen and amino acids) and elicits *structural perturbations* (irritation or damage) of muscle fibers. Hypothetically, providing the body with nutrients following such exercise not only facilitates the repletion of energy reserves and remodeling of damaged tissue, but actually does so in a supercompensated manner that ultimately heightens muscular development. Indeed, numerous studies support the efficacy of nutrient timing for acutely increasing muscle protein synthesis following a resistance training bout over and above that of placebo (602, 766, 768, 769). These findings provide compelling evidence that exercise sensitizes muscles to nutrient administration.

Anabolic Window of Opportunity

The concept of an anabolic window of opportunity was initially formulated from acute muscle protein synthesis data. In one of the earliest studies on the topic, Okamura and colleagues (550) found a significantly greater protein synthetic response when dogs were infused with amino acids immediately after 150 minutes of treadmill exercise compared to delaying administration for 2 hours. Subsequently, a human trial by Levenhagen and colleagues (416) showed that lower-body (and whole-body) protein synthesis of the legs increased significantly more when protein was ingested immediately following 60 minutes of cycling at 60% of $\dot{V}O_2$ max versus delaying consumption by 3 hours. A confounding issue with these studies is that both involved moderate-intensity, long-duration aerobic exercise. This raises the possibility that results were attributed to greater mitochondrial and perhaps other sarcoplasmic protein fractions as opposed to the synthesis of contractile elements. In contrast, Rasmussen and colleagues (602) investigated the acute impact of protein timing after resistance training and found no significant differences in the protein synthetic response between consuming nutrients 1 hour and consuming nutrients 3 hours postexercise.

The aforementioned studies, although providing interesting mechanistic insight into postexercise nutritional responses, are limited to generating hypotheses regarding hypertrophic adaptations as opposed to drawing practical conclusions about the efficacy of nutrient timing for building muscle. Acute measures of muscle protein synthesis taken in the postworkout period are often decoupled from the chronic upregulation of causative myogenic signals (148) and do not necessarily predict long-term hypertrophic adaptations from regimented resistance training (765). In addition, postworkout elevations in muscle protein synthesis in untrained subjects are not replicated in those who are resistance trained (12). The only way to determine whether a nutrient's timing produces a true hypertrophic effect is by performing training studies that measure changes in muscle size over time.

Effect of Postexercise Protein on Hypertrophy

A number of longitudinal studies have directly investigated the effects of postexercise protein ingestion on muscle growth. The results of these trials are contradictory, seemingly because of disparities in study design and methodology. In an attempt to achieve clarity on the topic, my lab conducted a meta-analysis of the protein timing literature (659). Inclusion criteria were that the studies had to involve randomized controlled trials in which one group received protein within 1 hour pre- or postworkout and the other did not for at least 2 hours after the exercise bout. Moreover, studies had to span at least 6 weeks and provide a minimum dose of 6 g of EAAs, an amount shown to produce a robust increase in muscle protein synthesis following resistance training (89, 360). A total of 23 studies were analyzed comprising 525 subjects. Simple pooled analysis of data showed a small but significant effect (0.20) on muscle hypertrophy favoring timed protein consumption. However, regression analysis found that virtually the entire effect was explained by greater protein consumption in the timing group versus the nontiming group (~1.7 g/kg vs. 1.3 g/kg, respectively). In other words, the average protein consumption in the nontimed groups was well below what is deemed necessary for maximizing the protein synthesis associated with resistance training. Only a few studies actually endeavored to match protein intake between conditions. A subanalysis of these studies revealed no effects associated with protein timing. The findings provide strong evidence that any effect of protein timing on muscle hypertrophy is relatively small, if there is one at all.

Effect of Postexercise Carbohydrate on Hypertrophy

The inclusion of carbohydrate in postworkout nutrition intake is often claimed to be synergistic to protein consumption with respect to promoting a hypertrophic response (334).

KEY POINT

Numerous studies support the efficacy of nutrient timing for acutely increasing muscle protein synthesis following a resistance training bout, but research has failed to demonstrate that protein timing has a long-term effect on muscle hypertrophy.

This assertion is primarily based on theorized anabolic actions of carbohydrate-mediated insulin release. However, although insulin has known anabolic properties (78, 221), emerging research shows that the hormone has a permissive rather than stimulatory role in regulating protein synthesis (577). Its secretion has little impact on postexercise anabolism at physiological levels (265), although evidence suggests a threshold below which plasma insulin levels cause a refractory response of muscle protein synthesis to the stimulatory effect of resistance training (369). Importantly, studies have failed to show any additive effects of carbohydrate on enhancing postexercise muscle protein synthesis when combined with amino acid provision (251, 381, 721).

The principal effects of insulin on lean body mass are related to its role in reducing muscle catabolism (174, 243, 305, 362). Although the precise mechanisms are not well defined at this time, anticatabolic effects are believed to involve insulin-mediated phosphorylation of PI3K/Akt, which in turn blunts activation of the Forkhead family of transcription factors (364). An inhibition of other components of the ubiquitin–proteasome pathway are also theorized to play a role in the process (265).

To take advantage of these anticatabolic properties, traditional nutrient timing lore proposes a benefit to spiking insulin levels as fast and high as possible following an exercise bout. Muscle protein breakdown is only slightly elevated immediately postexercise and then rapidly rises thereafter (398). When in the fasted state, proteoloysis is markedly increased at 195 min postexercise, and protein balance remains negative (584). The extent of protein breakdown increases by up to 50% at the 3-hour mark, and heightened proteolysis can persist for up to 24 hours after an intense resistance training bout (398). Given that muscle hypertrophy represents the difference between myofibrillar protein synthesis and proteolysis, a decrease in protein breakdown would conceivably enhance the accretion of contractile proteins and thus facilitate hypertrophy.

Although the concept of spiking insulin is logical in theory, the need to do so postexercise ultimately depends on when food was consumed preexercise. The impact of insulin on net muscle protein balance plateaus at 3 to 4 times fasting levels (a range of ~15 to 30 mU/L) (265, 610). Typical mixed meals achieve this effect 1 to 2 hours after consumption, and levels remain elevated for 3 to 6 hours (or more) depending on the size of the meal. For example, a solid meal of 75 g carbohydrate, 37 g protein, and 17 g fat raises insulin concentrations 3-fold over fasting conditions within a half hour after consumption and increases to 5-fold after 1 hour; at the 5-hour mark, levels remain double those seen during fasting (123). Hence, the need to rapidly reverse catabolic processes is relevant only in the absence of preworkout nutrient provision.

KEY POINT

There is no need to spike insulin postexercise via carbohydrate consumption with the goal of hypertrophy if exercise was not performed in a fasting state. The need to quickly replenish glycogen is only relevant for those who perform 2-a-day split resistance training bouts (i.e., morning and evening) in which the same muscles are worked during the respective sessions.

It also should be noted that amino acids are highly insulinemic. A 45 g dose of whey isolate produces insulin levels sufficient to maximize net muscle protein balance (15 to 30 mU/L) (590). Once this physiological threshold is attained via amino acid consumption, adding carbohydrate to the mix to further stimulate elevations in insulin is moot with respect to hypertrophic adaptations (265, 281, 721).

There is evidence that consuming carbohydrate immediately after exercise significantly increases the rate of muscle glycogen repletion; delaying intake by just 2 hours decreases the rate of resynthesis by as much as 50% (335). This is due to the potentiating effect of exercise on insulin-stimulated glucose uptake, which shows a strong positive correlation to the magnitude of glycogen use during the bout (615). Mechanisms responsible for this phenomenon include heightened translocation of the glucose transporter type 4 (GLUT4) protein responsible for facilitating entry of glucose into muscle (176, 355) and an increase in the activity of glycogen synthase—the principal enzyme involved in promoting glycogen storage (549). In combination, these factors expedite the uptake of glucose after exercise, accelerating the rate of glycogen replenishment.

Glycogen is considered critical to the performance of hypertrophy-type protocols (402). MacDougall and colleagues (443) found that 3 sets of elbow flexion exercises at 80% of 1RM performed to muscular failure decreased mixed-muscle glycogen concentration by 24%. Similar findings were reported for the vastus lateralis: 3 sets of 12RM depleted glycogen stores by 26.1%, and 6 sets led to a 38% reduction. Extrapolation of these results to a typical high-volume bodybuilding workout involving multiple exercises and sets for the same muscle group indicates that the majority of local glycogen stores are depleted during such training. Decrements in performance from glycogen depletion would conceivably impair the ability to maximize the hypertrophic response to exercise.

Despite a reliance on glycolysis during resistance training, the practical importance of rapid glycogen replenishment is questionable for the majority of lifters. Even if glycogen is completely depleted during exercise, full replenishment of these stores is accomplished within 24 hours regardless of whether carbohydrate intake is delayed postworkout (227, 559). Thus, the need to quickly replenish glycogen is only relevant for those who perform 2-a-day split resistance training bouts (i.e., morning and evening) in which the same muscles are worked during the respective sessions (40). The rate of glycogen repletion is not a limiting factor in those who consume sufficient carbohydrate over the course of a day. From a muscle-building standpoint, the focus should be directed at meeting the daily carbohydrate requirement as opposed to worrying about timing issues.

In terms of nutrient timing, there is compelling evidence that the body is primed for anabolism following intense exercise. Muscles become sensitized to nutrient intake so that muscle protein synthesis is blunted until amino acids are consumed. However, the body of research suggests that the anabolic window of opportunity is considerably larger than the 1-hour postworkout period often cited in the literature. The practical application of nutrient timing should therefore be considered for the entire periworkout period (before, during, and after workout). Although research is somewhat equivocal, it seems prudent to consume high-quality protein (at a dose of ~0.4 to 0.5 g/kg of lean body mass) both pre- and postexercise within about 4 to 6 hours of each other depending on meal size. For those who train partially or fully fasted, on the other hand, consuming protein immediately postworkout becomes increasingly more important to promote anabolism.

PRACTICAL APPLICATIONS

NUTRIENT TIMING GUIDELINES

It is important to consume high-quality protein (at a dose of ~0.4 to 0.5 g/kg of lean body mass) both pre- and postexercise within about 4 to 6 hours of each other depending on meal size. Those who resistance train partially or fully fasted should consume protein (at a dose of ~0.4 to 0.5 g/kg of lean body mass) as quickly as possible postworkout, preferably within 45 minutes of the bout. Those who perform 2-a-day (morning and evening workouts in the same day) should consume carbohydrate (at a dose of ~1.0 to 1.5 g/kg of lean body mass) within 1 hour postworkout.

TAKE-HOME POINTS

- A positive energy balance is necessary for maximizing the hypertrophic response to resistance training, but overconsumption ultimately is detrimental to gains.

- Those seeking to maximize hypertrophy should consume at least 1.7 g/kg/day of protein. Qualitative factors are not an issue for those eating a meat-based diet. Vegans must be cognizant of combining proteins so that they get sufficient quantities of the full complement of EAAs.

- Carbohydrate intake should be at least 3 g/kg/day to ensure that glycogen stores are fully stocked. Higher carbohydrate intakes may enhance performance and anabolism, but this may be specific to the individual.

- Dietary fat should comprise the balance of nutrient intake after setting protein and carbohydrate amounts. People should focus on obtaining a majority of fat from unsaturated sources.

- At least three meals consisting of a minimum of 25 g of high-quality protein should be consumed every 5 to 6 hours to maximize anabolism.

- Nutrient timing around the exercise bout should be considered in the context of the periworkout period. It seems prudent to consume high-quality protein (at a dose of ~0.4 to 0.5 g/kg of lean body mass) both pre- and postexercise within about 4 to 6 hours of each other depending on meal size. Those who train partially or fully fasted should consume protein as quickly as possible postworkout.

REFERENCES

1. Aagaard, P, Andersen, JL, Dyhre-Poulsen, P, Leffers, AM, Wagner, A, Magnusson, SP, Halkjaer-Kristensen, J, and Simonsen, EB. A mechanism for increased contractile strength of human pennate muscle in response to strength training: Changes in muscle architecture. *J Physiol.* 534: 613-623, 2001.

2. Aagaard, P, Simonsen, EB, Andersen, JL, Magnusson, P, and Dyhre-Poulsen, P. Neural adaptation to resistance training: Changes in evoked V-wave and H-reflex responses. *J Appl Physiol.* 1985(92): 2309-2318, 2002.

3. Aagaard, P, Simonsen, EB, Andersen, JL, Magnusson, P, and Dyhre-Poulsen, P. Increased rate of force development and neural drive of human skeletal muscle following resistance training. *J Appl Physiol.* 1985(93): 1318-1326, 2002.

4. Abdessemed, D, Duche, P, Hautier, C, Poumarat, G, and Bedu, M. Effect of recovery duration on muscular power and blood lactate during the bench press exercise. *Int J Sports Med.* 20: 368-373, 1999.

5. Abe , T, Beekley, MD, Hinata, S, Koizumi, K, and Sato, Y. Day-to-day change in muscle strength and MRI-measured skeletal muscle size during 7 days KAATSU resistance training: A case study. *Int J Kaatsu Training Res.* 1: 71-76, 2005.

6. Abe, T, Yasuda, T, Midorikawa, T, Sato, Y, Kearns, C, Inoue, K, Koizumi, K, and Ishii, N. Skeletal muscle size and circulating IGF-1 are increased after two weeks of twice daily KAATSU resistance training. *Int J Kaatsu Training Res.* 1: 6-12, 2005.

7. Abe, T, DeHoyos, DV, Pollock, ML, and Garzarella, L. Time course for strength and muscle thickness changes following upper and lower body resistance training in men and women. *Eur J Appl Physiol.* 81: 174-180, 2000.

8. Abe, T, Kearns, CF, and Sato, Y. Muscle size and strength are increased following walk training with restricted venous blood flow from the leg muscle, Kaatsu-walk training. *J Appl Physiol.* 100: 1460-1466, 2006.

9. Abernethy, PJ, Jurimae, J, Logan, PA, Taylor, AW, and Thayer, RE. Acute and chronic response of skeletal muscle to resistance exercise. *Sports Med.* 17: 22-38, 1994.

10. Ackel-D'Elia, C, Carnier, J, Bueno, CR, Jr, Campos, RM, Sanches, PL, Clemente, AP, Tufik, S, de Mello, MT, and Damaso, AR. Effects of different physical exercises on leptin concentration in obese adolescents. *Int J Sports Med.* 35: 164-171, 2014.

11. Adams, G. The molecular response of skeletal muscle to resistance training. *Deutsche Zeitschrift für Sportmedizin* 61: 61-67, 2010.

12. Adams, G, and Bamman, MM. Characterization and regulation of mechanical loading-induced compensatory muscle hypertrophy. *Comp Physiol.* (2)4: 2829-2870, 2012.

13. Adams, GR, and McCue, SA. Localized infusion of IGF-I results in skeletal muscle hypertrophy in rats. *J Appl Physiol.* 84: 1716-1722, 1998.

14. Adams, GR. Invited review: Autocrine/paracrine IGF-I and skeletal muscle adaptation. *J Appl Physiol.* 93: 1159-1167, 2002.

15. Adams, GR, Cheng, DC, Haddad, F, and Baldwin, KM. Skeletal muscle hypertrophy in response to isometric, lengthening, and shortening training bouts of equivalent duration. *J Appl Physiol.* 96: 1613-1618, 2004.

16. Adechian, S, Balage, M, Remond, D, Migne, C, Quignard-Boulange, A, Marset-Baglieri, A, Rousset, S, Boirie, Y, Gaudichon, C, Dardevet, D, and Mosoni, L. Protein feeding pattern, casein feeding, or milk-soluble protein feeding did not change the evolution of body composition during a short-term weight loss program. *Am J Physiol Endocrinol Metab.* 303: E973-E982, 2012.

17. Ahmadizad, S, Ghorbani, S, Ghasemikaram, M, and Bahmanzadeh, M. Effects of short-term non-periodized, linear periodized and daily undulating periodized resistance training on plasma adiponectin, leptin and insulin resistance. *Clin Biochem.* 47: 417-422, 2014.

18. Ahtiainen, JP, Pakarinen, A, Alen, M, Kraemer, WJ, and Hakkinen, K. Muscle hypertrophy, hormonal adaptations and strength development during strength training in strength-trained and untrained men. *Eur J Appl Physiol.* 89: 555-563, 2003.

19. Ahtiainen, JP, Hulmi, JJ, Kraemer, WJ, Lehti, M, Nyman, K, Selanne, H, Alen, M, Pakarinen, A, Komulainen, J, Kovanen, V, Mero, AA, and Hakkinen, K. Heavy resistance exercise training and skeletal muscle androgen receptor expression in younger and older men. *Steroids* 76: 183-192, 2011.

20. Ahtiainen, JP, Pakarinen, A, Alen, M, Kraemer, WJ, and Hakkinen, K. Short vs. long rest period between the sets in hypertrophic resistance training: Influence on muscle strength, size, and hormonal adaptations in trained men. *J Strength Cond Res.* 19: 572-582, 2005.

21. Akima, H, and Saito, A. Activation of quadriceps femoris including vastus intermedius during fatiguing dynamic knee extensions. *Eur J Appl Physiol.* 113: 2829-2840, 2013.

22. Alegre, LM, Jimenez, F, Gonzalo-Orden, JM, Martin-Acero, R, and Aguado, X. Effects of dynamic resistance training on fascicle length and isometric strength. *J Sports Sci.* 24: 501-508, 2006.

23. Alexander, JW. Immunonutrition: The role of omega-3 fatty acids. *Nutrition* 14: 627-633, 1998.

24. Allen, DG, Whitehead, NP, and Yeung, EW. Mechanisms of stretch-induced muscle damage in normal and dystrophic muscle: Role of ionic changes. *J Physiol.* 567: 723-735, 2005.

25. Alves Souza, RW, Aguiar, AF, Vechetti-Junior, IJ, Piedade, WP, Rocha Campos, GE, and Dal-Pai-Silva, M. Resistance training with excessive training load and insufficient recovery alters skeletal muscle mass-related protein expression. *J Strength Cond Res.* 28: 2338-2345, 2014.

26. Alway, SE, Grumbt, WH, Gonyea, WJ, and Stray-Gundersen, J. Contrasts in muscle and myofibers of elite male and female bodybuilders. *J Appl Physiol.* 1985(67): 24-31, 1989.

27. Alway, SE, Gonyea, WJ, and Davis, ME. Muscle fiber formation and fiber hypertrophy during the onset of stretch-overload. *Am J Physiol.* 259: C92-102, 1990.

28. Alway, SE, Grumbt, WH, Stray-Gundersen, J, and Gonyea, WJ. Effects of resistance training on elbow flexors of highly competitive bodybuilders. *J Appl Physiol.* 1985(72): 1512-1521, 1992.

29. American College of Sports Medicine. American College of Sports Medicine position stand. Progression models in resistance training for healthy adults. *Med Sci Sports Exerc.* 41: 687-708, 2009.

30. Amiridis, IG, Martin, A, Morlon, B, Martin, L, Cometti, G, Pousson, M, and van Hoecke, J. Co-activation and tension-regulating phenomena during isokinetic knee extension in sedentary and highly skilled humans. *Eur J Appl Physiol Occup Physiol.* 73: 149-156, 1996.

31. Andersen, MB, Pingel, J, Kjaer, M, and Langberg, H. Interleukin-6: A growth factor stimulating collagen synthesis in human tendon. *J Appl Physiol.* 1985(110): 1549-1554, 2011.

32. Andersen, P, and Henriksson, J. Capillary supply of the quadriceps femoris muscle of man: Adaptive response to exercise. *J Physiol.* 270: 677-690, 1977.

33. Andersen, V, Fimland, MS, Wiik, E, Skoglund, A, and Saeterbakken, AH. Effects of grip width on muscle strength and activation in the lat pull-down. *J Strength Cond Res.* 28: 1135-1142, 2014.

34. Anderson, KE, Rosner, W, Khan, MS, New, MI, Pang, SY, Wissel, PS, and Kappas, A. Diet-hormone interactions: Protein/carbohydrate ratio alters reciprocally the plasma levels of testosterone and cortisol and their respective binding globulins in man. *Life Sci.* 40: 1761-1768, 1987.

35. Antonio, J. Nonuniform response of skeletal muscle to heavy resistance training: Can bodybuilders induce regional muscle hypertrophy. *J Strength Cond Res.* 14: 102-113, 2000.

36. Antonio, J, and Gonyea, WJ. Role of muscle fiber hypertrophy and hyperplasia in intermittently stretched avian muscle. *J Appl Physiol.* 74: 1893-1898, 1993.

37. Antonio, J, and Gonyea, WJ. Progressive stretch overload of skeletal muscle results in hypertrophy before hyperplasia. *J Appl Physiol.* 1985(75): 1263-1271, 1993.

38. Aperghis, M, Velloso, CP, Hameed, M, Brothwood, T, Bradley, L, Bouloux, PM, Harridge, SD, and Goldspink, G. Serum IGF-I levels and IGF-I gene splicing in muscle of healthy young males receiving rhGH. *Growth Horm IGF Res.* 19: 61-67, 2009.

39. Apro, W, Wang, L, Ponten, M, Blomstrand, E, and Sahlin, K. Resistance exercise induced mTORC1 signaling is not impaired by subsequent endurance exercise in human skeletal muscle. *Am J Physiol Endocrinol Metab.* 305: E22-E32, 2013.

40. Aragon, AA, and Schoenfeld, BJ. Nutrient timing revisited: Is there a post-exercise anabolic window? *J Int Soc Sports Nutr.* 10(5), 2013.

41. Arazi, H, and Asadi, A. Effects of 8 weeks equal-volume resistance training with different workout frequency on maximal strength, endurance and body composition. *Int J Sports Sci Eng.* 5: 112-118, 2011.

42. Areta, JL, Burke, LM, Ross, ML, Camera, DM, West, DW, Broad, EM, Jeacocke, NA, Moore, DR, Stellingwerff, T, Phillips, SM, Hawley, JA, and Coffey, VG. Timing and distribution of protein ingestion during prolonged recovery from resistance exercise alters myofibrillar protein synthesis. *J Physiol.* 591: 2319-2331, 2013.

43. Arnal, MA, Mosoni, L, Boirie, Y, Houlier, ML, Morin, L, Verdier, E, Ritz, P, Antoine, JM, Prugnaud, J, Beaufrere, B, and Mirand, PP. Protein pulse feeding improves protein retention in elderly women. *Am J Clin Nutr.* 69: 1202-1208, 1999.

44. Arnal, MA, Mosoni, L, Boirie, Y, Houlier, ML, Morin, L, Verdier, E, Ritz, P, Antoine, JM, Prugnaud, J, Beaufrere, B, and Mirand, PP. Protein feeding pattern does not affect protein retention in young women. *J Nutr.* 130: 1700-1704, 2000.

45. Aronson, D, Violan, MA, Dufresne, SD, Zangen, D, Fielding, RA, and Goodyear, LJ. Exercise stimulates the mitogen-activated protein kinase pathway in human skeletal muscle. *J Clin Invest.* 99: 1251-1257, 1997.

46. Aronson, D, Wojtaszewski, JF, Thorell, A, Nygren, J, Zangen, D, Richter, EA, Ljungqvist, O, Fielding,

RA, and Goodyear, LJ. Extracellular-regulated protein kinase cascades are activated in response to injury in human skeletal muscle. *Am J Physiol.* 275: C555-561, 1998.

47. Atherton, PJ, Babraj, J, Smith, K, Singh, J, Rennie, MJ, and Wackerhage, H. Selective activation of AMPK-PGC-1alpha or PKB-TSC2-mTOR signaling can explain specific adaptive responses to endurance or resistance training-like electrical muscle stimulation. *FASEB J.* 19: 786-788, 2005.

48. Atherton, PJ, Etheridge, T, Watt, PW, Wilkinson, D, Selby, A, Rankin, D, Smith, K, and Rennie, MJ. Muscle full effect after oral protein: Time-dependent concordance and discordance between human muscle protein synthesis and mTORC1 signaling. *Am J Clin Nutr.* 92: 1080-1088, 2010.

49. Atherton, PJ, and Smith, K. Muscle protein synthesis in response to nutrition and exercise. *J Physiol.* 590: 1049-1057, 2012.

50. Atherton, PJ. Is there an optimal time for warfighters to supplement with protein? *J Nutr.* 143: 1848S-1851S, 2013.

51. Baechle, TR, and Earle, RW. *Essentials of Strength Training and Conditioning.* Champaign, IL: Human Kinetics, 2008.

52. Baker, D, Wilson, G, and Carolyn, R. Periodization: The effect on strength of manipulating volume and intensity. *J Strength Cond Res.* 8: 235-242, 1994.

53. Bamman, MM, Shipp, JR, Jiang, J, Gower, BA, Hunter, GR, Goodman, A, McLafferty, CL, Jr, and Urban, RJ. Mechanical load increases muscle IGF-I and androgen receptor mRNA concentrations in humans. *Am J Physiol Endocrinol Metab.* 280: E383-E390, 2001.

54. Bamman, MM, Hill, VJ, Adams, GR, Haddad, F, Wetzstein, CJ, Gower, BA, Ahmed, A, and Hunter, GR. Gender differences in resistance-training-induced myofiber hypertrophy among older adults. *J Gerontol A Biol Sci Med Sci.* 58: 108-116, 2003.

55. Bamman, MM. Take two NSAIDs and call on your satellite cells in the morning. *J Appl Physiol.* 103: 415-416, 2007.

56. Bamman, MM, Petrella, JK, Kim, JS, Mayhew, DL, and Cross, JM. Cluster analysis tests the importance of myogenic gene expression during myofiber hypertrophy in humans. *J Appl Physiol.* 102: 2232-2239, 2007.

57. Barash, IA, Mathew, L, Ryan, AF, Chen, J, and Lieber, RL. Rapid muscle-specific gene expression changes after a single bout of eccentric contractions in the mouse. *Am J Physiol Cell Physiol.* 286: C355-364, 2004.

58. Barnett, C, Kippers, V, and Turner, P. Effects of variations of the bench press exercise on the EMG activity of five shoulder muscles. *J Strength Cond Res.* 9: 222-227, 1995.

59. Barton, ER. Viral expression of insulin-like growth factor-I isoforms promotes different responses in skeletal muscle. *J Appl Physiol.* 100: 1778-1784, 2006.

60. Barton, ER, Morris, L, Musaro, A, Rosenthal, N, and Sweeney, HL. Muscle-specific expression of insulin-like growth factor I counters muscle decline in mdx mice. *J Cell Biol.* 157: 137-148, 2002.

61. Barton-Davis, ER, Shoturma, DI, and Sweeney, HL. Contribution of satellite cells to IGF-I induced hypertrophy of skeletal muscle. *Acta Physiol Scand.* 167: 301-305, 1999.

62. Bassel-Duby, R, and Olson, EN. Signaling pathways in skeletal muscle remodeling. *Ann Rev Biochem.* 75: 19-37, 2006.

63. Baum, C, Kennedy, DL, and Forbes, MB. Utilization of nonsteroidal antiinflammatory drugs. *Arthritis Rheum.* 28: 686-692, 1985.

64. Behm, DG. Neuromuscular implications and applications of resistance training. *J Strength Cond Res.* 9: 264-274, 1995.

65. Belcastro, AN, Shewchuk, LD, and Raj, DA. Exercise-induced muscle injury: A calpain hypothesis. *Mol Cell Biochem.* 179: 135-145, 1998.

66. Bell, GJ, Syrotuik, D, Martin, TP, Burnham, R, and Quinney, HA. Effect of concurrent strength and endurance training on skeletal muscle properties and hormone concentrations in humans. *Eur J Appl Physiol.* 81: 418-427, 2000.

67. Bellamy, LM, Joanisse, S, Grubb, A, Mitchell, CJ, McKay, BR, Phillips, SM, Baker, S, and Parise, G. The acute satellite cell response and skeletal muscle hypertrophy following resistance training. *PLoS One* 9: e109739, 2014.

68. Ben-Sira, D, Ayalon, A, and Tavi, M. The effect of different types of strength training on concentric strength in women. *J Strength Cond Res.* 9: 143-148, 1995.

69. Benton, MJ, Kasper, MJ, Raab, SA, Waggener, GT, and Swan, PD. Short-term effects of resistance training frequency on body composition and strength in middle-aged women. *J Strength Cond Res.* 25: 3142-3149, 2011.

70. Bentwich, I, Avniel, A, Karov, Y, Aharonov, R, Gilad, S, Barad, O, Barzilai, A, Einat, P, Einav, U, Meiri, E, Sharon, E, Spector, Y, and Bentwich, Z. Identification of hundreds of conserved and nonconserved human microRNAs. *Nat Genet.* 37: 766-770, 2005.

71. Benziane, B, Burton, TJ, Scanlan, B, Galuska, D, Canny, BJ, Chibalin, AV, Zierath, JR, and Stepto, NK. Divergent cell signaling after short-term intensified endurance training in human skeletal muscle. *Am J Physiol Endocrinol Metab.* 295: E1427-E1438, 2008.

72. Bergeron, K, Julien, P, Davis, TA, Myre, A, and Thivierge, MC. Long-chain n-3 fatty acids enhance neonatal insulin-regulated protein metabolism in piglets by differentially altering muscle lipid composition. *J Lipid Res.* 48: 2396-2410, 2007.

73. Bhasin, S, Storer, TW, Berman, N, Callegari, C, Clevenger, B, Phillips, J, Bunnell, TJ, Tricker, R, Shirazi, A, and Casaburi, R. The effects of supraphysiologic doses of testosterone on muscle size and strength in normal men. *N Engl J Med.* 335: 1-7, 1996.

74. Bhasin, S, Woodhouse, L, and Storer, TW. Proof of the effect of testosterone on skeletal muscle. *J Endocrinol.* 170: 27-38, 2001.

75. Bhasin, S, Woodhouse, L, Casaburi, R, Singh, AB, Mac, RP, Lee, M, Yarasheski, KE, Sinha-Hikim, I, Dzekov, C, Dzekov, J, Magliano, L, and Storer, TW. Older men are as responsive as young men to the anabolic effects of graded doses of testosterone on the skeletal muscle. *J Clin Endocrinol Metab.* 90: 678-688, 2005.

76. Bickel, CS, Cross, JM, and Bamman, MM. Exercise dosing to retain resistance training adaptations in young and older adults. *Med Sci Sports Exerc.* 43: 1177-1187, 2011.

77. Bickel, CS, Slade, J, Mahoney, E, Haddad, F, Dudley, GA, and Adams, GR. Time course of molecular responses of human skeletal muscle to acute bouts of resistance exercise. *J Appl Physiol.* 98: 482-488, 2005.

78. Biolo, G, Williams, BD, Fleming, RY, and Wolfe, RR. Insulin action on muscle protein kinetics and amino acid transport during recovery after resistance exercise. *Diabetes* 48: 949-957, 1999.

79. Blazevich, AJ, Gill, ND, Bronks, R, and Newton, RU. Training-specific muscle architecture adaptation after 5-wk training in athletes. *Med Sci Sports Exerc.* 35: 2013-2022, 2003.

80. Blazevich, AJ, Cannavan, D, Coleman, DR, and Horne, S. Influence of concentric and eccentric resistance training on architectural adaptation in human quadriceps muscles. *J Appl Physiol.* 103: 1565-1575, 2007.

81. Bloomquist, K, Langberg, H, Karlsen, S, Madsgaard, S, Boesen, M, and Raastad, T. Effect of range of motion in heavy load squatting on muscle and tendon adaptations. *Eur J Appl Physiol.* 113: 2133-2142, 2013.

82. Bodine, SC, Stitt, TN, Gonzalez, M, Kline, WO, Stover, GL, Bauerlein, R, Zlotchenko, E, Scrimgeour, A, Lawrence, JC, Glass, DJ, and Yancopoulos, GD. Akt/mTOR pathway is a crucial regulator of skeletal muscle hypertrophy and can prevent muscle atrophy in vivo. *Nat Cell Biol.* 3: 1014-1019, 2001.

83. Bodnar, D, Geyer, N, Ruzsnavszky, O, Olah, T, Hegyi, B, Sztretye, M, Fodor, J, Dienes, B, Balogh, A, Papp, Z, Szabo, L, Muller, G, Csernoch, L, and Szentesi, P. Hypermuscular mice with mutation in the myostatin gene display altered calcium signalling. *J Physiol.* 592: 1353-1365, 2014.

84. Bompa, T, and Haff, GG. *Theory and Methodology of Training.* Champaign, IL: Human Kinetics, 2009.

85. Bondesen, BA, Mills, ST, Kegley, KM, and Pavlath, GK. The COX-2 pathway is essential during early stages of skeletal muscle regeneration. *Am J Physiol Cell Physiol.* 287: C475-483, 2004.

86. Bondesen, BA, Mills, ST, Kegley, KM, and Pavlath, GK. The COX-2 pathway is essential during early stages of skeletal muscle regeneration. *Am J Physiol., Cell Physiol.* 287: 475-483, 2004.

87. Bondesen, BA, Mills, ST, and Pavlath, GK. The COX-2 pathway regulates growth of atrophied muscle via multiple mechanisms. *Am J Physiol., Cell Physiol.* 290: 1651-1659, 2006.

88. Borkman, M, Storlien, LH, Pan, DA, Jenkins, AB, Chisholm, DJ, and Campbell, LV. The relation between insulin sensitivity and the fatty-acid composition of skeletal-muscle phospholipids. *N Engl J Med.* 328: 238-244, 1993.

89. Borsheim, E, Tipton, KD, Wolf, SE, and Wolfe, RR. Essential amino acids and muscle protein recovery from resistance exercise. *Am J Physiol Endocrinol Metab.* 283: E648-E657, 2002.

90. Bottaro, M, Veloso, J, Wagner, D, and Gentil, P. Resistance training for strength and muscle thickness: Effect of number of sets and muscle group trained. *Sci Sports* 26: 259-264, 2011.

91. Botton, CE, Wilhelm, EN, Ughini, CC, Pinto, RS, and Lima, CS. Electromyographical analysis of the deltoid between different strength training exercises. *Medicina Sportiva.* 17: 67-71, 2013.

92. Brahm, H, Piehl-Aulin, K, Saltin, B, and Ljunghall, S. Net fluxes over working thigh of hormones, growth factors and biomarkers of bone metabolism during short lasting dynamic exercise. *Calcif Tissue Int.* 60: 175-180, 1997.

93. Breen, L, and Phillips, SM. Skeletal muscle protein metabolism in the elderly: Interventions to counteract the "anabolic resistance" of ageing. *Nutr Metab. (Lond.)* 8(68), 2011.

94. Brentano, MA, and Martins Kruel, LF. A review on strength exercise-induced muscle damage: Applications, adaptation mechanisms and limitations. *J Sports Med Phys Fitness* 51: 1-10, 2011.

95. Bressel, E, Willardson, JM, Thompson, B, and Fontana, FE. Effect of instruction, surface stability, and load intensity on trunk muscle activity. *J Electromyogr Kinesiol.* 19: e500-e504, 2009.

96. Broholm, C, and Pedersen, BK. Leukaemia inhibitory factor: An exercise-induced myokine. *Exerc Immunol Rev.* 16: 77-85, 2010.

97. Brown, D, Hikim, AP, Kovacheva, EL, and Sinha-Hikim, I. Mouse model of testosterone-induced muscle fiber hypertrophy: Involvement of p38 mitogen-activated protein kinase-mediated Notch signaling. *J Endocrinol.* 201: 129-139, 2009.

98. Brown, JM, Solomon, C, and Paton, M. Further evidence of functional differentiation within biceps brachii. *Electromyogr Clin Neurophysiol.* 33: 301-309, 1993.

99. Bruunsgaard, H, Galbo, H, Halkjaer-Kristensen, J, Johansen, TL, MacLean, DA, and Pedersen, BK. Exercise-induced increase in serum interleukin-6 in humans is related to muscle damage. *J Physiol.* 499 (Pt 3): 833-841, 1997.

100. Bruunsgaard, H. Physical activity and modulation of systemic low-level inflammation. *J Leukoc Biol.* 78: 819-835, 2005.

101. Bruusgaard, JC, Johansen, IB, Egner, IM, Rana, ZA, and Gundersen, K. Myonuclei acquired by overload exercise precede hypertrophy and are not lost on detraining. *Proc Natl Acad Sci USA* 107: 15111-15116, 2010.

102. Buford, TW, Anton, SD, Judge, AR, Marzetti, E, Wohlgemuth, SE, Carter, CS, Leeuwenburgh, C, Pahor, M, and Manini, TM. Models of accelerated sarcopenia: Critical pieces for solving the puzzle of age-related muscle atrophy. *Ageing Res Rev.* 9: 369-383, 2010.

103. Burd, NA, Dickinson, JM, Lemoine, JK, Carroll, CC, Sullivan, BE, Haus, JM, Jemiolo, B, Trappe, SW, Hughes, GM, Sanders, CE, Jr, and Trappe, TA. Effect of a cyclooxygenase-2 inhibitor on postexercise muscle protein synthesis in humans. *Am J Physiol Endocrinol Metab.* 298(2): E354-E361, 2010.

104. Burd, NA, Holwerda, AM, Selby, KC, West, DW, Staples, AW, Cain, NE, Cashaback, JG, Potvin, JR, Baker, SK, and Phillips, SM. Resistance exercise volume affects myofibrillar protein synthesis and anabolic signalling molecule phosphorylation in young men. *J Physiol.* 588: 3119-3130, 2010.

105. Burd, NA, West, DW, Staples, AW, Atherton, PJ, Baker, JM, Moore, DR, Holwerda, AM, Parise, G, Rennie, MJ, Baker, SK, and Phillips, SM. Low-load high volume resistance exercise stimulates muscle protein synthesis more than high-load low volume resistance exercise in young men. *PLoS One* 5: e12033, 2010.

106. Burd, NA, West, DW, Moore, DR, Atherton, PJ, Staples, AW, Prior, T, Tang, JE, Rennie, MJ, Baker, SK, and Phillips, SM. Enhanced amino acid sensitivity of myofibrillar protein synthesis persists for up to 24 h after resistance exercise in young men. *J Nutr.* 141: 568-573, 2011.

107. Burd, NA, Mitchell, CJ, Churchward-Venne, TA, and Phillips, SM. Bigger weights may not beget bigger muscles: Evidence from acute muscle pro-tein synthetic responses after resistance exercise. *Appl Physiol Nutr Metab.* 37: 551-554, 2012.

108. Buresh, R, Berg, K, and French, J. The effect of resistive exercise rest interval on hormonal response, strength, and hypertrophy with training. *J Strength Cond Res.* 23: 62-71, 2009.

109. Burian, M, and Geisslinger, G. COX-dependent mechanisms involved in the antinociceptive action of NSAIDs at central and peripheral sites. *Pharmacol Ther.* 107: 139-154, 2005.

110. Burnham, TR, Ruud, JD, and McGowan, R. Bench press training program with attached chains for female volleyball and basketball athletes. *Percept Mot Skills* 110: 61-68, 2010.

111. Burton, LA, and Sumukadas, D. Optimal management of sarcopenia. *Clin Interv Aging* 5: 217-228, 2010.

112. Burton, LC, Shapiro, S, and German, PS. Determinants of physical activity initiation and maintenance among community-dwelling older persons. *Prev Med.* 29: 422-430, 1999.

113. Cadore, EL, Izquierdo, M, Pinto, SS, Alberton, CL, Pinto, RS, Baroni, BM, Vaz, MA, Lanferdini, FJ, Radaelli, R, Gonzalez-Izal, M, Bottaro, M, and Kruel, LF. Neuromuscular adaptations to concurrent training in the elderly: Effects of intrasession exercise sequence. *Age (Dordr.)* 35: 891-903, 2013.

114. Cadore, EL, Gonzalez-Izal, M, Pallares, JG, Rodriguez-Falces, J, Hakkinen, K, Kraemer, WJ, Pinto, RS, and Izquierdo, M. Muscle conduction velocity, strength, neural activity, and morphological changes after eccentric and concentric training. *Scand J Med Sci Sports* 24(5): e343-e352, 2014.

115. Calder, AW, Chilibeck, PD, Webber, CE, and Sale, DG. Comparison of whole and split weight training routines in young women. *Can J Appl Physiol.* 19: 185-199, 1994.

116. Cambridge, ED, Sidorkewicz, N, Ikeda, DM, and McGill, SM. Progressive hip rehabilitation: The effects of resistance band placement on gluteal activation during two common exercises. *Clin Biomech. (Bristol, Avon)* 27: 719-724, 2012.

117. Camera, DM, West, DW, Burd, NA, Phillips, SM, Garnham, AP, Hawley, JA, and Coffey, VG. Low muscle glycogen concentration does not suppress the anabolic response to resistance exercise. *J Appl Physiol.* 113: 206-214, 2012.

118. Campbell, B, Kreider, RB, Ziegenfuss, T, La Bounty, P, Roberts, M, Burke, D, Landis, J, Lopez, H, and Antonio, J. International Society of Sports Nutrition position stand: Protein and exercise. *J Int Soc Sports Nutr.* 4: 8, 2007.

119. Campos, GER, Luecke, TJ, Wendeln, HK, Toma, K, Hagerman, FC, Murray, TF, Ragg, KE, Ratamess, NA, Kraemer, WJ, and Staron, RS. Muscular adaptations in response to three different resistance-training regimens: Specificity of repetition maximum training zones. *Eur J Appl Physiol.* 88: 50-60, 2002.

120. Candow, DG, and Burke, DG. Effect of short-term equal-volume resistance training with different workout frequency on muscle mass and strength in untrained men and women. *J Strength Cond Res.* 21: 204-207, 2007.

121. Candow, DG, and Chilibeck, PD. Timing of creatine or protein supplementation and resistance training in the elderly. *App. Physiol Nutr Metab.* 33: 184-190, 2008.

122. Cannon, J, and Marino, FE. Early-phase neuromuscular adaptations to high- and low-volume resistance training in untrained young and older women. *J Sports Sci.* 28: 1505-1514, 2010.

123. Capaldo, B, Gastaldelli, A, Antoniello, S, Auletta, M, Pardo, F, Ciociaro, D, Guida, R, Ferrannini, E, and Sacca, L. Splanchnic and leg substrate exchange after ingestion of a natural mixed meal in humans. *Diabetes* 48: 958-966, 1999.

124. Carneiro, NH, Ribeiro, AS, Nascimento, MA, Gobbo, LA, Schoenfeld, BJ, Achour Junior, A, Gobbi, S, Oliveira, AR, and Cyrino, ES. Effects of different resistance training frequencies on flexibility in older women. *Clin Interv Aging* 10: 531-538, 2015.

125. Carolan, B, and Cafarelli, E. Adaptations in coactivation after isometric resistance training. *J Appl Physiol.* 1985(73): 911-917, 1992.

126. Carpinelli, RN. The size principle and a critical analysis of the unsubstantiated heavier-is-better recommendation for resistance training. *J Exerc Sci Fit.* 6: 67-86, 2008.

127. Carrithers, JA, Carroll, CC, Coker, RH, Sullivan, DH, and Trappe, TA. Concurrent exercise and muscle protein synthesis: Implications for exercise countermeasures in space. *Aviat Space Environ Med.* 78: 457-462, 2007.

128. Carruthers, NJ, and Stemmer, PM. Methionine oxidation in the calmodulin-binding domain of calcineurin disrupts calmodulin binding and calcineurin activation. *Biochemistry (N.Y.)* 47: 3085-3095, 2008.

129. Chan, MHS, Carey, AL, Watt, MJ, and Febbraio, MA. Cytokine gene expression in human skeletal muscle during concentric contraction: Evidence that IL-8, like IL-6, is influenced by glycogen availability. *Am J Physiol Regul Integr Comp Physiol.* 287: 322-327, 2004.

130. Chan, ST, Johnson, AW, Moore, MH, Kapadia, CR, and Dudley, HA. Early weight gain and glycogen-obligated water during nutritional rehabilitation. *Hum Nutr Clin Nutr.* 36: 223-232, 1982.

131. Charette, SL, McEvoy, L, Pyka, G, Snow-Harter, C, Guido, D, Wiswell, RA, and Marcus, R. Muscle hypertrophy response to resistance training in older women. *J Appl Physiol.* 1985(70): 1912-1916, 1991.

132. Charifi, N, Kadi, F, Feasson, L, and Denis, C. Effects of endurance training on satellite cell frequency in skeletal muscle of old men. *Muscle Nerve* 28: 87-92, 2003.

133. Chen, TC, Lin, K, Chen, H, Lin, M, and Nosaka, K. Comparison in eccentric exercise-induced muscle damage among four limb muscles. *Eur J Appl Physiol.* 111: 211-223, 2011.

134. Chestnut, J, and Docherty, D. The effects of 4 and 10 repetition maximum weight-training protocols on neuromuscular adaptations in untrained men. *J Strength Cond Res.* 13: 353-359, 1999.

135. Chin, ER. Role of Ca2+/calmodulin-dependent kinases in skeletal muscle plasticity. *J Appl Physiol.* 99: 414-423, 2005.

136. Choi, J, Takahashi, H, and Itai, Y. The difference between effects of "power-up type" and "bulk-up type" strength training exercises: With special reference to muscle cross-sectional area. *Jpn J Phys Fitness Sports Med.* 47: 119-129, 1998.

137. Christian, JF, and Lawrence, JC. Control of protein synthesis by insulin. *Eurekah Bioscience* 1: 711-721, 2005.

138. Chtara, M, Chaouachi, A, Levin, GT, Chaouachi, M, Chamari, K, Amri, M, and Laursen, PB. Effect of concurrent endurance and circuit resistance training sequence on muscular strength and power development. *J Strength Cond Res.* 22: 1037-1045, 2008.

139. Churchley, EG, Coffey, VG, Pedersen, DJ, Shield, A, Carey, KA, Cameron-Smith, D, and Hawley, JA. Influence of preexercise muscle glycogen content on transcriptional activity of metabolic and myogenic genes in well-trained humans. *J Appl Physiol.* 102: 1604-1611, 2007.

140. Churchward-Venne, TA, Murphy, CH, Longland, TM, and Phillips, SM. Role of protein and amino acids in promoting lean mass accretion with resistance exercise and attenuating lean mass loss during energy deficit in humans. *Amino Acids* 45: 231-240, 2013.

141. Claflin, DR, Larkin, LM, Cederna, PS, Horowitz, JF, Alexander, NB, Cole, NM, Galecki, AT, Chen, S, Nyquist, LV, Carlson, BM, Faulkner, JA, and Ashton-Miller, JA. Effects of high- and low-velocity resistance training on the contractile properties of skeletal muscle fibers from young and older humans. *J Appl Physiol.* 1985(111): 1021-1030, 2011.

142. Clarke, MS, and Feeback, DL. Mechanical load induces sarcoplasmic wounding and FGF release in differentiated human skeletal muscle cultures. *FASEB J.* 10: 502-509, 1996.

143. Clarke, MS, Bamman, MM, and Feeback, DL. Bed rest decreases mechanically induced myofiber wounding and consequent wound-mediated FGF release. *J Appl Physiol.* 85: 593-600, 1998.

144. Clarkson, PM, Byrnes, WC, McCormick, KM, Turcotte, LP, and White, JS. Muscle soreness and serum creatine kinase activity following isometric, eccentric, and concentric exercise. *Int J Sports Med.* 7: 152-155, 1986.

145. Clarkson, PM, Nosaka, K, and Braun, B. Muscle function after exercise-induced muscle damage and rapid adaptation. *Med Sci Sports Exerc.* 24: 512-520, 1992.

146. Clarkson, PM, and Hubal, MJ. Exercise-induced muscle damage in humans. *Am J Phys Med Rehabil.* 81: 52-69, 2002.

147. Cobley, JN, Bartlett, JD, Kayani, A, Murray, SW, Louhelainen, J, Donovan, T, Waldron, S, Gregson, W, Burniston, JG, Morton, JP, and Close, GL. PGC-1alpha transcriptional response and mitochondrial adaptation to acute exercise is maintained in skeletal muscle of sedentary elderly males. *Biogerontology* 13: 621-631, 2012.

148. Coffey, VG, Shield, A, Canny, BJ, Carey, KA, Cameron-Smith, D, and Hawley, JA. Interaction of contractile activity and training history on mRNA abundance in skeletal muscle from trained athletes. *Am J Physiol Endocrinol Metab.* 290: E849-E855, 2006.

149. Coffey, VG, Zhong, Z, Shield, A, Canny, BJ, Chibalin, AV, Zierath, JR, and Hawley, JA. Early signaling responses to divergent exercise stimuli in skeletal muscle from well-trained humans. *FASEB J.* 20: 190-192, 2006.

150. Coffey, VG, Jemiolo, B, Edge, J, Garnham, AP, Trappe, SW, and Hawley, JA. Effect of consecutive repeated sprint and resistance exercise bouts on acute adaptive responses in human skeletal muscle. *Am J Physiol Regul Integr Comp Physiol.* 297: R1441-1451, 2009.

151. Coffey, VG, Pilegaard, H, Garnham, AP, O'Brien, BJ, and Hawley, JA. Consecutive bouts of diverse contractile activity alter acute responses in human skeletal muscle. *J Appl Physiol.* 1985(106): 1187-1197, 2009.

152. Coggan, AR, Spina, RJ, King, DS, Rogers, MA, Brown, M, Nemeth, PM, and Holloszy, JO. Skeletal muscle adaptations to endurance training in 60- to 70-yr-old men and women. *J Appl Physiol.* 1985(72): 1780-1786, 1992.

153. Collins, MA, and Snow, TK. Are adaptations to combined endurance and strength training affected by the sequence of training? *J Sports Sci.* 11: 485-491, 1993.

154. Conboy, IM, Conboy, MJ, Wagers, AJ, Girma, ER, Weissman, IL, and Rando, TA. Rejuvenation of aged progenitor cells by exposure to a young systemic environment. *Nature* 433: 760-764, 2005.

155. Contreras, B, Cronin, J, Schoenfeld, BJ, Nates, R, and Sonmez, GT. Are all hip extension exercises created equal? *Strength Cond J.* 35: 17-22, 2013.

156. Contreras, B, Vigotsky, AD, Schoenfeld, BJ, Beardsley, C, and Cronin, J. A comparison of gluteus maximus, biceps femoris, and vastus lateralis EMG activity in the back squat and barbell hip thrust exercises. *J Appl Biomech.* 31(6): 452-458, 2015.

157. Cook, SB, Murphy, BG, and Labarbera, KE. Neuromuscular function after a bout of low-load blood flow-restricted exercise. *Med Sci Sports Exerc.* 45: 67-74, 2013.

158. Cornelison, DD, and Wold, BJ. Single-cell analysis of regulatory gene expression in quiescent and activated mouse skeletal muscle satellite cells. *Dev Biol.* 191: 270-283, 1997.

159. Correa, CS, Teixeira, BC, Bittencourt, A, Lemos, L, Marques, NR, Radaelli, R, Kruger, RL, Reischak-Oliveira, A, and Pinto, RS. Effects of high and low volume of strength training on muscle strength, muscle volume and lipid profile in postmenopausal women. *J Exerc Sci Fit.* 12: 62-67, 2014.

160. Creer, A, Gallagher, P, Slivka, D, Jemiolo, B, Fink, W, and Trappe, S. Influence of muscle glycogen availability on ERK1/2 and Akt signaling after resistance exercise in human skeletal muscle. *J Appl Physiol.* 99: 950-956, 2005.

161. Crewther, B, Keogh, J, Cronin, J, and Cook, C. Possible stimuli for strength and power adaptation: Acute hormonal responses. *Sports Med.* 36: 215-238, 2006.

162. Crewther, BT, Cook, C, Cardinale, M, Weatherby, RP, and Lowe, T. Two emerging concepts for elite athletes: The short-term effects of testosterone and cortisol on the neuromuscular system and the dose-response training role of these endogenous hormones. *Sports Med.* 41: 103-123, 2011.

163. Critchley, D. Instructing pelvic floor contraction facilitates transversus abdominis thickness increase during low-abdominal hollowing. *Physiother Res Int.* 7: 65-75, 2002.

164. Croisier, JL, Camus, G, Venneman, I, Deby-Dupont, G, Juchmes-Ferir, A, Lamy, M, Crielaard, JM, Deby, C, and Duchateau, J. Effects of training on exercise-induced muscle damage and interleukin 6 production. *Muscle Nerve* 22: 208-212, 1999.

165. Crossland, H, Kazi, AA, Lang, CH, Timmons, JA, Pierre, P, Wilkinson, DJ, Smith, K, Szewczyk, NJ, and Atherton, PJ. Focal adhesion kinase is required for IGF-I-mediated growth of skeletal muscle cells via a TSC2/mTOR/S6K1-associated pathway. *Am J Physiol Endocrinol Metab.* 305: E183-E193, 2013.

166. Cuthbertson, DJ, Babraj, J, Smith, K, Wilkes, E, Fedele, MJ, Esser, K, and Rennie, M. Anabolic signaling and protein synthesis in human skeletal muscle after dynamic shortening or lengthening exercise. *Am J Physiol Endocrinol Metab.* 290: E731-E738, 2006.

167. Dahmane, R, Djordjevic, S, Simunic, B, and Valencic, V. Spatial fiber type distribution in normal human muscle: Histochemical and tensiomyographical evaluation. *J Biomech.* 38: 2451-2459, 2005.

168. Dangott, B, Schultz, E, and Mozdziak, PE. Dietary creatine monohydrate supplementation increases satellite cell mitotic activity during compensatory hypertrophy. *Int J Sports Med.* 21: 13-16, 2000.

169. Davidsen, PK, Gallagher, IJ, Hartman, JW, Tarnopolsky, MA, Dela, F, Helge, JW, Timmons, JA, and Phillips, SM. High responders to resistance exercise training demonstrate differential regulation of skeletal muscle microRNA expression. *J Appl Physiol.* 110: 309-317, 2011.

170. Davitt, PM, Pellegrino, JK, Schanzer, JR, Tjionas, H, and Arent, SM. The effects of a combined resistance training and endurance exercise program in inactive college female subjects: Does order matter? *J Strength Cond Res.* 28: 1937-1945, 2014.

171. de Lima, C, Boullosa, DA, Frollini, AB, Donatto, FF, Leite, RD, Gonelli, PR, Montebello, MI, Prestes, J, and Cesar, MC. Linear and daily undulating resistance training periodizations have differential beneficial effects in young sedentary women. *Int J Sports Med.* 33: 723-727, 2012.

172. de Souza, TP, Jr, Fleck, SJ, Simao, R, Dubas, JP, Pereira, B, de Brito Pacheco, EM, da Silva, AC, and de Oliveira, PR. Comparison between constant and decreasing rest intervals: Influence on maximal strength and hypertrophy. *J Strength Cond Res.* 24: 1843-1850, 2010.

173. Debold, EP. Recent insights into the molecular basis of muscular fatigue. *Med Sci Sports Exerc.* 44(8): 1440-1452, 2012.

174. Denne, SC, Liechty, EA, Liu, YM, Brechtel, G, and Baron, AD. Proteolysis in skeletal muscle and whole body in response to euglycemic hyperinsulinemia in normal adults. *Am J Physiol.* 261: E809-E814, 1991.

175. Dennis, PB, Jaeschke, A, Saitoh, M, Fowler, B, Kozma, SC, and Thomas, G. Mammalian TOR: A homeostatic ATP sensor. *Science* 294: 1102-1105, 2001.

176. Derave, W, Lund, S, Holman, GD, Wojtaszewski, J, Pedersen, O, and Richter, EA. Contraction-stimulated muscle glucose transport and GLUT-4 surface content are dependent on glycogen content. *Am J Physiol.* 277: E1103-E1110, 1999.

177. Deutz, NE, and Wolfe, RR. Is there a maximal anabolic response to protein intake with a meal? *Clin Nutr.* 32: 309-313, 2013.

178. Devaney, JM, Tosi, LL, Fritz, DT, Gordish-Dressman, HA, Jiang, S, Orkunoglu-Suer, FE, Gordon, AH, Harmon, BT, Thompson, PD, Clarkson, PM, Angelopoulos, TJ, Gordon, PM, Moyna, NM, Pescatello, LS, Visich, PS, Zoeller, RF, Brandoli, C, Hoffman, EP, and Rogers, MB. Differences in fat and muscle mass associated with a functional human polymorphism in a post-transcriptional BMP2 gene regulatory element. *J Cell Biochem.* 107: 1073-1082, 2009.

179. Dhawan, J, and Rando, TA. Stem cells in postnatal myogenesis: Molecular mechanisms of satellite cell quiescence, activation and replenishment. *Trends Cell Biol.* 15: 666-673, 2005.

180. Di Donato, DM, West, DW, Churchward-Venne, TA, Breen, L, Baker, SK, and Phillips, SM. Influence of aerobic exercise intensity on myofibrillar and mitochondrial protein synthesis in young men during early and late postexercise recovery. *Am J Physiol Endocrinol Metab.* 306: E1025-E1032, 2014.

181. Dideriksen, K, Reitelseder, S, and Holm, L. Influence of amino acids, dietary protein, and physical activity on muscle mass development in humans. *Nutrients* 5: 852-876, 2013.

182. Dieli-Conwright, CM, Spektor, TM, Rice, JC, Sattler, FR, and Schroeder, ET. Influence of hormone replacement therapy on eccentric exercise induced myogenic gene expression in postmenopausal women. *J Appl Physiol.* 1985(107): 1381-1388, 2009.

183. Dimitrova, NA, and Dimitrov, GV. Interpretation of EMG changes with fatigue: Facts, pitfalls, and fallacies. *J Electromyogr Kinesiol.* 13: 13-36, 2003.

184. Doessing, S, Heinemeier, KM, Holm, L, Mackey, AL, Schjerling, P, Rennie, M, Smith, K, Reitelseder, S, Kappelgaard, AM, Rasmussen, MH, Flyvbjerg, A, and Kjaer, M. Growth hormone stimulates the collagen synthesis in human tendon and skeletal muscle without affecting myofibrillar protein synthesis. *J Physiol.* 588: 341-351, 2010.

185. Donges, CE, Burd, NA, Duffield, R, Smith, GC, West, DW, Short, MJ, Mackenzie, R, Plank, LD, Shepherd, PR, Phillips, SM, and Edge, JA. Concurrent resistance and aerobic exercise stimulates both myofibrillar and mitochondrial protein synthesis in sedentary middle-aged men. *J Appl Physiol.* 1985(112): 1992-2001, 2012.

186. Dorgan, JF, Judd, JT, Longcope, C, Brown, C, Schatzkin, A, Clevidence, BA, Campbell, WS, Nair, PP, Franz, C, Kahle, L, and Taylor, PR. Effects of dietary fat and fiber on plasma and urine androgens and estrogens in men: A controlled feeding study. *Am J Clin Nutr.* 64: 850-855, 1996.

187. Dowling, JJ, Konert, E, Ljucovic, P, and Andrews, DM. Are humans able to voluntarily elicit maximum muscle force? *Neurosci Lett.* 179: 25-28, 1994.

188. Dreyer, HC, Fujita, S, Cadenas, JG, Chinkes, DL, Volpi, E, and Rasmussen, BB. Resistance exercise increases AMPK activity and reduces 4E-BP1 phosphorylation and protein synthesis in human skeletal muscle. *J Physiol.* 576: 613-624, 2006.

189. Drummond, MJ, Fujita, S, Abe, T, Dreyer, HC, Volpi, E, and Rasmussen, BB. Human muscle gene expression following resistance exercise and blood flow restriction. *Med Sci Sports Exerc.* 40: 691-698, 2008.

190. Drummond, MJ, Dreyer, HC, Fry, CS, Glynn, EL, and Rasmussen, BB. Nutritional and contractile regulation of human skeletal muscle protein synthesis and mTORC1 signaling. *J Appl Physiol.* 1985(106): 1374-1384, 2009.

191. Duchateau, J, Semmler, JG, and Enoka, RM. Training adaptations in the behavior of human motor units. *J Appl Physiol.* 101: 1766-1775, 2006.

192. Dunn, SE, Burns, JL, and Michel, RN. Calcineurin is required for skeletal muscle hypertrophy. *J Biol Chem.* 274: 21908-21912, 1999.

193. Dunn, SE, Chin, ER, and Michel, RN. Matching of calcineurin activity to upstream effectors is critical for skeletal muscle fiber growth. *J Cell Biol.* 151: 663-672, 2000.

194. Durand, RJ, Castracane, VD, Hollander, DB, Tryniecki, JL, Bamman, MM, O'Neal, S, Hebert, EP, and Kraemer, RR. Hormonal responses from concentric and eccentric muscle contractions. *Med Sci Sports Exerc.* 35: 937-943, 2003.

195. Ebbeling, CB, and Clarkson, PM. Exercise-induced muscle damage and adaptation. *Sports Med.* 7: 207-234, 1989.

196. Ebben, WP, Feldmann, CR, Dayne, A, Mitsche, D, Alexander, P, and Knetzger, KJ. Muscle activation during lower body resistance training. *Int J Sports Med.* 30: 1-8, 2009.

197. Edmonds, MS, and Baker, DH. Amino acid excesses for young pigs: Effects of excess methionine, tryptophan, threonine or leucine. *J Anim Sci.* 64: 1664-1671, 1987.

198. Edstrom, L, and Ekblom, B. Differences in sizes of red and white muscle fibres in vastus lateralis of musculus quadriceps femoris of normal individuals and athletes. Relation to physical performance. *Scand J Clin Lab Invest.* 30: 175-181, 1972.

199. Egner, IM, Bruusgaard, JC, Eftestol, E, and Gundersen, K. A cellular memory mechanism aids overload hypertrophy in muscle long after an episodic exposure to anabolic steroids. *J Physiol.* 591: 6221-6230, 2013.

200. Ehrnborg, C, and Rosen, T. Physiological and pharmacological basis for the ergogenic effects of growth hormone in elite sports. *Asian J Androl.* 10: 373-383, 2008.

201. Eliasson, J, Elfegoun, T, Nilsson, J, Kohnke, R, Ekblom, B, and Blomstrand, E. Maximal lengthening contractions increase p70 S6 kinase phosphorylation in human skeletal muscle in the absence of nutritional supply. *Am J Physiol Endocrinol Metab.* 291: 1197-1205, 2006.

202. Elkina, Y, von Haehling, S, Anker, SD, and Springer, J. The role of myostatin in muscle wasting: An overview. *J Cachexia Sarcopenia Muscle* 2: 143-151, 2011.

203. English, AW, Wolf, SL, and Segal, RL. Compartmentalization of muscles and their motor nuclei: The partitioning hypothesis. *Phys Ther.* 73: 857-867, 1993.

204. Enoka, RM. Eccentric contractions require unique activation strategies by the nervous system. *J Appl Physiol.* 81: 2339-2346, 1996.

205. Escamilla, RF, Fleisig, GS, Zheng, N, Barrentine, SW, Wilk, KE, and Andrews, JR. Biomechanics of the knee during closed kinetic chain and open kinetic chain exercises. *Med Sci Sports Exerc.* 30: 556-569, 1998.

206. Essen-Gustavsson, B, and Tesch, PA. Glycogen and triglyceride utilization in relation to muscle metabolic characteristics in men performing heavy-resistance exercise. *Eur J Appl Physiol Occup Physiol.* 61: 5-10, 1990.

207. Evans, W. Functional and metabolic consequences of sarcopenia. *J Nutr.* 127: 998S-1003S, 1997.

208. Evans, WJ, and Cannon, JG. The metabolic effects of exercise-induced muscle damage. *Exerc Sport Sci Rev.* 19: 99-125, 1991.

209. Farthing, JP, and Chilibeck, PD. The effects of eccentric and concentric training at different velocities on muscle hypertrophy. *Eur J Appl Physiol.* 89: 578-586, 2003.

210. Farup, J, Kjolhede, T, Sorensen, H, Dalgas, U, Moller, AB, Vestergaard, PF, Ringgaard, S, Bojsen-Moller, J, and Vissing, K. Muscle morphological and strength adaptations to endurance vs. resistance training. *J Strength Cond Res.* 26: 398-407, 2012.

211. Farup, J, Rahbek, SK, Riis, S, Vendelbo, MH, Paoli, F, and Vissing, K. Influence of exercise contraction mode and protein supplementation on human skeletal muscle satellite cell content and muscle fiber growth. *J Appl Physiol.* 1985(117): 898-909, 2014.

212. Farup, J, Rahbek, SK, Vendelbo, MH, Matzon, A, Hindhede, J, Bejder, A, Ringgard, S, and Vissing, K. Whey protein hydrolysate augments tendon and muscle hypertrophy independent of resistance exercise contraction mode. *Scand J Med Sci Sports* 24: 788-798, 2014.

213. Febbraio, MA, and Pedersen, BK. Contraction-induced myokine production and release: Is skeletal muscle an endocrine organ? *Exerc Sport Sci Rev.* 33: 114-119, 2005.

214. Febbraio, MA, and Pedersen, BK. Muscle-derived interleukin-6: Mechanisms for activation and possible biological roles. *FASEB J.* 16: 1335-1347, 2002.

215. Fernandez-Gonzalo, R, Lundberg, TR, and Tesch, PA. Acute molecular responses in untrained and trained muscle subjected to aerobic and resistance exercise training versus resistance training alone. *Acta Physiol. (Oxf.)* 209: 283-294, 2013.

216. Finkenzeller, G, Newsome, W, Lang, F, and Haussinger, D. Increase of c-jun mRNA upon hypo-osmotic cell swelling of rat hepatoma cells. *FEBS Lett.* 340: 163-166, 1994.

217. Fisher, J, Steele, J, Bruce-Low, S, and Smith, D. Evidence-based resistance training recommendations. *Med Sportiva* 15: 147-162, 2011.

218. Fisher, JP, Carlson, L, Steele, J, and Smith, D. The effects of pre-exhaustion, exercise order, and rest intervals in a full-body resistance training intervention. *Appl Physiol Nutr Metab.* 39: 1265-1270, 2014.

219. Flann, KL, LaStayo, PC, McClain, DA, Hazel, M, and Lindstedt, SL. Muscle damage and muscle remodeling: No pain, no gain? *J Exp Biol.* 214: 674-679, 2011.

220. Fluck, M. Regulation of protein synthesis in skeletal muscle. *Dtsch Z Sportmed.* 63: 75-80, 2012.

221. Fluckey, JD, Vary, TC, Jefferson, LS, and Farrell, PA. Augmented insulin action on rates of protein synthesis after resistance exercise in rats. *Am J Physiol.* 270: E313-E319, 1996.

222. Folland, JP, Irish, CS, Roberts, JC, Tarr, JE, and Jones, DA. Fatigue is not a necessary stimulus for strength gains during resistance training. *Br J Sports Med.* 36: 370-373, 2002.

223. Fonseca, RM, Roschel, H, Tricoli, V, de Souza, EO, Wilson, JM, Laurentino, GC, Aihara, AY, de Souza Leao, AR, and Ugrinowitsch, C. Changes in exercises are more effective than in loading schemes to improve muscle strength. *J Strength Cond Res.* 28(11): 3085-3092, 2014.

224. Formigli, L, Lombardo, LD, Adembri, C, Brunelleschi, S, Ferrari, E, and Novelli, GP. Neutrophils as mediators of human skeletal muscle ischemia-reperfusion syndrome. *Hum Pathol.* 23: 627-634, 1992.

225. Fornaro, M, Hinken, AC, Needle, S, Hu, E, Trendelenburg, AU, Mayer, A, Rosenstiel, A, Chang, C, Meier, V, Billin, AN, Becherer, JD, Brace, AD, Evans, WJ, Glass, DJ, and Russell, AJ. Mechano-growth factor peptide, the COOH terminus of unprocessed insulin-like growth factor 1, has no apparent effect on myoblasts or primary muscle stem cells. *Am J Physiol Endocrinol Metab.* 306: E150-E156, 2014.

226. Foster, WH, Tidball, JG, and Wang, Y. P38gamma activity is required for maintenance of slow skeletal muscle size. *Muscle Nerve* 45: 266-273, 2012.

227. Fox, AK, Kaufman, AE, and Horowitz, JF. Adding fat calories to meals after exercise does not alter glucose tolerance. *J Appl Physiol.* 97: 11-16, 2004.

228. Franchi, MV, Atherton, PJ, Reeves, ND, Fluck, M, Williams, J, Mitchell, WK, Selby, A, Beltran Valls, RM, and Narici, MV. Architectural, functional and molecular responses to concentric and eccentric loading in human skeletal muscle. *Acta Physiol. (Oxf.)* 210: 642-654, 2014.

229. Frey, JW, Farley, EE, O'Neil, TK, Burkholder, TJ, and Hornberger, TA. Evidence that mechanosensors with distinct biomechanical properties allow for specificity in mechanotransduction. *Biophys J.* 97: 347-356, 2009.

230. Frigeri, A, Nicchia, GP, Verbavatz, JM, Valenti, G, and Svelto, M. Expression of aquaporin-4 in fast-twitch fibers of mammalian skeletal muscle. *J Clin Invest.* 102: 695-703, 1998.

231. Fry, AC, and Kraemer, WJ. Resistance exercise overtraining and overreaching: Neuroendocrine responses. *Sports Med.* 23: 106-129, 1997.

232. Fry, AC. The role of resistance exercise intensity on muscle fibre adaptations. *Sports Med.* 34: 663-679, 2004.

233. Fry, CS, Glynn, EL, Drummond, MJ, Timmerman, KL, Fujita, S, Abe, T, Dhanani, S, Volpi, E, and Rasmussen, BB. Blood flow restriction exercise stimulates mTORC1 signaling and muscle protein synthesis in older men. *J Appl Physiol.* 108: 1199-1209, 2010.

234. Fry, CS, Drummond, MJ, Glynn, EL, Dickinson, JM, Gundermann, DM, Timmerman, KL, Walker, DK, Dhanani, S, Volpi, E, and Rasmussen, BB. Aging impairs contraction-induced human skeletal muscle mTORC1 signaling and protein synthesis. *Skelet Muscle* 1(1): 11, 2011.

235. Fujino, H, Xu, W, and Regan, JW. Prostaglandin E2 induced functional expression of early growth response factor-1 by EP4, but not EP2, prostanoid receptors via the phosphatidylinositol 3-kinase and extracellular signal-regulated kinases. *J Biol Chem.* 278: 12151-12156, 2003.

236. Fujita, T, Brechue, WF, Kurita, K, Sato, Y, and Abe, T. Increased muscle volume and strength following six days of low-intensity resistance training with restricted muscle blood flow. *Int J KAATSU Training Res.* 4: 1-8, 2008.

237. Fujita, S, Abe, T, Drummond, MJ, Cadenas, JG, Dreyer, HC, Sato, Y, Volpi, E, and Rasmussen, BB. Blood flow restriction during low-intensity resistance exercise increases S6K1 phosphorylation and muscle protein synthesis. *J Appl Physiol.* 103: 903-910, 2007.

238. Fyfe, JJ, Bishop, DJ, and Stepto, NK. Interference between concurrent resistance and endurance exercise: Molecular bases and the role of individual training variables. *Sports Med.* 44: 743-762, 2014.

239. Galvao, DA, and Taaffe, DR. Resistance exercise dosage in older adults: Single- versus multiset effects on physical performance and body composition. *J Am Geriatr Soc.* 53: 2090-2097, 2005.

240. Garcia-Lopez, D, Hernandez-Sanchez, S, Martin, E, Marin, PJ, Zarzosa, F, and Herrero, AJ. Free-weight augmentation with elastic bands improves bench-press kinematics in professional rugby players. *J Strength Cond Res.*, 2014.

241. Garma, T, Kobayashi, C, Haddad, F, Adams, GR, Bodell, PW, and Baldwin, KM. Similar acute molecular responses to equivalent volumes of isometric, lengthening, or shortening mode resistance exercise. *J Appl Physiol.* 102: 135-143, 2007.

242. Garthe, I, Raastad, T, Refsnes, PE, and Sundgot-Borgen, J. Effect of nutritional intervention on body composition and performance in elite athletes. *Eur J Sport Sci.* 13: 295-303, 2013.

243. Gelfand, RA, and Barrett, EJ. Effect of physiologic hyperinsulinemia on skeletal muscle protein synthesis and breakdown in man. *J Clin Invest.* 80: 1-6, 1987.

244. Gentil, P, Fischer, B, Martorelli, AS, Lima, RM, and Bottaro, M. Effects of equal-volume resistance training performed one or two times a week in upper body muscle size and strength of untrained young men. *J Sports Med Phys Fitness* 55: 144-149, 2015.

245. Gibala, MJ, MacDougall, JD, Tarnopolsky, MA, Stauber, WT, and Elorriaga, A. Changes in human skeletal muscle ultrastructure and force production after acute resistance exercise. *J Appl Physiol.* 78: 702-708, 1995.

246. Gibala, MJ, Interisano, SA, Tarnopolsky, MA, Roy, BD, MacDonald, JR, Yarasheski, KE, and MacDougall, JD. Myofibrillar disruption following acute concentric and eccentric resistance exercise in strength-trained men. *Can J Physiol Pharmacol.* 78: 656-661, 2000.

247. Giessing, J, Fisher, J, Steele, J, Rothe, F, Raubold, K, and Eichmann, B. The effects of low volume resistance training with and without advanced techniques in trained participants. *J Sports Med Phys Fitness*, 2014.

248. Gingras, AA, White, PJ, Chouinard, PY, Julien, P, Davis, TA, Dombrowski, L, Couture, Y, Dubreuil, P, Myre, A, Bergeron, K, Marette, A, and Thivierge, MC. Long-chain omega-3 fatty acids regulate bovine whole-body protein metabolism by promoting muscle insulin signalling to the Akt-mTOR-S6K1 pathway and insulin sensitivity. *J Physiol.* 579: 269-284, 2007.

249. Glass, SC, and Armstrong, T. Electromyographical activity of the pectoralis muscle during incline and decline bench presses. *J Strength Cond Res.* 11: 163-167, 1997.

250. Glass, DJ. PI3 kinase regulation of skeletal muscle hypertrophy and atrophy. *Curr Top Microbiol Immunol.* 346: 267-278, 2010.

251. Glynn, EL, Fry, CS, Timmerman, KL, Drummond, MJ, Volpi, E, and Rasmussen, BB. Addition of carbohydrate or alanine to an essential amino acid mixture does not enhance human skeletal muscle protein anabolism. *J Nutr.* 143: 307-314, 2013.

252. Godfrey, RJ, Whyte, GP, Buckley, J, and Quinlivan, R. The role of lactate in the exercise-induced human growth hormone response: Evidence from McArdle disease. *Br J Sports Med.* 43: 521-525, 2009.

253. Goldberg, AL, Etlinger, JD, Goldspink, DF, and Jablecki, C. Mechanism of work-induced hypertrophy of skeletal muscle. *Med Sci Sports* 7: 185-198, 1975.

254. Goldspink, G. Mechanical signals, IGF-I gene splicing, and muscle adaptation. *Physiology (Bethesda)* 20: 232-238, 2005.

255. Goldspink, G. Impairment of IGF-I gene splicing and MGF expression associated with muscle wasting. *Int J Biochem Cell Biol.* 38: 481-489, 2006.

256. Gollnick, PD, Karlsson, J, Piehl, K, and Saltin, B. Selective glycogen depletion in skeletal muscle fibres of man following sustained contractions. *J Physiol.* 241: 59-67, 1974.

257. Gollnick, PD, and Saltin, B. Significance of skeletal muscle oxidative enzyme enhancement with endurance training. *Clin Physiol.* 2: 1-12, 1982.

258. Gomez-Cabrera, MC, Domenech, E, and Vina, J. Moderate exercise is an antioxidant: Upregulation of antioxidant genes by training. *Free Radic Biol Med.* 44: 126-131, 2008.

259. Goodman, CA, Mayhew, DL, and Hornberger, TA. Recent progress toward understanding the molecular mechanisms that regulate skeletal muscle mass. *Cell Signal.* 23: 1896-1906, 2011.

260. Goodman, CA, and Hornberger, TA. New roles for Smad signaling and phosphatidic acid in the regulation of skeletal muscle mass. *F1000Prime Rep.* 6: 20-20. eCollection 2014, 2014.

261. Gordon, SE, Kraemer, WJ, Vos, NH, Lynch, JM, and Knuttgen, HG. Effect of acid-base balance on the growth hormone response to acute high-intensity cycle exercise. *J Appl Physiol.* 76: 821-829, 1994.

262. Goto, K, Ishii, N, Kizuka, T, and Takamatsu, K. The impact of metabolic stress on hormonal responses and muscular adaptations. *Med Sci Sports Exerc.* 37: 955-963, 2005.

263. Gotshalk, LA, Loebel, CC, Nindl, BC, Putukian, M, Sebastianelli, WJ, Newton, RU, Hakkinen, K, and Kraemer, WJ. Hormonal responses of multiset versus single-set heavy-resistance exercise protocols. *Can J Appl Physiol.* 22: 244-255, 1997.

264. Gravelle, BL, and Blessing, DL. Physiological adaptation in women concurrently training for strength and endurance. *J Strength Cond Res.* 14: 5-13, 2000.

265. Greenhaff, PL, Karagounis, LG, Peirce, N, Simpson, EJ, Hazell, M, Layfield, R, Wackerhage, H, Smith, K, Atherton, P, Selby, A, and Rennie, MJ. Disassociation between the effects of amino acids and insulin on signaling, ubiquitin ligases, and protein turnover in human muscle. *Am J Physiol Endocrinol Metab.* 295: E595-E604, 2008.

266. Gundersen, K. Excitation-transcription coupling in skeletal muscle: The molecular pathways of exercise. *Biol Rev Camb Philos Soc.* 86: 564-600, 2011.

267. Gute, DC, Ishida, T, Yarimizu, K, and Korthuis, RJ. Inflammatory responses to ischemia and reperfusion in skeletal muscle. *Mol Cell Biochem.* 179: 169-187, 1998.

268. Guyton, A. *Textbook of Medical Physiology.* Philadelphia, PA: WB Saunders, 1986.

269. Habermeyer, P, Kaiser, E, Knappe, M, Kreusser, T, and Wiedemann, E. Functional anatomy and biomechanics of the long biceps tendon. *Unfallchirurg* 90: 319-329, 1987.

270. Hackett, DA, Johnson, NA, and Chow, CM. Training practices and ergogenic aids used by male bodybuilders. *J Strength Cond Res.* 27: 1609-1617, 2013.

271. Haddad, F, and Adams, GR. Selected contribution: Acute cellular and molecular responses to resistance exercise. *J Appl Physiol.* 1985(93): 394-403, 2002.

272. Haddad, F, and Adams, GR. Inhibition of MAP/ERK kinase prevents IGF-I-induced hypertrophy in rat muscles. *J Appl Physiol.* 96: 203-210, 2004.

273. Hakkinen, K, and Pakarinen, A. Acute hormonal responses to two different fatiguing heavy-resistance protocols in male athletes. *J Appl Physiol.* 74: 882-887, 1993.

274. Hakkinen, K, and Kallinen, M. Distribution of strength training volume into one or two daily sessions and neuromuscular adaptations in female athletes. *Electromyogr Clin Neurophysiol.* 34: 117-124, 1994.

275. Hakkinen, K, Newton, RU, Gordon, SE, McCormick, M, Volek, JS, Nindl, BC, Gotshalk, LA, Campbell, WW, Evans, WJ, Hakkinen, A, Humphries, BJ, and Kraemer, WJ. Changes in muscle morphology, electromyographic activity, and force production characteristics during progressive strength training in young and older men. *J Gerontol A Biol Sci Med Sci.* 53: B415-423, 1998.

276. Hakkinen, K, Alen, M, Kallinen, M, Newton, RU, and Kraemer, WJ. Neuromuscular adaptation during prolonged strength training, detraining and re-strength-training in middle-aged and elderly people. *Eur J Appl Physiol.* 83: 51-62, 2000.

277. Hakkinen, K, Pakarinen, A, Kraemer, WJ, Newton, RU, and Alen, M. Basal concentrations and acute responses of serum hormones and strength development during heavy resistance training in middle-aged and elderly men and women. *J Gerontol A Biol Sci Med Sci.* 55: B95-105, 2000.

278. Hakkinen, K, Pakarinen, A, Kraemer, WJ, Hakkinen, A, Valkeinen, H, and Alen, M. Selective muscle hypertrophy, changes in EMG and force, and serum hormones during strength training in older women. *J Appl Physiol.* 91: 569-580, 2001.

279. Hamalainen, EK, Adlercreutz, H, Puska, P, and Pietinen, P. Decrease of serum total and free testosterone during a low-fat high-fibre diet. *J Steroid Biochem.* 18: 369-370, 1983.

280. Hameed, M, Lange, KH, Andersen, JL, Schjerling, P, Kjaer, M, Harridge, SD, and Goldspink, G. The effect of recombinant human growth hormone and resistance training on IGF-I mRNA expression in the muscles of elderly men. *J Physiol.* 555: 231-240, 2004.

281. Hamer, HM, Wall, BT, Kiskini, A, de Lange, A, Groen, BB, Bakker, JA, Gijsen, AP, Verdijk, LB, and van Loon, LJ. Carbohydrate co-ingestion with protein does not further augment post-prandial muscle protein accretion in older men. *Nutr Metab. (Lond.)* 10(1): 15, 2013.

282. Hand, BD, Kostek, MC, Ferrell, RE, Delmonico, MJ, Douglass, LW, Roth, SM, Hagberg, JM, and Hurley, BF. Influence of promoter region variants of insulin-like growth factor pathway genes on the strength-training response of muscle phenotypes in older adults. *J Appl Physiol.* 103: 1678-1687, 2007.

283. Handayaningsih, A, Iguchi, G, Fukuoka, H, Nishizawa, H, Takahashi, M, Yamamoto, M, Herningtyas, E, Okimura, Y, Kaji, H, Chihara, K, Seino, S, and Takahashi, Y. Reactive oxygen species play an essential role in IGF-I signaling and IGF-I-induced myocyte hypertrophy in C2C12 myocytes. *Endocrinology* 152: 912-921, 2011.

284. Hansen, M, and Kjaer, M. Influence of sex and estrogen on musculotendinous protein turnover at rest and after exercise. *Exerc Sport Sci Rev.* 42: 183-192, 2014.

285. Hansen, S, Kvorning, T, Kjaer, M, and Sjogaard, G. The effect of short-term strength training on human skeletal muscle: The importance of physiologically elevated hormone levels. *Scand J Med Sci Sports* 11: 347-354, 2001.

286. Hanssen, KE, Kvamme, NH, Nilsen, TS, Ronnestad, B, Ambjornsen, IK, Norheim, F, Kadi, F, Hallen, J, Drevon, CA, and Raastad, T. The effect of strength training volume on satellite cells, myogenic regulatory factors, and growth factors. *Scand J Med Sci Sports* 23: 728-739, 2013.

287. Harber, MP, Konopka, AR, Douglass, MD, Minchev, K, Kaminsky, LA, Trappe, TA, and Trappe, S. Aerobic exercise training improves whole muscle and single myofiber size and function in older women. *Am J Physiol Regul Integr Comp Physiol.* 297: R1452-459, 2009.

288. Harber, MP, Konopka, AR, Undem, MK, Hinkley, JM, Minchev, K, Kaminsky, LA, Trappe, TA, and Trappe, S. Aerobic exercise training induces skeletal muscle hypertrophy and age-dependent adaptations in myofiber function in young and older men. *J Appl Physiol.* 1985(113): 1495-1504, 2012.

289. Harridge, SD. Plasticity of human skeletal muscle: Gene expression to in vivo function. *Exp Physiol.* 92: 783-797, 2007.

290. Harries, SK, Lubans, DR, and Callister, R. Comparison of resistance training progression models on maximal strength in sub-elite adolescent rugby union players. *J Sci Med Sport,* 19(2): 163-169, 2015.

291. Hartman, MJ, Clark, B, Bembens, DA, Kilgore, JL, and Bemben, MG. Comparisons between twice-daily and once-daily training sessions in male weight lifters. *Int J Sports Physiol Perform.* 2: 159-169, 2007.

292. Haussinger, D, Lang, F, and Gerok, W. Regulation of cell function by the cellular hydration state. *Am J Physiol.* 267: E343-E355, 1994.

293. Haussinger, D. The role of cellular hydration in the regulation of cell function. *Biochem J.* 313 (Pt 3): 697-710, 1996.

294. Hawley, JA, Burke, LM, Phillips, SM, and Spriet, LL. Nutritional modulation of training-induced skeletal muscle adaptations. *J Appl Physiol.* 1985(110): 834-845, 2011.

295. Hawley, JA. Molecular responses to strength and endurance training: Are they incompatible? *Appl Physiol Nutr Metab* 34: 355-361, 2009.

296. Hebert-Losier, K, Schneiders, AG, Garcia, JA, Sullivan, SJ, and Simoneau, GG. Influence of knee flexion angle and age on triceps surae muscle activity during heel raises. *J Strength Cond Res.* 26: 3124-3133, 2012.

297. Hedayatpour, N, and Falla, D. Non-uniform muscle adaptations to eccentric exercise and the implications for training and sport. *J Electromyogr Kinesiol.* 22: 329-333, 2012.

298. Helms, E, Fitschen, PJ, Aragon, A, Cronin, J, and Schoenfeld, BJ. Recommendations for natural bodybuilding contest preparation: Resistance and cardiovascular training. *J Sports Med Phys Fitness,* 55(3): 164-178, 2014.

299. Helms, ER, Aragon, AA, and Fitschen, PJ. Evidence-based recommendations for natural bodybuilding contest preparation: Nutrition and supplementation. *J Int Soc Sports Nutr.* 11: 20, 2014.

300. Helms, ER, Zinn, C, Rowlands, DS, and Brown, SR. A systematic review of dietary protein during caloric restriction in resistance trained lean athletes: A case for higher intakes. *Int J Sport Nutr Exerc Metab.* 24: 127-138, 2014.

301. Henneman, E, Somjen, G, and Carpenter, DO. Functional significance of cell size in spinal motoneurons. *J Neurophysiol.* 28: 560-580, 1965.

302. Hepburn, D, and Maughan, RJ. Glycogen availability as a limiting factor in the performance of isometric exercise. *J Physiol.* 342: 52P-53P, 1982.

303. Herman-Montemayor, JR, Hikida, RS, and Staron, RS. Early-phase satellite cell and myonuclear domain adaptations to slow-speed versus traditional resistance training programs. *J Strength Cond Res.* 29(11): 3105-3114, 2015.

304. Heron, MI, and Richmond, FJ. In-series fiber architecture in long human muscles. *J Morphol.* 216: 35-45, 1993.

305. Heslin, MJ, Newman, E, Wolf, RF, Pisters, PW, and Brennan, MF. Effect of hyperinsulinemia on whole body and skeletal muscle leucine carbon kinetics in humans. *Am J Physiol.* 262: E911-E918, 1992.

306. Hickson, RC. Interference of strength development by simultaneously training for strength and endurance. *Eur J Appl Physiol Occup Physiol.* 45: 255-263, 1980.

307. Higbie, EJ, Cureton, KJ, Warren, GL, 3rd, and Prior, BM. Effects of concentric and eccentric training on muscle strength, cross-sectional area, and neural activation. *J Appl Physiol.* 1985(81): 2173-2181, 1996.

308. Hill, M, and Goldspink, G. Expression and splicing of the insulin-like growth factor gene in rodent muscle is associated with muscle satellite (stem) cell activation following local tissue damage. *J Physiol. (Lond.)* 549: 409-418, 2003.

309. Hill, M, Wernig, A, and Goldspink, G. Muscle satellite (stem) cell activation during local tissue injury and repair. *J Anat.* 203: 89-99, 2003.

310. Hoeger, WW, Barette, SL, Hale, DF, and Hopkins, DR. Relationship between repetitions and selected percentages of one repetition maximum. *J Appl Sport Sci Res.* 1: 11-13, 1987.

311. Holm, L, Reitelseder, S, Pedersen, TG, Doessing, S, Petersen, SG, Flyvbjerg, A, Andersen, JL, Aagaard, P, and Kjaer, M. Changes in muscle size and MHC composition in response to resistance exercise with heavy and light loading intensity. *J Appl Physiol.* 105: 1454-1461, 2008.

312. Hoppeler, H. Exercise-induced ultrastructural changes in skeletal muscle. *Int J Sports Med.* 7: 187-204, 1986.

313. Hornberger, TA, McLoughlin, TJ, Leszczynski, JK, Armstrong, DD, Jameson, RR, Bowen, PE, Hwang, ES, Hou, H, Moustafa, ME, Carlson, BA, Hatfield, DL, Diamond, AM, and Esser, KA. Selenoprotein-deficient transgenic mice exhibit enhanced exercise-induced muscle growth. *J Nutr.* 133: 3091-3097, 2003.

314. Hornberger, TA, and Esser, KA. Mechanotransduction and the regulation of protein synthesis in skeletal muscle. *Proc Nutr Soc.* 63: 331-335, 2004.

315. Hornberger, TA, Chu, WK, Mak, YW, Hsiung, JW, Huang, SA, and Chien, S. The role of phospholipase D and phosphatidic acid in the mechanical activation of mTOR signaling in skeletal muscle. *Proc Natl Acad Sci USA.* 103: 4741-4746, 2006.

316. Hornberger, TA, Chu, WK, Mak, YW, Hsiung, JW, Huang, SA, and Chien, S. The role of phospholipase D and phosphatidic acid in the mechanical activation of mTOR signaling in skeletal muscle. *Proc Natl Acad Sci USA* 103: 4741-4746, 2006.

317. Horsley, V, and Pavlath, GK. Prostaglandin F2(alpha) stimulates growth of skeletal muscle cells via an NFATC2-dependent pathway. *J Cell Biol.* 161: 111-118, 2003.

318. Hortobagyi, T, Hill, JP, Houmard, JA, Fraser, DD, Lambert, NJ, and Israel, RG. Adaptive responses to muscle lengthening and shortening in humans. *J Appl Physiol.* 1985(80): 765-772, 1996.

319. Hortobagyi, T, Dempsey, L, Fraser, D, Zheng, D, Hamilton, G, Lambert, J, and Dohm, L. Changes in muscle strength, muscle fibre size and myofibrillar gene expression after immobilization and retraining in humans. *J Physiol.* 524 Pt 1: 293-304, 2000.

320. Housh, DJ, Housh, TJ, Johnson, GO, and Chu, WK. Hypertrophic response to unilateral concentric isokinetic resistance training. *J Appl Physiol.* 1985(73): 65-70, 1992.

321. Houtman, CJ, Stegeman, DF, Van Dijk, JP, and Zwarts, MJ. Changes in muscle fiber conduction velocity indicate recruitment of distinct motor unit populations. *J Appl Physiol.* 95: 1045-1054, 2003.

322. Howatson, G, and Milak, A. Exercise-induced muscle damage following a bout of sport specific repeated sprints. *J Strength Cond Res.* 23: 2419-2424, 2009.

323. Howell, JN, Chleboun, G, and Conatser, R. Muscle stiffness, strength loss, swelling and soreness following exercise-induced injury in humans. *J Physiol. (Lond.)* 464: 183-196, 1993.

324. Hubal, MJ, Gordish-Dressman, H, Thompson, PD, Price, TB, Hoffman, EP, Angelopoulos, TJ, Gordon, PM, Moyna, NM, Pescatello, LS, Visich, PS, Zoeller, RF, Seip, RL, and Clarkson, PM. Variability in muscle size and strength gain after unilateral resistance training. *Med Sci Sports Exerc.* 37: 964-972, 2005.

325. Hudelmaier, M, Wirth, W, Himmer, M, Ring-Dimitriou, S, Sanger, A, and Eckstein, F. Effect of exercise intervention on thigh muscle volume and anatomical cross-sectional areas: Quantitative assessment using MRI. *Magn Reson Med.* 64: 1713-1720, 2010.

326. Hudson, MB, and Price, SR. Calcineurin: A poorly understood regulator of muscle mass. *Int J Biochem Cell Biol.* 45: 2173-2178, 2013.

327. Hulmi, JJ, Walker, S, Ahtiainen, JP, Nyman, K, Kraemer, WJ, and Hakkinen, K. Molecular signaling in muscle is affected by the specificity of resistance exercise protocol. *Scand J Med Sci Sports* 22: 240-248, 2012.

328. Hung, YJ, and Gross, MT. Effect of foot position on electromyographic activity of the vastus medialis oblique and vastus lateralis during lower-extremity weight-bearing activities. *J Orthop Sports Phys Ther.* 29: 93-102; discussion 103-105, 1999.

329. Huxley, AF. The origin of force in skeletal muscle. *Ciba Found Symp.* 31: 271-290, 1975.

330. Iida, K, Itoh, E, Kim, DS, del Rincon, JP, Coschigano, KT, Kopchick, JJ, and Thorner, MO. Muscle mechano growth factor is preferentially induced by growth hormone in growth hormone-deficient lit/lit mice. *J Physiol.* 560: 341-349, 2004.

331. Imanaka, M, Iida, K, Murawaki, A, Nishizawa, H, Fukuoka, H, Takeno, R, Takahashi, Y, Okimura, Y, Kaji, H, and Chihara, K. Growth hormone stimulates mechano growth factor expression and activates myoblast transformation in C2C12 cells. *Kobe J Med Sci.* 54: E46-E54, 2008.

332. Ingemann-Hansen, T, Halkjaer-Kristensen, J, and Halskov, O. Skeletal muscle phosphagen and lactate concentrations in ischaemic dynamic exercise. *Eur J Appl Physiol Occup Physiol.* 46: 261-270, 1981.

333. Ivey, FM, Roth, SM, Ferrell, RE, Tracy, BL, Lemmer, JT, Hurlbut, DE, Martel, GF, Siegel, EL, Fozard, JL, Jeffrey Metter, E, Fleg, JL, and Hurley, BF. Effects of age, gender, and myostatin genotype on the hypertrophic response to heavy resistance strength training. *J Gerontol A Biol Sci Med Sci.* 55: M641-648, 2000.

334. Ivy, J, and Ferguson-Stegall, L. Nutrient timing: The means to improved exercise performance, recovery, and training. *Am J Lifestyle Med.* 1-14, 2013.

335. Ivy, JL. Glycogen resynthesis after exercise: Effect of carbohydrate intake. *Int J Sports Med.* 19 Suppl 2: S142-145, 1998.

336. Izquierdo, M, Ibanez, J, Hakkinen, K, Kraemer, WJ, Larrion, JL, and Gorostiaga, EM. Once weekly combined resistance and cardiovascular training in healthy older men. *Med Sci Sports Exerc.* 36: 435-443, 2004.

337. Izquierdo, M, Hakkinen, K, Ibanez, J, Kraemer, WJ, and Gorostiaga, EM. Effects of combined resistance and cardiovascular training on strength, power, muscle cross-sectional area, and endurance markers in middle-aged men. *Eur J Appl Physiol.* 94: 70-75, 2005.

338. Izquierdo, M, Ibanez, J, Gonzalez-Badillo, JJ, Hakkinen, K, Ratamess, NA, Kraemer, WJ, French, DN, Eslava, J, Altadill, A, Asiain, X, and Gorostiaga, EM. Differential effects of strength training leading to failure versus not to failure on hormonal responses, strength, and muscle power gains. *J Appl Physiol.* 100: 1647-1656, 2006.

339. Jacinto, E, and Hall, MN. Tor signalling in bugs, brain and brawn. *Nat Rev Mol Cell Biol.* 4: 117-126, 2003.

340. Jackson, MJ. Free radicals generated by contracting muscle: By-products of metabolism or key regula-

tors of muscle function? *Free Radic Biol Med.* 44: 132-141, 2008.

341. Ji, LL, Gomez-Cabrera, MC, and Vina, J. Exercise and hormesis: Activation of cellular antioxidant signaling pathway. *Ann NY Acad Sci.* 1067: 425-435, 2006.

342. Johnston, BD. moving too rapidly in strength training will unload muscles and limit full range strength development adaptation. *J Exerc Physiol Online* 8: 36-45, 2005.

343. Jones, DA, and Rutherford, OM. Human muscle strength training: The effects of three different regimens and the nature of the resultant changes. *J Physiol. (Lond.)* 391: 1-11, 1987.

344. Jones, TW, Howatson, G, Russell, M, and French, DN. Performance and neuromuscular adaptations following differing ratios of concurrent strength and endurance training. *J Strength Cond Res.* 27: 3342-3351, 2013.

345. Jubrias, SA, Esselman, PC, Price, LB, Cress, ME, and Conley, KE. Large energetic adaptations of elderly muscle to resistance and endurance training. *J Appl Physiol.* 1985(90): 1663-1670, 2001.

346. Junior, V, Gentil, P, Oliveira, E, and Carmo, J. Comparison among the EMG activity of the pectoralis major, anterior deltoidis and triceps brachii during the bench press and peck deck exercises. *Rev Bras Med Esporte.* 13: 43-46, 2007.

347. Kadi, F, Charifi, N, Denis, C, and Lexell, J. Satellite cells and myonuclei in young and elderly women and men. *Muscle Nerve* 29: 120-127, 2004.

348. Kadi, F, Schjerling, P, Andersen, LL, Charifi, N, Madsen, JL, Christensen, LR, and Andersen, JL. The effects of heavy resistance training and detraining on satellite cells in human skeletal muscles. *J Physiol.* 558: 1005-1012, 2004.

349. Kamen, G, and Knight, CA. Training-related adaptations in motor unit discharge rate in young and older adults. *J Gerontol A Biol Sci Med Sci.* 59: 1334-1338, 2004.

350. Kami, K, and Senba, E. Localization of leukemia inhibitory factor and interleukin-6 messenger ribonucleic acids in regenerating rat skeletal muscle. *Muscle Nerve* 21: 819-822, 1998.

351. Karst, GM, and Willett, GM. Effects of specific exercise instructions on abdominal muscle activity during trunk curl exercises. *J Orthop Sports Phys Ther.* 34: 4-12, 2004.

352. Katch, VL, Katch, FI, Moffatt, R, and Gittleson, M. Muscular development and lean body weight in body builders and weight lifters. *Med Sci Sports Exerc.* 12: 340-344, 1980.

353. Katsanos, CS, Kobayashi, H, Sheffield-Moore, M, Aarsland, A, and Wolfe, RR. A high proportion of leucine is required for optimal stimulation of the rate of muscle protein synthesis by essential amino acids in the elderly. *Am J Physiol Endocrinol Metab.* 291: E381-E387, 2006.

354. Kawada, S, and Ishii, N. Skeletal muscle hypertrophy after chronic restriction of venous blood flow in rats. *Med Sci Sports Exerc.* 37: 1144-1150, 2005.

355. Kawanaka, K, Nolte, LA, Han, DH, Hansen, PA, and Holloszy, JO. Mechanisms underlying impaired GLUT-4 translocation in glycogen-supercompensated muscles of exercised rats. *Am J Physiol Endocrinol Metab.* 279: E1311-E1318, 2000.

356. Keeler, LK, Finkelstein, LH, Miller, W, and Fernhall, B. Early-phase adaptations of traditional-speed vs. superslow resistance training on strength and aerobic capacity in sedentary individuals. *J Strength Cond Res.* 15: 309-314, 2001.

357. Kefaloyianni, E, Gaitanaki, C, and Beis, I. ERK1/2 and p38-MAPK signalling pathways, through MSK1, are involved in NF-kappaB transactivation during oxidative stress in skeletal myoblasts. *Cell Signal.* 18: 2238-2251, 2006.

358. Kelley, G. Mechanical overload and skeletal muscle fiber hyperplasia: A meta-analysis. *J Appl Physiol.* 81: 1584-1588, 1996.

359. Keogh, JWL, Wilson, GJ, and Weatherby, RP. A cross-sectional comparison of different resistance training techniques in the bench press. *J Strength Cond Res.* 13: 247-258, 1999.

360. Kerksick, C, Harvey, T, Stout, J, Campbell, B, Wilborn, C, Kreider, R, Kalman, D, Ziegenfuss, T, Lopez, H, Landis, J, Ivy, JL, and Antonio, J. International Society of Sports Nutrition position stand: Nutrient timing. *J Int Soc Sports Nutr.* 5: 17, 2008.

361. Kerksick, CM, Wilborn, CD, Campbell, BI, Roberts, MD, Rasmussen, CJ, Greenwood, M, and Kreider, RB. Early-phase adaptations to a split-body, linear periodization resistance training program in college-aged and middle-aged men. *J Strength Cond Res.* 23: 962-971, 2009.

362. Kettelhut, IC, Wing, SS, and Goldberg, AL. Endocrine regulation of protein breakdown in skeletal muscle. *Diabetes Metab Rev.* 4: 751-772, 1988.

363. Kidgell, DJ, Sale, MV, and Semmler, JG. Motor unit synchronization measured by cross-correlation is not influenced by short-term strength training of a hand muscle. *Exp Brain Res.* 175: 745-753, 2006.

364. Kim, DH, Kim, JY, Yu, BP, and Chung, HY. The activation of NF-kappaB through Akt-induced FOXO1 phosphorylation during aging and its modulation by calorie restriction. *Biogerontology* 9: 33-47, 2008.

365. Kim, H, Barton, E, Muja, N, Yakar, S, Pennisi, P, and Leroith, D. Intact insulin and insulin-like growth factor-I receptor signaling is required for growth hormone effects on skeletal muscle growth and function in vivo. *Endocrinology* 146: 1772-1779, 2005.

366. Kim, JS, Cross, JM, and Bamman, MM. Impact of resistance loading on myostatin expression and cell cycle regulation in young and older men and women. *Am J Physiol Endocrinol Metab.* 288: E1110-E1119, 2005.

367. Kim, JS, Petrella, JK, Cross, JM, and Bamman, MM. Load-mediated downregulation of myostatin mRNA is not sufficient to promote myofiber hypertrophy in humans: A cluster analysis. *J Appl Physiol.* 1985(103): 1488-1495, 2007.

368. Kim, SY, Ko, JB, Farthing, JP, and Butcher, SJ. Investigation of supraspinatus muscle architecture following concentric and eccentric training. *J Sci Med Sport* 18(4): 378-382, 2014.

369. Kimball, SR. Integration of signals generated by nutrients, hormones, and exercise in skeletal muscle. *Am J Clin Nutr.* 99: 237S-242S, 2014.

370. Klover, P, and Hennighausen, L. Postnatal body growth is dependent on the transcription factors signal transducers and activators of transcription 5a/b in muscle: A role for autocrine/paracrine insulin-like growth factor I. *Endocrinology* 148: 1489-1497, 2007.

371. Knight, CA, and Kamen, G. Adaptations in muscular activation of the knee extensor muscles with strength training in young and older adults. *J Electromyogr Kinesiol.* 11: 405-412, 2001.

372. Koh, TJ, and Pizza, FX. Do inflammatory cells influence skeletal muscle hypertrophy? *Front Biosci. (Elite Ed.)* 1: 60-71, 2009.

373. Kohn, TA, Essen-Gustavsson, B, and Myburgh, KH. Specific muscle adaptations in type II fibers after high-intensity interval training of well-trained runners. *Scand J Med Sci Sports* 21: 765-772, 2011.

374. Kok, LY, Hamer, PW, and Bishop, DJ. Enhancing muscular qualities in untrained women: Linear versus undulating periodization. *Med Sci Sports Exerc.* 41: 1797-1807, 2009.

375. Komi, PV, and Buskirk, ER. Effect of eccentric and concentric muscle conditioning on tension and electrical activity of human muscle. *Ergonomics* 15: 417-434, 1972.

376. Komulainen, J, Kalliokoski, R, Koskinen, SO, Drost, MR, Kuipers, H, and Hesselink, MK. Controlled lengthening or shortening contraction-induced damage is followed by fiber hypertrophy in rat skeletal muscle. *Int J Sports Med.* 21: 107-112, 2000.

377. Kon, M, Ikeda, T, Homma, T, and Suzuki, Y. Effects of low-intensity resistance exercise under acute systemic hypoxia on hormonal responses. *J Strength Cond Res.* 26: 611-617, 2012.

378. Konopka, AR, Douglass, MD, Kaminsky, LA, Jemiolo, B, Trappe, TA, Trappe, S, and Harber, MP. Molecular adaptations to aerobic exercise training in skeletal muscle of older women. *J Gerontol A Biol Sci Med Sci.* 65: 1201-1207, 2010.

379. Konopka, AR, and Harber, MP. Skeletal muscle hypertrophy after aerobic exercise training. *Exerc Sport Sci Rev.* 42(2): 53-61, 2014.

380. Koopman, R, Zorenc, AH, Gransier, RJ, Cameron-Smith, D, and van Loon, LJ. Increase in S6K1 phosphorylation in human skeletal muscle following resistance exercise occurs mainly in type II muscle fibers. *Am J Physiol Endocrinol Metab.* 290: E1245-E1252, 2006.

381. Koopman, R, Beelen, M, Stellingwerff, T, Pennings, B, Saris, WH, Kies, AK, Kuipers, H, and van Loon, LJ. Coingestion of carbohydrate with protein does not further augment postexercise muscle protein synthesis. *Am J Physiol Endocrinol Metab.* 293: E833-E842, 2007.

382. Kosek, DJ, Kim, JS, Petrella, JK, Cross, JM, and Bamman, MM. Efficacy of 3 days/wk resistance training on myofiber hypertrophy and myogenic mechanisms in young vs. older adults. *J Appl Physiol.* 101: 531-544, 2006.

383. Kraemer, WJ. A series of studies: The physiological basis for strength training in American football: Fact over philosophy. *J Strength Cond Res.* 11: 131-134, 1997.

384. Kraemer, WJ, Noble, BJ, Clark, MJ, and Culver, BW. Physiologic responses to heavy-resistance exercise with very short rest periods. *Int J Sports Med.* 8: 247-252, 1987.

385. Kraemer, WJ, Marchitelli, L, Gordon, SE, Harman, E, Dziados, JE, Mello, R, Frykman, P, McCurry, D, and Fleck, SJ. Hormonal and growth factor responses to heavy resistance exercise protocols. *J Appl Physiol.* 69: 1442-1450, 1990.

386. Kraemer, WJ, Gordon, SE, Fleck, SJ, Marchitelli, LJ, Mello, R, Dziados, JE, Friedl, K, Harman, E, Maresh, C, and Fry, AC. Endogenous anabolic hormonal and growth factor responses to heavy resistance exercise in males and females. *Int J Sports Med.* 12: 228-235, 1991.

387. Kraemer, WJ, Fleck, SJ, Dziados, JE, Harman, EA, Marchitelli, LJ, Gordon, SE, Mello, R, Frykman, PN, Koziris, LP, and Triplett, NT. Changes in hormonal concentrations after different heavy-resistance exercise protocols in women. *J Appl Physiol.* 75: 594-604, 1993.

388. Kraemer, WJ, Aguilera, BA, Terada, M, Newton, RU, Lynch, JM, Rosendaal, G, McBride, JM, Gordon, SE, and Hakkinen, K. Responses of IGF-I to endogenous increases in growth hormone after heavy-resistance exercise. *J Appl Physiol.* 79: 1310-1315, 1995.

389. Kraemer, WJ, Patton, JF, Gordon, SE, Harman, EA, Deschenes, MR, Reynolds, K, Newton, RU, Triplett, NT, and Dziados, JE. Compatibility of high-intensity strength and endurance training on hormonal and skeletal muscle adaptations. *J Appl Physiol.* 1985(78): 976-989, 1995.

390. Kraemer, WJ, and Ratamess, NA. Fundamentals of resistance training: Progression and exercise prescription. *Med Sci Sports Exerc.* 36: 674-688, 2004.

391. Kraemer, WJ, and Ratamess, NA. Hormonal responses and adaptations to resistance exercise and training. *Sports Med.* 35: 339-361, 2005.

392. Kraemer, WJ, Adams, K, Cafarelli, E, Dudley, GA, Dooly, C, Feigenbaum, MS, Fleck, SJ, Franklin, B, Fry, AC, Hoffman, JR, Newton, RU, Potteiger, J, Stone, MH, Ratamess, NA, and Triplett-McBride, T. American College of Sports Medicine position stand. Progression models in resistance training for healthy adults. *Med Sci Sports Exerc.* 34: 364-380, 2002.

393. Kramer, HF, and Goodyear, LJ. Exercise, MAPK, and NF-kappaB signaling in skeletal muscle. *J Appl Physiol.* 1985(103): 388-395, 2007.

394. Krentz, JR, Quest, B, Farthing, JP, Quest, DW, and Chilibeck, PD. The effects of ibuprofen on muscle hypertrophy, strength, and soreness during resistance training. *Appl Physiol Nutr Metab.* 33: 470-475, 2008.

395. Krentz, JR, and Farthing, JP. Neural and morphological changes in response to a 20-day intense eccentric training protocol. *Eur J Appl Physiol.* 110: 333-340, 2010.

396. Krieger, JW. Single vs. multiple sets of resistance exercise for muscle hypertrophy: A meta-analysis. *J Strength Cond Res.* 24: 1150-1159, 2010.

397. Kuipers, H. Exercise-induced muscle damage. *Int J Sports Med.* 15: 132-135, 1994.

398. Kumar, V, Atherton, P, Smith, K, and Rennie, MJ. Human muscle protein synthesis and breakdown during and after exercise. *J Appl Physiol.* 106: 2026-2039, 2009.

399. Kumar, V, Selby, A, Rankin, D, Patel, R, Atherton, P, Hildebrandt, W, Williams, J, Smith, K, Seynnes, O, Hiscock, N, and Rennie, MJ. Age-related differences in the dose-response relationship of muscle protein synthesis to resistance exercise in young and old men. *J Physiol.* 587: 211-217, 2009.

400. Kvorning, T, Andersen, M, Brixen, K, and Madsen, K. Suppression of endogenous testosterone production attenuates the response to strength training: A randomized, placebo-controlled, and blinded intervention study. *Am J Physiol Endocrinol Metab.* 291: E1325-E1332, 2006.

401. Kvorning, T, Andersen, M, Brixen, K, Schjerling, P, Suetta, C, and Madsen, K. Suppression of testosterone does not blunt mRNA expression of myoD, myogenin, IGF, myostatin or androgen receptor post strength training in humans. *J Physiol.* 578: 579-593, 2007.

402. Lambert, CP, and Flynn, MG. Fatigue during high-intensity intermittent exercise: Application to bodybuilding. *Sports Med.* 32: 511-522, 2002.

403. Lambert, IH, Hoffmann, EK, and Pedersen, SF. Cell volume regulation: Physiology and pathophysiology. *Acta Physiol. (Oxf.)* 194: 255-282, 2008.

404. Lane, AR, Duke, JW, and Hackney, AC. Influence of dietary carbohydrate intake on the free testosterone: Cortisol ratio responses to short-term intensive exercise training. *Eur J Appl Physiol.* 108: 1125-1131, 2010.

405. Lang, F, Busch, GL, Ritter, M, Volkl, H, Waldegger, S, Gulbins, E, and Haussinger, D. Functional significance of cell volume regulatory mechanisms. *Physiol Rev.* 78: 247-306, 1998.

406. Lang, F. Mechanisms and significance of cell volume regulation. *J Am Coll Nutr.* 26: 613S-623S, 2007.

407. Lange, KH, Andersen, JL, Beyer, N, Isaksson, F, Larsson, B, Rasmussen, MH, Juul, A, Bulow, J, and Kjaer, M. GH administration changes myosin heavy chain isoforms in skeletal muscle but does not augment muscle strength or hypertrophy, either alone or combined with resistance exercise training in healthy elderly men. *J Clin Endocrinol Metab.* 87: 513-523, 2002.

408. Langfort, J, Zarzeczny, R, Pilis, W, Nazar, K, and Kaciuba-Uscitko, H. The effect of a low-carbohydrate diet on performance, hormonal and metabolic responses to a 30-s bout of supramaximal exercise. *Eur J Appl Physiol Occup Physiol.* 76: 128-133, 1997.

409. Laurentino, GC, Ugrinowitsch, C, Roschel, H, Aoki, MS, Soares, AG, Neves, M, Jr, Aihara, AY, Fernandes Ada, R, and Tricoli, V. Strength training with blood flow restriction diminishes myostatin gene expression. *Med Sci Sports Exerc.* 44: 406-412, 2012.

410. Layman, DK. Protein quantity and quality at levels above the RDA improves adult weight loss. *J Am Coll Nutr.* 23: 631S-636S, 2004.

411. Le Bozec, S, Maton, B, and Cnockaert, JC. The synergy of elbow extensor muscles during dynamic work in man. I. Elbow extension. *Eur J Appl Physiol Occup Physiol.* 44: 255-269, 1980.

412. Leger, B, Cartoni, R, Praz, M, Lamon, S, Deriaz, O, Crettenand, A, Gobelet, C, Rohmer, P, Konzelmann, M, Luthi, F, and Russell, AP. Akt signalling through GSK-3beta, mTOR and Foxo1 is involved in human skeletal muscle hypertrophy and atrophy. *J Physiol.* 576: 923-933, 2006.

413. Lehman, GJ, Buchan, DD, Lundy, A, Myers, N, and Nalborczyk, A. Variations in muscle activation levels during traditional latissimus dorsi weight training exercises: An experimental study. *Dyn Med.* 3: 4, 2004.

414. Lehman, N, Ledford, B, Di Fulvio, M, Frondorf, K, McPhail, LC, and Gomez-Cambronero, J. Phospholipase D2-derived phosphatidic acid binds to and activates ribosomal p70 S6 kinase independently of mTOR. *FASEB J.* 21: 1075-1087, 2007.

415. Lemon, PW, Tarnopolsky, MA, MacDougall, JD, and Atkinson, SA. Protein requirements and muscle mass/strength changes during intensive training in novice bodybuilders. *J Appl Physiol.* 73: 767-775, 1992.

416. Levenhagen, DK, Gresham, JD, Carlson, MG, Maron, DJ, Borel, MJ, and Flakoll, PJ. Postexercise nutrient intake timing in humans is critical to recovery of leg glucose and protein homeostasis. *Am J Physiol Endocrinol Metab.* 280: E982-E993, 2001.

417. Leveritt, M, and Abernethy, PJ. Effects of carbohydrate restriction on strength performance. *J Strength Cond Res.* 13: 52-57, 1999.

418. Levy, AS, Kelly, BT, Lintner, SA, Osbahr, DC, and Speer, KP. Function of the long head of the biceps at the shoulder: Electromyographic analysis. *J Shoulder Elbow Surg.* 10: 250-255, 2001.

419. Lewis, CL, and Sahrmann, SA. Muscle activation and movement patterns during prone hip extension exercise in women. *J Athl Train.* 44: 238-248, 2009.

420. Lexell, J, Henriksson-Larsen, K, Winblad, B, and Sjostrom, M. Distribution of different fiber types in human skeletal muscles: Effects of aging studied in whole muscle cross sections. *Muscle Nerve* 6: 588-595, 1983.

421. Lexell, J, Downham, D, and Sjostrom, M. Distribution of different fibre types in human skeletal muscles. Fibre type arrangement in m. vastus lateralis from three groups of healthy men between 15 and 83 years. *J Neurol Sci.* 72: 211-222, 1986.

422. Lima-Silva, AE, Pires, FO, Bertuzzi, R, Silva-Cavalcante, MD, Oliveira, RS, Kiss, MA, and Bishop, D. Effects of a low- or a high-carbohydrate diet on performance, energy system contribution, and metabolic responses during supramaximal exercise. *Appl Physiol Nutr Metab.* 38: 928-934, 2013.

423. Lindman, R, Eriksson, A, and Thornell, LE. Fiber type composition of the human female trapezius muscle: Enzyme-histochemical characteristics. *Am J Anat.* 190: 385-392, 1991.

424. Loebel, C, and Kraemer, W. A brief review: Testosterone and resistance exercise in men. *J Strength Cond Res.* 12: 57-63, 1998.

425. Loenneke, JP, Wilson, GJ, and Wilson, JM. A mechanistic approach to blood flow occlusion. *Int J Sports Med.* 31: 1-4, 2010.

426. Loenneke, JP, Fahs, CA, Wilson, JM, and Bemben, MG. Blood flow restriction: The metabolite/volume threshold theory. *Med Hypotheses.* 77: 748-752, 2011.

427. Loenneke, JP, Wilson, JM, Marin, PJ, Zourdos, MC, and Bemben, MG. Low intensity blood flow restriction training: A meta-analysis. *Eur J Appl Physiol.* 112(5): 1849-1859, 2011.

428. Loenneke, JP, Thiebaud, RS, and Abe, T. Does blood flow restriction result in skeletal muscle damage? A critical review of available evidence. *Scand J Med Sci Sports* 24: e415-e422, 2014.

429. Lovell, DI, Cuneo, R, and Gass, GC. Can aerobic training improve muscle strength and power in older men? *J Aging Phys Act.* 18: 14-26, 2010.

430. Low, SY, Rennie, MJ, and Taylor, PM. Signaling elements involved in amino acid transport responses to altered muscle cell volume. *FASEB J.* 11: 1111-1117, 1997.

431. Lu, SS, Lau, CP, Tung, YF, Huang, SW, Chen, YH, Shih, HC, Tsai, SC, Lu, CC, Wang, SW, Chen, JJ, Chien, EJ, Chien, CH, and Wang, PS. Lactate and the effects of exercise on testosterone secretion: Evidence for the involvement of a cAMP-mediated mechanism. *Med Sci Sports Exerc.* 29: 1048-1054, 1997.

432. Lundberg, TR, Fernandez-Gonzalo, R, Gustafsson, T, and Tesch, PA. Aerobic exercise alters skeletal muscle molecular responses to resistance exercise. *Med Sci Sports Exerc.* 44: 1680-1688, 2012.

433. Lundberg, TR, Fernandez-Gonzalo, R, and Tesch, PA. Exercise-induced AMPK activation does not interfere with muscle hypertrophy in response to resistance training in men. *J Appl Physiol.* 1985(116): 611-620, 2014.

434. Lupu, F, Terwilliger, JD, Lee, K, Segre, GV, and Efstratiadis, A. Roles of growth hormone and insulin-like growth factor 1 in mouse postnatal growth. *Dev Biol.* 229: 141-162, 2001.

435. Lusk, SJ, Hale, BD, and Russell, DM. Grip width and forearm orientation effects on muscle activity during the lat pull-down. *J Strength Cond Res.* 24: 1895-1900, 2010.

436. Lynch, CJ, Hutson, SM, Patson, BJ, Vaval, A, and Vary, TC. Tissue-specific effects of chronic dietary leucine and norleucine supplementation on protein synthesis in rats. *Am J Physiol Endocrinol Metab.* 283: E824-E835, 2002.

437. Lynn, R, and Morgan, DL. Decline running produces more sarcomeres in rat vastus intermedius muscle fibers than does incline running. *J Appl Physiol.* 77: 1439-1444, 1994.

438. Lynn, SK, and Costigan, PA. Changes in the medial-lateral hamstring activation ratio with foot rotation during lower limb exercise. *J Electromyogr Kinesiol.* 19: e197-e205, 2009.

439. MacDougall, JD, Ward, GR, Sale, DG, and Sutton, JR. Biochemical adaptation of human skeletal muscle to heavy resistance training and immobilization. *J Appl Physiol.* 43: 700-703, 1977.

440. MacDougall, JD, Sale, DG, Elder, GC, and Sutton, JR. Muscle ultrastructural characteristics of elite powerlifters and bodybuilders. *Eur J Appl Physiol. Occup. Physiol.* 48: 117-126, 1982.

441. MacDougall, JD, Sale, DG, Alway, SE, and Sutton, JR. Muscle fiber number in biceps brachii in bodybuilders and control subjects. *J Appl Physiol.* 57: 1399-1403, 1984.

442. MacDougall, JD, Gibala, MJ, Tarnopolsky, MA, MacDonald, JR, Interisano, SA, and Yarasheski, KE. The time course for elevated muscle protein synthesis following heavy resistance exercise. *Can J Appl Physiol.* 20: 480-486, 1995.

443. MacDougall, JD, Ray, S, Sale, DG, McCartney, N, Lee, P, and Garner, S. Muscle substrate utilization and lactate production. *Can J Appl Physiol.* 24: 209-215, 1999.

444. Machado, M, Koch, AJ, Willardson, JM, Pereira, LS, Cardoso, MI, Motta, MK, Pereira, R, and Monteiro, AN. Effect of varying rest intervals between sets of assistance exercises on creatine kinase and lactate dehydrogenase responses. *J Strength Cond Res.* 25: 1339-1345, 2011.

445. Mackey, AL, Kjaer, M, Dandanell, S, Mikkelsen, KH, Holm, L, Dossing, S, Kadi, F, Koskinen, SO, Jensen, CH, Schroder, HD, and Langberg, H. The influence of anti-inflammatory medication on exercise-induced myogenic precursor cell responses in humans. *J Appl Physiol.* 103: 425-431, 2007.

446. MacNeil, LG, Melov, S, Hubbard, AE, Baker, SK, and Tarnopolsky, MA. Eccentric exercise activates novel transcriptional regulation of hypertrophic signaling pathways not affected by hormone changes. *PLoS One* 5: e10695, 2010.

447. Madarame, H, Neya, M, Ochi, E, Nakazato, K, Sato, Y, and Ishii, N. Cross-transfer effects of resistance training with blood flow restriction. *Med Sci Sports Exerc.* 40: 258-263, 2008.

448. Malm, C. Exercise-induced muscle damage and inflammation: Fact or fiction? *Acta Physiol Scand.* 171: 233-239, 2001.

449. Mamerow, MM, Mettler, JA, English, KL, Casperson, SL, Arentson-Lantz, E, Sheffield-Moore, M, Layman, DK, and Paddon-Jones, D. Dietary protein distribution positively influences 24-h muscle protein synthesis in healthy adults. *J Nutr.* 144(6): 876-880, 2014.

450. Manini, TM, and Clark, BC. Blood flow restricted exercise and skeletal muscle health. *Exerc Sport Sci Rev.* 37: 78-85, 2009.

451. Manini, TM, Vincent, KR, Leeuwenburgh, CL, Lees, HA, Kavazis, AN, Borst, SE, and Clark, BC. Myogenic and proteolytic mRNA expression following blood flow restricted exercise. *Acta Physiol. (Oxf.)* 201: 255-263, 2011.

452. Marchant, DC, Greig, M, and Scott, C. Attentional focusing instructions influence force production and muscular activity during isokinetic elbow flexions. *J Strength Cond Res.* 23: 2358-2366, 2009.

453. Marchetti, PH, and Uchida, MC. Effects of the pull-over exercise on the pectoralis major and latissimus dorsi muscles as evaluated by EMG. *J Appl Biomech.* 27: 380-384, 2011.

454. Martineau, LC, and Gardiner, PF. Insight into skeletal muscle mechanotransduction: MAPK activation is quantitatively related to tension. *J Appl Physiol.* 91: 693-702, 2001.

455. Martineau, LC, and Gardiner, PF. Skeletal muscle is sensitive to the tension-time integral but not to the rate of change of tension, as assessed by mechanically induced signaling. *J Biomech.* 35: 657-663, 2002.

456. Martins, KJ, St-Louis, M, Murdoch, GK, MacLean, IM, McDonald, P, Dixon, WT, Putman, CT, and Michel, RN. Nitric oxide synthase inhibition prevents activity-induced calcineurin-NFATc1 signalling and fast-to-slow skeletal muscle fibre type conversions. *J Physiol.* 590: 1427-1442, 2012.

457. Marzolini, S, Oh, PI, Thomas, SG, and Goodman, JM. Aerobic and resistance training in coronary disease: Single versus multiple sets. *Med Sci Sports Exerc.* 40: 1557-1564, 2008.

458. Mascher, H, Andersson, H, Nilsson, PA, Ekblom, B, and Blomstrand, E. Changes in signalling pathways regulating protein synthesis in human muscle in the recovery period after endurance exercise. *Acta Physiol. (Oxf.)* 191: 67-75, 2007.

459. Mascher, H, Tannerstedt, J, Brink-Elfegoun, T, Ekblom, B, Gustafsson, T, and Blomstrand, E. Repeated resistance exercise training induces different changes in mRNA expression of MAFbx and MuRF-1 in human skeletal muscle. *Am J Physiol Endocrinol Metab.* 294: E43-E51, 2008.

460. Mascher, H, Ekblom, B, Rooyackers, O, and Blomstrand, E. Enhanced rates of muscle protein synthesis and elevated mTOR signalling following endurance exercise in human subjects. *Acta Physiol. (Oxf.)* 202: 175-184, 2011.

461. Masuda, K, Choi, JY, Shimojo, H, and Katsuta, S. Maintenance of myoglobin concentration in human skeletal muscle after heavy resistance training. *Eur J Appl Physiol Occup Physiol.* 79: 347-352, 1999.

462. Matheny, RW, Merritt, E, Zannikos, SV, Farrar, RP, and Adamo, ML. Serum IGF-I-deficiency does not prevent compensatory skeletal muscle hypertrophy in resistance exercise. *Exp Biol Med. (Maywood)* 234: 164-170, 2009.

463. Mayhew, DL, Hornberger, TA, Lincoln, HC, and Bamman, MM. Eukaryotic initiation factor 2B epsilon induces cap-dependent translation and skeletal muscle hypertrophy. *J Physiol.* 589: 3023-3037, 2011.

464. Mayhew, TP, Rothstein, JM, Finucane, SD, and Lamb, RL. Muscular adaptation to concentric and eccentric exercise at equal power levels. *Med Sci Sports Exerc.* 27: 868-873, 1995.

465. Mazzetti, S, Douglass, M, Yocum, A, and Harber, M. Effect of explosive versus slow contractions and exercise intensity on energy expenditure. *Med Sci Sports Exerc.* 39: 1291-1301, 2007.

466. McAllister, MJ, Schilling, BK, Hammond, KG, Weiss, LW, and Farney, TM. Effect of grip width on electromyographic activity during the upright row. *J Strength Cond Res.* 27: 181-187, 2013.

467. McBride, A, Ghilagaber, S, Nikolaev, A, and Hardie, DG. The glycogen-binding domain on the AMPK beta subunit allows the kinase to act as a glycogen sensor. *Cell Metab.* 9: 23-34, 2009.

468. McBride, JM, Blaak, JB, and Triplett-McBride, T. Effect of resistance exercise volume and complexity on EMG, strength, and regional body composition. *Eur J Appl Physiol.* 90: 626-632, 2003.

469. McCall, GE, Byrnes, WC, Fleck, SJ, Dickinson, A, and Kraemer, WJ. Acute and chronic hormonal responses to resistance training designed to promote muscle hypertrophy. *Can J Appl Physiol.* 24: 96-107, 1999.

470. McCarthy, JJ, and Esser, KA. Counterpoint: Satellite cell addition is not obligatory for skeletal muscle hypertrophy. *J Appl Physiol.* 103: 1100-1102, 2007.

471. McCaulley, GO, McBride, JM, Cormie, P, Hudson, MB, Nuzzo, JL, Quindry, JC, and Triplett, NT. Acute hormonal and neuromuscular responses to hypertrophy, strength and power type resistance exercise. *Eur J Appl Physiol.* 105: 695-704, 2009.

472. McCaw, ST, and Melrose, DR. Stance width and bar load effects on leg muscle activity during the parallel squat. *Med Sci Sports Exerc.* 31: 428-436, 1999.

473. McCroskery, S, Thomas, M, Maxwell, L, Sharma, M, and Kambadur, R. Myostatin negatively regulates satellite cell activation and self-renewal. *J Cell Biol.* 162: 1135-1147, 2003.

474. McGee, SL, Mustard, KJ, Hardie, DG, and Baar, K. Normal hypertrophy accompanied by phosphorylation and activation of AMP-activated protein kinase alpha1 following overload in LKB1 knockout mice. *J Physiol.* 586: 1731-1741, 2008.

475. McGinley, C, Shafat, A, and Donnelly, AE. Does antioxidant vitamin supplementation protect against muscle damage? *Sports Med.* 39: 1011-1032, 2009.

476. McHugh, MP, Connolly, DA, Eston, RG, and Gleim, GW. Electromyographic analysis of exercise resulting in symptoms of muscle damage. *J Sports Sci.* 18: 163-172, 2000.

477. McHugh, MP. Recent advances in the understanding of the repeated bout effect: The protective effect against muscle damage from a single bout of eccentric exercise. *Scand J Med Sci Sports* 13: 88-97, 2003.

478. McIver, CM, Wycherley, TP, and Clifton, PM. MTOR signaling and ubiquitin-proteosome gene expression in the preservation of fat free mass following high protein, calorie restricted weight loss. *Nutr Metab. (Lond.)* 9: 83-7075-9-83, 2012.

479. McKay, BR, O'Reilly, CE, Phillips, SM, Tarnopolsky, MA, and Parise, G. Co-expression of IGF-1 family members with myogenic regulatory factors following acute damaging muscle-lengthening contractions in humans. *J Physiol.* 586: 5549-5560, 2008.

480. McLester, JR, Bishop, P, and Guilliams, ME. Comparison of 1 day and 3 days per week of equal-volume resistance training in experienced subjects. *J Strength Cond Res.* 14: 273-281, 2000.

481. McMahon, G, Morse, CI, Burden, A, Winwood, K, and Onambele, GL. Muscular adaptations and insulin-like growth factor-I (IGF-I) responses to resistance training are stretch-mediated. *Muscle Nerve* 49(1): 108-119, 2013.

482. McMahon, GE, Morse, CI, Burden, A, Winwood, K, and Onambele, GL. Impact of range of motion during ecologically valid resistance training protocols on muscle size, subcutaneous fat, and strength. *J Strength Cond Res.* 28: 245-255, 2014.

483. McPhee, JS, Williams, AG, Degens, H, and Jones, DA. Inter-individual variability in adaptation of the leg muscles following a standardised endurance training programme in young women. *Eur J Appl Physiol.* 109: 1111-1118, 2010.

484. McPherron, AC, Lawler, AM, and Lee, SJ. Regulation of skeletal muscle mass in mice by a new TGF-beta superfamily member. *Nature* 387: 83-90, 1997.

485. Medeiros, HS, Jr, Mello, RS, Amorim, MZ, Koch, AJ, and Machado, M. Planned intensity reduction to maintain repetitions within recommended hypertrophy range. *Int J Sports Physiol Perform.* 8: 384-390, 2013.

486. Mendias, CL, Tatsumi, R, and Allen, RE. Role of cyclooxygenase-1 and -2 in satellite cell proliferation, differentiation, and fusion. *Muscle Nerve* 30: 497-500, 2004.

487. Mero, AA, Hulmi, JJ, Salmijarvi, H, Katajavuori, M, Haverinen, M, Holviala, J, Ridanpaa, T, Hakkinen, K, Kovanen, V, Ahtiainen, JP, and Selanne, H. Resistance training induced increase in muscle fiber size in young and older men. *Eur J Appl Physiol.* 113: 641-650, 2013.

488. Meyer, RA. Does blood flow restriction enhance hypertrophic signaling in skeletal muscle? *J Appl Physiol.* 100: 1443-1444, 2006.

489. Michaud, M, Balardy, L, Moulis, G, Gaudin, C, Peyrot, C, Vellas, B, Cesari, M, and Nourhashemi, F. Proinflammatory cytokines, aging, and age-related diseases. *J Am Med Dir Assoc.* 14: 877-882, 2013.

490. Michel, RN, Dunn, SE, and Chin, ER. Calcineurin and skeletal muscle growth. *Proc Nutr Soc.* 63: 341-349, 2004.

491. Mikkelsen, UR, Langberg, H, Helmark, IC, Skovgaard, D, Andersen, LL, Kjaer, M, and Mackey, AL. Local NSAID infusion inhibits satellite cell proliferation in human skeletal muscle after eccentric exercise. *J Appl Physiol.* 107: 1600-1611, 2009.

492. Mikkelsen, UR, Schjerling, P, Helmark, IC, Reitelseder, S, Holm, L, Skovgaard, D, Langberg, H, Kjaer, M, and Heinemeier, KM. Local NSAID infusion does not affect protein synthesis and gene expression in human muscle after eccentric exercise. *Scand J Med Sci Sports* 21: 630-644, 2011.

493. Mikkola, J, Rusko, H, Izquierdo, M, Gorostiaga, EM, and Hakkinen, K. Neuromuscular and cardiovascular adaptations during concurrent strength and endurance training in untrained men. *Int J Sports Med.* 33: 702-710, 2012.

494. Miller, BF, Olesen, JL, Hansen, M, Dossing, S, Crameri, RM, Welling, RJ, Langberg, H, Flyvbjerg, A, Kjaer, M, Babraj, JA, Smith, K, and Rennie, MJ. Coordinated collagen and muscle protein synthesis in human patella tendon and quadriceps muscle after exercise. *J Physiol.* 567: 1021-1033, 2005.

495. Miller, KJ, Garland, SJ, Ivanova, T, and Ohtsuki, T. Motor-unit behavior in humans during fatiguing arm movements. *J Neurophysiol.* 75: 1629-1636, 1996.

496. Mitchell, CJ, Churchward-Venne, TA, West, DD, Burd, NA, Breen, L, Baker, SK, and Phillips, SM. Resistance exercise load does not determine training-mediated hypertrophic gains in young men. *J Appl Physiol.*, 2012.

497. Mitchell, CJ, Churchward-Venne, TA, Bellamy, L, Parise, G, Baker, SK, and Phillips, SM. Muscular and systemic correlates of resistance training-induced muscle hypertrophy. *PLoS One* 8: e78636, 2013.

498. Mitchell, JB, DiLauro, PC, Pizza, FX, and Cavender, DL. The effect of preexercise carbohydrate status on resistance exercise performance. *Int J Sport Nutr.* 7: 185-196, 1997.

499. Miyamoto, N, Wakahara, T, Ema, R, and Kawakami, Y. Non-uniform muscle oxygenation despite uniform neuromuscular activity within the vastus lateralis during fatiguing heavy resistance exercise. *Clin Physiol Funct Imaging* 33: 463-469, 2013.

500. Miyazaki, M, and Esser, KA. Cellular mechanisms regulating protein synthesis and skeletal muscle hypertrophy in animals. *J Appl Physiol.* 106: 1367-1373, 2009.

501. Miyazaki, M, McCarthy, JJ, Fedele, MJ, and Esser, KA. Early activation of mTORC1 signalling in response to mechanical overload is independent of phosphoinositide 3-kinase/Akt signalling. *J Physiol.* 589: 1831-1846, 2011.

502. Monteiro, AG, Aoki, MS, Evangelista, AL, Alveno, DA, Monteiro, GA, Picarro Ida, C, and Ugrinowitsch, C. Nonlinear periodization maximizes strength gains in split resistance training routines. *J Strength Cond Res.* 23: 1321-1326, 2009.

503. Mookerjee, S, and Ratamess, N. Comparison of strength differences and joint action durations between full and partial range-of-motion bench press exercise. *J Strength Cond Res.* 13: 76-81, 1999.

504. Moore, DR, Del Bel, NC, Nizi, KI, Hartman, JW, Tang, JE, Armstrong, D, and Phillips, SM. Resistance training reduces fasted- and fed-state leucine turnover and increases dietary nitrogen retention in previously untrained young men. *J Nutr.* 137: 985-991, 2007.

505. Moore, DR, Robinson, MJ, Fry, JL, Tang, JE, Glover, EI, Wilkinson, SB, Prior, T, Tarnopolsky, MA, and Phillips, SM. Ingested protein dose response of muscle and albumin protein synthesis after resistance exercise in young men. *Am J Clin Nutr.* 89: 161-168, 2009.

506. Moore, DR, Young, M, and Phillips, SM. Similar increases in muscle size and strength in young men after training with maximal shortening or lengthening contractions when matched for total work. *Eur J Appl Physiol.* 112: 1587-1592, 2012.

507. Moore, DR, Phillips, SM, Babraj, JA, Smith, K, and Rennie, MJ. Myofibrillar and collagen protein synthesis in human skeletal muscle in young men after maximal shortening and lengthening contractions. *Am J Physiol Endocrinol Metab.* 288: 1153-1159, 2005.

508. Moore, DR, Young, M, and Phillips, SM. Similar increases in muscle size and strength in young men after training with maximal shortening or lengthening contractions when matched for total work. *Eur J Appl Physiol.* 112(4): 1587-1592, 2011.

509. Moritani, T, and deVries, HA. Neural factors versus hypertrophy in the time course of muscle strength gain. *Am J Phys Med.* 58: 115-130, 1979.

510. Moritani, T, and deVries, HA. Potential for gross muscle hypertrophy in older men. *J Gerontol.* 35: 672-682, 1980.

511. Mosher, DS, Quignon, P, Bustamante, CD, Sutter, NB, Mellersh, CS, Parker, HG, and Ostrander, EA. A mutation in the myostatin gene increases muscle mass and enhances racing performance in heterozygote dogs. *PLoS Genet.* 3: e79, 2007.

512. Moss, FP, and Leblond, CP. Satellite cells as the source of nuclei in muscles of growing rats. *Anat Rec.* 170: 421-435, 1971.

513. Munn, J, Herbert, RD, Hancock, MJ, and Gandevia, SC. Resistance training for strength: Effect of number of sets and contraction speed. *Med Sci Sports Exerc.* 37: 1622-1626, 2005.

514. Murphy, MG. Dietary fatty acids and membrane protein function. *J Nutr Biochem.* 1: 68-79, 1990.

515. Nader, GA, and Esser, KA. Intracellular signaling specificity in skeletal muscle in response to different modes of exercise. *J Appl Physiol.* 1985(90): 1936-1942, 2001.

516. Nader, GA, von Walden, F, Liu, C, Lindvall, J, Gutmann, L, Pistilli, EE, and Gordon, PM. Resistance exercise training modulates acute gene expression during human skeletal muscle hypertrophy. *J Appl Physiol.* 1985(116): 693-702, 2014.

517. Nakashima, K, and Yakabe, Y. AMPK activation stimulates myofibrillar protein degradation and expression of atrophy-related ubiquitin ligases by increasing FOXO transcription factors in C2C12 myotubes. *Biosci Biotechnol Biochem.* 71: 1650-1656, 2007.

518. Nardone, A, and Schieppati, M. Shift of activity from slow to fast muscle during voluntary lengthening contractions of the triceps surae muscles in humans. *J Physiol. (Lond.)* 395: 363-381, 1988.

519. Narici, MV, Roi, GS, Landoni, L, Minetti, AE, and Cerretelli, P. Changes in force, cross-sectional area and neural activation during strength training and detraining of the human quadriceps. *Eur J Appl Physiol Occup Physiol.* 59: 310-319, 1989.

520. Narici, MV, Hoppeler, H, Kayser, B, Landoni, L, Claassen, H, Gavardi, C, Conti, M, and Cerretelli, P. Human quadriceps cross-sectional area, torque and neural activation during 6 months strength training. *Acta Physiol Scand.* 157: 175-186, 1996.

521. Naya, FJ, Mercer, B, Shelton, J, Richardson, JA, Williams, RS, and Olson, EN. Stimulation of slow skeletal muscle fiber gene expression by calcineurin in vivo. *J Biol Chem.* 275: 4545-4548, 2000.

522. Neils, CM, Udermann, BE, Brice, GA, Winchester, JB, and McGuigan, MR. Influence of contraction velocity in untrained individuals over the initial early phase of resistance training. *J Strength Cond Res.* 19: 883-887, 2005.

523. Netreba, A, Popov, D, Bravyy, Y, Lyubaeva, E, Terada, M, Ohira, T, Okabe, H, Vinogradova, O, and Ohira, Y. Responses of knee extensor muscles to leg press training of various types in human. *Ross Fiziol Zh Im I M Sechenova.* 99: 406-416, 2013.

524. Netreba, AI, Popov, DV, Liubaeva, EV, Bravyi, I, Prostova, AB, Lemesheva, I, and Vinogradova, OL. Physiological effects of using the low intensity strength training without relaxation in single-joint and multi-joint movements. *Ross Fiziol Zh Im I M Sechenova.* 93: 27-38, 2007.

525. Netreba, AI, Popov, DV, Bravyi, I, Misina, SS, and Vinogradova, OL. Physiological effects of low-intensity strength training without relaxation. *Fiziol Cheloveka.* 35: 97-102, 2009.

526. Nguyen, HX, and Tidball, JG. Null mutation of gp91phox reduces muscle membrane lysis during muscle inflammation in mice. *J Physiol. (Lond.)* 553: 833-841, 2003.

527. Nicholson, G, Mcloughlin, G, Bissas, A, and Ispoglou, T. Do the acute biochemical and neuromuscular responses justify the classification of strength and hypertrophy-type resistance exercise? *J Strength Cond Res.* 28(11): 3188-3199, 2014.

528. Nickols-Richardson, SM, Miller, LE, Wootten, DF, Ramp, WK, and Herbert, WG. Concentric and eccentric isokinetic resistance training similarly increases muscular strength, fat-free soft tissue mass, and specific bone mineral measurements in young women. *Osteoporos Int.* 18: 789-796, 2007.

529. Nielsen, AR, Mounier, R, Plomgaard, P, Mortensen, OH, Penkowa, M, Speerschneider, T, Pilegaard, H, and Pedersen, BK. Expression of interleukin-15 in human skeletal muscle effect of exercise and muscle fibre type composition. *J Physiol.* 584: 305-312, 2007.

530. Nielsen, AR, and Pedersen, BK. The biological roles of exercise-induced cytokines: IL-6, IL-8, and IL-15. *Appl Physiol Nutr Metab.* 32: 833-839, 2007.

531. Nindl, BC, Hymer, WC, Deaver, DR, and Kraemer, WJ. Growth hormone pulsatility profile characteristics following acute heavy resistance exercise. *J Appl Physiol.* 91: 163-172, 2001.

532. Ninos, JC, Irrgang, JJ, Burdett, R, and Weiss, JR. Electromyographic analysis of the squat performed in self-selected lower extremity neutral rotation and 30 degrees of lower extremity turn-out from the self-selected neutral position. *J Orthop Sports Phys Ther.* 25: 307-315, 1997.

533. Nishimura, A, Sugita, M, Kato, K, Fukuda, A, Sudo, A, and Uchida, A. Hypoxia increases muscle hypertrophy induced by resistance training. *Int J Sports Physiol. Perform.* 5: 497-508, 2010.

534. Nogueira, W, Gentil, P, Mello, SN, Oliveira, RJ, Bezerra, AJ, and Bottaro, M. Effects of power training on muscle thickness of older men. *Int J Sports Med.* 30: 200-204, 2009.

535. Noorkoiv, M, Nosaka, K, and Blazevich, AJ. Neuromuscular adaptations associated with knee joint angle-specific force change. *Med Sci Sports Exerc.* 46: 1525-1537, 2014.

536. Noreen, EE, Sass, MJ, Crowe, ML, Pabon, VA, Brandauer, J, and Averill, LK. Effects of supplemental fish oil on resting metabolic rate, body composition, and salivary cortisol in healthy adults. *J Int Soc Sports Nutr.* 7: 31-2783-7-31, 2010.

537. Nosaka, K, Lavender, A, Newton, M, and Sacco, P. Muscle damage in resistance training: Is muscle damage necessary for strength gain and muscle hypertrophy? *IJSHS.* 1: 1-8, 2003.

538. Nosaka, K, and Clarkson, PM. Changes in indicators of inflammation after eccentric exercise of the elbow flexors. *Med Sci Sports Exerc.* 28: 953-961, 1996.

539. Novak, ML, Billich, W, Smith, SM, Sukhija, KB, McLoughlin, TJ, Hornberger, TA, and Koh, TJ. COX-2 inhibitor reduces skeletal muscle hypertrophy in mice. *Am J Physiol Regul Integr Comp Physiol.* 296: R1132-1139, 2009.

540. O'Bryant, HS, Byrd, R, and Stone, MH. Cycle ergometer performance and maximum leg and hip strength adaptations to two different methods of weight training. *J Appl Sport Sci Res.* 2: 27-30, 1988.

541. Ochi, E, Ishii, N, and Nakazato, K. Time course change of IGF1/Akt/mTOR/p70s6k pathway activation in rat gastrocnemius muscle during repeated bouts of eccentric exercise. *JSSM.* 9: 170-175, 2010.

542. O'Connor, RS, and Pavlath, GK. Point:Counterpoint: Satellite cell addition is/is not obligatory for skeletal muscle hypertrophy. *J Appl Physiol.* 103: 1099-1100, 2007.

543. Ogasawara, R, Loenneke, JP, Thiebaud, RS, and Abe, T. Low-load bench press training to fatigue results in muscle hypertrophy similar to high-load bench press training. *Int J Clin Med.* 4: 114-121, 2013.

544. Ogasawara, R, Yasuda, T, Sakamaki, M, Ozaki, H, and Abe, T. Effects of periodic and continued resistance training on muscle CSA and strength in previously untrained men. *Clin Physiol Funct Imaging* 31: 399-404, 2011.

545. Ogasawara, R, Kobayashi, K, Tsutaki, A, Lee, K, Abe, T, Fujita, S, Nakazato, K, and Ishii, N. mTOR signaling response to resistance exercise is altered by chronic resistance training and detraining in skeletal muscle. *J Appl Physiol.* 114(7): 934-940, 2013.

546. Ogasawara, R, Yasuda, T, Ishii, N, and Abe, T. Comparison of muscle hypertrophy following 6-month of continuous and periodic strength training. *Eur J Appl Physiol.* 113: 975-985, 2013.

547. Ogawa, K, Sanada, K, Machida, S, Okutsu, M, and Suzuki, K. Resistance exercise training-induced muscle hypertrophy was associated with reduction of inflammatory markers in elderly women. *Mediators Inflamm.* 2010: 171023, 2010.

548. Ogborn, D, and Schoenfeld, BJ. The role of fiber types in muscle hypertrophy: Implications for loading strategies. *Strength Cond J.* 36: 20-25, 2014.

549. O'Gorman, DJ, Del Aguila, LF, Williamson, DL, Krishnan, RK, and Kirwan, JP. Insulin and exercise differentially regulate PI3-kinase and glycogen synthase in human skeletal muscle. *J Appl Physiol.* 89: 1412-1419, 2000.

550. Okamura, K, Doi, T, Hamada, K, Sakurai, M, Matsumoto, K, Imaizumi, K, Yoshioka, Y, Shimizu, S, and Suzuki, M. Effect of amino acid and glucose administration during postexercise recovery on protein kinetics in dogs. *Am J Physiol.* 272: E1023-E1030, 1997.

551. O'Neil, TK, Duffy, LR, Frey, JW, and Hornberger, TA. The role of phosphoinositide 3-kinase and phosphatidic acid in the regulation of mammalian target of rapamycin following eccentric contractions. *J Physiol.* 587: 3691-3701, 2009.

552. Ortenblad, N, Westerblad, H, and Nielsen, J. Muscle glycogen stores and fatigue. *J Physiol.* 591: 4405-4413, 2013.

553. Oshowski, K, Wilson, GJ, Weatherby, R, Murphy, PW, and Little, AD. The effect of weight training volume on hormonal output and muscular size and function. *J Strength Cond Res.* 11: 149-154, 1997.

554. Otis, JS, Burkholder, TJ, and Pavlath, GK. Stretch-induced myoblast proliferation is dependent on the COX2 pathway. *Exp Cell Res.* 310: 417-425, 2005.

555. Palmer, RM. Prostaglandins and the control of muscle protein synthesis and degradation. *Prostaglandins Leukot Essent Fatty Acids* 39: 95-104, 1990.

556. Panissa, VL, Tricoli, VA, Julio, UF, Da Silva, NR, Neto, RM, Carmo, EC, and Franchini, E. Acute effect of high-intensity aerobic exercise performed on treadmill and cycle ergometer on strength performance. *J Strength Cond Res.*, 2014.

557. Paoli, A, Marcolin, G, and Petrone, N. The effect of stance width on the electromyographical activity of eight superficial thigh muscles during back squat with different bar loads. *J Strength Cond Res.* 23: 246-250, 2009.

558. Paoli, A, Grimaldi, K, D'Agostino, D, Cenci, L, Moro, T, Bianco, A, and Palma, A. Ketogenic diet does not affect strength performance in elite artistic gymnasts. *J Int Soc Sports Nutr.* 9: 34, 2012.

559. Parkin, JA, Carey, MF, Martin, IK, Stojanovska, L, and Febbraio, MA. Muscle glycogen storage following prolonged exercise: Effect of timing of ingestion of high glycemic index food. *Med Sci Sports Exerc.* 29: 220-224, 1997.

560. Parsons, SA, Millay, DP, Wilkins, BJ, Bueno, OF, Tsika, GL, Neilson, JR, Liberatore, CM, Yutzey, KE, Crabtree, GR, Tsika, RW, and Molkentin, JD. Genetic loss of calcineurin blocks mechanical overload-induced skeletal muscle fiber type switching but not hypertrophy. *J Biol Chem.* 279: 26192-26200, 2004.

561. Pasiakos, SM. Exercise and amino acid anabolic cell signaling and the regulation of skeletal muscle mass. *Nutrients* 4: 740-758, 2012.

562. Pasiakos, SM, and Carbone, JW. Assessment of skeletal muscle proteolysis and the regulatory response to nutrition and exercise. *IUBMB Life* 66: 478-484, 2014.

563. Paul, AC, and Rosenthal, N. Different modes of hypertrophy in skeletal muscle fibers. *J Cell Biol.* 156: 751-760, 2002.

564. Paulsen, G, Egner, IM, Drange, M, Langberg, H, Benestad, HB, Fjeld, JG, Hallen, J, and Raastad, T. A COX-2 inhibitor reduces muscle soreness, but does not influence recovery and adaptation after eccentric exercise. *Scand J Med Sci Sports* 20: e195-e207, 2010.

565. Pedersen, BK, Ostrowski, K, Rohde, T, and Bruunsgaard, H. The cytokine response to strenuous exercise. *Can J Physiol Pharmacol.* 76: 505-511, 1998.

566. Pedersen, BK. Muscles and their myokines. *J Exp Biol.* 214: 337-346, 2011.

567. Pedersen, BK, and Febbraio, MA. Muscles, exercise and obesity: Skeletal muscle as a secretory organ. *Nat Rev Endocrinol.* 8: 457-465, 2012.

568. Pescatello, LS, Devaney, JM, Hubal, MJ, Thompson, PD, and Hoffman, EP. Highlights from the functional single nucleotide polymorphisms associated with human muscle size and strength or FAMuSS study. *Biomed Res Int.* 2013: 643575, 2013.

569. Petersen, SG, Beyer, N, Hansen, M, Holm, L, Aagaard, P, Mackey, AL, and Kjaer, M. Nonsteroidal anti-inflammatory drug or glucosamine reduced pain and improved muscle strength with resistance training in a randomized controlled trial of knee osteoarthritis patients. *Arch Phys Med Rehabil.* 92: 1185-1193, 2011.

570. Petersen, SG, Miller, BF, Hansen, M, Kjaer, M, and Holm, L. Exercise and NSAIDs: Effect on muscle protein synthesis in patients with knee osteoarthritis. *Med Sci Sports Exerc.* 43: 425-431, 2011.

571. Peterson, MD, Rhea, MR, and Alvar, BA. Applications of the dose-response for muscular strength development: A review of meta-analytic efficacy and reliability for designing training prescription. *J Strength Cond Res.* 19: 950-958, 2005.

572. Peterson, MD, Sen, A, and Gordon, PM. Influence of resistance exercise on lean body mass in aging adults: A meta-analysis. *Med Sci Sports Exerc.* 43: 249-258, 2011.

573. Petrella, JK, Kim, JS, Cross, JM, Kosek, DJ, and Bamman, MM. Efficacy of myonuclear addition may explain differential myofiber growth among resistance-trained young and older men and women. *Am J Physiol Endocrinol Metab.* 291: E937-E946, 2006.

574. Petrella, JK, Kim, J, Mayhew, DL, Cross, JM, and Bamman, MM. Potent myofiber hypertrophy during resistance training in humans is associated with satellite cell-mediated myonuclear addition: A cluster analysis. *J Appl Physiol.* 104: 1736-1742, 2008.

575. Phillips, SM, Tipton, KD, Aarsland, A, Wolf, SE, and Wolfe, RR. Mixed muscle protein synthesis and breakdown after resistance exercise in humans. *Am J Physiol.* 273: E99-E107, 1997.

576. Phillips, SM. Physiologic and molecular bases of muscle hypertrophy and atrophy: Impact of resistance exercise on human skeletal muscle (protein and exercise dose effects). *Appl Physiol Nutr Metab.* 34: 403-410, 2009.

577. Phillips, SM. The science of muscle hypertrophy: Making dietary protein count. *Proc Nutr Soc.* 70: 100-103, 2011.

578. Phillips, SM, and Van Loon, LJ. Dietary protein for athletes: From requirements to optimum adaptation. *J Sports Sci.* 29 Suppl 1: S29-S38, 2011.

579. Pierce, JR, Clark, BC, Ploutz-Snyder, LL, and Kanaley, JA. Growth hormone and muscle function responses to skeletal muscle ischemia. *J Appl Physiol.* 101: 1588-1595, 2006.

580. Pillon, NJ, Bilan, PJ, Fink, LN, and Klip, A. Crosstalk between skeletal muscle and immune cells: Muscle-derived mediators and metabolic implications. *Am J Physiol Endocrinol Metab.* 304: E453-E465, 2013.

581. Pinto, RS, Gomes, N, Radaelli, R, Botton, CE, Brown, LE, and Bottaro, M. Effect of range of motion on muscle strength and thickness. *J Strength Cond Res.* 26: 2140-2145, 2012.

582. Pistilli, EE, Devaney, JM, Gordish-Dressman, H, Bradbury, MK, Seip, RL, Thompson, PD, Angelopoulos, TJ, Clarkson, PM, Moyna, NM, Pescatello, LS, Visich, PS, Zoeller, RF, Gordon, PM, and Hoffman, EP. Interleukin-15 and interleukin-15R alpha SNPs and associations with muscle, bone, and predictors of the metabolic syndrome. *Cytokine.* 43: 45-53, 2008.

583. Pistilli, EE, and Quinn, LS. From anabolic to oxidative: Reconsidering the roles of IL-15 and IL-15Ralpha in skeletal muscle. *Exerc Sport Sci Rev.* 41: 100-106, 2013.

584. Pitkanen, HT, Nykanen, T, Knuutinen, J, Lahti, K, Keinanen, O, Alen, M, Komi, PV, and Mero, AA. Free amino acid pool and muscle protein balance after resistance exercise. *Med Sci Sports Exerc.* 35: 784-792, 2003.

585. Ploutz, LL, Tesch, PA, Biro, RL, and Dudley, GA. Effect of resistance training on muscle use during exercise. *J Appl Physiol.* 1985(76): 1675-1681, 1994.

586. Poliquin, C. Five steps to increasing the effectiveness of your strength training program. *Natl Strength Cond Assoc J.* 10: 34-39, 1988.

587. Pollanen, E, Ronkainen, PH, Suominen, H, Takala, T, Koskinen, S, Puolakka, J, Sipila, S, and Kovanen, V. Muscular transcriptome in postmenopausal women with or without hormone replacement. *Rejuvenation Res.* 10: 485-500, 2007.

588. Popov, DV, Tsvirkun, DV, Netreba, AI, Tarasova, OS, Prostova, AB, Larina, IM, Borovik, AS, and Vinogradova, OL. Hormonal adaptation determines the increase in muscle mass and strength during low-intensity strength training without relaxation. *Fiziol Cheloveka.* 32: 121-127, 2006.

589. Popov, DV, Lysenko, EA, Bachinin, AV, Miller, TF, Kurochkina, NS, Kravchenko, IV, Furalyov, VA, and Vinogradova, OL. Influence of resistance exercise intensity and metabolic stress on anabolic signaling and expression of myogenic genes in skeletal muscle. *Muscle Nerve* 51: 434-442, 2015.

590. Power, O, Hallihan, A, and Jakeman, P. Human insulinotropic response to oral ingestion of native and hydrolysed whey protein. *Amino Acids* 37: 333-339, 2009.

591. Prestes, J, De Lima, C, Frollini, AB, Donatto, FF, and Conte, M. Comparison of linear and reverse linear periodization effects on maximal strength and body composition. *J Strength Cond Res.* 23: 266-274, 2009.

592. Prestes, J, Frollini, AB, de Lima, C, Donatto, FF, Foschini, D, de Cassia Marqueti, R, Figueira, A, Jr, and Fleck, SJ. Comparison between linear and daily undulating periodized resistance training to increase strength. *J Strength Cond Res.* 23: 2437-2442, 2009.

593. Proske, U, and Morgan, DL. Muscle damage from eccentric exercise: Mechanism, mechanical signs, adaptation and clinical applications. *J Physiol.* 537: 333-345, 2001.

594. Pucci, AR, Griffin, L, and Cafarelli, E. Maximal motor unit firing rates during isometric resistance training in men. *Exp Physiol.* 91: 171-178, 2006.

595. Quinn, LS, Anderson, BG, Conner, JD, Pistilli, EE, and Wolden-Hanson, T. Overexpression of inter-leukin-15 in mice promotes resistance to diet-induced obesity, increased insulin sensitivity, and markers of oxidative skeletal muscle metabolism. *Int J Interferon Cytokine Mediator Res.* 3: 29-42, 2011.

596. Quinn, LS. Interleukin-15: A muscle-derived cytokine regulating fat-to-lean body composition. *J Anim Sci.* 86: E75-E83, 2008.

597. Radaelli, R, Botton, CE, Wilhelm, EN, Bottaro, M, Lacerda, F, Gaya, A, Moraes, K, Peruzzolo, A, Brown, LE, and Pinto, RS. Low- and high-volume strength training induces similar neuromuscular improvements in muscle quality in elderly women. *Exp Gerontol.* 48: 710-716, 2013.

598. Radaelli, R, Botton, CE, Wilhelm, EN, Bottaro, M, Brown, LE, Lacerda, F, Gaya, A, Moraes, K, Peruzzolo, A, and Pinto, RS. Time course of low- and high-volume strength training on neuromuscular adaptations and muscle quality in older women. *Age (Dordr.)* 36: 881-892, 2014.

599. Radaelli, R, Fleck, SJ, Leite, T, Leite, RD, Pinto, RS, Fernandes, L, and Simao, R. Dose response of 1, 3 and 5 sets of resistance exercise on strength, local muscular endurance and hypertrophy. *J Strength Cond Res.* 29(5): 1349-1358, 2014.

600. Radaelli, R, Wilhelm, EN, Botton, CE, Rech, A, Bottaro, M, Brown, LE, and Pinto, RS. Effects of single vs. multiple-set short-term strength training in elderly women. *Age (Dordr.)* 36: 9720, 2014.

601. Rana, SR, Chleboun, GS, Gilders, RM, Hagerman, FC, Herman, JR, Hikida, RS, Kushnick, MR, Staron, RS, and Toma, K. Comparison of early phase adaptations for traditional strength and endurance, and low velocity resistance training programs in college-aged women. *J Strength Cond Res.* 22: 119-127, 2008.

602. Rasmussen, BB, Tipton, KD, Miller, SL, Wolf, SE, and Wolfe, RR. An oral essential amino acid-car-bohydrate supplement enhances muscle protein anabolism after resistance exercise. *J Appl Physiol.* 88: 386-392, 2000.

603. Ratamess, NA, Falvo, MJ, Mangine, GT, Hoffman, JR, Faigenbaum, AD, and Kang, J. The effect of rest interval length on metabolic responses to the bench press exercise. *Eur J Appl Physiol.* 100: 1-17, 2007.

604. Raught, B, and Gingras, AC. eIF4E activity is regulated at multiple levels. *Int J Biochem. Cell Biol.* 31: 43-57, 1999.

605. Reeves, GV, Kraemer, RR, Hollander, DB, Clavier, J, Thomas, C, Francois, M, and Castracane, VD. Comparison of hormone responses following light resistance exercise with partial vascular occlusion and moderately difficult resistance exercise without occlusion. *J Appl Physiol.* 101: 1616-1622, 2006.

606. Reeves, ND, Maganaris, CN, Longo, S, and Narici, MV. Differential adaptations to eccentric versus conventional resistance training in older humans. *Exp Physiol.* 94: 825-833, 2009.

607. Reidy, PT, Walker, DK, Dickinson, JM, Gundermann, DM, Drummond, MJ, Timmerman, KL, Fry, CS, Borack, MS, Cope, MB, Mukherjea, R, Jennings, K, Volpi, E, and Rasmussen, BB. Protein blend ingestion following resistance exercise promotes human muscle protein synthesis. *J Nutr.* 143: 410-416, 2013.

608. Reihmane, D, and Dela, F. Interleukin-6: Possible biological roles during exercise. *Eur J Sport Sci.* 14: 242-250, 2014.

609. Renault, V, Thornell, LE, Eriksson, PO, Butler-Browne, G, and Mouly, V. Regenerative potential of human skeletal muscle during aging. *Aging Cell.* 1: 132-139, 2002.

610. Rennie, MJ, Bohe, J, Smith, K, Wackerhage, H, and Greenhaff, P. Branched-chain amino acids as fuels and anabolic signals in human muscle. *J Nutr.* 136: 264S-8S, 2006.

611. Rhea, MR, Alvar, BA, Ball, SD, and Burkett, LN. Three sets of weight training superior to 1 set with equal intensity for eliciting strength. *J Strength Cond Res.* 16: 525-529, 2002.

612. Ribeiro, AS, Souza, MF, Pina, FLC, Nascimento, MA, dos Santos, L, Antunes, M, Schoenfeld, BJ, and Cyrino, ES. Resistance training in older women: Comparison of single vs. multiple sets on muscle strength and body composition. *Isokinet Exerc Sci.* 23: 53-60, 2015.

613. Ribeiro, AS, Avelar, A, Schoenfeld, BJ, Ritti Dias, RM, Altimari, LR, and Cyrino, ES. Resistance training promotes increase in intracellular hydration in men and women. *Eur J Sport. Sci.* 14: 578-585, 2014.

614. Ribeiro, AS, Schoenfeld, BJ, Silva, DR, Pina, FL, Guariglia, DA, Porto, M, Maesta, N, Burini, RC, and Cyrino, ES. Effect of two- versus three-way split resistance training routines on body composition and muscular strength in bodybuilders: A pilot study. *Int J Sport Nutr Exerc Metab.*, 2015.

615. Richter, EA, Derave, W, and Wojtaszewski, JF. Glucose, exercise and insulin: Emerging concepts. *J Physiol.* 535: 313-322, 2001.

616. Riechman, SE, Balasekaran, G, Roth, SM, and Ferrell, RE. Association of interleukin-15 protein and interleukin-15 receptor genetic variation with resistance exercise training responses. *J Appl Physiol.* 97: 2214-2219, 2004.

617. Riemann, BL, Limbaugh, GK, Eitner, JD, and LeFavi, RG. Medial and lateral gastrocnemius activation differences during heel-raise exercise with three different foot positions. *J Strength Cond Res.* 25: 634-639, 2011.

618. Rieu, I, Magne, H, Savary-Auzeloux, I, Averous, J, Bos, C, Peyron, MA, Combaret, L, and Dardevet, D. Reduction of low grade inflammation restores blunting of postprandial muscle anabolism and limits sarcopenia in old rats. *J Physiol.* 587: 5483-5492, 2009.

619. Rigamonti, AE, Locatelli, L, Cella, SG, Bonomo, SM, Giunta, M, Molinari, F, Sartorio, A, and Muller, EE. Muscle expressions of MGF, IGF-IEa, and myostatin in intact and hypophysectomized rats: Effects of rhGH and testosterone alone or combined. *Horm Metab Res.* 41: 23-29, 2009.

620. Robbins, DW, Goodale, TL, Docherty, D, Behm, DG, and Tran, QT. The effects of load and training pattern on acute neuromuscular responses in the upper body. *J Strength Cond Res.* 24: 2996-3007, 2010.

621. Rodemann, HP, and Goldberg, AL. Arachidonic acid, prostaglandin E2 and F2 alpha influence rates of protein turnover in skeletal and cardiac muscle. *J Biol Chem.* 257: 1632-1638, 1982.

622. Roig, M, O'Brien, K, Kirk, G, Murray, R, McKinnon, P, Shadgan, B, and Reid, WD. The effects of eccentric versus concentric resistance training on muscle strength and mass in healthy adults: A systematic review with meta-analysis. *Br J Sports Med.* 43: 556-568, 2009.

623. Rommel, C, Bodine, SC, Clarke, BA, Rossman, R, Nunez, L, Stitt, TN, Yancopoulos, GD, and Glass, DJ. Mediation of IGF-1-induced skeletal myotube hypertrophy by PI(3)K/Akt/mTOR and PI(3)K/Akt/GSK3 pathways. *Nat Cell Biol.* 3: 1009-1013, 2001.

624. Ronnestad, BR, Egeland, W, Kvamme, NH, Refsnes, PE, Kadi, F, and Raastad, T. Dissimilar effects of one- and three-set strength training on strength and muscle mass gains in upper and lower body in untrained subjects. *J Strength Cond Res.* 21: 157-163, 2007.

625. Ronnestad, BR, Nygaard, H, and Raastad, T. Physiological elevation of endogenous hormones results in superior strength training adaptation. *Eur J Appl Physiol.* 111: 2249-2259, 2011.

626. Rooney, KJ, Herbert, RD, and Balnave, RJ. Fatigue contributes to the strength training stimulus. *Med Sci Sports Exerc.* 26: 1160-1164, 1994.

627. Roschel, H, Ugrinowistch, C, Barroso, R, Batista, MA, Souza, EO, Aoki, MS, Siqueira-Filho, MA, Zanuto, R, Carvalho, CR, Neves, M, Mello, MT, and Tricoli, V. Effect of eccentric exercise velocity on akt/mtor/p70(s6k) signaling in human skeletal muscle. *Appl Physiol Nutr Metab.* 36: 283-290, 2011.

628. Rosqvist, F, Iggman, D, Kullberg, J, Cedernaes, J, Johansson, HE, Larsson, A, Johansson, L, Ahlstrom, H, Arner, P, Dahlman, I, and Riserus, U. Overfeeding polyunsaturated and saturated fat causes distinct effects on liver and visceral fat accumulation in humans. *Diabetes* 63: 2356-2368, 2014.

629. Roth, SM, Martel, GF, Ivey, FM, Lemmer, JT, Metter, EJ, Hurley, BF, and Rogers, MA. Skeletal muscle satellite cell populations in healthy young and older men and women. *Anat Rec.* 260: 351-358, 2000.

630. Roth, SM, Ivey, FM, Martel, GF, Lemmer, JT, Hurlbut, DE, Siegel, EL, Metter, EJ, Fleg, JL, Fozard, JL, Kostek, MC, Wernick, DM, and Hurley, BF. Muscle size responses to strength training in young and older men and women. *J Am Geriatr Soc.* 49: 1428-1433, 2001.

631. Roux, PP, and Blenis, J. ERK and p38 MAPK-activated protein kinases: A family of protein kinases with diverse biological functions. *Microbiol Mol Biol Rev.* 68: 320-344, 2004.

632. Rozenek, R, Ward, P, Long, S, and Garhammer, J. Effects of high-calorie supplements on body composition and muscular strength following resistance training. *J Sports Med Phys Fitness* 42: 340-347, 2002.

633. Rubin, MR, Kraemer, WJ, Maresh, CM, Volek, JS, Ratamess, NA, Vanheest, JL, Silvestre, R, French, DN, Sharman, MJ, Judelson, DA, Gomez, AL, Vescovi, JD, and Hymer, WC. High-affinity growth hormone binding protein and acute heavy resistance exercise. *Med Sci Sports Exerc.* 37: 395-403, 2005.

634. Russell, B, Dix, DJ, Haller, DL, and Jacobs-El, J. Repair of injured skeletal muscle: A molecular approach. *Med Sci Sports Exerc.* 24: 189-196, 1992.

635. Ryan, AM, Reynolds, JV, Healy, L, Byrne, M, Moore, J, Brannelly, N, McHugh, A, McCormack, D, and Flood, P. Enteral nutrition enriched with eicosapentaenoic acid (EPA) preserves lean body mass following esophageal cancer surgery: Results of a double-blinded randomized controlled trial. *Ann Surg.* 249: 355-363, 2009.

636. Sabourin, LA, and Rudnicki, MA. The molecular regulation of myogenesis. *Clin Genet.* 57: 16-25, 2000.

637. Saclier, M, Yacoub-Youssef, H, Mackey, AL, Arnold, L, Ardjoune, H, Magnan, M, Sailhan, F, Chelly, J, Pavlath, GK, Mounier, R, Kjaer, M, and Chazaud,

B. Differentially activated macrophages orchestrate myogenic precursor cell fate during human skeletal muscle regeneration. *Stem Cells* 31: 384-396, 2013.

638. Sahlin, K, Soderlund, K, Tonkonogi, M, and Hirakoba, K. Phosphocreatine content in single fibers of human muscle after sustained submaximal exercise. *Am J Physiol*. 273: C172-178, 1997.

639. Sale, DG, MacDougall, JD, Alway, SE, and Sutton, JR. Voluntary strength and muscle characteristics in untrained men and women and male bodybuilders. *J Appl Physiol*. 1985(62): 1786-1793, 1987.

640. Sale, DG. Neural adaptation to resistance training. *Med Sci Sports Exerc*. 20: S135-45, 1988.

641. Sallinen, J, Pakarinen, A, Ahtiainen, J, Kraemer, WJ, Volek, JS, and Hakkinen, K. Relationship between diet and serum anabolic hormone responses to heavy-resistance exercise in men. *Int J Sports Med*. 25: 627-633, 2004.

642. Sampson, JA, and Groeller, H. Is repetition failure critical for the development of muscle hypertrophy and strength? *Scand J Med Sci Sports*, 2015.

643. Sandri, M. Signaling in muscle atrophy and hypertrophy. *Physiology (Bethesda)* 23: 160-170, 2008.

644. Saxton, JM, Donnelly, AE, and Roper, HP. Indices of free-radical-mediated damage following maximum voluntary eccentric and concentric muscular work. *Eur J Appl Physiol Occup Physiol*. 68: 189-193, 1994.

645. Schaafsma, G. The protein digestibility-corrected amino acid score. *J Nutr*. 130: 1865S-1867S, 2000.

646. Schliess, F, Schreiber, R, and Haussinger, D. Activation of extracellular signal-regulated kinases Erk-1 and Erk-2 by cell swelling in H4IIE hepatoma cells. *Biochem J*. 309 (Pt 1): 13-17, 1995.

647. Schliess, F, Richter, L, vom Dahl, S, and Haussinger, D. Cell hydration and mTOR-dependent signalling. *Acta Physiol. (Oxf.)* 187: 223-229, 2006.

648. Schmidtbleicher, D, and Buehrle, M. Neuronal adaptation and increase of cross-sectional area studying different strength training methods. In: Jonsson GB, ed. *Biomechanics* (vol. X-B, pp. 615-620). Champaign, IL: Human Kinetics, 1987.

649. Schoenfeld, B, Kolber, MJ, and Haimes, JE. The upright row: Implications for preventing subacromial impingement. *Strength Cond J*. 33: 25-28, 2011.

650. Schoenfeld, B. The use of specialized training techniques to maximize muscle hypertrophy. *Strength Cond J*. 33: 60-65, 2011.

651. Schoenfeld, B, Pope, ZK, Henselmans, M, and Krieger, J. Longer inter-set rest periods enhance muscle strength and hypertrophy in resistance-trained men. In press.

652. Schoenfeld, BJ. *The M.A.X. Muscle Plan*. Champaign, IL: Human Kinetics, 2012.

653. Schoenfeld, BJ, Contreras, B, Vigotsky, A, Sonmez, GT, and Fontana, F. Upper body muscle activation during low- versus high-load resistance exercise in the bench press. Unpublished manuscript, 2016.

654. Schoenfeld, BJ. Potential mechanisms for a role of metabolic stress in hypertrophic adaptations to resistance training. *Sports Med*. In press.

655. Schoenfeld, B, Sonmez, RG, Kolber, MJ, Contreras, B, Harris, R, and Ozen, S. Effect of hand position on EMG activity of the posterior shoulder musculature during a horizontal abduction exercise. *J Strength Cond Res*. 27: 2644-2649, 2013.

656. Schoenfeld, BJ. The mechanisms of muscle hypertrophy and their application to resistance training. *J Strength Cond Res*. 24: 2857-2872, 2010.

657. Schoenfeld, BJ. Does exercise-induced muscle damage play a role in skeletal muscle hypertrophy? *J Strength Cond Res*. 26: 1441-1453, 2012.

658. Schoenfeld, BJ. Postexercise hypertrophic adaptations: A reexamination of the hormone hypothesis and its applicability to resistance training program design. *J Strength Cond Res*. 27: 1720-1730, 2013.

659. Schoenfeld, BJ, Aragon, AA, and Krieger, JW. The effect of protein timing on muscle strength and hypertrophy: A meta-analysis. *J Int Soc Sports Nutr*. 10: 53, 2013.

660. Schoenfeld, BJ, Contreras, B, Willardson, JM, Fontana, F, and Tiryaki-Sonmez, G. Muscle activation during low- versus high-load resistance training in well-trained men. *Eur J Appl Physiol*. 114: 2491-2497, 2014.

661. Schoenfeld, BJ, Ratamess, NA, Peterson, MD, Contreras, B, Tiryaki-Sonmez, G, and Alvar, BA. Effects of different volume-equated resistance training loading strategies on muscular adaptations in well-trained men. *J Strength Cond Res*. 28: 2909-2918, 2014.

662. Schoenfeld, BJ, Wilson, JM, Lowery, RP, and Krieger, JW. Muscular adaptations in low- versus high-load resistance training: A meta-analysis. *Eur J Sport Sci*. 16(1): 1-10, 2014.

663. Schoenfeld, BJ, Contreras, B, Tiryaki-Sonmez, G, Wilson, JM, Kolber, MJ, and Peterson, MD. Regional differences in muscle activation during hamstrings exercise. *J Strength Cond Res*. 29: 159-164, 2015.

664. Schoenfeld, BJ, Ogborn, DI, and Krieger, JW. Effect of repetition duration during resistance training on muscle hypertrophy: A systematic review and meta-analysis. *Sports Med*. 45(4): 577-585, 2015.

665. Schoenfeld, BJ, Peterson, MD, Ogborn, D, Contreras, B, and Sonmez, GT. Effects of low- versus high-load resistance training on muscle strength and hypertrophy in well-trained men. *J Strength Cond Res*. 29: 2954-2963, 2015.

666. Schoenfeld, BJ, Ratamess, NA, Peterson, MD, Contreras, B, and Tiryaki-Sonmez, G. Influence of resistance training frequency on muscular adaptations in well-trained men. *J Strength Cond Res.* 29: 1821-1829, 2015.

667. Schott, J, McCully, K, and Rutherford, OM. The role of metabolites in strength training. II. Short versus long isometric contractions. *Eur J Appl Physiol Occup Physiol.* 71: 337-341, 1995.

668. Schott, J, McCully, K, and Rutherford, OM. The role of metabolites in strength training. II. Short versus long isometric contractions. *Eur J Appl Physiol Occup Physiol.* 71: 337-341, 1995.

669. Schuelke, M, Wagner, KR, Stolz, LE, Hubner, C, Riebel, T, Komen, W, Braun, T, Tobin, JF, and Lee, SJ. Myostatin mutation associated with gross muscle hypertrophy in a child. *N Engl J Med.* 350: 2682-2688, 2004.

670. Schuenke, MD, Herman, JR, Gliders, RM, Hagerman, FC, Hikida, RS, Rana, SR, Ragg, KE, and Staron, RS. Early-phase muscular adaptations in response to slow-speed versus traditional resistance-training regimens. *Eur J Appl Physiol.* 112: 3585-3595, 2012.

671. Schultz, E, Jaryszak, DL, and Valliere, CR. Response of satellite cells to focal skeletal muscle injury. *Muscle Nerve* 8: 217-222, 1985.

672. Schwane, JA, Johnson, SR, Vandenakker, CB, and Armstrong, RB. Delayed-onset muscular soreness and plasma CPK and LDH activities after downhill running. *Med Sci Sports Exerc.* 15: 51-56, 1983.

673. Schwartz, RS, Shuman, WP, Larson, V, Cain, KC, Fellingham, GW, Beard, JC, Kahn, SE, Stratton, JR, Cerqueira, MD, and Abrass, IB. The effect of intensive endurance exercise training on body fat distribution in young and older men. *Metabolism* 40: 545-551, 1991.

674. Scott, BR, Slattery, KM, and Dascombe, BJ. Intermittent hypoxic resistance training: Is metabolic stress the key moderator? *Med Hypotheses* 84: 145-149, 2015.

675. Sculthorpe, N, Solomon, AM, Sinanan, AC, Bouloux, PM, Grace, F, and Lewis, MP. Androgens affect myogenesis in vitro and increase local IGF-1 expression. *Med Sci Sports Exerc.* 44: 610-615, 2012.

676. Segal, RL. Neuromuscular compartments in the human biceps brachii muscle. *Neurosci Lett.* 140: 98-102, 1992.

677. Seger, JY, Arvidsson, B, and Thorstensson, A. Specific effects of eccentric and concentric training on muscle strength and morphology in humans. *Eur J Appl Physiol Occup Physiol.* 79: 49-57, 1998.

678. Selye, H. Stress and the general adaptation syndrome. *Br Med J.* 1: 1383-1392, 1950.

679. Semmler, JG, and Nordstrom, MA. Motor unit discharge and force tremor in skill- and strength-trained individuals. *Exp Brain Res.* 119: 27-38, 1998.

680. Semsarian, C, Wu, MJ, Ju, YK, Marciniec, T, Yeoh, T, Allen, DG, Harvey, RP, and Graham, RM. Skeletal muscle hypertrophy is mediated by a Ca2+-dependent calcineurin signalling pathway. *Nature* 400: 576-581, 1999.

681. Sengupta, S, Peterson, TR, and Sabatini, DM. Regulation of the mTOR complex 1 pathway by nutrients, growth factors, and stress. *Mol Cell.* 40: 310-322, 2010.

682. Serrano, AL, Baeza-Raja, B, Perdiguero, E, Jardi, M, and Munoz-Canoves, P. Interleukin-6 is an essential regulator of satellite cell-mediated skeletal muscle hypertrophy. *Cell Metab.* 7: 33-44, 2008.

683. Seynnes, OR, de Boer, M, and Narici, MV. Early skeletal muscle hypertrophy and architectural changes in response to high-intensity resistance training. *J Appl Physiol.* 102: 368-373, 2007.

684. Shepstone, TN, Tang, JE, Dallaire, S, Schuenke, MD, Staron, RS, and Phillips, SM. Short-term high- vs. low-velocity isokinetic lengthening training results in greater hypertrophy of the elbow flexors in young men. *J Appl Physiol.* 1985(98): 1768-1776, 2005.

685. Shinohara, M, Kouzaki, M, Yoshihisa, T, and Fukunaga, T. Efficacy of tourniquet ischemia for strength training with low resistance. *Eur J Appl Physiol Occup Physiol.* 77: 189-191, 1998.

686. Short, KR, Vittone, JL, Bigelow, ML, Proctor, DN, and Nair, KS. Age and aerobic exercise training effects on whole body and muscle protein metabolism. *Am J Physiol Endocrinol Metab.* 286: E92-E101, 2004.

687. Siff, M. *Supertraining.* Denver, CO: Supertraining Institute, 2009.

688. Signorile, JF, Lew, KM, Stoutenberg, M, Pluchino, A, Lewis, JE, and Gao, J. Range of motion and leg rotation affect electromyography activation levels of the superficial quadriceps muscles during leg extension. *J Strength Cond Res.* 28: 2536-2545, 2014.

689. Sillanpaa, E, Laaksonen, DE, Hakkinen, A, Karavirta, L, Jensen, B, Kraemer, WJ, Nyman, K, and Hakkinen, K. Body composition, fitness, and metabolic health during strength and endurance training and their combination in middle-aged and older women. *Eur J Appl Physiol.* 106: 285-296, 2009.

690. Silva, RF, Cadore, EL, Kothe, G, Guedes, M, Alberton, CL, Pinto, SS, Pinto, RS, Trindade, G, and Kruel, LF. Concurrent training with different aerobic exercises. *Int J Sports Med.* 33: 627-634, 2012.

691. Simao, R, Spineti, J, de Salles, BF, Oliveira, LF, Matta, T, Miranda, F, Miranda, H, and Costa, PB. Influence of exercise order on maximum strength and muscle thickness in untrained men. *J Sports Sci Med.* 9: 1-7, 2010.

692. Simao, R, de Salles, BF, Figueiredo, T, Dias, I, and Willardson, JM. Exercise order in resistance training. *Sports Med.* 42: 251-265, 2012.

693. Simao, R, Spineti, J, de Salles, BF, Matta, T, Fernandes, L, Fleck, SJ, Rhea, MR, and Strom-Olsen, HE. Comparison between nonlinear and linear periodized resistance training: Hypertrophic and strength effects. *J Strength Cond Res.* 26: 1389-1395, 2012.

694. Simoneau, JA, and Bouchard, C. Genetic determinism of fiber type proportion in human skeletal muscle. *FASEB J.* 9: 1091-1095, 1995.

695. Singh, MA, Ding, W, Manfredi, TJ, Solares, GS, O'Neill, EF, Clements, KM, Ryan, ND, Kehayias, JJ, Fielding, RA, and Evans, WJ. Insulin-like growth factor I in skeletal muscle after weight-lifting exercise in frail elders. *Am J Physiol.* 277: E135-E143, 1999.

696. Sinha-Hikim, I, Cornford, M, Gaytan, H, Lee, ML, and Bhasin, S. Effects of testosterone supplementation on skeletal muscle fiber hypertrophy and satellite cells in community-dwelling older men. *J Clin Endocrinol Metab.* 91: 3024-3033, 2006.

697. Sipila, S, and Suominen, H. Effects of strength and endurance training on thigh and leg muscle mass and composition in elderly women. *J Appl Physiol.* 1985(78): 334-340, 1995.

698. Sjogaard, G, Adams, RP, and Saltin, B. Water and ion shifts in skeletal muscle of humans with intense dynamic knee extension. *Am J Physiol.* 248: R190-6, 1985.

699. Sjogaard, G. Water and electrolyte fluxes during exercise and their relation to muscle fatigue. *Acta Physiol Scand Suppl.* 556: 129-136, 1986.

700. Slater, G, and Phillips, SM. Nutrition guidelines for strength sports: Sprinting, weightlifting, throwing events, and bodybuilding. *J Sports Sci.* 29 Suppl 1: S67-77, 2011.

701. Smilios, I, Pilianidis, T, Karamouzis, M, and Tokmakidis, SP. Hormonal responses after various resistance exercise protocols. *Med Sci Sports Exerc.* 35: 644-654, 2003.

702. Smith, GI, Atherton, P, Villareal, DT, Frimel, TN, Rankin, D, Rennie, MJ, and Mittendorfer, B. Differences in muscle protein synthesis and anabolic signaling in the postabsorptive state and in response to food in 65-80 year old men and women. *PLoS One* 3: e1875, 2008.

703. Smith, GI, Atherton, P, Reeds, DN, Mohammed, BS, Rankin, D, Rennie, MJ, and Mittendorfer, B. Dietary omega-3 fatty acid supplementation increases the rate of muscle protein synthesis in older adults: A randomized controlled trial. *Am J Clin Nutr.* 93: 402-412, 2011.

704. Smith, GI, Villareal, DT, Sinacore, DR, Shah, K, and Mittendorfer, B. Muscle protein synthesis response to exercise training in obese, older men and women. *Med Sci Sports Exerc.* 44: 1259-1266, 2012.

705. Smith, RC, and Rutherford, OM. The role of metabolites in strength training. I. A comparison of eccentric and concentric contractions. *Eur J Appl Physiol Occup Physiol.* 71: 332-336, 1995.

706. Snyder, BJ, and Leech, JR. Voluntary increase in latissimus dorsi muscle activity during the lat pulldown following expert instruction. *J Strength Cond Res.* 23: 2204-2209, 2009.

707. Snyder, BJ, and Fry, WR. Effect of verbal instruction on muscle activity during the bench press exercise. *J Strength Cond Res.* 26: 2394-2400, 2012.

708. Solomon, AM, and Bouloux, PM. Modifying muscle mass: The endocrine perspective. *J Endocrinol.* 191: 349-360, 2006.

709. Soltow, QA, Betters, JL, Sellman, JE, Lira, VA, Long, JH, and Criswell, DS. Ibuprofen inhibits skeletal muscle hypertrophy in rats. *Med Sci Sports Exerc.* 38: 840-846, 2006.

710. Soltow, QA, Betters, JL, Sellman, JE, Lira, VA, Long, JHD, and Criswell, DS. Ibuprofen inhibits skeletal muscle hypertrophy in rats. *Med Sci Sports Exerc.* 38: 840-846, 2006.

711. Sonmez, GT, Schoenfeld, BJ, and Vatansever-Ozen, S. Omega-3 fatty acids and exercise: A review of their combined effects on body composition and physical performance. *Biomed Hum Kinetics* 3: 23-29, 2011.

712. Sooneste, H, Tanimoto, M, Kakigi, R, Saga, N, and Katamoto, S. Effects of training volume on strength and hypertrophy in young men. *J Strength Cond Res.* 27: 8-13, 2013.

713. Sotiropoulos, A, Ohanna, M, Kedzia, C, Menon, RK, Kopchick, JJ, Kelly, PA, and Pende, M. Growth hormone promotes skeletal muscle cell fusion independent of insulin-like growth factor 1 up-regulation. *Proc Natl Acad Sci USA* 103: 7315-7320, 2006.

714. Souza, EO, Ugrinowitsch, C, Tricoli, V, Roschel, H, Lowery, RP, Aihara, AY, Leao, ARS, and Wilson, JM. Early adaptations to six weeks of non-periodized and periodized strength training regimens in recreational males. *J Sports Sci Med.* 13: 604-609, 2014.

715. Souza-Junior, TP, Willardson, JM, Bloomer, R, Leite, RD, Fleck, SJ, Oliveira, PR, and Simao, R. Strength and hypertrophy responses to constant and decreasing rest intervals in trained men using creatine supplementation. *J Int Soc Sports Nutr.* 8: 17, 2011.

716. Spangenburg, EE, Le Roith, D, Ward, CW, and Bodine, SC. A functional insulin-like growth factor receptor is not necessary for load-induced skeletal muscle hypertrophy. *J Physiol.* 586: 283-291, 2008.

717. Spangenburg, EE. Changes in muscle mass with mechanical load: Possible cellular mechanisms. *Appl Physiol Nutr Metab.* 34: 328-335, 2009.

718. Spiering, BA, Kraemer, WJ, Anderson, JM, Armstrong, LE, Nindl, BC, Volek, JS, and Maresh, CM. Resistance exercise biology: Manipulation of resistance exercise programme variables determines the responses of cellular and molecular signalling pathways. *Sports Med.* 38: 527-540, 2008.

719. Spiering, BA, Kraemer, WJ, Vingren, JL, Ratamess, NA, Anderson, JM, Armstrong, LE, Nindl, BC, Volek, JS, Hakkinen, K, and Maresh, CM. Elevated endogenous testosterone concentrations potentiate muscle androgen receptor responses to resistance exercise. *J Steroid Biochem Mol Biol.* 114: 195-199, 2009.

720. Spineti, J, de Salles, BF, Rhea, MR, Lavigne, D, Matta, T, Miranda, F, Fernandes, L, and Simao, R. Influence of exercise order on maximum strength and muscle volume in nonlinear periodized resistance training. *J Strength Cond Res.* 24: 2962-2969, 2010.

721. Staples, AW, Burd, NA, West, DW, Currie, KD, Atherton, PJ, Moore, DR, Rennie, MJ, Macdonald, MJ, Baker, SK, and Phillips, SM. Carbohydrate does not augment exercise-induced protein accretion versus protein alone. *Med Sci Sports Exerc.* 43: 1154-1161, 2011.

722. Starkey, DB, Pollock, ML, Ishida, Y, Welsch, MA, Brechue, WF, Graves, JE, and Feigenbaum, MS. Effect of resistance training volume on strength and muscle thickness. *Med Sci Sports Exerc.* 28: 1311-1320, 1996.

723. Staron, RS, Leonardi, MJ, Karapondo, DL, Malicky, ES, Falkel, JE, Hagerman, FC, and Hikida, RS. Strength and skeletal muscle adaptations in heavy-resistance-trained women after detraining and retraining. *J Appl Physiol.* 70: 631-640, 1991.

724. Stepto, NK, Coffey, VG, Carey, AL, Ponnampalam, AP, Canny, BJ, Powell, D, and Hawley, JA. Global gene expression in skeletal muscle from well-trained strength and endurance athletes. *Med Sci Sports Exerc.* 41: 546-565, 2009.

725. Stewart, CE, and Rittweger, J. Adaptive processes in skeletal muscle: Molecular regulators and genetic influences. *J Musculoskelet Neuronal Interact.* 6: 73-86, 2006.

726. Stewart, VH, Saunders, DH, and Greig, CA. Responsiveness of muscle size and strength to physical training in very elderly people: A systematic review. *Scand J Med Sci Sports.* 24: e1-e10, 2014.

727. Stone, MH, O'Bryant, HS, Schilling, BK, and R.L. Johnson, RL. Periodization: Effects of manipulating volume and intensity. Part 1. *Strength Cond J.* 21: 56-62, 1999.

728. Stone, MH, Potteiger, JA, Pierce, KC, Proulx, CM, O´Bryant, HS, Johnson, RL, and Stone, ME. Comparison of the effects of three different weight-training programs on the one repetition maximum squat. *J Strength Cond Res.* 14: 332-337, 2000.

729. Stone, MH, O'Bryant, H, and Garhammer, J. A hypothetical model for strength training. *J Sports Med Phys Fitness* 21: 342-351, 1981.

730. Street, SF. Lateral transmission of tension in frog myofibers: A myofibrillar network and transverse cytoskeletal connections are possible transmitters. *J Cell Physiol.* 114: 346-364, 1983.

731. Suga, T, Okita, K, Morita, N, Yokota, T, Hirabayashi, K, Horiuchi, M, Takada, S, Omokawa, M, Kinugawa, S, and Tsutsui, H. Dose effect on intramuscular metabolic stress during low-intensity resistance exercise with blood flow restriction. *J Appl Physiol.* 108: 1563-1567, 2010.

732. Suga, T, Okita, K, Morita, N, Yokota, T, Hirabayashi, K, Horiuchi, M, Takada, S, Takahashi, T, Omokawa, M, Kinugawa, S, and Tsutsui, H. Intramuscular metabolism during low-intensity resistance exercise with blood flow restriction. *J Appl Physiol.* 106: 1119-1124, 2009.

733. Sundstrup, E, Jakobsen, MD, Andersen, CH, Zebis, MK, Mortensen, OS, and Andersen, LL. Muscle activation strategies during strength training with heavy loading vs. repetitions to failure. *J Strength Cond Res.* 26: 1897-1903, 2012.

734. Suzuki, YJ, and Ford, GD. Redox regulation of signal transduction in cardiac and smooth muscle. *J Mol Cell Cardiol.* 31: 345-353, 1999.

735. Takada, S, Okita, K, Suga, T, Omokawa, M, Kadoguchi, T, Sato, T, Takahashi, M, Yokota, T, Hirabayashi, K, Morita, N, Horiuchi, M, Kinugawa, S, and Tsutsui, H. Low-intensity exercise can increase muscle mass and strength proportionally to enhanced metabolic stress under ischemic conditions. *J Appl Physiol.* 1985(113): 199-205, 2012.

736. Takano, H, Morita, T, Iida, H, Asada, K, Kato, M, Uno, K, Hirose, K, Matsumoto, A, Takenaka, K, Hirata, Y, Eto, F, Nagai, R, Sato, Y, and Nakajima, T. Hemodynamic and hormonal responses to a short-term low-intensity resistance exercise with the reduction of muscle blood flow. *Eur J Appl Physiol.* 95: 65-73, 2005.

737. Takarada, Y, Nakamura, Y, Aruga, S, Onda, T, Miyazaki, S, and Ishii, N. Rapid increase in plasma growth hormone after low-intensity resistance exercise with vascular occlusion. *J Appl Physiol.* 88: 61-65, 2000.

738. Takarada, Y, Takazawa, H, Sato, Y, Takebayashi, S, Tanaka, Y, and Ishii, N. Effects of resistance exercise combined with moderate vascular occlusion on muscular function in humans. *J Appl Physiol.* 88: 2097-2106, 2000.

739. Talmadge, RJ, Otis, JS, Rittler, MR, Garcia, ND, Spencer, SR, Lees, SJ, and Naya, FJ. Calcineurin activation influences muscle phenotype in a muscle-specific fashion. *BMC Cell Biol.* 5: 28, 2004.

740. Tamaki, T, Uchiyama, S, Tamura, T, and Nakano, S. Changes in muscle oxygenation during weight-lifting exercise. *Eur J Appl Physiol Occup Physiol.* 68: 465-469, 1994.

741. Tang, JE, Perco, JG, Moore, DR, Wilkinson, SB, and Phillips, SM. Resistance training alters the response of fed state mixed muscle protein synthesis in

young men. *Am J Physiol Regul Integr Comp Physiol.* 294: R172-178, 2008.

742. Tang, JE, Moore, DR, Kujbida, GW, Tarnopolsky, MA, and Phillips, SM. Ingestion of whey hydrolysate, casein, or soy protein isolate: Effects on mixed muscle protein synthesis at rest and following resistance exercise in young men. *J Appl Physiol.* 1985(107): 987-992, 2009.

743. Tanimoto, M, and Ishii, N. Effects of low-intensity resistance exercise with slow movement and tonic force generation on muscular function in young men. *J Appl Physiol.* 100: 1150-1157, 2006.

744. Tanimoto, M, Sanada, K, Yamamoto, K, Kawano, H, Gando, Y, Tabata, I, Ishii, N, and Miyachi, M. Effects of whole-body low-intensity resistance training with slow movement and tonic force generation on muscular size and strength in young men. *J Strength Cond Res.* 22: 1926-1938, 2008.

745. Tarnopolsky, MA, Atkinson, SA, MacDougall, JD, Chesley, A, Phillips, S, and Schwarcz, HP. Evaluation of protein requirements for trained strength athletes. *J Appl Physiol.* 1985(73): 1986-1995, 1992.

746. Tatsumi, R, and Allen, RE. Active hepatocyte growth factor is present in skeletal muscle extracellular matrix. *Muscle Nerve* 30: 654-658, 2004.

747. Tatsumi, R. Mechano-biology of skeletal muscle hypertrophy and regeneration: Possible mechanism of stretch-induced activation of resident myogenic stem cells. *Anim Sci J.* 81: 11-20, 2010.

748. Tatsumi, R, Hattori, A, Ikeuchi, Y, Anderson, JE, and Allen, RE. Release of hepatocyte growth factor from mechanically stretched skeletal muscle satellite cells and role of pH and nitric oxide. *Mol Biol Cell.* 13: 2909-2918, 2002.

749. Taylor, LW, Wilborn, CD, Kreider, RB, and Willoughby, DS. Effects of resistance exercise intensity on extracellular signal-regulated kinase 1/2 mitogen-activated protein kinase activation in men. *J Strength Cond Res.* 26: 599-607, 2012.

750. Tee, JC, Bosch, AN, and Lambert, MI. Metabolic consequences of exercise-induced muscle damage. *Sports Med.* 37: 827-836, 2007.

751. Tee, JC, Bosch, AN, and Lambert, MI. Metabolic consequences of exercise-induced muscle damage. *Sports Med.* 37: 827-836, 2007.

752. ter Haar Romeny, BM, Denier van der Gon, JJ, and Gielen, CC. Changes in recruitment order of motor units in the human biceps muscle. *Exp Neurol.* 78: 360-368, 1982.

753. ter Haar Romeny, BM, van der Gon, JJ, and Gielen, CC. Relation between location of a motor unit in the human biceps brachii and its critical firing levels for different tasks. *Exp Neurol.* 85: 631-650, 1984.

754. Terzis, G, Georgiadis, G, Stratakos, G, Vogiatzis, I, Kavouras, S, Manta, P, Mascher, H, and Blomstrand, E. Resistance exercise-induced increase in muscle mass correlates with p70S6 kinase phosphorylation in human subjects. *Eur J Appl Physiol.* 102: 145-152, 2008.

755. Terzis, G, Spengos, K, Mascher, H, Georgiadis, G, Manta, P, and Blomstrand, E. The degree of p70 S6k and S6 phosphorylation in human skeletal muscle in response to resistance exercise depends on the training volume. *Eur J Appl Physiol.* 110: 835-843, 2010.

756. Tesch, PA, Ploutz-Snyder, LL, Ystrom, L, Castro, MJ, and Dudley, GA. Skeletal muscle glycogen loss evoked by resistance exercise. *J Strength Cond Res.* 12: 67-73, 1998.

757. Tesch, PA, and Larsson, L. Muscle hypertrophy in bodybuilders. *Eur J Appl Physiol Occup Physiol.* 49: 301-306, 1982.

758. Tesch, PA, Colliander, EB, and Kaiser, P. Muscle metabolism during intense, heavy-resistance exercise. *Eur J Appl Physiol Occup Physiol.* 55: 362-366, 1986.

759. Tesch, PA. Skeletal muscle adaptations consequent to long-term heavy resistance exercise. *Med Sci Sports Exerc.* 20: S132-134, 1988.

760. Thannickal, VJ, and Fanburg, BL. Reactive oxygen species in cell signaling. *Am J Physiol Lung Cell Mol Physiol.* 279: L1005-1028, 2000.

761. Thomas, G, and Hall, MN. TOR signalling and control of cell growth. *Curr Opin Cell Biol.* 9: 782-787, 1997.

762. Thomson, DM, and Gordon, SE. Impaired overload-induced muscle growth is associated with diminished translational signalling in aged rat fast-twitch skeletal muscle. *J Physiol.* 574: 291-305, 2006.

763. Tidball, JG. Mechanical signal transduction in skeletal muscle growth and adaptation. *J Appl Physiol.* 98: 1900-1908, 2005.

764. Tidball, JG. Inflammatory processes in muscle injury and repair. *Am J Physiol Regul Integr Comp Physiol.* 288: 345-353, 2005.

765. Timmons, JA. Variability in training-induced skeletal muscle adaptation. *J Appl Physiol.* 110: 846-853, 2011.

766. Tipton, KD, Ferrando, AA, Phillips, SM, Doyle, D, Jr, and Wolfe, RR. Postexercise net protein synthesis in human muscle from orally administered amino acids. *Am J Physiol.* 276: E628-E634, 1999.

767. Tipton, KD, Gurkin, BE, Matin, S, and Wolfe, RR. Nonessential amino acids are not necessary to stimulate net muscle protein synthesis in healthy volunteers. *J Nutr Biochem.* 10: 89-95, 1999.

768. Tipton, KD, Elliott, TA, Cree, MG, Wolf, SE, Sanford, AP, and Wolfe, RR. Ingestion of casein and whey proteins result in muscle anabolism after resistance exercise. *Med Sci Sports Exerc.* 36: 2073-2081, 2004.

769. Tipton, KD, Elliott, TA, Ferrando, AA, Aarsland, AA, and Wolfe, RR. Stimulation of muscle anabolism by resistance exercise and ingestion of leucine plus protein. *Appl Physiol Nutr Metab.* 34: 151-161, 2009.

770. Toft, AD, Jensen, LB, Bruunsgaard, H, Ibfelt, T, Halkjaer-Kristensen, J, Febbraio, M, and Pedersen, BK. Cytokine response to eccentric exercise in young and elderly humans. *Am J Physiol, Cell Physiol.* 283: 289-295, 2002.

771. Toigo, M, and Boutellier, U. New fundamental resistance exercise determinants of molecular and cellular muscle adaptations. *Eur J Appl Physiol.* 97: 643-663, 2006.

772. Tomiya, A, Aizawa, T, Nagatomi, R, Sensui, H, and Kokubun, S. Myofibers express IL-6 after eccentric exercise. *Am J Sports Med.* 32: 503-508, 2004.

773. Trappe, S, Harber, M, Creer, A, Gallagher, P, Slivka, D, Minchev, K, and Whitsett, D. Single muscle fiber adaptations with marathon training. *J Appl Physiol.* 1985(101): 721-727, 2006.

774. Trappe, TA, White, F, Lambert, CP, Cesar, D, Hellerstein, M, and Evans, WJ. Effect of ibuprofen and acetaminophen on postexercise muscle protein synthesis. *Am J Physiol Endocrinol Metab.* 282: E551-E556, 2002.

775. Trappe, TA, Raue, U, and Tesch, PA. Human soleus muscle protein synthesis following resistance exercise. *Acta Physiol Scand.* 182: 189-196, 2004.

776. Trappe, TA, Carroll, CC, Dickinson, JM, LeMoine, JK, Haus, JM, Sullivan, BE, Lee, JD, Jemiolo, B, Weinheimer, EM, and Hollon, CJ. Influence of acetaminophen and ibuprofen on skeletal muscle adaptations to resistance exercise in older adults. *Am J Physiol Regul Integr Comp Physiol.* 300: R655-662, 2011.

777. Trebs, AA, Brandenburg, JP, and Pitney, WA. An electromyography analysis of 3 muscles surrounding the shoulder joint during the performance of a chest press exercise at several angles. *J Strength Cond Res.* 24: 1925-1930, 2010.

778. Turner, DL, Hoppeler, H, Claassen, H, Vock, P, Kayser, B, Schena, F, and Ferretti, G. Effects of endurance training on oxidative capacity and structural composition of human arm and leg muscles. *Acta Physiol Scand.* 161: 459-464, 1997.

779. Uchiyama, S, Tsukamoto, H, Yoshimura, S, and Tamaki, T. Relationship between oxidative stress in muscle tissue and weight-lifting-induced muscle damage. *Pflugers Arch.* 452: 109-116, 2006.

780. Urban, RJ, Bodenburg, YH, Gilkison, C, Foxworth, J, Coggan, AR, Wolfe, RR, and Ferrando, A. Testosterone administration to elderly men increases skeletal muscle strength and protein synthesis. *Am J Physiol.* 269: E820-E826, 1995.

781. Usher-Smith, JA, Fraser, JA, Bailey, PS, Griffin, JL, and Huang, CL. The influence of intracellular lactate and H+ on cell volume in amphibian skeletal muscle. *J Physiol.* 573: 799-818, 2006.

782. Van Cutsem, M, Duchateau, J, and Hainaut, K. Changes in single motor unit behaviour contribute to the increase in contraction speed after dynamic training in humans. *J Physiol.* 513 (Pt 1): 295-305, 1998.

783. Van Roie, E, Delecluse, C, Coudyzer, W, Boonen, S, and Bautmans, I. Strength training at high versus low external resistance in older adults: Effects on muscle volume, muscle strength, and force-velocity characteristics. *Exp Gerontol.* 48: 1351-1361, 2013.

784. van Wessel, T, de Haan, A, van der Laarse, WJ, and Jaspers, RT. The muscle fiber type-fiber size paradox: Hypertrophy or oxidative metabolism? *Eur J Appl Physiol.* 110: 665-694, 2010.

785. Vance, J, Wulf, G, Tollner, T, McNevin, N, and Mercer, J. EMG activity as a function of the performer's focus of attention. *J Mot Behav.* 36: 450-459, 2004.

786. Vandenburgh, HH, Hatfaludy, S, Sohar, I, and Shansky, J. Stretch-induced prostaglandins and protein turnover in cultured skeletal muscle. *Am J Physiol.* 259: C232-240, 1990.

787. Vane, JR, and Botting, RM. Anti-inflammatory drugs and their mechanism of action. *Inflamm Res.* 47 Suppl 2: S78-87, 1998.

788. Veldhuis, JD, Keenan, DM, Mielke, K, Miles, JM, and Bowers, CY. Testosterone supplementation in healthy older men drives GH and IGF-I secretion without potentiating peptidyl secretagogue efficacy. *Eur J Endocrinol.* 153: 577-586, 2005.

789. Velloso, CP. Regulation of muscle mass by growth hormone and IGF-I. *Br J Pharmacol.* 154: 557-568, 2008.

790. Verdijk, LB, Koopman, R, Schaart, G, Meijer, K, Savelberg, HH, and van Loon, LJ. Satellite cell content is specifically reduced in type II skeletal muscle fibers in the elderly. *Am J Physiol Endocrinol Metab.* 292: E151-E157, 2007.

791. Vierck, J, O'Reilly, B, Hossner, K, Antonio, J, Byrne, K, Bucci, L, and Dodson, M. Satellite cell regulation following myotrauma caused by resistance exercise. *Cell Biol Int.* 24: 263-272, 2000.

792. Vijayan, K, Thompson, JL, Norenberg, KM, Fitts, RH, and Riley, DA. Fiber-type susceptibility to eccentric contraction-induced damage of hindlimb-unloaded rat AL muscles. *J Appl Physiol.* 90: 770-776, 2001.

793. Vikne, H, Refsnes, PE, Ekmark, M, Medbo, JI, Gundersen, V, and Gundersen, K. Muscular performance after concentric and eccentric exercise in trained men. *Med Sci Sports Exerc.* 38: 1770-1781, 2006.

794. Villanueva, MG, Lane, CJ, and Schroeder, ET. Short rest interval lengths between sets optimally

enhance body composition and performance with 8 weeks of strength resistance training in older men. *Eur J Appl Physiol.* 115: 295-308, 2015.

795. Vingren, JL, Kraemer, WJ, Ratamess, NA, Anderson, JM, Volek, JS, and Maresh, CM. Testosterone physiology in resistance exercise and training: The up-stream regulatory elements. *Sports Med.* 40: 1037-1053, 2010.

796. Viru, M, Jansson, E, Viru, A, and Sundberg, CJ. Effect of restricted blood flow on exercise-induced hormone changes in healthy men. *Eur J Appl Physiol Occup Physiol.* 77: 517-522, 1998.

797. Vissing, K, McGee, S, Farup, J, Kjolhede, T, Vendelbo, M, and Jessen, N. Differentiated mTOR but not AMPK signaling after strength vs endurance exercise in training-accustomed individuals. *Scand J Med Sci Sports.* 23: 355-366, 2013.

798. Vissing, K, Rahbek, SK, Lamon, S, Farup, J, Stefanetti, RJ, Wallace, MA, Vendelbo, MH, and Russell, A. Effect of resistance exercise contraction mode and protein supplementation on members of the STARS signalling pathway. *J Physiol.* 591: 3749-3763, 2013.

799. Volek, JS, Kraemer, WJ, Bush, JA, Incledon, T, and Boetes, M. Testosterone and cortisol in relationship to dietary nutrients and resistance exercise. *J Appl Physiol.* 1985(82): 49-54, 1997.

800. Volek, JS, Gomez, AL, Love, DM, Avery, NG, Sharman, MJ, and Kraemer, WJ. Effects of a high-fat diet on postabsorptive and postprandial testosterone responses to a fat-rich meal. *Metabolism* 50: 1351-1355, 2001.

801. Vollestad, NK, Vaage, O, and Hermansen, L. Muscle glycogen depletion patterns in type I and subgroups of type II fibres during prolonged severe exercise in man. *Acta Physiol Scand.* 122: 433-441, 1984.

802. Wakahara, T, Miyamoto, N, Sugisaki, N, Murata, K, Kanehisa, H, Kawakami, Y, Fukunaga, T, and Yanai, T. Association between regional differences in muscle activation in one session of resistance exercise and in muscle hypertrophy after resistance training. *Eur J Appl Physiol.* 112: 1569-1576, 2012.

803. Wakahara, T, Fukutani, A, Kawakami, Y, and Yanai, T. Nonuniform muscle hypertrophy: Its relation to muscle activation in training session. *Med Sci Sports Exerc.* 45: 2158-2165, 2013.

804. Wang, Q, and McPherron, AC. Myostatin inhibition induces muscle fibre hypertrophy prior to satellite cell activation. *J Physiol.* 590: 2151-2165, 2012.

805. Wang, XD, Kawano, F, Matsuoka, Y, Fukunaga, K, Terada, M, Sudoh, M, Ishihara, A, and Ohira, Y. Mechanical load-dependent regulation of satellite cell and fiber size in rat soleus muscle. *Am J Physiol, Cell Physiol.* 290: 981-989, 2006.

806. Warner, DC, Schnepf, G, Barrett, MS, Dian, D, and Swigonski, NL. Prevalence, attitudes, and behaviors related to the use of nonsteroidal anti-inflammatory drugs (NSAIDs) in student athletes. *J Adolesc Health* 30: 150-153, 2002.

807. Watanabe, Y, Tanimoto, M, Ohgane, A, Sanada, K, Miyachi, M, and Ishii, N. Increased muscle size and strength from slow-movement, low-intensity resistance exercise and tonic force generation. *J Aging Phys Act.* 21: 71-84, 2013.

808. Watanabe, Y, Madarame, H, Ogasawara, R, Nakazato, K, and Ishii, N. Effect of very low-intensity resistance training with slow movement on muscle size and strength in healthy older adults. *Clin Physiol Funct Imaging* 34: 463-470, 2014.

809. Waters, DL, Baumgartner, RN, Garry, PJ, and Vellas, B. Advantages of dietary, exercise-related, and therapeutic interventions to prevent and treat sarcopenia in adult patients: An update. *Clin Interv Aging* 5: 259-270, 2010.

810. Wax, B, Kavazis, AN, and Brown, SP. Effects of supplemental carbohydrate ingestion during superimposed electromyostimulation exercise in elite weightlifters. *J Strength Cond Res.* 27: 3084-3090, 2013.

811. Weiss, LW, Coney, HD, and Clark, FC. Gross measures of exercise-induced muscular hypertrophy. *J Orthop Sports Phys Ther.* 30: 143-148, 2000.

812. Welle, S, Thornton, C, and Statt, M. Myofibrillar protein synthesis in young and old human subjects after three months of resistance training. *Am J Physiol.* 268: E422-E427, 1995.

813. Welle, S, Totterman, S, and Thornton, C. Effect of age on muscle hypertrophy induced by resistance training. *J Gerontol A Biol Sci Med Sci.* 51: M270-275, 1996.

814. Wernbom, M, Augustsson, J, and Thomee, R. The influence of frequency, intensity, volume and mode of strength training on whole muscle cross-sectional area in humans. *Sports Med.* 37: 225-264, 2007.

815. Wernbom, M, Paulsen, G, Nilsen, TS, Hisdal, J, and Raastad, T. Contractile function and sarcolemmal permeability after acute low-load resistance exercise with blood flow restriction. *Eur J Appl Physiol.* 112: 2051-2063, 2012.

816. Wernig, A, Irintchev, A, and Weisshaupt, P. Muscle injury, cross-sectional area and fibre type distribution in mouse soleus after intermittent wheel-running. *J Physiol.* 428: 639-652, 1990.

817. West, DW, Kujbida, GW, Moore, DR, Atherton, P, Burd, NA, Padzik, JP, De Lisio, M, Tang, JE, Parise, G, Rennie, MJ, Baker, SK, and Phillips, SM. Resistance exercise-induced increases in putative anabolic hormones do not enhance muscle protein synthesis or intracellular signalling in young men. *J Physiol.* 587: 5239-5247, 2009.

818. West, DW, Burd, NA, Tang, JE, Moore, DR, Staples, AW, Holwerda, AM, Baker, SK, and Phillips, SM. Elevations in ostensibly anabolic hormones with resistance exercise enhance neither training-induced muscle hypertrophy nor strength of the elbow flexors. *J Appl Physiol.* 108: 60-67, 2010.

819. West, DW, and Phillips, SM. Anabolic processes in human skeletal muscle: Restoring the identities of growth hormone and testosterone. *Phys Sportsmed.* 38: 97-104, 2010.

820. West, DW, and Phillips, SM. Associations of exercise-induced hormone profiles and gains in strength and hypertrophy in a large cohort after weight training. *Eur J Appl Physiol.* 112: 2693-2702, 2012.

821. West, DW, Cotie, LM, Mitchell, CJ, Churchward-Venne, TA, MacDonald, MJ, and Phillips, SM. Resistance exercise order does not determine postexercise delivery of testosterone, growth hormone, and IGF-1 to skeletal muscle. *Appl Physiol Nutr Metab.* 38: 220-226, 2013.

822. Westcott, WL, Winett, RA, Anderson, ES, Wojcik, JR, Loud, RL, Cleggett, E, and Glover, S. Effects of regular and slow speed resistance training on muscle strength. *J Sports Med Phys Fitness* 41: 154-158, 2001.

823. Whitehouse, AS, and Tisdale, MJ. Downregulation of ubiquitin-dependent proteolysis by eicosapentaenoic acid in acute starvation. *Biochem Biophys Res Commun.* 285: 598-602, 2001.

824. Wickiewicz, TL, Roy, RR, Powell, PL, and Edgerton, VR. Muscle architecture of the human lower limb. *Clin Orthop Relat Res.* 179: 275-283, 1983.

825. Widegren, U, Ryder, JW, and Zierath, JR. Mitogen-activated protein kinase signal transduction in skeletal muscle: Effects of exercise and muscle contraction. *Acta Physiol Scand.* 172: 227-238, 2001.

826. Wilk, KE, Escamilla, RF, Fleisig, GS, Barrentine, SW, Andrews, JR, and Boyd, ML. A comparison of tibiofemoral joint forces and electromyographic activity during open and closed kinetic chain exercises. *Am J Sports Med.* 24: 518-527, 1996.

827. Wilkinson, SB, Tarnopolsky, MA, Macdonald, MJ, Macdonald, JR, Armstrong, D, and Phillips, SM. Consumption of fluid skim milk promotes greater muscle protein accretion after resistance exercise than does consumption of an isonitrogenous and isoenergetic soy-protein beverage. *Am J Clin Nutr.* 85: 1031-1040, 2007.

828. Wilkinson, SB, Phillips, SM, Atherton, PJ, Patel, R, Yarasheski, KE, Tarnopolsky, MA, and Rennie, MJ. Differential effects of resistance and endurance exercise in the fed state on signalling molecule phosphorylation and protein synthesis in human muscle. *J Physiol.* 586: 3701-3717, 2008.

829. Willardson, JM, Norton, L, and Wilson, G. Training to failure and beyond in mainstream resistance exercise programs. *Strength Cond J.* 32: 21-29, 2010.

830. Willoughby, DS. The effects of mesocycle-length weight training programs involving periodization and partially equated volumes on upper and lower body strength. *J Strength Cond Res.* 7: 2-8, 1993.

831. Wilson, JM, Marin, PJ, Rhea, MR, Wilson, SM, Loenneke, JP, and Anderson, JC. Concurrent training: A meta-analysis examining interference of aerobic and resistance exercises. *J Strength Cond Res.* 26: 2293-2307, 2012.

832. Wilson, JM, Lowery, RP, Joy, JM, Loenneke, JP, and Naimo, MA. Practical blood flow restriction training increases acute determinants of hypertrophy without increasing indices of muscle damage. *J Strength Cond Res.* 27(11): 3068-3075, 2013.

833. Winter, JN, Jefferson, LS, and Kimball, SR. ERK and Akt signaling pathways function through parallel mechanisms to promote mTORC1 signaling. *Am J Physiol Cell Physiol.* 300: C1172-1180, 2011.

834. Witard, OC, Jackman, SR, Breen, L, Smith, K, Selby, A, and Tipton, KD. Myofibrillar muscle protein synthesis rates subsequent to a meal in response to increasing doses of whey protein at rest and after resistance exercise. *Am J Clin Nutr.* 99: 86-95, 2014.

835. Wojtaszewski, JF, MacDonald, C, Nielsen, JN, Hellsten, Y, Hardie, DG, Kemp, BE, Kiens, B, and Richter, EA. Regulation of 5'AMP-activated protein kinase activity and substrate utilization in exercising human skeletal muscle. *Am J Physiol Endocrinol Metab.* 284: E813-E822, 2003.

836. Woodley, SJ, and Mercer, SR. Hamstring muscles: Architecture and innervation. *Cells Tissues Organs* 179: 125-141, 2005.

837. Worrell, TW, Karst, G, Adamczyk, D, Moore, R, Stanley, C, Steimel, B, and Steimel, S. Influence of joint position on electromyographic and torque generation during maximal voluntary isometric contractions of the hamstrings and gluteus maximus muscles. *J Orthop Sports Phys Ther.* 31: 730-740, 2001.

838. Wright, GA, Delong, T, and Gehlsen, G. Electromyographic activity of the hamstrings during performance of the leg curl, stiff-leg deadlift and back squat movements. *J Strength Cond Res.* 13: 168-174, 1999.

839. Wu, G. Amino acids: Metabolism, functions, and nutrition. *Amino Acids* 37: 1-17, 2009.

840. Wulf, G. Attentional focus and motor learning: A review of 15 years. *Int Rev Sport Exerc Psych.* 6: 77-104, 2013.

841. Yamada, S, Buffinger, N, DiMario, J, and Strohman, RC. Fibroblast growth factor is stored in fiber extracellular matrix and plays a role in regulating muscle hypertrophy. *Med Sci Sports Exerc.* 21: 173-180, 1989.

842. Yamaguchi, A, Fujikawa, T, Shimada, S, Kanbayashi, I, Tateoka, M, Soya, H, Takeda, H, Morita,

I, Matsubara, K, and Hirai, T. Muscle IGF-I Ea, MGF, and myostatin mRNA expressions after compensatory overload in hypophysectomized rats. *Pflugers Arch.* 453: 203-210, 2006.

843. Yamashita, N. EMG activities in mono- and bi-articular thigh muscles in combined hip and knee extension. *Eur J Appl Physiol Occup Physiol.* 58: 274-277, 1988.

844. Yang, SY, and Goldspink, G. Different roles of the IGF-I Ec peptide (MGF) and mature IGF-I in myoblast proliferation and differentiation. *FEBS Lett.* 522: 156-160, 2002.

845. Yang, Y, Breen, L, Burd, NA, Hector, AJ, Churchward-Venne, TA, Josse, AR, Tarnopolsky, MA, and Phillips, SM. Resistance exercise enhances myofibrillar protein synthesis with graded intakes of whey protein in older men. *Br J Nutr.* 108(10): 1780-1788, 2012.

846. Yao, W, Fuglevand, RJ, and Enoka, RM. Motor-unit synchronization increases EMG amplitude and decreases force steadiness of simulated contractions. *J Neurophysiol.* 83: 441-452, 2000.

847. Yarasheski, KE, Campbell, JA, Smith, K, Rennie, MJ, Holloszy, JO, and Bier, DM. Effect of growth hormone and resistance exercise on muscle growth in young men. *Am J Physiol.* 262: E261-E267, 1992.

848. Yarasheski, KE, Zachwieja, JJ, Campbell, JA, and Bier, DM. Effect of growth hormone and resistance exercise on muscle growth and strength in older men. *Am J Physiol.* 268: E268-E276, 1995.

849. Yarasheski, KE. Managing sarcopenia with progressive resistance exercise training. *J Nutr Health Aging* 6: 349-356, 2002.

850. Yasuda, T, Abe, T, Sato, Y, Midorikawa, T, Kearns, CF, Inoue, K, Ryushi, T, and Ishii, N. Muscle fiber cross-sectional area is increased after two weeks of twice daily KAATSU-resistance training. *Int J KAATSU Train Res.* 1: 65-70, 2005.

851. Youdas, JW, Amundson, CL, Cicero, KS, Hahn, JJ, Harezlak, DT, and Hollman, JH. Surface electromyographic activation patterns and elbow joint motion during a pull-up, chin-up, or perfect-pullup rotational exercise. *J Strength Cond Res.* 24: 3404-3414, 2010.

852. Young, WB, and Bilby, GE. The effect of voluntary effort to influence speed of contraction on strength, muscular power, and hypertrophy development. *J Strength Cond Res.* 7: 172-178, 1993.

853. Young, K, and Davies, CT. Effect of diet on human muscle weakness following prolonged exercise. *Eur J Appl Physiol Occup Physiol.* 53: 81-85, 1984.

854. Zacker, RJ. Health-related implications and management of sarcopenia. *JAAPA.* 19: 24-29, 2006.

855. Zammit, PS. All muscle satellite cells are equal, but are some more equal than others? *J Cell Sci.* 121: 2975-2982, 2008.

856. Zanchi, NE, and Lancha, AH, Jr. Mechanical stimuli of skeletal muscle: Implications on mTOR/p70s6k and protein synthesis. *Eur J Appl Physiol.* 102: 253-263, 2008.

857. Zanou, N, and Gailly, P. Skeletal muscle hypertrophy and regeneration: Interplay between the myogenic regulatory factors (MRFs) and insulin-like growth factors (IGFs) pathways. *Cell Mol Life Sci.* 70: 4117-4130, 2013.

858. Zatsiorsky, VM, and Kraemer, WJ. *Science and Practice of Strength Training.* Champaign, IL: Human Kinetics, 2006.

859. Zebis, MK, Skotte, J, Andersen, CH, Mortensen, P, Petersen, HH, Viskaer, TC, Jensen, TL, Bencke, J, and Andersen, LL. Kettlebell swing targets semitendinosus and supine leg curl targets biceps femoris: An EMG study with rehabilitation implications. *Br J Sports Med.* 47: 1192-1198, 2013.

860. Zhao, W, Pan, J, Zhao, Z, Wu, Y, Bauman, WA, and Cardozo, CP. Testosterone protects against dexamethasone-induced muscle atrophy, protein degradation and MAFbx upregulation. *J Steroid Biochem Mol Biol.* 110: 125-129, 2008.

861. Zou, K, Meador, BM, Johnson, B, Huntsman, HD, Mahmassani, Z, Valero, MC, Huey, KA, and Boppart, MD. The alpha(7)beta(1)-integrin increases muscle hypertrophy following multiple bouts of eccentric exercise. *J Appl Physiol.* 111: 1134-1141, 2011.

AUTHOR INDEX

Note: The italicized *f* and *t* following page numbers refer to figures and tables, respectively.

A

Aagaard, P 5, 6, 44, 47, 65, 66t
Aarsland, AA 9, 71, 112, 142, 151
Abdessemed, D 76
Abe, T 19, 38, 39, 40, 41, 43, 65, 66t, 110, 112, 113, 130
Abernethy, PJ 11, 106, 145
Abrass, IB 95, 97t
Achour Junior, A 59t
Ackel-D'Elia, C 99
Adamczyk, D 122
Adamo, ML 16
Adams, GR 5, 6, 9, 13, 15, 22, 25, 26, 33, 46, 48, 57, 71, 101, 110, 151
Adams, K 38
Adams, RP 40
Adechian, S 6, 150
Adembri, C 43
Adlercreutz, H 148
Aguado, X 10
Aguiar, AF 130
Aguilera, BA 19, 40
Aharonov, R 106
Ahlstrom, H 148
Ahmadizad, S 6, 126
Ahmed, A 110
Ahtiainen, JP 6, 18, 20, 61, 63, 77, 79t, 109, 113, 148
Aihara, AY 39, 69, 70t, 123t, 127, 129t
Aizawa, T 23
Akima, H 39
Alberton, CL 101, 103t
Alegre, LM 10
Alen, M 6, 18, 20, 68, 69, 77, 79t, 113, 152
Alexander, JW 6, 148
Alexander, NB 83t
Alexander, P 123
Allen, DG 15, 42, 71
Allen, RE 26, 46, 47
Altadill, A 89
Altimari, LR 11
Alvar, BA 37, 55t, 56, 64, 111, 113
Alveno, DA 125, 126, 127, 129t
Alves Souza, RW 130
Alway, SE 11, 14, 15, 107, 110, 112, 113
Ambjornsen, IK 25, 53

American College of Sports Medicine 82
Amiridis, IG 7
Amorim, MZ 77
Amri, M 103
Amundson, CL 119
Andersen, CH 88, 123
Andersen, JL 5, 6, 13, 17, 19, 44, 65, 66t
Andersen, LL 13, 88, 123
Andersen, MB 18, 19, 23
Andersen, P 98
Andersen, V 6, 119
Anderson, BG 24
Anderson, ES 81
Anderson, JC 99, 101, 102, 104
Anderson, JE 26, 46
Anderson, JM 17, 18, 62, 81, 88
Anderson, KE 6, 146
Andersson, H 93
Andrews, DM 5
Andrews, JR 123
Angelopoulos, TJ 105, 106, 110
Anker, SD 33
Antoine, JM 150
Anton, SD 108f
Antoniello, S 153
Antonio, J 12, 15, 17, 42, 46, 117, 143, 151, 152
Antunes, M 55t
Aoki, MS 39, 81, 125, 126, 127, 129t
Aperghis, M 17
Apro, W 100
Aragon, AA 51, 56, 57, 63, 70, 124, 147, 152, 153
Arazi, H 59t
Ardjoune, H 24
Arent, SM 104
Arentson-Lantz, E 150
Areta, JL 149
Armstrong, DD 45,14
Armstrong, LE 18, 62, 81, 88
Armstrong, RB 43
Armstrong, T 120
Arnal, MA 150
Arner, P 148
Arnold, L 24
Aronson, D 34
Aruga, S 19, 20, 37, 39, 40, 43, 45
Arvidsson, B 75t
Asada, K 19, 20, 40
Asadi, A 59t

Ashton-Miller, JA 83t
Asiain, X 89
Atherton, PJ 8, 12, 20, 31, 63, 65, 71, 72, 73t, 88, 93, 98, 109, 110, 112, 140, 141, 148, 149, 150, 152, 153
Atkinson, SA 142
Augustsson, J 52, 56, 57, 61
Auletta, M 153
Avelar, A 11
Averill, LK 148
Averous, J 2
Avery, NG 148
Avniel, A 106
Ayalon, A 72t

B

Baar, K 36
Babraj, JA 71, 93, 112
Bachinin, AV 63
Baechle, TR 125
Baeza-Raja, B 21, 23
Bahmanzadeh, M 6, 126
Bailey, PS 40
Baker, DH 125, 126t, 127, 128t, 142
Baker, JM 12, 63
Baker, SK 12, 13, 20, 21, 23, 34, 44, 45, 51, 54t, 63, 65, 66t, 85, 88, 98, 106, 152, 153
Bakker, JA 153
Balage, M 6, 150
Balardy, L 24
Balasekaran, G 23, 46, 106
Baldwin, KM 48, 71
Ball, SD 55t
Balnave, RJ 36
Balogh, A 24
Bamman, MM 5, 6, 13, 15, 16, 22, 24, 25, 26, 40, 45, 46, 47, 48, 62, 70, 79, 101, 105, 106, 107, 109, 110, 151
Barad, O 106
Barash, IA 44
Barette, SL 61
Barnett, C 120
Baron, AD 18, 146
Baroni, BM 103t
Barrentine, SW 123
Barrett, EJ 18, 152
Barrett, MS 47
Barroso, R 81
Bartlett, JD 99
Barton, ER 17, 23, 46
Barton-Davis, ER 13

191

Lew, KM 87, 123
Lewis, CL 118
Lewis, JE 87, 123
Lewis, MP 18
Lexell, J 108, 109
Liberatore, CM 45
Lieber, RL 44
Liechty, EA 18, 146
Liete, T 52, 54t
Lima, CS 121
Lima, RM 60t
Lima-Silva, AE 146
Limbaugh, GK 124
Lin, K 42
Lin, M 42
Lindman, R 68
Lindstedt, SL 44
Lindvall, J 25, 112
Lintner, SA 121
Lira, VA 46, 47
Little, AD 54t
Liu, C 25, 112
Liu, YM 18, 146
Liubaeva, EV 63
Ljucovic, P 5
Ljunghall, S 16
Ljungqvist, O 34
Locatelli, L 17
Loebel, CC 18, 19, 41
Loenneke, JP 19, 37, 38, 40, 41, 49, 65, 66t, 99, 101, 102, 104
Logan, PA 11, 106
Lonbardo, LD 43
Long, JH 46, 47
Long, S 139
Longcope, C 148
Longland, TM 139
Longo, S 72, 75t
Lopez, H 143, 151, 152
Loud, RL 81
Louhelainen, J 99
Love, DM 148
Lovell, DI 96t
Low, SY 40
Lowe, T 19
Lowery, RP 49, 65, 127, 129t
Lu, CC 40
Lu, SS 40
Lubans, DR 127, 128t
Luecke, TJ 5, 37, 38, 64, 65, 66t
Lund, S 153
Lundberg, TR 25, 98, 99, 100, 104
Lundy, A 119
Lupu, F 17
Lusk, SJ 119
Luthi, F 65, 66t
Lynch, CJ 142
Lynch, JM 19, 20, 37, 40
Lynn, R 10
Lynn, SK 124

Lysenko, EA 63
Lyubaeva, E 63

M
Mac, RP 18
MacDonald, C 146
MacDonald, JR 43, 57, 71, 112, 143
MacDonald, MJ 85, 86, 143, 152, 153
MacDougall, JD 11, 15, 36, 38, 42, 43, 57, 71, 107, 110, 112, 142, 153
Machado, M 57, 77
Machida, S 110, 111
Mackenzie, R 98, 100
Mackey, AL 17, 24, 46, 47
MacLean, DA 46
MacLean, IM 34
MacNeil, LG 34, 44, 45
Madarame, H 20, 85
Madsen, JL 13
Madsen, K 18, 19
Madsgaard, S 87, 88t
Maesta, N 57, 60t
Maganaris, CN 72, 75t
Magliano, L 18
Magnan, M 24
Magne, H 24
Magnusson, SP 5, 6, 44
Mahmassani, Z 16, 30, 31
Mahoney, E 57
Mak, YW 29, 35
Malam, C 42
Malicky, ES 5
Mamerow, MM 150
Manfredi, TJ 108
Mangine, GT 76
Manini, TM 39, 108f
Manta, P 33, 51
Marchant, DC 118
Marchetti, PH 120, 121
Marchitelli, LJ 19, 36, 40, 41
Marciniec, T 15
Marcolin, G 122
Marcus, R 5, 110
Maresh, CM 17, 18, 19, 40, 62, 81, 88
Marette, A 148
Marin, PJ 37, 99, 101, 102, 104, 121
Marino, FE 53t
Maron, DJ 151
Marques, NR 53t
Marset-Baglieri, A 6, 150
Martel, GF 109, 110
Martin, A 7
Martin, E 121
Martin, IK 153
Martin, L 7
Martin, TP 103
Martin-Acero, R 10
Martineau, LC 29, 45, 63
Martins, KJ 34
Martins Kruel, LF 42, 43

Martorelli, AS 60t
Marzetti, E 108f
Marzolini, S 53t
Mascher, H 33, 51, 93
Masuda, K 37, 63
Matheny, RW 16
Mathew, L 44
Matin, S 151
Maton, B 121
Matsubara, K 17
Matsumoto, A 19, 20, 40
Matsumoto, K 151
Matsuoka, Y 48
Matta, T 82, 85, 86t, 127, 129t
Matzon, A 73t
Maughan, RJ 145
Maxwell, L 24
Mayer, A 23
Mayhew, DL 9, 13, 22, 31, 33, 35, 36, 45, 99, 105, 106, 107, 109, 146
Mayhew, TP 71, 74t
Mazzetti, S 81
McAllister, MJ 121
McBride, A 146
McBride, JM 19, 40, 41, 54t
McCall, GE 20
McCarthy, JJ 13, 16, 29, 33
McCartney, N 36, 38, 153
McCaulley, GO 19, 41
McCaw, ST 122, 123
McClain, DA 44
McCormack, D 148
McCormick, KM 42
McCormick, M 109
McCroskery, S 24
McCue, SA 22
McCully, K 36, 90
McCurry, D 19, 36, 40, 41
McDonald, P 34
McEvoy, L 5, 110
McGee, SL 33, 36, 93, 99
McGill, SM 123
McGinley, C 45, 48
McGowan, R 121
McGuigan, MR 83t
McHugh, A 148
McHugh, MP 42, 70
McIver, CM 139, 140, 143
McKay, BR 13, 48, 106
McKinnon, P 71
McLafferty, CL, Jr 48, 70, 79
McLester, JR 58, 60t
McLoughlin, G 77
McLoughlin, TJ 45, 47
McMahon, GE 87, 88t
McNevin, N 118
McPhail, LC 29, 35
McPhee, JS 97t
McPherron, AC 24, 25
Meador, MB 16, 30, 31

SUBJECT INDEX

ABOUT THE AUTHOR

Brad Schoenfeld, PhD, CSCS, CSPS, FNSCA, is widely regarded as one of the leading strength and fitness experts in the United States. The 2011 NSCA Personal Trainer of the Year is a lifetime drug-free bodybuilder who has won numerous natural bodybuilding titles, including the All-Natural Physique and Power Conference (ANPPC) Tri-State Naturals and USA Mixed Pairs crowns. As a personal trainer, Schoenfeld has worked with numerous elite-level physique athletes, including many top pros. Also, he was elected to the National Strength and Conditioning Association's Board of Directors in 2012.

Schoenfeld is the author of multiple consumer-oriented fitness books, including *The M.A.X. Muscle Plan* and *Strong and Sculpted* (formerly *Sculpting Her Body Perfect*). He is a regular columnist for *Muscular Development* magazine, has been published or featured in virtually every major fitness magazine (including *Muscle and Fitness, MuscleMag, Ironman, Oxygen,* and *Shape*), and has appeared on hundreds of television shows and radio programs across the United States. He also serves as a fitness expert and contributor to www.bodybuilding.com, www.diet.com, and www.t-nation.com.

Schoenfeld earned his PhD in health promotion and wellness at Rocky Mountain University, where his research focused on elucidating the mechanisms of muscle hypertrophy and their application to resistance training. He has published more than 80 peer-reviewed scientific papers and serves on the editorial advisory boards for several journals, including the *Journal of Strength and Conditioning Research* and *Journal of the International Society of Sports Nutrition*. He is an assistant professor of exercise science at Lehman College in the Bronx, New York, and heads their human performance laboratory.

Visit his blog at www.workout911.com.